Adobe InDesign

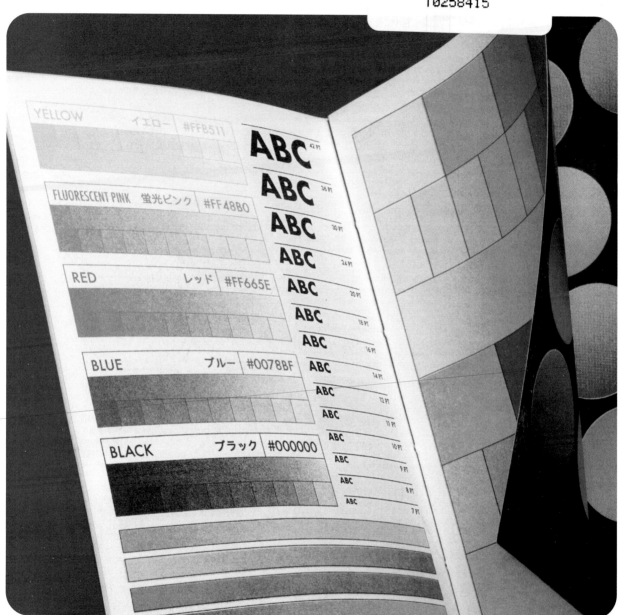

Classroom in a Book®

The official training workbook from Adobe

Kelly Kordes Anton & Tina DeJarld

Executive Editor: Laura Norman
Senior Production Editor: Tracey Croom
Technical Reviewer: Jonathan Gordon
Copyeditor: Elizabeth Welch
Composition: Kelly Anton, Tina DeJarld
Proofreader: Kim Wimpsett
Indexer: Tina DeJarld
Cover Illustration: Julia Schimautz, behance.net/juliaschim4d1d
Interior Designer: Mimi Heft

ISBN-13: 978-0-13-796744-5
ISBN-10: 0-13-796744-6

2 2023

WHERE ARE THE LESSON FILES?

Purchase of this Classroom in a Book in any format gives you access to the lesson files you'll need to complete the exercises in the book.

1 Go to adobepress.com/InDesignCIB2023.

2 Sign in or create a new account.

3 Click Submit.

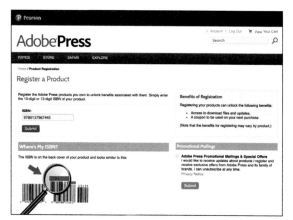

● **Note:** If you encounter problems registering your product or accessing the lesson files or web edition, go to adobepress.com/support for assistance.

4 Answer the questions as proof of purchase.

5 The lesson files can be accessed through the Registered Products tab on your Account page.

6 Click the Access Bonus Content link below the title of your product to proceed to the download page. Click the lesson file links to download them to your computer.

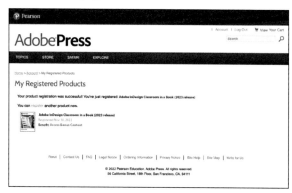

● **Note:** If you purchased a digital product directly from adobepress.com or peachpit.com, your product will already be registered. However, you still need to follow the registration steps and answer the proof of purchase question before the Access Bonus Content link will appear under the product on your Registered Products tab.

About the Authors

Kelly Kordes Anton has written and edited dozens of books and training resources on publishing technologies and InDesign, including 10 previous editions of *Adobe InDesign Classroom in a Book*. She is a freelance writer based in Littleton, Colorado, and she also writes about ergonomics, lean manufacturing, and lifestyles.

Tina DeJarld has worked on the front lines of taking designs from the computer screen to real-world production since before InDesign 1.0. She is highly accomplished in both prepress and graphic design production and passionate about building files that will work correctly. Tina has handled thousands of large and complex projects, becoming an expert on InDesign best practices and techniques. Tina is currently a senior production artist at PXP Studios, a production studio in Chicago.

Acknowledgments

This book would not have been possible without the contributions of several invaluable collaborators. The authors would like to thank Anshul Sharma and Laura Norman for putting together a strong team; Jonathan Gordon, technical editor, for ensuring the accuracy of every word on every page; Megan Ahearn, keystroker, for testing every step in every lesson; Elizabeth Welch, copyeditor, and Kim Wimpsett, proofreader, for making sure every i was dotted and every t was crossed; and Tracey Croom, senior production editor at Pearson, for overseeing the entire production process and keeping everybody informed and on track. In addition, we appreciate the invaluable influence of John Cruise, whose contributions remain throughout this book.

CONTENTS

GETTING STARTED

▶ **Tip:** To learn about seamless integration with other Adobe Creative Cloud (CC) components, see Bart Van de Wiele's book, *Adobe Photoshop, Illustrator, and InDesign Collaboration and Workflow Classroom in a Book* (Adobe Press, 2022).

Welcome to Adobe® InDesign® (2023 release), a powerful page-design and production application that offers precision, control, and seamless integration with other Adobe professional graphics software. Writers, artists, designers, and publishers can communicate to a broader audience than ever before through an unprecedented variety of media.

Using InDesign, you can produce professional-quality, full-color documents and print them using a variety of output devices, including desktop printers, high-resolution imaging devices, and high-volume color printing presses. In addition, you can design publications for a broad range of electronic devices, such as tablets, smartphones, and e-readers, and export InDesign documents in key formats, including PDF, HTML, and EPUB. Within the Adobe Creative Suite, InDesign is the application that pulls all the content together and provides the output you need.

About Classroom in a Book

Adobe InDesign Classroom in a Book® (2023 release) is part of the official training series for Adobe graphics and publishing software developed with the support of Adobe product experts. Given the feature-rich nature of the software, this book focuses on the core features of InDesign.

The Classroom in a Book lessons are designed so that you can learn at your own pace. If you're new to Adobe InDesign, you'll master the fundamentals and learn to put the software to work for you. If you've already been using InDesign, you'll find that this book teaches many advanced features and best practices, including tips and techniques for using the latest version of InDesign.

A few notes about the lessons: Each lesson provides step-by-step instructions for creating a specific project. You can follow the book from start to finish or do only the lessons that meet your interests and needs. Each lesson concludes with optional tasks that let you further explore the features covered in the lesson, as well as a set of review questions and answers. When instructions differ by platform, Windows commands appear first, followed by the macOS commands, with the platform noted in parentheses.

Prerequisites

▶ **Tip:** To review basic computer techniques, see the help resources included with your operating system.

Before beginning to use *Adobe InDesign Classroom in a Book (2023 release)*, you should have a working knowledge of your computer and its operating system. Make sure that you know how to use the mouse and standard menus and commands along with how to open, save, and close files.

Installing the software

Before you begin using *Adobe InDesign Classroom in a Book (2023 release)*, make sure that your system is set up correctly and that you've installed the proper software and hardware.

The Adobe InDesign software is not included with this book; you must subscribe to the software separately (visit adobe.com/products/indesign). In addition to InDesign, some lessons in this book have steps that can be performed with other Adobe applications. You must install these applications from Adobe Creative Cloud onto your computer by following the onscreen instructions.

Adobe Creative Cloud desktop app

▶ **Tip:** You can use the Creative Cloud desktop application to access your Adobe Account, update and manage applications, sync and share files, manage fonts and CC libraries, and access libraries of stock photography and design assets.

In addition to Adobe InDesign, this training requires the Adobe Creative Cloud desktop application, which provides a central location for managing the dozens of apps and services included in a Creative Cloud membership. Adobe periodically provides updates to software.

The Creative Cloud desktop application is installed automatically when you download your first Creative Cloud product. If you have Adobe Application Manager installed, it auto-updates to the Creative Cloud desktop application. If the Creative Cloud desktop application is not installed on your computer, click Download Creative Cloud at adobe.com/creativecloud/desktop-app.html.

Classroom in a Book fonts

Most of the fonts used in the Classroom in a Book lesson files are installed with InDesign. Some fonts are not installed with InDesign but are instead available through Adobe Fonts, an online font service that offers free access to a vast library of fonts for your use. To access Adobe Fonts, log in to your Creative Cloud account.

Online content

Your purchase of this Classroom in a Book includes online materials provided by way of your Account page on adobepress.com. These include lesson files and the Web Edition.

Lesson files

To work through the projects in this book, you will need to download the lesson files by following the instructions below.

Web Edition

The Web Edition is an online interactive version of the book providing an enhanced learning experience. Your Web Edition can be accessed from any device with a connection to the internet, and it contains:

* The complete text of the book

* Hours of instructional video keyed to the text

* Interactive quizzes

Accessing the lesson files and Web Edition

You must register your purchase on adobepress.com to access the online content:

1 Go to adobepress.com/InDesignCIB2023.

2 Sign in or create a new account.

3 Click Submit.

4 Answer the question as proof of purchase.

5 The lesson files can be accessed from the Registered Products tab on your Account page.

 * Click the Access Bonus Content link below the title of your product to proceed to the download page.

 * Click the lesson file link(s) to download them to your computer.

6 The Web Edition can be accessed from the Digital Purchases tab on your Account page. Click the Launch link to access the product.

 If you purchased a digital product directly from adobepress.com or peachpit.com, your product will already be registered. However, you still need to follow the registration steps and answer the proof of purchase question before the Access Bonus Content link will appear under the product on your Registered Products tab.

● **Note:** If you encounter problems registering your product or accessing the lesson files or Web Edition, go to adobepress.com/support for assistance.

Saving and restoring the InDesign Defaults file

The InDesign Defaults file stores program preferences and default settings, such as tool settings and the default unit of measurement. To ensure that the preferences and default settings of your InDesign program match those used in this book, move

the current InDesign Defaults file to a different location before you begin working on the lessons.

1 Quit Adobe InDesign.

2 Locate the InDesign Defaults file on your operating system.

● **Note:** If hidden files are visible and you still cannot locate the preferences file, use your operating system's Find File feature and search for "InDesign Defaults."

- Windows: The InDesign Defaults file is located in the folder [*startup drive*]\ Users\[*username*]\AppData\Roaming\Adobe\InDesign\Version 18.0\en_US\ InDesign Defaults.

 The AppData folder is hidden by default on Windows 10. To display the AppData folder, click Appearance And Personalization in the Control panel, and then click File Explorer Options.

- macOS: The InDesign Defaults file is located in the folder [*startup drive*]/ Users/*[username]*/Library/Preferences/Adobe InDesign/Version 18.0/en_US/ InDesign Defaults.

 To access the Library folder, choose Go > Go To Folder from the Finder menu. Type ~/**Library** in the Go To The Folder box, and then click OK or Go.

3 If you want to restore customized preferences, move the file to another folder on your hard drive. Otherwise, you can delete the file.

4 Start Adobe InDesign to automatically create a new InDesign Defaults file with all preferences and defaults set to their original factory settings.

If you want to restore your customized InDesign Defaults file that you moved to another location, quit InDesign. Locate your saved InDesign Defaults file, drag it back into its original folder, and replace the current InDesign Defaults file.

Training resources

● **Note:** Every year, Adobe adds features that make InDesign more powerful and easier to use—for example, additional collaboration tools and easy access to a robust font library, templates, color themes, and stock photography. Use these resources to stay abreast of changes and learn more.

Adobe InDesign Classroom in a Book (2023 release) is not meant to be a comprehensive reference for every feature. Only the commands and options used in the lessons are explained in this book. Refer to these resources for more details and support:

Adobe InDesign Learn & Support: helpx.adobe.com/indesign.html is where you can find and browse Help and Support content on Adobe.com. Adobe InDesign Help and Adobe InDesign Support Center are accessible from the Help menu in InDesign.

Adobe Support Community: community.adobe.com lets you tap into peer-to-peer discussions, questions, and answers on Adobe products.

Adobe InDesign product home page: adobe.com/products/indesign provides information about new features and intuitive ways to create professional layouts.

Adobe Add-ons: creative.adobe.com/addons is a central resource for finding tools, services, extensions, and more to supplement and extend your Adobe products.

Resources for educators: adobe.com/education and edex.adobe.com offer a treasure trove of information for instructors who teach classes on Adobe software. Find solutions for education at all levels, including free curricula that use an integrated approach to teaching Adobe software and that can be used to prepare for the Adobe Certified Associate exams.

Adobe Authorized Training Centers: Adobe Authorized Training Centers (AATCs) employ only Adobe Certified Instructors and offer instructor-led courses and training on Adobe products. A directory of AATCs is available at learning.adobe.com/partner-finder.

Pearson's Commitment to Diversity, Equity, and Inclusion

Pearson is dedicated to creating bias-free content that reflects the diversity of all learners. We embrace the many dimensions of diversity, including but not limited to race, ethnicity, gender, socioeconomic status, ability, age, sexual orientation, and religious or political beliefs.

Education is a powerful force for equity and change in our world. It has the potential to deliver opportunities that improve lives and enable economic mobility. As we work with authors to create content for every product and service, we acknowledge our responsibility to demonstrate inclusivity and incorporate diverse scholarship so that everyone can achieve their potential through learning. As the world's leading learning company, we have a duty to help drive change and live up to our purpose to help more people create a better life for themselves and to create a better world.

Our ambition is to purposefully contribute to a world where:

- Everyone has an equitable and lifelong opportunity to succeed through learning.
- Our educational products and services are inclusive and represent the rich diversity of learners.
- Our educational content accurately reflects the histories and experiences of the learners we serve.
- Our educational content prompts deeper discussions with learners and motivates them to expand their own learning (and worldview).

While we work hard to present unbiased content, we want to hear from you about any concerns or needs with this Pearson product so that we can investigate and address them. Please contact us with concerns about any potential bias at pearson.com/report-bias.html.

1 INTRODUCING THE WORKSPACE

Lesson overview

In this lesson, you'll learn how to do the following:

- Open documents.

- Select and use tools.

- View information in the Properties panel.

- Use the Control panel.

- Manage document windows.

- Work with panels.

- Customize the workspace.

- Change the magnification of a document.

- Navigate through a document.

- Use context menus and panel menus.

- Change Interface preferences.

 This lesson will take about 45 minutes to complete. To get the lesson files used in this chapter, download them from the web page for this book at adobepress.com/InDesignCIB2023. For more information, see "Accessing the lesson files and Web Edition" in the Getting Started section at the beginning of this book.

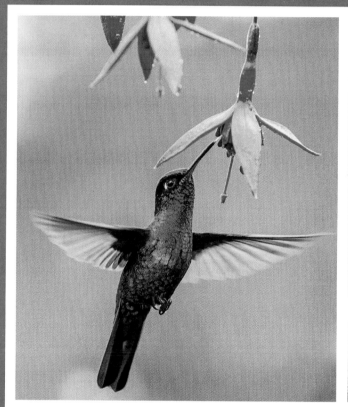

Plant a Humming-bird Garden

Learn to select and tend flowers that attract hummingbirds, flourish in our climate and create fabulous flowerbeds.

The intuitive Adobe InDesign interface makes it easy to create compelling layouts. It is important to understand the InDesign work area to make the most of its powerful layout and design capabilities. The customizable work area consists of the document window, menus, pasteboard, and panels such as the Tools, Properties, and Control panels.

Getting started

In this lesson, you'll practice using tools and panels and navigating through a simple layout. You will use this document only to explore the InDesign work area. The lesson file represents the final version of the document—you will not make permanent changes to objects, add graphics, or modify text. Rather, you will reverse any changes you make using Edit > Undo. Building a habit with the Undo feature helps you experiment and recover from any mistakes.

● **Note:** If you have not already downloaded the project files for this lesson to your computer from your Account page, make sure to do so now. See "Getting Started" at the beginning of the book.

1 To ensure that the preferences and default settings of your InDesign program match those used in this lesson, move the InDesign Defaults file to a different folder following the procedure in "Saving and restoring the InDesign Defaults file" on pages 3–4.

2 Start InDesign. The InDesign Home screen displays.

3 Click the Open button. (If the Home screen does not display, choose File > Open from the InDesign menu bar.)

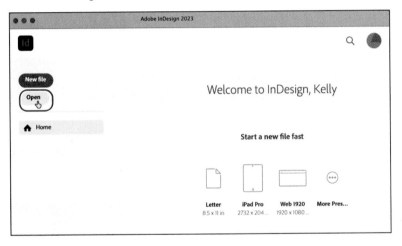

● **Note:** To better view the interface onscreen or in print, the screen captures in this book reflect the Medium Light interface rather than the default setting of Medium Dark. In addition, some screen captures illustrate User Interface Scaling for a closer look at interface elements. You can modify interface settings in Preferences.

4 Open the 01_Start.indd file in the Lesson01 folder, located inside the Lessons folder within the InDesignCIB folder on your hard drive.

5 If an alert informs you that the document contains links to sources that have been modified, click Update Modified Links.

6 If any learning resource panels display, close them by clicking Ignore or a close box.

7 Choose File > Save As, rename the file **01_Intro.indd**, and save it in the Lesson01 folder.

8 Using the scroll bars on the document window, scroll down to see the second page of the postcard, and then scroll back up to the first page of the postcard.

Looking at the workspace

The InDesign work area encompasses everything you see when you first open or create a document. By default, InDesign shows tools and panels available in the Essentials workspace. You can customize the InDesign work area to suit your work style. For example, you can choose to display only the panels you frequently use, minimize and rearrange panel groups, resize windows, and so on. By default you will see the following:

- The menu bar at the top of the screen

- The Tools panel, docked at the left side of the screen

- The Properties panel and other commonly used panels, docked at the right side of the screen

The configuration of the panels in the work area is referred to as the "workspace." You can save your custom workspace setup or choose among special-purpose set-ups, such as Interactive For PDF, Printing And Proofing, and Typography.

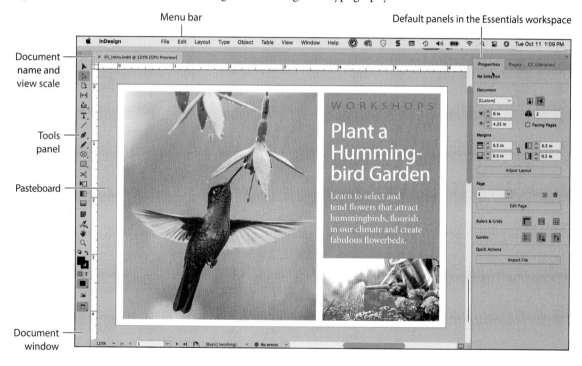

Selecting and using tools

▶ **Tip:** The building blocks of InDesign pages are objects, which include frames (for containing text and graphics) and lines.

The Tools panel contains tools for creating and modifying page objects, adding and formatting text and images, and working with color. By default, the Tools panel is docked to the upper-left corner of the work area. In this exercise, you will select and experiment with several tools.

Using the Selection tool

The Selection tool lets you move and resize objects, and it lets you select objects for formatting, such as applying a fill color. Here, you will click to select the Selection tool. Later, you will experiment with other methods of selecting tools.

1 Locate the Tools panel at the far-left side of the screen.

● **Note:** If you do not see tool tips when pointing at tools, select Tools Tips in InDesign Preferences. To do this, choose Edit > Preferences > Interface (Windows) or InDesign > Preferences > Interface (macOS). Tool Tips settings are under Cursor And Gesture Options.

2 Point at each tool in the Tools panel to see its name.

3 Click the Selection tool (▶) at the top of the Tools panel.

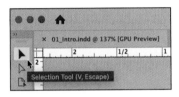

4 Click near the hummingbird's head to select the graphics frame containing the hummingbird photograph.

5 Drag the frame up and to the left to see how frames move.

 The frame's location on the page is shown near the Selection tool pointer and in the Properties panel at the right. In addition to viewing information in this panel, you can make adjustments to selected objects. For example, you can crop the image to control the portions that display.

6 After you release the mouse button, press Ctrl+Z (Windows) or Command+Z (macOS) to undo the move.

7 With the Selection tool still selected, click other objects on the page and drag them to new locations. The page contains another image in a graphics frame, a rectangular text frame, and an elliptical text frame. Undo each move immediately after you do it.

Using the Type tool

Now you will switch to the Type tool, which lets you enter, edit, and format text much like you would in a word processor or email application. Rather than clicking to select it, you will use its keyboard shortcut.

1 Point at the Type tool (T.) to display its tool tip. The letter shown in parentheses indicates a single-letter keyboard shortcut for selecting this tool. In this case, the letter is T.

2 Point at various other tools to see their single-letter keyboard shortcuts.

3 Press T on the keyboard to select the Type tool. Click after the word "flowerbeds" and the period on the right side of the postcard.

4 Type a space and a few characters to get a feel for the Type tool.

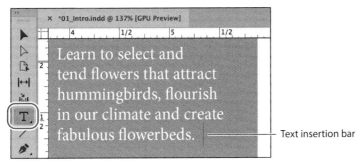
Text insertion bar

5 Press Ctrl+Z (Windows) or Command+Z (macOS) to undo any changes to the postcard text.

6 With the Type tool still selected, click in other words and revise the text. Undo each change after you finish typing.

Using the Line tool and Hand tool

Now you will switch to the Line tool, which lets you create horizontal, vertical, and diagonal lines. Once you have experimented with the Line tool, you will select the Hand tool temporarily by holding its keyboard shortcut: H. When you release the keyboard shortcut, InDesign reverts to the previously selected tool. This technique is useful for quickly using a tool—for example, you might use the Hand tool to move to another area of a page and then create a line there.

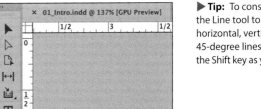

1 Click the Line tool (/) to select it.

2 Drag to create a line anywhere on the page.

● **Note:** The single-letter shortcuts do not work when the text insertion bar is in text.

▶ **Tip:** As you learn InDesign and experiment with layouts, remember that you can undo as many changes as you want.

▶ **Tip:** To constrain the Line tool to creating horizontal, vertical, or 45-degree lines, press the Shift key as you draw.

3 With the Line tool still selected, press and hold the H key on the keyboard. While you hold the H key, the Hand tool (🖐) is selected.

4 Drag the Hand tool around to view another area of the page. When you release the H key, the Line tool remains selected.

5 Press Ctrl+Z (Windows) or Command+Z (macOS) to undo the line creation.

Using the Rectangle Frame tool and the Ellipse Frame tool

So far, you have selected tools that display on the Tools panel in three ways: (1) clicking them, (2) pressing a keyboard shortcut, and (3) holding a keyboard shortcut to select the tool temporarily. Now, you will select a tool that is not visible on the Tools panel. A small triangle in the lower-right corner of a tool indicates a menu of additional hidden tools.

The triangle indicates a menu of additional tools.

In this exercise, you will create frames by selecting and using the Rectangle Frame tool and then the Ellipse Frame tool. When designing a document, you would create these frames to contain imported graphics and text.

1 Choose View > Screen Mode > Normal so that you can see the frames that contain graphics and text.

2 Press F on the keyboard to select the Rectangle Frame tool (⊠).

▶ **Tip:** To easily create a square or circle, press the Shift key while you draw with the Rectangle Frame tool or with the Ellipse Frame tool.

3 Scroll to the left to view the pasteboard surrounding the document. Click and drag to create a rectangular graphics frame.

4 Press Ctrl+Z (Windows) or Command+Z (macOS) to undo the frame creation.

5 To see the Ellipse Frame tool, press and hold the Rectangle Frame tool to display additional hidden tools.

6 Select the Ellipse Frame tool (⊗), and notice how it replaces the Rectangle Frame tool.

▶ **Tip:** You can Alt-click (Windows) or Option-click (macOS) a tool in the Tools panel to alternate between the tools in a menu.

7 Drag to create an oval graphics frame anywhere on the page or pasteboard.

8 Notice the object placement information shown in the Transform area of the Properties panel. Press Ctrl+Z or Command+Z as many times as necessary to undo the frame creation.

▶ **Tip:** Other options in the Properties panel allow you to format any selected object. For example, you can apply a fill color (background color) or stroke (outline width, style, and color) to the object.

9 Press and hold the Ellipse Frame tool to display the menu, and choose the Rectangle Frame tool to display it again. This is the default tool that displays.

10 Review the remaining hidden tools. Click each tool with a triangle and hold down the mouse button to see its menu of additional tools.

The tools with menus for hidden tools include Content Collector, Type, Pen, Pencil, Rectangle Frame, Rectangle, Free Transform, Color Theme, View Options, and Screen Mode.

Reviewing the Control panel

InDesign provides many more panels than are shown in the default Essentials workspace. In this exercise, you will switch to the Advanced workspace to view the Control panel, which displays immediately below the menu bar and offers quick access to expansive options for editing selected objects. Depending on your screen size, you may prefer to use the Control panel as it takes up less space than the Properties panel.

As with the Properties panel, the Control panel is context sensitive, which means it displays settings based on what you have selected on the page. Additionally, the Control panel displays more or fewer settings depending on the size of your screen.

▶ **Tip:** To customize the options showing in the Control panel, click the gear icon (⚙) at the far-right side of the panel.

1 To see the panels and menu commands used in this lesson, choose Window > Workspace > [Advanced], and then choose Window > Workspace > Reset Advanced. Notice the Control panel across the top of the screen.

2 If necessary, choose View > Screen Mode > Normal so that you can see the frames that contain graphics and text.

3 In the Tools panel, select the Direct Selection tool (▷).

4 Click the hummingbird image. The Control panel provides options for controlling the size and position of the graphics frame, the scale of the image, and other attributes.

▶ **Tip:** You can also move and resize objects by entering values in Control panel fields and by dragging objects with the mouse.

5 In the Control panel, click the up and down arrows next to the Scale X Percentage and Scale Y Percentage fields to see how you can resize the image.

6 Press Ctrl+Z (Windows) or Command+Z (macOS) as many times as necessary to undo any changes.

7 In the Tools panel, select the Type tool (T).

8 Click in the word "Hummingbird" in the headline. The Control panel now provides options for controlling paragraph and character formatting. If necessary, click Character Formatting Controls (A) at the far-left side of the Control panel.

▶ **Tip:** Press the Shift key while clicking the up and down arrows to increase the size in larger increments.

9 Double-click to select the word "Hummingbird" and click once on the down arrow on the Font Size field, as shown, to decrease the size of the type.

10 Press Ctrl+Z or Command+Z to undo the change.

11 Click the pasteboard (the blank area outside the pages) to deselect the text.

Reviewing the document window and pasteboard

The document window and pasteboard have the following characteristics:

- Controls for displaying different pages in the document are in the lower-left corner of the document window.

- Each page or spread is surrounded by its own pasteboard.

- You can use the pasteboard as a work area or a storage area—for example, to place design elements not yet included in the page layout.

▶ **Tip:** You can change the size of the pasteboard in Preferences > Guides & Pasteboard > Pasteboard Options.

Now, you will look at the pasteboard and review features on the document window.

1 To see all the pages in the document and the pasteboard, you will decrease the view scale. Click the Zoom Level menu in the lower-left corner of the document window, and then select 75% from the menu.

In the 75% view, you will see a circular text frame on the pasteboard to the right of page 1.

2 In the Tools panel, select the Selection tool (▶).

3 Click the circular text frame, which contains the words "free community workshop series." Drag the frame from the pasteboard to the document page and see how it looks in various spots.

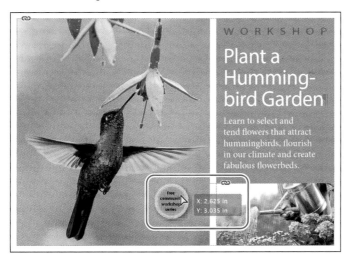

4 Press Ctrl+Z (Windows) or Command+Z (macOS) to undo the change.

5 Choose View > Fit Page In Window.

6 In the lower-left corner of the document window, click the arrow next to the Page Number field to display a menu of document pages and parent pages.

7 Choose 2 from the menu to display page 2 in the document window.

8 Click the arrow to the left of the Page Number field to turn back to page 1.

9 Choose View > Screen Mode > Preview to hide the frame guides.

Working with multiple document windows

▶ **Tip:** The techniques you use here for arranging document windows can be used with different views of the same document and for any other open documents.

When you open multiple documents, each document displays in its own tab of the main document window. You can also open multiple windows for a single document so that you can see different parts of the layout at one time. Essentially, you can see more than one view of a document at the same time. Here, you'll create a second window so that you can see how changes to the headline affect the entire page.

1 Choose Window > Arrange > New Window For 01_Intro.indd.

A new window, titled 01_Intro.indd:2, opens. The original window is now titled 01_Intro.indd:1.

2 Select the Zoom tool (🔍) in the Tools panel.

3 In the second window, 01_Intro.indd:2, click three times on the word "WORKSHOP" to zoom in on the text.

Notice that the other window stays at its original magnification.

4 Press T on the keyboard to select the Type tool (T).

5 In the second window, click at the end of the word "WORKSHOP" and add an "S" to make it plural: WORKSHOPS.

Notice the change in both windows.

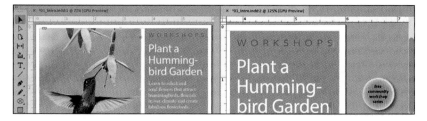

6 Press Ctrl+Z (Windows) or Command+Z (macOS) to restore the word "WORKSHOP."

7 Choose Window > Arrange > New Window For 01_Intro.indd to create an additional window.

8 Choose options from the Window > Arrange submenu to see the various ways to arrange open windows.

9 Choose Window > Arrange > Consolidate All Windows. This creates a tab for each window.

▶ **Tip:** Opening a document in multiple windows is helpful for seeing how changes in one area of a page or document affect other areas. For example, if you have an article that continues toward the back of a magazine, you might open a window for each page that contains the article. This allows you to see how the edits impact the text flow across all pages.

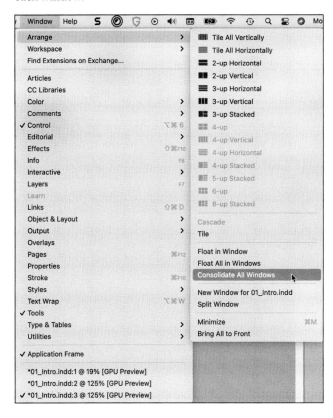

10 Click the tabs in the upper-left corner (below the Control panel) to control which document window to display.

11 Click the Close Document Window button on all the additional tabs, leaving one open. It doesn't matter which one remains open.

● **Note:** The tabs may display in reverse order on your screen.

12 If necessary, choose View > Fit Page In Window.

Working with panels

▶ Tip: As you become comfortable with InDesign, experiment with configuring the panels and workspace to best meet your needs. You will soon find out which panels you use the most, where you like to keep them, and what sizes are best for your needs. You may even prefer to store panels on a second monitor.

InDesign provides many panels that provide quick access to commonly used tools and features. By default, various useful panels are docked at the right side of the screen. (Think of a dock as a collection of panels "glued" together.) The panels that display are different depending on the selected workspace, and each workspace remembers its panel configuration.

You can reorganize panels in various ways. Here, you'll experiment with opening, collapsing, grouping, stacking, and closing the default panels in the Advanced workspace. Feel free to experiment with panels as much as you want, as selecting Window > Workspace > Reset Advanced will restore the panels to their original locations.

Opening and closing panels

To display a hidden panel, choose the panel name from the Window menu (or a submenu of the Window menu). Various text-formatting panels are available in the Type menu as well. If the panel name has a checkmark in the menu, it is already open and in front of any other panels in its panel group. In this exercise, you will open, use, and close the Info panel, which provides feedback about anything you select in the document.

1 Choose Window > Info to open the Info panel.

2 In the Tools panel, select the Selection tool (▶).

3 Point at and click various objects on the page to view their details.

▶ Tip: When a panel is floating, you can click its close box (✖) to close it.

4 Choose Window > Info again to close the Info panel.

 Many panels have keyboard shortcuts shown in the Window menu. The keyboard shortcuts let you toggle panels open and closed.

5 Press Ctrl+Alt+6 (Windows) or Command+Option+6 (macOS) to close the Control panel. Press the keyboard shortcut again to reopen it.

Expanding and collapsing panels

In this exercise, you will expand and collapse a panel, hide the panel names, and expand all the panels in the dock.

1 In the dock to the right of the document window, click the Pages panel icon to expand the Pages panel.

 Clicking a panel icon is handy if you want to open a panel, use it briefly, and then close it.

Double arrow

The Pages panel icon

▶ Tip: It may be difficult to remember all the techniques and terminology involved in managing the panels onscreen. The most important thing to remember is that you can always open and close a panel from the Window menu. Other than that, click around and experiment to see how the panels work.

2 When you've finished using the Pages panel, click the double arrow (≫) to the right of the panel names or click the Pages panel icon again to collapse the panel.

3 To reduce the width of the panel dock, drag the left edge of the panel dock to the right until the names are hidden.

▶ Tip: Click the double arrow button (≫) to expand and collapse panels.

Drag the left edge of the panel dock to collapse the panels into icons.

The panels are collapsed into icons.

4 To expand all the panels in the dock so that you can see all their controls, click the double arrow (≪) in the upper-right corner of the dock. For the next exercise, you will leave the panels expanded.

Rearranging and customizing panels

In this exercise, you will drag a single panel out of the dock to create a free-floating panel. Then, you will drag another panel into that panel to create a custom panel group. You will also ungroup the panels, stack them, and minimize them.

●**Note:** If necessary, click the double arrow (**‹‹**) in the upper-right corner of the dock to expand all of the panels.

1 Locate the Paragraph Styles panel toward the bottom of the panels docked at the right. You will detach this from the dock to create a floating panel.

2 Click the Paragraph Styles tab in the dock, and then drag the panel away from the dock. This removes the panel from the dock.

Drag the bar up to adjust the height of the panel.

Now you will add the Character Styles panel to the floating Paragraph Styles panel to create a panel group.

▶**Tip:** Grouping the Character Styles and Paragraph Styles panels can be helpful for formatting text. You can put this panel group in a handy location while leaving the remaining panels collapsed and out of the way.

3 Locate the Character Styles panel toward the bottom of the panel dock. Drag its tab into the gray area to the right of the Paragraph Styles panel tab.

4 Release the mouse button when the blue line appears along the perimeter of the Paragraph Styles panel.

5 To ungroup the panels, drag one of the panel tabs out of the panel group.

 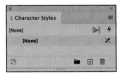

You can also stack floating panels in a vertical arrangement. You'll try that now.

6 Drag the tab of the Character Styles panel to the bottom of the Paragraph Styles panel. Release the mouse button when a blue line appears.

▶ **Tip:** A detached panel is called a "floating panel." To minimize or maximize a floating panel, double-click its name, or click the double arrow (◀◀) to the left of the panel name.

The panels are now stacked rather than grouped. Stacked panels attach vertically to each other. You can move the panels as a unit by dragging the topmost title bar. Next, you'll experiment with resizing the stacked panels.

7 Drag the lower-right corner of the panel stack to resize it.

8 Regroup the panels by dragging the tab of the Character Styles panel up next to the Paragraph Styles panel tab.

▶ **Tip:** For floating panels, you can change the width and height by dragging the lower-right or lower-left corner, change the height by dragging the bottom, and change the width by dragging the left or right edge of the panel.

9 Minimize the panel group by double-clicking the gray area to the right of a panel's tab. Double-click the area again to expand the panels.

Leave the panels this way to be saved with a workspace in a later exercise.

Moving the Tools panel and Control panel

When working in the Advanced workspace, it's likely that you will keep the Tools panel and the Control panel open all the time. However, as with all other panels, you can move them to best suit your own work style. Here, you will experiment with moving these two panels.

▶ **Tip:** To undock the
Tools panel, you can
drag either the title bar
or the gray dotted bar
just below the title bar.

1 To undock the Tools panel and make it float in the workspace, drag the panel by its dotted bar (|||||||) to pull it into the pasteboard.

When the Tools panel is floating, it can be a two-column vertical panel, a single-column vertical panel, or a single-column horizontal row. The Tools panel must be floating (not docked) to display horizontally.

2 With the Tools panel floating, click the double arrow (>>) at the top of the panel.

The Tools panel becomes one horizontal row.

3 Click the double arrow () in the Tools panel to turn it into a two-column vertical panel.

4 To dock the Tools panel again, drag the dotted bar (||||||||) at the top of the Tools panel to the far-left edge of the screen.

5 Release the Tools panel when a blue line appears along the edge of the workspace. Click the double arrow again to return to the default Tools panel.

The Control panel can be moved if you don't like it docked at the top of the document window.

6 In the Control panel, drag the vertical dotted bar () at the left into the document window. Release the mouse button to make the panel float.

▶ **Tip:** You can also
dock the Control panel
by dragging the dotted
bar until a horizontal
blue line appears at the
docking position.

7 To dock the panel again, click the Control panel menu button (≡) at the far right and choose Dock At Top.

Customizing the workspace

A workspace is a configuration of panels and menus. (The configuration of document windows, however, is not saved in workspaces.) InDesign provides a variety of workspaces for special purposes, such as Interactive For PDF, Printing And Proofing, and Typography. You cannot modify the provided workspaces, but you can save your own. In this exercise, you will save the panel configuration from the previous exercises.

1 Choose Window > Workspace > New Workspace.

2 In the New Workspace dialog, type **Styles** in the Name field. If necessary, select Panel Locations and Menu Customization.

3 Click OK. If an alert displays indicating that the workspace already exists, click OK to replace the existing workspace.

▶ **Tip:** To further customize the workspace, you can control which commands appear in the InDesign menus by choosing Edit > Menus. For example, you might prefer shorter menus for use on a smaller laptop screen, or you might want to streamline the commands available to a new user. You can save the menu customization with your saved workspaces.

4 Choose Window > Workspace to see that your custom workspace is selected.

5 The name of the selected workspace (Styles) also displays in the Workspace Switcher menu at the far right of the Control panel. Click this menu and select a different workspace.

6 To see the different panel and menu configurations, choose each option from the Window > Workspace submenu or the Workspace Switcher menu in the upper-right corner of the document window.

7 To restore the workspace, choose Window > Workspace > Advanced, and then choose Window > Workspace > Reset Advanced.

Changing the magnification of a document

Controls in InDesign let you view documents at any zoom level from 5% to 4000%. When a document is open, the current magnification percentage is displayed next to the filename in the document's tab.

In a document's title bar, the percentage next to the name indicates the zoom level.

Using the view commands

You can easily enlarge or reduce the view of a document by doing any of the following:

- Choose View > Zoom In to enlarge the display by one preset increment.
- Choose View > Zoom Out to reduce the display by one preset increment.
- Choose View > Fit Page In Window to center and display the page in the window.
- Choose View > Fit Spread In Window to center and display the current spread in the window. (A spread is multiple pages displayed side-by-side.)
- Choose View > Actual Size to display the document at 100%.
- Choose a percentage from the Zoom Level menu (in the lower-left corner of the document window) to enlarge or reduce the display by any preset increment.
- Type a percentage in the Zoom Level field by clicking in the field, typing the desired viewing percentage, and then pressing the Enter (Windows) or Return (macOS) key.

- Press Ctrl+= (Windows) or Command+= (macOS) to increase the magnification by one preset increment.
- Press Ctrl+− (Windows) or Command+− (macOS) to decrease the magnification by one preset increment.

Using the Zoom tool

In addition to the view commands, you can use the Zoom tool to magnify and reduce the view of a document. You might zoom in on a text frame to revise text, for example. In this exercise, you will experiment with the Zoom tool.

▶ **Tip:** When clicking with the Zoom tool to increase the zoom level, target the item you want to zoom in on to avoid zooming in to random areas of a page.

1 Choose View > Actual Size to view the document at 100%.

2 Select the Zoom tool (🔍) in the Tools panel and position it near the hummingbird on the left side of page 1. Notice that a plus sign appears in the center of the Zoom tool.

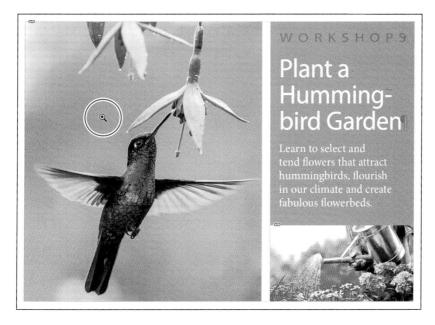

3 Click three times. The view changes to the next preset magnification, centered on the point where you clicked.

The preset magnifications include 5%, 12.5%, 25%, 50%, 75%, 100%, 125%, 150%, 200%, 300%, 400%, 600%, 800%, 1200%, 1600%, 2400%, 3200%, and 4000%.

Now you'll reduce the view.

4 Position the Zoom tool over the hummingbird image and hold down the Alt (Windows) or Option (macOS) key. A minus sign appears in the center of the Zoom tool.

5 While holding the Alt or Option key, click three times to reduce the view scale.

To magnify a specific area, you can drag the Zoom tool around that area. The percentage by which the area is magnified depends on the size of the marquee: the smaller the marquee, the larger the degree of magnification.

6 Scroll as necessary to see the text starting with "Learn to select."

● **Note:** If you have a Mac with a compatible graphics processing unit (GPU) card, your Zoom tool offers Animated Zoom. See the sidebar on the next page for details.

7 With the Zoom tool still selected, zoom in on the text frame.

Learn to select and tend flowers that attract hummingbirds, flourish in our climate and create fabulous flowerbeds.

8 Choose View > Fit Page In Window.

Note: Your Windows or macOS system preferences may override some InDesign keyboard shortcuts. If a shortcut is not working, consider revising your system's keyboard shortcut preferences.

9 Because the Zoom tool is used frequently during the design and editing processes, you can temporarily select it from the keyboard at any time without deselecting the tool you are using. To try this:

- Click the Selection tool (▶) in the Tools panel and position it anywhere in the document window.

- Hold down Ctrl+spacebar (Windows) or Command+spacebar (macOS) so that the Selection tool icon allows you to zoom, and then click the hummingbird to magnify the view.

Note: In macOS, hold the spacebar first and then add the Command key. Otherwise, Command+spacebar may activate Siri.

- Hold down Ctrl+Alt+spacebar (Windows) or Command+Option+spacebar (macOS) to reduce the view.

- When you release the keys, the pointer returns to the Selection tool.

10 Choose View > Screen Mode > Preview, and then choose View > Fit Page In Window to center the page again.

Using Animated Zoom

If you have a Mac with a compatible graphics processing unit (GPU) card, InDesign provides enhanced view features. The Display Performance (View menu) is set to High Quality and Animated Zoom (InDesign > Preferences > GPU Performance) is enabled by default.

Animated Zoom offers smooth, animated displays when using the Zoom tool:

- Press and hold: Zoom in to the center.

- Press Option and hold: Zoom out from the center.

- Press and drag to the right: Zoom in.

- Press and drag to the left: Zoom out.

- Press Shift while dragging: Access standard marquee zoom.

You can disable this feature by selecting View > Preview On CPU.

Navigating through a document

InDesign offers several different ways to navigate through a document, including using the Pages panel, the Hand tool, the Go To Page dialog, scroll bars, and controls in the document window. As you work with InDesign, you will find that you prefer certain methods over others. Once you find a method you like, remember any shortcuts to make that method easier.

▶ **Tip:** To navigate pages, you can also use commands in the Layout menu: First Page, Previous Page, Next Page, Last Page, Next Spread, and Previous Spread.

Navigating pages

You can navigate document pages using the Pages panel, the page icons at the bottom of the document window, the scroll bars, or a variety of other methods. The Pages panel displays an icon for each page in the document. Double-clicking any page icon or page number in the panel brings that page or spread into view. In this exercise, you will experiment with turning pages.

1 Click the Pages panel icon to expand the Pages panel, if necessary.

2 Double-click the page 2 icon to display the second page centered in the document window.

3 Double-click the page 1 icon to center the first page in the document window.

4 To return to the second page of the document, use the menu in the lower-left corner of the document window. Click the down arrow, and choose 2.

You will now use the arrow buttons at the bottom of the document window to display a different page.

▶ **Tip:** When View > Fit Spread In Window is selected, the navigation controls in the document window are for spreads rather than pages.

5 Click the Previous Page button (left-facing arrow) next to the Page Number field to switch pages until the first page is displayed.

6 Click the Next Page button (the right-facing arrow) next to the Page Number field until the second page is displayed.

▶ **Tip:** The keyboard shortcut for Layout > Go To Page is Ctrl+J (Windows) or Command+J (macOS). If you're entering edits on a longer document, this shortcut is worth remembering.

7 Choose Layout > Go To Page.

8 In the Page field, type **1** or select 1 from the menu. Click OK.

Using the Hand tool

The Hand tool in the Tools panel lets you "push" the pages of a document around until the area you want to see is visible. In this exercise, you will experiment with the Hand tool.

▶ **Tip:** When you're using the Selection tool, you can press the spacebar to temporarily access the Hand tool. When you're using the Type tool, press the Alt (Windows) or Option (macOS) key to use the Hand tool.

1 Choose 400% from the Zoom Level menu on the lower-left corner of the document window.

2 Select the Hand tool (🖐).

3 Drag in any direction to move the page around, and then drag upward in the document window to display page 2.

4 With the Hand tool still selected, click the page and hold the mouse button down to power zoom.

5 With the mouse button still held down, drag to zoom into the area of the page you want to view.

6 Double-click the Hand tool in the Tools panel to fit the page in the document window.

Using context menus

Context menus display commands relevant to the active tool or selection. For example, if a text frame is selected, the context menu lets you access the Text Frame Options dialog, the Lock command, the Effects submenu, and more. To display a context menu, right-click as follows: Position the pointer over a selected object or anywhere in the document window and click with the right mouse button. If you have a one-button mouse, press Control and hold down the mouse button.

1 Using the Selection tool (▶), click any object on the page, such as the text frame containing the postcard's return address starting with "Urban Oasis Gardens."

2 Right-click the text frame. Note the available options; a partial list is shown here.

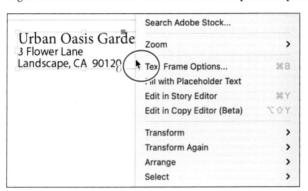

▶ **Tip:** You can display a context menu when entering or editing text. The Type context menu lets you insert special characters, check spelling, and perform other text-related tasks. For example, if you need to enter a copyright symbol (©), right-click and choose Insert Special Character > Symbols > Copyright Symbol.

3 Continue to right-click different types of objects on page 1 and page 2 to display their context menus to see the available commands.

4 When you're finished reviewing the context menus, use the scroll bars to return to page 2, if necessary.

Using panel menus

Most panels have additional panel-specific options. Clicking the panel menu button displays a menu of additional commands related to the panel's function along with options for customizing the panel. In this exercise, you will change the display of the Swatches panel.

1 Locate the Swatches panel on the dock. (If necessary, choose Window > Color > Swatches to display it.) Drag the Swatches panel out of the dock at the right to create a free-floating panel.

2 If necessary, click the double arrow (⟫) in its title bar to expand the Swatches panel.

3 In the upper-right corner of the Swatches panel, click the panel menu button (≡) to display the panel menu.

You can use the Swatches panel menu to create new color swatches, load swatches from another document, and more.

4 Choose Large Thumbnail from the Swatches panel menu to see how a panel's display can be customized. Note the other options on the menu as well.

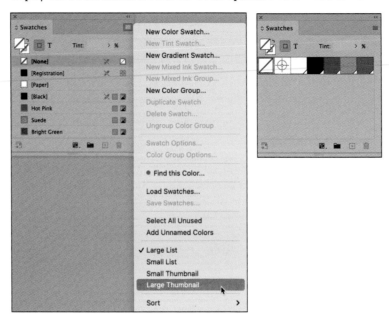

5 To restore the panel, choose Large List from the Swatches panel menu.

Modifying Interface preferences

● **Note:** The screen captures in this book show the Medium Light interface. You can use any color theme that you prefer.

You can customize the InDesign interface through preferences, including changing the overall color, the way various tools work, how the panels are configured, and how the interface scales based on screen resolution. Some settings in the Preferences dialog affect the application (InDesign itself), whereas others affect only the active document. For example, changes to Autocorrect preferences are document-specific as preferred spellings may change among clients. If you change the document-specific preferences while no documents are open, the changes affect all new documents (without affecting existing documents). Here, you will look at Interface preferences that affect how InDesign works with all documents.

1 Choose Edit > Preferences > Interface (Windows) or InDesign > Preferences > Interface (macOS) to customize the appearance of InDesign.

2 In the Appearance area, experiment with other options for the Color Theme.

3 Leave the setting at your preference. (Medium Dark is the default; the screen captures in this book represent the Medium Light interface.)

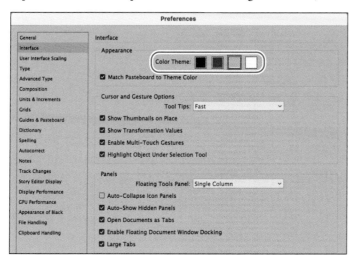

4 Click User Interface Scaling at the left to see the scaling options available for scaling interface controls according to your screen resolution.

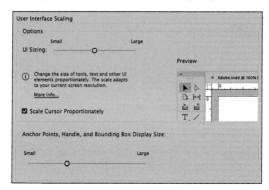

5 In the Preferences dialog, click through the list at the left to see other options for customizing InDesign. For example, the Units & Increments tab lets you specify the measurement system (points, picas, inches) on the ruler.

6 When you are finished reviewing Preferences, click OK.

Congratulations! You've learned the basics of InDesign interface elements, such as tools and panels, that you will use to complete the lessons in this book. Revisit this lesson as necessary for a refresher on panel management, zooming, and more.

Exploring on your own

▶ **Tip:** For complete and up-to-date information about using InDesign panels, tools, and other application features, use the Help menu.

Using the 01_Intro.indd document, continue to explore the tools, panels, navigation, and magnification options.

- Choose Window > Utilities > Tool Hints to display information about the selected tool. Select various tools to learn more about them.

- Choose Window > Editorial > Notes to display the Notes panel group, which includes the Assignments panel and the Track Changes panel. You can use these panels to collaborate on documents.

- Learn more about existing key commands and how you can change them by exploring the Keyboard Shortcuts dialog (Edit > Keyboard Shortcuts).

- Review the menu configurations and how you can edit them in the Menu Customization dialog (Edit > Menus).

- Try organizing your panels to meet your needs, and create your own workspace by choosing Window > Workspace > New Workspace.

- Select objects and use the Properties panel or the Control panel to change formatting.

- Using the Type tool (T.), edit and format the text.

Review questions

1 What are some ways you can change the magnification (zoom level) of a document?

2 How do you select tools in InDesign?

3 What are three ways to display a panel?

4 How do you create a panel group?

5 What are some ways you can customize the InDesign interface through Preferences?

Review answers

1 You can choose commands from the View menu to zoom in, zoom out, fit the page to the window, and more. You can also use the Zoom tool in the Tools panel and click or drag over a document to enlarge or reduce the view. In addition, you can use keyboard shortcuts to increase or reduce the magnification. Finally, you can also use the Zoom Level field on the lower-left corner of the document window.

2 You can click to select a tool in the Tools panel. Or, if the Type tool is not selected (that is, if no text insertion bar is in text), you can press the tool's keyboard shortcut. For example, you can press **V** to select the Selection tool from the keyboard; press and hold the keyboard shortcut to temporarily select the tool. Select hidden tools by positioning the pointer over a tool in the Tools panel and holding down the mouse button. When the menu appears, select the tool. Finally, you can Alt-click (Windows) or Option-click (macOS) a tool to cycle through its hidden tools.

3 To make a panel display, click its icon, click its tab, or choose its name from the Window menu. For example, choose Window > Object & Layout > Align. You can also access type-specific panels from the Type menu. For example, choose Type > Character or Type > Paragraph Styles.

4 Drag a panel off the dock to create a free-floating panel. Drag the tab of any other panel into the tab bar of the new, free-floating panel. A panel group can be moved and resized as one panel.

5 In the Preferences dialog box, adjust options such as the color of the background and panels, how panels display, and how the interface scales according to screen resolution.

2 GETTING TO KNOW INDESIGN

Lesson overview

In this lesson, you'll learn how to do the following:

- View layout aids.

- Type and style text.

- Import text and thread text frames.

- Import a graphic.

- Move, rotate, fill, and stroke (outline) an object.

- Add a QR code.

- Automate formatting with paragraph, character, and object styles.

- Check on potential production issues with the Preflight panel.

- Preview a document in Presentation mode.

 This lesson will take about 60 minutes to complete. To get the lesson files used in this chapter, download them from the web page for this book at adobepress.com/InDesignCIB2023. For more information, see "Accessing the lesson files and Web Edition" in the Getting Started section at the beginning of this book.

edible blossoms

Bistro & Bar

Relax in our elegant dining room or charming patio and enjoy the creations of our bartender, chef and gardener! Our irresistible appetizers, seasonal entrées and home-made desserts feature fruits, flowers and herbs grown right here in our stunning Urban Oasis Gardens.

Starters & Small Plates

Sip a rosé martini, try zucchini blossom fritters *(V)* or braised dandelion greens *(V, GF)* for appetizers, and share small plates such as orange ginger seared scallops or chive flower flatbread.

Entrées & Desserts

Indulge in our chef's daily creations, such as lavender honey grilled chicken or fresh basil pesto *(V)* and be sure to leave room for scrumptious violet macarons or candied pansies *(V, GF)*.

see the full menu

The building blocks of an Adobe InDesign layout are objects, text, and graphics. Layout aids such as guides help with size and placement, and styles let you format page elements automatically.

Getting started

The document for this lesson is a standard-size postcard designed to be printed and mailed. In addition, the postcard can be exported as a JPEG to use in email marketing. As you will see in this lesson, the building blocks of an InDesign document are essentially the same, regardless of the output media. In this lesson, you will add the text, images, and formatting necessary to finish the postcard.

● **Note:** If you have not already downloaded the project files for this lesson to your computer from your Account page, make sure to do so now. See "Getting Started" at the beginning of the book.

1 To ensure that the preferences and default settings of your Adobe InDesign program match those used in this lesson, move the InDesign Defaults file to a different folder following the procedure in "Saving and restoring the InDesign Defaults file" on pages 3–4.

2 Start Adobe InDesign.

3 When the InDesign Home screen displays, click the Open button at the left. (If the Home screen does not display, choose File > Open from the InDesign menu bar.)

4 Open the 02_Start.indd file in the Lesson02 folder, located inside the Lessons folder within the InDesignCIB folder on your hard drive.

5 If an alert informs you that the document contains links to sources that have been modified, click Update Modified Links.

6 Choose File > Save As, rename the file **02_Postcard.indd**, and save it in the Lesson02 folder.

● **Note:** To better view the interface onscreen or in print, the screen captures in this book reflect the Medium Light interface rather than the default setting of Medium Dark. In addition, some screen captures illustrate User Interface Scaling for a closer look at interface elements. You can modify interface settings in Preferences.

7 This lesson uses the default Essentials workspace. If necessary, choose Window > Workspace > [Essentials], and then choose Window > Workspace > Reset Essentials.

8 If you want to see what the finished document looks like, open the 02_End.indd file in the same folder. You can leave this document open to act as a guide as you work.

9 When you're ready to resume working on the lesson document, display it by clicking its tab in the upper-left corner of the document window.

Viewing guides

Revising or completing an existing document, as you will do in this lesson, is typical work for entry-level InDesign users. Currently, the postcard document is displayed in Preview mode, which displays artwork in a standard window, hiding nonprinting elements such as guides, grids, frame edges, and hidden characters. To work on this document, you will view guides and hidden characters (such as spaces and tabs).

1 Click and hold down the Screen Mode button at the bottom of the Tools panel, and choose Normal (▣) from the menu.

Any layout aids previously enabled now display. For example, light blue nonprinting lines now indicate existing text frames and objects because frame edges were already displayed (View > Extras > Show Frame Edges). You will now enable other layout aids.

2 Choose View > Grids & Guides > Show Guides.

When guides are displayed, it's easy to position objects with precision, including automatically snapping text frames and graphics frames into place. The guides do not print and do not indicate the print or export area.

3 Choose Type > Show Hidden Characters.

Displaying hidden (nonprinting) characters—such as tabs, spaces, and paragraph returns—helps you precisely select and style text. In general, it's a good idea to show hidden characters whenever you are editing or formatting text.

▶ **Tip:** The lesson document starts out in Preview Screen Mode and then you switch to Normal Screen Mode. The other modes are Bleed, for reviewing the predefined bleed area for objects that extend beyond the page boundaries; Slug, for displaying the area outside the bleed area that can contain information such as printer instructions; and Presentation, which fills the screen and works well for presenting design ideas to clients.

▶ **Tip:** As you become comfortable working with InDesign, you will discover which Screen Modes and layout aids work best for you.

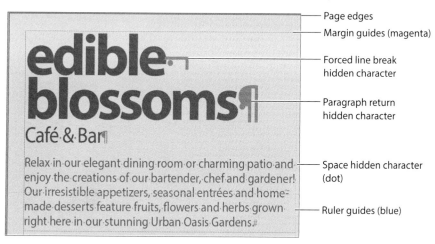

Page edges

Margin guides (magenta)

Forced line break hidden character

Paragraph return hidden character

Space hidden character (dot)

Ruler guides (blue)

4 As you work on this document, use the skills you learned in Lesson 1 to move panels, scroll, and zoom as necessary.

Adding text

With InDesign, most text is contained by a text frame. (Text can be contained in table cells and flow along paths as well.) You can type text directly into a text frame or import text files from word-processing programs. When importing text files, you can add the text to existing frames or create new frames to contain the text. If text doesn't fit within a single frame, you can link multiple text frames using a process called "threading." You will learn more about flowing text, including dividing text frames into columns, in Lesson 6, "Flowing Text."

Typing and styling text

You're ready to start working on the incomplete postcard. To get started, you'll edit and style the text under the headline.

▶ **Tip:** Use the Type tool to edit text, format text, and create new text frames.

1 Select the Type tool (**T.**), and click immediately after the word "Café."

2 Press Backspace (Windows) or Delete (macOS) four times to delete the word "Café."

| &·Bar¶ |
| Relax·in·our·elegant·dining·room·or·charming·patio·and· enjoy·the·creations·of·our·bartender,·chef·and·gardener! |

▶ **Tip:** When you enter edits, consider copying and pasting text from the notes in Acrobat or InDesign to ensure that you don't introduce typographical errors.

3 Type **Bistro** in the text frame so that the restaurant's descriptor is changed from "Café & Bar" to "Bistro & Bar."

| Bistro·&·Bar¶ |
| Relax·in·our·elegant·dining·room·or·charming·patio·and· enjoy·the·creations·of·our·bartender,·chef·and·gardener! |

4 With the insertion point still in the text, triple-click to select "Bistro & Bar."

5 Locate the Character controls of the Properties panel at the right. From the Font Style menu, select Bold.

▶ **Tip:** Using the Type tool, you can double-click to select a word, triple-click to select a line, and click four times to select a paragraph.

6 Click outside the text frame to deselect the text.

7 Choose File > Save to save your work.

Options for styling and placing text

In the Essentials workspace, the Properties panel displays at the right to provide quick access to the most common text formatting options. InDesign provides other options for formatting characters and paragraphs and for positioning text within a frame. Common text formatting options include:

- **Character formats:** Style, Size, Leading, All Caps
- **Paragraph formats:** Alignments such as Center, Indents, Space Before/After
- **Text Frame Options:** Columns, Inset Spacing, Vertical Justification

The Control panel, Paragraph panel (Type > Paragraph), and Character panel (Type > Character) provide all the controls you need to style text. To control the positioning of the text within its frame, such as dividing text into columns, choose Object > Text Frame Options. Many of these styling options also are available in the Control panel (Window > Workspace > Advanced).

Importing and flowing text

In most publishing workflows, writers and editors use word processors. When the text is almost final, they send the files to graphic designers. To complete the postcard, you will import a Microsoft Word file into a text frame at the bottom of the page using the Place command. You will then thread (link) the first text frame to the second frame. All the text in a series of threaded text frames is called a "story."

1 Using the Selection tool (▶), click a blank area of the pasteboard to make sure no objects are selected.

2 Choose File > Place. At the bottom of the Place dialog, make sure that Show Import Options is not selected. (On macOS, click Options if necessary to see Show Import Options.)

● **Note:** To see where to place the text, view the finished lesson document, 02_End.indd.

3 Navigate to the Lesson02 folder in the Lessons folder, and double-click the Bistro.docx file.

The pointer changes to a loaded text icon (⬚). You'll add this text to the text frame in the lower-left quadrant of the postcard. (The text frames are outlined by light blue nonprinting lines.)

▶ **Tip:** When the loaded text icon is displayed, you have several choices: You can drag to create a new text frame, click inside an existing frame, or click to create a new text frame within the page's column guides.

4 Position the loaded text icon in the text frame, and then click.

An out port on the text frame; the red plus sign indicates overset text.

The text in the Word file fills the frame, but it may not all fit. A red plus sign (+) in the out port of the frame (in the frame's lower-right corner) indicates overset text. You will thread the two bottom text frames so that the text flows through them.

5 Using the Selection tool, select the text frame that now contains the text.

6 Click the out port (+) of the selected frame to display the loaded text icon. Click in the text frame immediately to the right.

▶ **Tip:** You can create columns by threading individual text frames or by dividing text frames into multiple columns using the General tab of the Text Frame Options dialog (Object menu). Some designers prefer separate text frames for more layout flexibility.

Starters & Small Plates¶

Sip a rosé martini,
try zucchini blossom
fritters (V) or braised
dandelion greens (V,
GF) for appetizers, and
share small plates such

At this point, text likely remains overset. You will resolve this problem by formatting the text with styles later in this lesson.

● **Note:** Due to variations in font versions, you may see slightly different text in your frames.

Starters & Small Plates¶

Sip a rosé martini,
try zucchini blossom
fritters (V) or braised
dandelion greens (V,
GF) for appetizers,
and share small plates

such as orange ginger
seared scallops or chive
flower flatbread.¶

Entrées & Desserts¶

Indulge in our chef's
daily creations, such as

7 Choose File > Save.

Working with styles

InDesign provides paragraph styles, character styles, and object styles for quickly and consistently formatting text and objects. Another significant reason to use styles is that you can make global changes—such as changing the body text font or adjusting drop shadows—by simply editing the style. This can save you hours in making revisions to long documents such as books.

▶ **Tip:** A paragraph
style can include
nested styles that
format the beginning
of a paragraph and lines
within a paragraph. This
automates common
paragraph formatting,
such as starting a para-
graph with a drop cap
followed by all capital
letters on the first line.

Styles work as follows:

- A paragraph style includes all text formatting attributes—such as font, size, and alignment—and it applies to all the text in a paragraph. You can select a paragraph for formatting by clicking in it, highlighting any part it, or highlighting all of it.

- A character style includes only character attributes—such as font style (bold or italic) and color—and it applies only to selected text within a paragraph. Character styles are generally applied to call attention to specific text within a paragraph.

- An object style lets you apply formatting—such as fill and stroke color, stroke styles and corner effects, transparency, drop shadows, feathering, text frame options, and text wrap—to selected objects.

The object style for this text frame specifies the inset (that indents the text from the edges of the frame), the stroke around the edges of the frame, and the drop shadow behind it.

Starters & Small Plates

Sip a rosé martini, try zucchini blossom fritters *(V)* or braised dandelion greens *(V, GF)* for appe~~tizers, and share small plates such as orange ginger seared scallops or chive flower flatbread.

Paragraph styles specify formats such as alignment and basic character formats such as font and line spacing.

Character styles specify variations from the character formats in the paragraph style.

Applying paragraph styles

▶ **Tip:** In many pub-
lishing environments,
including marketing
and advertising, the
text in a publication
is referred to as "copy,"
which is why the writers
and editors are called
"copywriters" and
"copyeditors."

Because the postcard is part of a series, all the paragraph styles you need are already created. You will first apply the Body Copy style to all the text in the two threaded text frames, and then you will apply the Subhead style to the headings.

1 Using the Type tool (T), click in one of the text frames containing the newly imported text.

2 Choose Edit > Select All to select all the text in the story.

3 Click the Paragraph Styles button at the top of the Properties panel. Click the Paragraph Styles menu and select the Body Copy style to format the entire story.

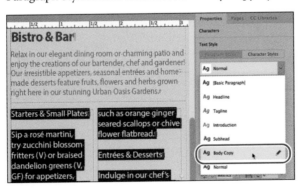

4 Using the Type tool, click in the first line of text in the story: "Starters & Small Plates."

As you can see from the hidden character (the paragraph return) at the end of the line, this line is actually its own paragraph. Therefore, it can be formatted with a paragraph style.

5 Select the Subhead style from the Paragraph Styles menu in the Properties panel.

6 Apply the Subhead paragraph style to the "Entrées & Desserts" subhead as well.

7 Choose Edit > Deselect All, and then choose File > Save.

● **Note:** If a plus sign (+) displays next to the applied style (Body Copy or Subhead), it indicates that the text formatting does not precisely match the style's formatting. To resolve this, click Clear Overrides (¶✸) at the bottom of the Paragraph Styles panel. You will learn more about styles in Lesson 9, "Working with Styles."

Formatting text for the character style

Highlighting key words in a paragraph can draw readers into the text. For the postcard copy, you will format the abbreviations for vegetarian foods (V) and gluten-free foods (GF) to make them "pop" and then create a character style based on that formatting. You can then quickly apply the character style to other selected words.

1 Using the Zoom tool (🔍), zoom in on the first text frame in the lower-left quadrant of the postcard. This frame contains the subhead "Starters & Small Plates."

2 Using the Type tool (T,), select the "(V)" in the first paragraph of body copy; be sure to include the parentheses.

3 In the Character controls of the Properties panel at the right, select Italic from the Type Style menu.

4 Click the Fill box (T) to display the document's color swatches. Click the red swatch named Red-Bright to apply the color to the text.

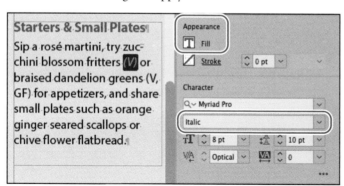

5 Click the pasteboard to deselect the text and view your changes.

6 Choose File > Save.

Creating and applying a character style

Now that you have formatted the text, you are ready to create a character style based on that formatting.

1 Using the Type tool (**T.**), select the newly formatted "(V)."

2 Choose Type > Character Styles to display the Character Styles panel.

3 Select New Character Style from the panel menu (≡).

● Note: If the New Character Style dialog does not open immediately, double-click Character Style 1 in the Character Styles panel.

The New Character Style dialog opens with a new style named Character Style 1. This new style includes the characteristics of the selected text, as indicated in the Style Settings area of the dialog.

4 In the Style Name field, type **Red Italic**.

5 At the bottom of the New Character Style dialog, select Apply Style To Selection.

6 Click OK.

7 Using the Type tool, select the "(V, GF)" later in the first paragraph.

8 Click Red Italic in the Character Styles panel.

Because you applied a character style instead of a paragraph style, the formatting affected only the selected text, not the entire paragraph.

9 Using the Type tool, select the "(V)" next to "fresh basil pesto" in the text frame at right.

10 Click Red Italic in the Character Styles panel.

11 Repeat the process to apply the Red Italic character style to the "(V, GF)" and the trailing period at the end of the paragraph.

▶ **Tip:** Typesetters often apply the same style to any punctuation following text formatted with a different style. (For example, if a word is italicized, you would italicize a comma after it.) This may vary based on design preferences or a publisher's style guide. The key is to be consistent.

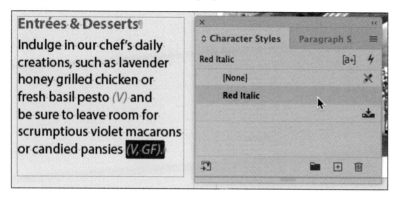

12 Choose Type > Character Styles to close the panel, and then choose File > Save.

Working with graphics

To add one of the final design elements to the postcard, you'll import, resize, and position a graphic. Graphics used in InDesign documents are placed inside frames. In InDesign, you can use the Selection tool (▶) to resize a graphics frame and to position the graphic within the frame. You will learn more about working with graphics in Lesson 11, "Importing and Modifying Graphics."

1 Choose View > Fit Page In Window.

You will position the graphic in the upper-right quadrant of the postcard.

2 Make sure that no objects are selected by choosing Edit > Deselect All.

3 Click the Import File button, the last option on the Properties panel at the right. In the Place dialog, make sure that Show Import Options is not selected.

4 Navigate to the Lesson02 folder in the Lessons folder, and double-click the DiningRoom.jpg file.

▶ **Tip:** You can place a graphic into an existing frame or create a new frame as you place the graphic. You can also drag graphic files from your computer's desktop onto an InDesign page or pasteboard.

The loaded graphics icon (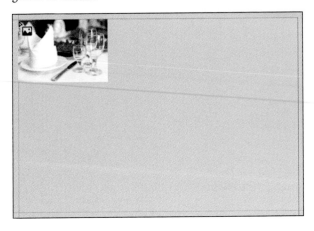) displays a preview of the graphic. If you click the page, InDesign places the graphic at full size, inside an identically sized graphics frame. In this case, however, you will scale the graphic as you add it to the page. The resulting graphics frame will have the same dimensions as the graphic. The graphic will be placed in the upper-right quadrant of the postcard.

● **Note:** To see where to place the graphic, consult the finished lesson document, 02_End.indd.

5 Position the loaded graphics icon at the intersection of the light blue and pink guides as shown.

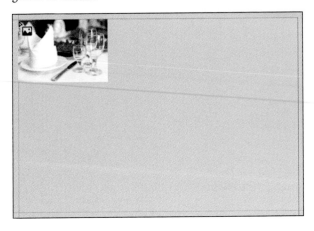

▶**Tip:** When you create a frame while placing a graphic on the page, the graphic is automatically scaled to fit within the frame. Use the scaling controls in the Properties panel and the Control panel to precisely adjust the graphic size. You will learn more about sizing in Lesson 11.

6 Drag down and to the right until the pointer touches the guide on the right side of the page.

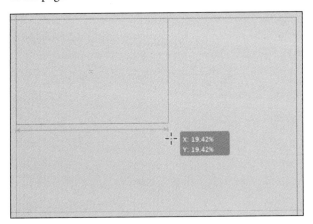

When you release the mouse button, the graphic is added to the page and a graphics frame is created automatically.

You will now experiment with cropping a graphic by decreasing the size of the frame, and you will try moving the graphic within the frame. You will undo these changes.

7 Using the Selection tool (▶), select the middle handle at the bottom of the graphics frame and drag it up. You can crop the image by dragging any of its eight resizing handles.

Use the Selection tool to crop a graphic by reducing the size of its frame.

8 Press Ctrl+Z (Windows) or Command+Z (macOS) to undo the crop.

9 Still using the Selection tool, position the pointer over the graphic to display the content grabber (◎) in the center of the graphic.

10 Click the content grabber to select the graphic, and then drag up to position the image within the frame as you please.

▶ **Tip:** To reposition a graphic with more control, press the Shift key while dragging. This constrains the movement to horizontal, vertical, and 45-degree angles. Click and pause briefly before moving the graphic within a frame to see the cropped part of the graphic ghosted but visible outside the frame area.

11 Press Ctrl+Z (Windows) or Command+Z (macOS) to undo the image move.
The eventual position of the graphic should be where you placed it in step 6.

12 Choose File > Save.

Working with objects

▶ **Tip:** You will learn more about objects in Lesson 4, "Working with Objects."

The building blocks of InDesign pages are objects: text frames, graphics frames, lines, and more. In general, you move and resize objects with the Selection tool. Objects can have a fill color (background color) and a stroke color (outline or border), which you can customize by specifying the width and style. You can move objects around freely, snap them to other objects, and place them with precision according to guides or values you enter. In addition, you can resize and scale objects and specify how text wraps around them. Here, you will experiment with a few object-related features, including adding a QR code for easy web access.

Moving and rotating an object

A flower graphic created by converting flower characters from the Zapf Dingbats font into outlines (Type > Create Outlines) is on the pasteboard to the left of the page. You will move this graphic to the right of the restaurant name, "edible blossoms." Then, you will rotate the object and adjust its placement.

1 Choose View > Fit Page In Window to center the page in the document window. Scroll left to see the flower graphic on the pasteboard.

2 Using the Selection tool (▶), click the flower graphic.

3 Drag the graphic to the right of the headline, "edible blossoms."

With the object still selected, you will fine-tune the placement using the Properties panel.

▶ **Tip:** When you enter values in the Properties panel or Control panel X and Y fields, the object is repositioned according to its reference point. You can view and change the reference point (▦) by clicking a box immediately to the left of the X and Y fields.

4 In the Transform controls of the Properties panel, click the More Options button (⋯) if necessary. To specify the object's placement in relation to its reference point (upper-left corner), type the following values in the fields:

X: **1.85 in**

Y: **.05 in**

Rotation angle (△): **–10**

You can tab between the fields, and then press Enter (Windows) or Return (macOS) to apply the changes.

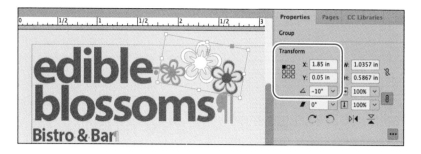

5 Choose File > Save.

Changing an object's stroke and fill

When an object is selected, you can change its stroke (outline or border) weight and color. In addition, you can apply a fill (background) color.

1 Choose Edit > Deselect All to make sure nothing is selected.

2 To better focus on the objects, choose Type > Hide Hidden Characters.

3 Click the Direct Selection (▷) tool on the Tools panel, and then click the white flower in the graphic to select it.

● **Note:** The flower graphic is a group of objects. The Direct Selection tool lets you select a single object within a group. You can also select a single object in a group by double-clicking it with the Selection tool.

4 In the Appearance controls of the Properties panel, click the Fill box (☐) to display the document's swatches. Click the Green-Dark swatch.

5 Press the V key on the keyboard to switch to the Selection tool (▶). Click to select the black horizontal line at the bottom of the page.

6 In the Appearance controls of the Properties panel, click the Stroke box (■) to display the document's swatches. Click the Green-Medium swatch.

7 Click the pasteboard to deselect all objects.

8 Choose File > Save.

Adding a QR Code

Consumers often expect advertising pieces to include a QR code so they can quickly visit a website for more information. The code is a graphic (generated by InDesign) that is inside a graphics frame. Here, you will add a QR code below the "see the full menu" text in the lower middle part of the postcard.

1 Choose Edit > Deselect All to make sure nothing is selected.

2 Choose Object > Generate QR Code.

● **Note:** Because the postcard in this lesson is for a fictional restaurant, you will create a QR code to the main Adobe website. When creating your own designs, you may type or paste any URL in the Content field.

3 In the Content tab of the Generate QR Code dialog, leave the Type setting at Plain Text. Type **https://www.adobe.com** in the Content field.

4 Click the Color tab, and then select Green-Dark in the list of swatches. This creates a QR code that matches the color theme of the postcard.

5 Click OK to load the pointer with the QR code. Drag the pointer below the "see the full menu" text to place the QR code. Keep the graphics frame selected so you can fine-tune its placement.

6 In the Transform controls of the Properties panel, type the following values in the fields:

● **Note:** Remember, you can tab between the fields, and then press Enter/Return to apply changes made in the Properties panel.

X: **3.6 in**

Y: **3.25 in**

W: **.5 in**

H: **.5 in**

7 To resize the QR code and center it within the frame, click Fit Content Proportionally (◨) in the Frame Fitting controls of the Properties panel.

8 Click the pasteboard to deselect all objects.

9 Choose File > Save.

Working with object styles

As with paragraph and character styles, you can quickly and consistently format objects by saving attributes as styles. In this exercise, you will apply an existing object style to the two threaded text frames containing the body copy.

1 Choose View > Fit Page In Window.

2 Choose Window > Styles > Object Styles to display the Object Styles panel.

3 Using the Selection tool (▶), click the text frame at the left containing the "Starters & Small Plates" subhead.

4 Click the Green Stroke And Drop Shadow style in the Object Styles panel.

5 Click the second text frame, which contains the "Entrées & Desserts" subhead.

6 Click the Green Stroke And Drop Shadow style in the Object Styles panel.

7 Select the text frame at the left and drag the bottom down until the paragraph fits in the frame. Then, select the text frame at the right and drag the bottom down to match the height of the text frame at the left.

8 Choose Edit > Deselect All.

9 Click the Object Styles panel's close box, and then choose File > Save.

Preflighting as you work

Whenever you start working on a document—whether you're creating a document from scratch or revising an existing document—you will need to know the intended output of the document (print and/or digital display) and keep an eye on output issues. For example, are all the lines in the document thick enough to print, and will the colors display and print properly? You will learn more about all these issues throughout the lessons in this book.

In publishing, the process of evaluating a document for potential output issues is known as "preflighting." The InDesign Live Preflight feature lets you monitor documents as you're working to prevent problems from occurring. To customize Live Preflight, you can create or import production rules (called "preflight profiles") against which InDesign checks your documents. The default profile supplied with InDesign flags issues such as missing fonts (fonts that are not active on your system) and overset text (text that does not fit in its frame).

In this exercise, you will check the document against the embedded Mailhouse profile, which the printer supplied to prevent common issues, such as the use of RGB colors in documents intended for CMYK output on a printing press.

▶ **Tip:** Keep an eye on the lower-left corner of the document window to see if any preflight errors arise. You can double-click the word "error" to open the Preflight panel for details on any errors.

1 Choose Window > Output > Preflight to open the Preflight panel; the Mailhouse profile is selected.

Using the Mailhouse preflight profile, InDesign finds 9 errors, as indicated next to the red Preflight icon (●) in the lower-left corner of the Preflight panel. According to the Error list in the Preflight panel, the problems are in the COLOR category.

2 To view the error, click the arrow next to COLOR in the Preflight panel.

▶ **Tip:** To quickly navigate to the object with the error, click the page number link in the Preflight panel.

3 Click the arrow next to Color Space Not Allowed, and then click the first instance of Text Frame in the list.

4 To display details for the error, click the arrow next to Info at the bottom of the Preflight panel.

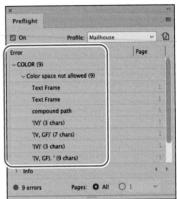

The Problem is reported as "Content Uses RGB." The Fix area offers the following suggestion: "Apply a swatch that uses a supported color space or mode, or edit the current swatch and specify a different color mode."

5 Choose Window > Color > Swatches to display the document's color swatches.

6 Double-click the Red-Bright swatch. In the Swatch Options dialog, select CMYK from the Color Mode menu (scroll up to locate the CMYK option if necessary). Click OK.

Because the Color Space Not Allowed error was resolved, InDesign now reports No Errors in the Preflight panel and in the lower-left corner of the document window.

7 Close the Preflight panel and the Swatches panel, and then choose File > Save.

Viewing the document in Presentation mode

In Presentation mode, the InDesign interface is hidden entirely, and the document fills the whole screen. This mode works well for presenting design ideas to clients.

1 Press and hold down the Screen Mode button (⊞) at the bottom of the Tools panel, and select Presentation (▢).

2 After viewing the document, press Esc (Escape) to exit Presentation mode. The document displays in its previous screen mode, Normal.

3 To view the document without layout aids, choose View > Screen Mode > Preview.

4 Choose View > Actual Size to see the document at its output size.

5 Choose File > Save.

Congratulations! You've learned many InDesign basics.

▶ **Tip:** You cannot edit documents in Presentation mode, but you can make changes in any other screen mode.

Exploring on your own

To learn more about InDesign, try the following within the postcard layout:

- Change the text formatting by choosing other options in the Properties panel.

- Apply different paragraph and character styles to text. Apply the object style to different objects.

- Move and resize objects and graphics.

- Create a QR code that links to your favorite restaurant. You can test the QR code by pointing your smartphone camera at the screen.

▶ **Tip:** If you're connected to the internet, click the Adobe Stock field in the upper-right corner of the document window. This takes you to the Adobe Stock image library, where you can download previews and purchase images.

InDesign best practices

While completing the postcard in this lesson, you experimented with the basic building blocks of a document and the best practices for creating a document. When you create a document following best practices, the document is easy to format, revise, and replicate consistently. Some of these techniques are listed here.

- **Avoid stacking objects.** Format one object rather than using multiple objects. For example, the two text frames containing the postcard's body text have a text inset, stroke weight, stroke color, and drop shadow applied. A new user might be tempted to create this look by stacking multiple frames. Using multiple objects creates extra work when moving, aligning, and formatting objects.

- **Thread text frames.** New InDesign users are often tempted to place or paste text into separate, freestanding text frames. The text in these frames needs to be selected and formatted individually. If you flow the text through threaded frames, it remains as a single body of text called a "story." Benefits of working with a story as opposed to disjointed frames of text include the following: you can select all the text in a story for formatting, you can limit the use of Find/Change and Check Spelling to the text in a story, and you can export all the text in a story. When you're working on a longer document, such as a book, threading text frames is crucial to controlling the text placement.

- **Use styles for all formatting.** InDesign provides styles for formatting objects, paragraphs, lines within paragraphs, characters, tables, and table cells. With styles, you can quickly and consistently format everything in a document. In addition, if you decide to change a format, you can update the style to make a global change. For example, in the postcard, if you wanted to change the font used in the body copy, all you would need to do is edit the character formats of the Body Copy paragraph style. Styles can be updated to reflect new formatting, and styles can be shared among documents as well.

- **Preflight early and often.** As soon as you receive a document to work on, find out how it will be used (print and/or digital display) and use the Preflight feature to make sure the document will output correctly. For example, if the document is missing a font, you will need to acquire and activate that font before you continue working on the document.

- **Try to automate repetitive tasks.** InDesign has many sophisticated features whose purpose you may not understand until you need them. For example, if you're constantly having to change the format of phone numbers (from using parentheses to hyphens), you can do that automatically using Wildcards in Find/Change. If you need to build a table of contents or index, you'll find features to help with both. Whenever you find yourself doing anything tedious, the InDesign Help file, or even a simple Google search, can help you find a better way.

You will learn more about all these features as you work through the lessons.

Review questions

1 What tool allows you to create text frames?

2 What tool allows you to thread text frames?

3 What symbol indicates that a text frame has more text than it can display—that is, overset text?

4 What tool allows you to move both frames and graphics within frames?

5 Where is the command for creating a QR code?

6 How can you tell if an aspect of a layout will cause output problems?

7 List two best practices for creating InDesign documents.

Review answers

1 You create text frames with the Type tool.

2 You thread text frames with the Selection tool.

3 A red plus sign in the lower-right corner of a text frame indicates overset text.

4 The Selection tool lets you drag a graphics frame (and its graphic) to move it, and it lets you move a graphic within its frame.

5 The Generate QR Code command is in the Object menu.

6 The Preflight panel reports errors when something in the layout does not comply with the selected preflight profile. For example, if the selected profile specifies no RGB color usage but an RGB color or image is used in the document, an error is reported. Preflight errors are also reported in the lower-left corner of the document window.

7 InDesign best practices include the following: avoid stacking objects, thread text frames, use styles for all formatting, preflight early and often, and try to automate repetitive tasks.

3 SETTING UP A DOCUMENT AND WORKING WITH PAGES

Lesson overview

In this lesson, you'll learn how to do the following:

- Create a new document and set document defaults.
- Save custom document settings as a document preset.
- Lay out a parent page.
- Create an additional parent page.
- Apply a parent page to document pages.
- Add pages to a document.
- Rearrange and delete pages.
- Change the size of pages.
- Create sections and specify page numbering.
- Lay out document pages.
- Prepare artwork to print to the edge of the paper.
- Rotate a document page.

This lesson will take about 90 minutes to complete. To get the lesson files used in this chapter, download them from the web page for this book at adobepress.com/InDesignCIB2023. For more information, see "Accessing the lesson files and Web Edition" in the Getting Started section at the beginning of this book.

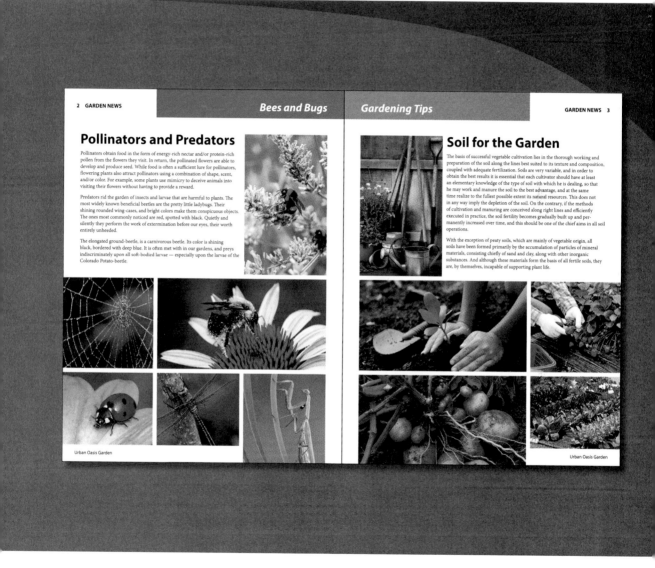

By taking advantage of features that help you set up
the publications you create, you can ensure consistent
page layout, simplify your production process, and
work as quickly and efficiently as possible.

Getting started

In this lesson, you'll set up an eight-page newsletter with an insert and then place text and graphics on one of the document's facing-page spreads.

● **Note:** If you have not already downloaded the project files for this lesson to your computer from your Account page, make sure to do so now. See "Getting Started" at the beginning of the book.

1 To ensure that the preferences and default settings of your InDesign program match those used in this lesson, move the InDesign Defaults file to a different folder following the procedure in "Saving and restoring the InDesign Defaults file" on pages 3–4.

2 Start InDesign. To see what the finished document looks like, open the 03_End.indd file in the Lesson03 folder, located inside the Lessons folder within the InDesignCIB folder on your hard drive.

● **Note:** If an alert informs you that the document contains links to sources that have been modified, click Update Modified Links.

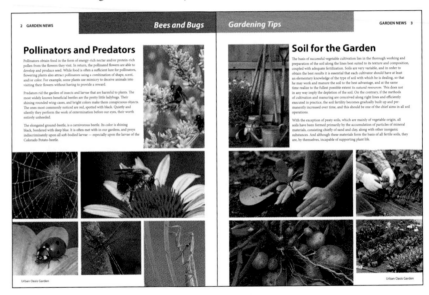

● **Note:** To better view the interface onscreen or in print, the screen captures in this book reflect the Medium Light interface rather than the default setting of Medium Dark. In addition, some screen captures illustrate User Interface Scaling for a closer look at interface elements. You can modify interface settings in Preferences.

3 Scroll through the document to view other pages. To see the guidelines and placeholder frames on the pages, choose View > Screen Mode > Normal. Navigate back to pages 2–3, which are the only document pages you'll lay out in this lesson. You will also lay out a pair of parent page spreads.

4 Close the 03_End.indd file after you have finished examining it.

5 To ensure that the panels and menu commands match those used in this lesson, choose Window > Workspace > [Advanced], and then choose Window > Workspace > Reset Advanced. To begin working, you'll learn how to create a new document.

Creating a new document

First, you will experiment with creating a new document the simplest way.

1 Choose File > New > Document or click the New File button on the InDesign home page.

2 Notice the categories: Recent, Saved, Print, Web, and Mobile. The Print, Web, and Mobile categories store document settings, called "presets," that are appropriate for each purpose. Each preset stores settings such as commonly used page sizes, default color swatches, and different measurement units (pixels for Web and Mobile, for example). The choice is governed by the intent of your layout. The Recent category stores your recently used settings so that you can use them again. The Saved category stores presets that you make. Choosing one of these saved document presets when you're starting a new project saves time and ensures consistency. This feature allows you to store the setup for many different projects so that they are always ready to use.

▶ **Tip:** You can use any supported unit of measurement in any dialog or panel. If you want to use a measurement unit that differs from the default, simply type the indicator for the unit you want to use, such as *p* for picas, *pt* for points, *px* for pixels, *cm* for centimeters, *mm* for millimeters, and either *in* or " (inch marks) for inches, after the value you enter in a box.

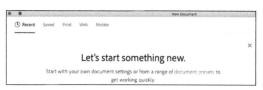

3 Choose Print and click Create. Examine the workspace. For example, choose Window > Color > Swatches, and notice that the default swatches are CMYK.

4 Choose File > New > Document, click Mobile, and then click Create. Notice the differences between this new document and the one created using the Print category. For example, compare the colors in the Swatches panel and the units of measurement on the rulers in the two documents.

5 To close both files without saving, choose File > Close, and click Don't Save (if necessary).

Creating and saving custom document settings

Now you will create a preset for an eight-page newsletter. Part of the preset includes document settings, such as the number of pages, page size, columns, and margins. You can save the correct details for any particular project in a preset, rather than having to set them up again each time. Make sure you have closed all files first.

1 Choose Edit > Preferences > Units & Increments (Windows) or InDesign > Preferences > Units & Increments (macOS). Change the Horizontal and Vertical settings to Inches to follow along with the steps in this lesson. Click OK.

2 Choose File > Document Presets > Define.

3 Click New in the Document Presets dialog.

4 In the New Document Preset dialog, set the following:

- In the Document Preset field, type **Newsletter**.

- For Intent, choose Print.

- In the Number Of Pages field, type **8**.

- Make sure that the Facing Pages option is selected.

- Choose Letter for Page Size.

● **Note:** "Gutter" is the term for the space between columns.

- In the Columns area, type **3** for Number, and for Gutter, click the down arrow once to set the gutter at .125 inches.

- In the Margins area, make sure that the Make All Settings The Same icon in the center of the margin settings is deselected (🔗) (broken chain) so that you can enter custom settings for each margin. Type **1.3125** for Top, **.375** for Bottom, **.5** for Inside, and **.25** for Outside.

▶ **Tip:** The bleed values specify an area outside the perimeter of each page that is used to print design elements that will extend to the edge of the paper in the finished piece, such as pictures or a colored background. The bleed area is trimmed and discarded after the printing process.

5 Click the triangle to the left of Bleed And Slug to display additional controls. Highlight or delete the text (0 in) in the Top field of the Bleed option, and then enter **0p9** (the picas measurement system). Then ensure that the Make All Settings The Same icon (🔗) is selected (unbroken chain) so that the same value is used for Bottom, Inside, and Outside. Press the Tab key and notice that InDesign automatically converts measurements expressed using other measurement units (in this case, picas and points) to the default equivalents (in this case, inches). (The standard Bleed value is one-eighth of an inch [.125], or 0p9.)

6 Click OK in both dialogs to save the document preset.

Creating a new document from a preset

Each time you create a new document, you can choose a document preset as the starting point rather than specifying multiple document settings, such as the number of pages, the page size, the number of columns, and more. In this exercise, you'll use the Newsletter preset that you just created.

1 Choose File > New > Document.

2 In the New Document dialog, click Saved at the top, and then click the Newsletter preset.

3 Click Create at the bottom right of the dialog (not shown).

InDesign creates a new document using all the specifications from the document preset, including the page size, margins, columns, and number of pages.

4 Open the Pages panel by clicking its icon in the panel dock (📘) or choosing Window > Pages. If necessary, drag the bottom of the panel downward until all eight document page icons are visible.

In the Pages panel, the icon for page 1 is highlighted, and the page number below the icon is displayed within a highlighted rectangle to indicate that page 1 is currently displayed in the document window. The Pages panel is divided into two sections by a horizontal line. The upper area displays thumbnails of the document's parent pages. A parent page is like a template that you can apply to any page in a document. Parent pages contain elements, such as headers, footers, and page numbers, that appear on all document pages. (You'll work with parent pages later in this lesson.) The area below the line of the Pages panel displays thumbnails of document pages.

▶ **Tip:** You can also create a new document based on a document preset by choosing File > Document Presets > [Preset_Name]. If you press the Shift key when selecting a preset, the New Document dialog is bypassed, and a new document based on that preset opens.

5 Choose File > Save As, name the file **03_Setup.indd**, navigate to the Lesson03 folder, and click Save.

About page numbering

There are two kinds of page numbering in any kind of multipage print publication. One is a result of the way paper folds to create the physical pages, regardless of anything printed on the pages. The other is the label printed on the pages. The label, or "folio," that appears on the document pages can have many possible configurations and can differ from the physical pages. For example, the label can have sections that restart the numbering with each section, such as Roman numerals in the front of a publication. In the Pages panel, the page thumbnails show the physical structure of a document, and the numbers below the thumbnails show the label.

Any printed material that has a spine, such as a magazine or a book, follows a structure dictated by folding paper. The simplest example is to fold a piece of paper in half. Each resulting rectangle is a page. If you nest two folded pieces of paper into each other and staple them at the fold (the spine), you have created an eight-page booklet. The first page (the cover) of this booklet is to the right of the fold (the spine). Open the first page and you have one page to the left of the spine (or fold), page 2, and one page to the right of the spine, page 3.

When you create a document with facing pages, InDesign shows you this structure in the Pages panel. Page 1 (outside cover) is to the right of the center line, which represents the spine. Page 2 (inside cover) is to the left. All odd number pages are to the right of the spine, and all even number pages are to the left.

spine
(fold)

Working with parent pages

Before you add graphics and text frames to a document, you may want to set up the parent pages, which serve as templates for your document pages. Any object that you add to a parent page automatically appears on the document pages to which the parent page has been applied. Setting up parent pages is a strategy to make it easier to keep a design structure consistent throughout a document, rather than starting over with each new page or duplicating the last page you worked on. Parent pages can also automate page numbering, contain repeating elements so that you have to create and position them only once, and have the advantage that any changes to these elements also appear on the document pages based on that parent page.

In this document, you'll create two parent page spreads to contain elements such as headers, footers, and placeholder frames for text and graphics. By creating multiple parent pages, you allow for variation within a consistent design theme.

Adding guides to the parent page

Guides are nonprinting lines that help you lay out a document precisely. Guides placed on a parent page appear on any document pages to which that parent is applied. For this document, you'll add several guides that, along with the existing column guides, act as a grid to help you position graphics frames, text frames, and other objects.

1 In the upper area of the Pages panel, double-click the name A-Parent. The parent spread's left and right pages are displayed in the document window.

2 Choose Layout > Create Guides.

3 Select Preview to display your changes as you make them.

4 For the Rows option, type **4** in the Number field and **.125** in the Gutter field.

5 For the Columns option, type **2** in the Number field and **0** in the Gutter field.

6 For Fit Guides To, select Page and notice how the horizontal and vertical guides appear on your parent pages, along with the margin and column guides that you established when you created the Newsletter preset.

▶ **Tip:** If the two pages of the parent page spread are not centered in the document window, double-click the Hand tool in the Tools panel to center them.

▶ **Tip:** The Create Guides command (Layout menu) can also be used when working on a document page as well as a parent page.

Selecting Margins instead of Page causes the guides to fit within the margin boundaries rather than the page boundaries. One choice may work better with a particular design than the other.

7 Click OK. You can close the Pages panel if you like.

Dragging guides from rulers

You can also add guides to a page or spread by dragging guides from the horizontal (top) and vertical (left side) rulers at the edge of the document window.

In this exercise, you will place headers above the top margin of the page and footers below the bottom margin. To position the headers and footers accurately, you will add two horizontal guides and two vertical guides.

1 Open the Transform panel (Window > Object & Layout > Transform). Without clicking in your document, move the pointer around the document window and watch the horizontal and vertical rulers as the pointer moves. Notice how the hairline indicators in the rulers correspond to the pointer's position. Also notice that the dimmed X and Y values in the Control panel and the Transform panel indicate the position of the pointer.

2 Press Ctrl (Windows) or Command (macOS) and position your pointer on the horizontal ruler anywhere above the spread. Drag a ruler guide down to .375. The Y value is displayed next to the pointer while you drag and is also displayed in the Y field in the Control panel and the Transform panel. If the Y value doesn't display .375 as you drag, place the guide as close as you can, and then—with the

● **Note:** When a guide is selected, the color becomes darker than when it is not selected.

guide still selected—highlight the Y value in the Control panel or the Transform panel, enter **.375**, and then press Enter (Windows) or Return (macOS).

● **Note:** The controls in the Transform panel are similar to those in the Control panel. You can use either panel to make many common modifications, such as changing position, size, scale, and angle of rotation.

Pressing Ctrl/Command when you create a guide causes the guide to extend across both pages of the spread, as well as across the pasteboard on either side. If you don't press Ctrl/Command, the guide will extend only across the page on which you release the mouse button.

3 Press Ctrl/Command and drag one more ruler guide down from the horizontal ruler to 10.75 on the vertical ruler.

▶ **Tip:** Pressing Alt (Windows) or Option (macOS) while dragging a guide from the horizontal ruler changes the guide to a vertical guide and also changes a vertical guide to a horizontal guide when dragging a guide from the vertical ruler.

4 Press Ctrl/Command and drag a ruler guide from the vertical ruler to the .5 position on the horizontal ruler. Watch the X value in the Control panel as you drag.

▶ **Tip:** To snap guides to ruler tick marks, press Shift while dragging the ruler.

5 Press Ctrl/Command and drag another guide from the vertical ruler to the 16.5 position on the horizontal ruler.

6 Close or dock the Transform panel, and then choose File > Save.

Step And Repeat, paste and delete guides

A key concept to understand about InDesign guides is that they behave like other objects. You can use many of the same techniques with guides that you use for working with any objects. One powerful technique is Step And Repeat.

1 Navigate to page 6 by double-clicking the icon for page 6 in the Pages panel. Drag a guide from the vertical ruler to 1 inch from the left.

2 With this guide still selected, choose Layout > Ruler Guides. Under the Color menu, click to see the color list and choose Red. It can be quite helpful to use a different color for guides that are for different purposes or on different layers. (You'll learn about layers in the next lesson.) Click OK. Click on the page away from the guide to see the new color. Using the Selection tool (▶), drag across the guide to select it again.

3 Open the Step And Repeat dialog (Edit > Step And Repeat). Click Preview to see the changes while you work. Enter **3** for the repeat count and **.75** for the Horizontal offset. Click OK.

● **Note:** If you accidentally deselect this new guide, drag across the guide to select it (with the Selection tool). When selected, the color of the guide will be darker.

4 Using the Selection tool, drag across all four guides you just created to select them. Choose Copy from the Edit menu.

5 Double-click page 8 in the Pages panel. Choose Paste In Place from the Edit menu. Click an empty area of the page (to deselect) so that you can see the red guides. The guides will be in the same place on page 8 as they are on page 6. This technique can be useful when you want to duplicate a design but not on enough pages to warrant creating another parent page. You can also copy and paste guides between documents.

6 If you decide to change your layout, it's helpful to delete guides you no longer need. Unneeded guides become clutter. Again, using the Selection tool, drag across the four guides you just pasted onto page 8 to select them. Choose Edit > Clear.

Creating a text frame on the parent page

Any text or graphic that you place on a parent page appears on document pages to which the parent is applied. To create a header, you'll add a publication title ("Garden News") and a page number marker to the top of the left (verso) and right (recto) pages of the document's facing-page parent spread.

▶ **Tip:** A header is text placed at the top of a page and is separate from the main body text. A header can include information such as page number, publication name, or issue date. When placed at the bottom of a page, such text is called a "footer."

1 Navigate to the left parent page by double-clicking it in the Pages panel, and make sure that you can see the top of the page. If necessary, zoom in and use the scroll bars or Hand tool (✋).

2 Select the Type tool (**T**) in the Tools panel. On the left parent page, click near where the two ruler guides intersect above the leftmost column and drag to create a text frame, as shown here. You'll position it exactly in a later step.

3 With the insertion point in the new text frame, choose Type > Insert Special Character > Markers > Current Page Number.

The letter A appears in your text frame, which is the placeholder character for automatic page numbering on the A parent page. On document pages based on this parent page, the correct page number is displayed, such as "4" on the document's page 4.

4 To add an em space after the page number, right-click with the insertion point after the letter A to display a context menu, and then choose Insert White Space > Em Space. Or choose Type > Insert White Space > Em Space.

▶ **Tip:** An em space is the width of the current font size. For example, when working with 12-point text, an em space is 12 points wide. The term originated in the days of metal type and described the width of the capital letter "M."

5 Type **Garden News** after the em space. Notice that the text frame displays with a dotted line rather than a solid line. Objects on parent pages display with dotted lines to distinguish them from objects on document pages.

A	Garden News

The dotted lines of frames on parent page objects may appear solid when you zoom in above 350%.

● **Note:** You can apply text attributes with the frame selected rather than selecting text with the cursor. This is a very useful feature. For example, you can select several text frames and apply the same attributes to all of them at the same time.

6 Press the Escape key to change to the Selection tool while keeping the text frame selected. Choose the Type tool and make sure Character Formatting Controls (A) is selected in the Control panel. Choose Myriad Pro from the Font menu, and from the Style menu, select Bold. Then choose Type > Change Case > UPPERCASE.

7 With the frame still selected, choose Object > Text Frame Options. Under Inset Spacing, turn off the Make All Settings The Same icon (🔳) and set the Left and Right insets to **.125**. Under Vertical Justification, choose Center from the Align menu, and click OK.

8 To size and position the text frame, click the Selection tool (▶). Set the reference point on the Control panel to the center-left position, and type these settings: X **.25**, Y **.5**, W **3**, and H **.3125**.

Next, you'll duplicate the header on the left parent page, position the copy on the right parent page, and adjust the text so that it's a mirror opposite of the left header.

1 Choose View > Fit Spread In Window to display both parent pages.

▶ **Tip:** Pressing the Shift key while Alt-dragging (Windows) or Option-dragging (macOS) a text frame, movement is constrained to vertical, horizontal, and 45-degree angles.

2 Using the Selection tool (▶), select the header text frame on the left parent page. To make a copy of this text frame, hold down the Shift key and Alt key (Windows) or Option key (macOS), and drag the text frame to the right parent page so that it approximately mirrors the left parent page, as shown here.

Another key concept is that InDesign can do math for you. When you have to move something an exact amount or position something in an exact location, type the math in the Control panel, rather than figuring out the result on your own. The reference point controls which side of the frame moves to the new position. In this case, we want the frame to end one-quarter inch (.25) from the edge of the paper on the right page, so we want to target the right side of the frame.

3 With this duplicate text frame still selected, change the reference point in the Control panel to a right position. Type **17–.25** for the X value and press the Tab key. (17 is the width of the spread, minus .25 to move it .25 to the left of the edge.) The right edge of this text frame is now at 16.75 inches.

4 Select the Type tool (T), and then click the Align Right button in the Control panel. On smaller screens, you may need to click the Paragraph Formatting Tools (¶) button before you see the Paragraph Alignment buttons.

The text is now right-aligned within the header frame on the right parent page. Now you'll move the page number to the right side of the words "Garden News" so that the page numbers will print on the outside edges of the pages, not toward the spine, which is more useful to the reader and best practice in publishing.

▶ **Tip:** Page numbers are placed near the outside edges of the paper because it's easier for readers to see the numbers when flipping through a printed publication.

5 Delete the em space and the "A" at the beginning of the right page header.

6 Press Ctrl/Command. Then, press the right arrow key twice to move the insertion point to the end of "Garden News" and choose Type > Insert White Space > Em Space. Choose Type > Insert Special Character > Markers > Current Page Number to insert the Current Page Number character after the em space.

A GARDEN NEWS		GARDEN NEWS A

Left and right headers

7 Choose View > Fit Spread In Window to display both parent pages. To create footers from duplicates of the headers, select both headers with the Selection tool (▶). Press Shift and Alt (Windows) or Option (macOS), and drag down below the pink bottom margin guide. This creates a copy of both text frames.

8 With both frames still selected, select the Type tool (T). In the Control panel, change the font from Bold to Regular and set the size to 10 points by clicking the down arrow next to Font Size twice. Then choose Type > Change Case > Title Case. Switch back to the Selection tool (▶) and, in the Alignment area of the Control panel, click the Align Bottom button.

● **Note:** On smaller screens, fewer tools are available in the Control panel. If you don't see the text alignment tools in the Control panel, choose Object > Text Frame Options, and in the Vertical Justification area choose Bottom.

9 Select the Type tool and place the insertion point in the left footer. Zoom in to make it easier to see. Triple-click to select all the text and replace it by typing **Urban Oasis Garden**. Select and copy this new text, move to the right footer, select all the text there, paste the new text (Urban Oasis Garden), and then click the Align Right button. Choose Edit > Deselect All, and return to Fit Spread In Window view.

Urban Oasis Garden		Urban Oasis Garden

Left and right footers.

10 Scroll through the document to see these parent items applied and notice the page numbers changing. Return to the A-Parent spread. Choose File > Save.

Renaming the parent page

When a document contains multiple parent pages, you may want to assign a descriptive name to each parent page to make them easier to identify, rather than leaving the default names. You will rename this first parent page "3-column Layout."

1 Choose Window > Pages if the Pages panel is not open. Confirm that the A-Parent page is still selected. Choose Parent Options For "A-Parent" from the Pages panel menu (≡).

2 In the Name field, type **3-column Layout**, and click OK.

Adding placeholder frames for text

► Tip: To set up a parent page spread with different margin and column settings for the left and right pages, you can double-click an individual page in the parent page spread and then change the selected page's settings by choosing Layout > Margins And Columns.

Each document page in the newsletter will contain text and graphics. Because the main text frame and graphics frame are in the same position on each page, one technique is to create a placeholder text frame and a placeholder graphics frame on the pages of the parent spread.

1 Double-click the left page icon of the A-3-column Layout parent in the Pages panel to center the left page of the spread in the document window.

2 Select the Type tool (T). Click where the top margin guide (pink) intersects with the .5 inch guide you drew (light blue) in the upper-left area of the page, and drag to create a text frame that extends horizontally across two columns and vertically down to the fourth horizontal guide.

3 Choose Fit Spread In Window if you zoomed in to create the text frame.

4 With the Selection tool (▶), click the text frame you just created. Then press Alt (Windows) or Option (macOS), and drag across to the right page to create a copy. Position this text frame so that it begins at the second column on the right page. The left position will be at 11.625 on the ruler guide. Verify by choosing a left reference point and looking at the X value in the Control panel or the Properties panel.

5 Click a blank area of the page or pasteboard, or choose Edit > Deselect All.

6 Choose File > Save.

Adding placeholder frames for graphics

You have now created placeholder text frames for the main text on each page. Next, you'll add two graphics frames to the A-3-column Layout parent. Similar to the text frames you created, these frames act as placeholders for graphics you'll later place on document pages, helping you to maintain a consistent design.

Although the Rectangle tool (□.) and the Rectangle Frame tool (⊠.) are more or less interchangeable, the Rectangle Frame tool, which includes nonprinting diagonal lines within that form an X, is commonly used to create placeholders for graphics that will be imported.

1 Select the Rectangle Frame tool (⊠.) in the Tools panel.

2 Position the crosshair pointer at the intersection of the top margin guide and the first column guide on the right page.

Drag down and to the left to create a frame that extends horizontally one column width and vertically to the ruler guide at 5.4375 in (the fourth horizontal guide). The resulting frame will be 2.5 inches wide (W) and 4.125 inches tall (H).

3 Create an identical placeholder graphics frame in the mirror position on the left page by either drawing another frame or duplicating this frame.

● **Note:** It's not necessary to add placeholder frames to every document you create. For example, one-page documents, such as posters, business cards, and ads, may not benefit from parent pages and placeholder frames.

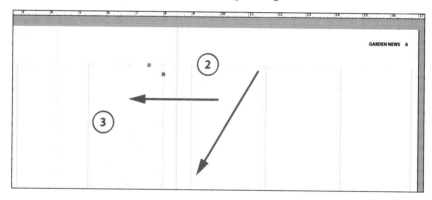

4 Use the Selection tool to click a blank area of the page or pasteboard, or choose Edit > Deselect All.

5 Choose File > Save.

Creating an additional parent page

You can create multiple parent pages within a document. You can build them independently from each other or base one parent page on another parent page. If you base a parent page on another parent page, any change made to the first parent is automatically applied to the second parent page. This is referred to as a "parent–child" relationship between the pages. In the example you'll create next, the second parent page has the same margins, headers, and footers as the first but a different number of columns.

▶ **Tip:** The ability to create parent–child relationships between parent pages is ideal for publications like newsletters and magazines with folios that include the date of publication. Each time you create a new publication, begin by changing the date on the first parent page, which automatically changes the date on all parent pages based on the first one.

To accommodate different layouts, you will create a separate parent page spread that uses a two-column format, and then you'll modify the two-column layout.

1 In the Pages panel, choose New Parent from the Pages panel menu (≡).

2 In the Name field, type **2-column Layout**.

3 From the Based On Parent menu, choose A-3-column Layout, and click OK. The new parent spread is displayed in the document window.

4 In the Pages panel, click the horizontal bar that separates the parent page icons from document page icons and drag down until the B-2-column parent page icons are visible.

Notice that the letter "A" is displayed on the B-2-column Layout parent page thumbnails in the Pages panel. This letter indicates that the A-3-column Layout parent serves as the foundation for the B-2-column Layout parent. If you change the A-3-column Layout parent, the changes will also apply to the B-2-column Layout parent. You may also notice that you cannot easily select objects, such as the footer frames, that came from the Based On parent page. You'll learn about selecting and overriding parent page items in the next exercise.

The Current Page Number character changes to B on the B Parent page.

5 Choose Layout > Margins And Columns. In the Columns field, set the number of columns to **2**, and then click OK.

Overriding parent objects

The document pages that will use the two-column layout do not require placeholder frames, which will be one of the differences between the two parent pages. Next, you'll remove the placeholder frames from the B-2-column Layout parent.

▶ **Tip:** To override multiple parent page items, hold down Shift+Ctrl (Windows) or Shift+Command (macOS), and with the Selection tool, drag a marquee around the objects you want to override.

1 Using the Selection tool (▶), click within the graphics frame on the left page of the B-2-column Layout parent. Nothing happens. Because this frame is inherited from the Based On parent page, you can't select it with a simple click.

2 Hold down Shift+Ctrl (Windows) or Shift+Command (macOS), and then click within the graphics frame. The frame is now selected, and you have overridden its status as a Based On parent item. Press Backspace or Delete to delete the frame.

3 Use the same method to delete the placeholder graphics frame on the right page, as well as the placeholder text frames on the left and right pages. The header and footer objects, as well as the guides from A-3-column Layout parent, remain.

4 Choose File > Save.

Modifying a Based On parent

To complete your work laying out the newsletter's parent pages, you'll add several header elements to the top of the A-3-column Layout parent. Then you'll view the B parent and see how the new objects are automatically added to that parent page spread because it's based on A.

Rather than manually laying out the additional header and footer frames, you'll import a "snippet" that contains several objects that are already formatted. A snippet is a file that contains InDesign objects, including their location relative to one another on a page or spread. Snippets can be imported into a layout with the Place command (File menu) the same way you import graphic files. You'll use snippets again later in this lesson, and you'll learn more about snippets in Lesson 11, "Importing and Modifying Graphics."

1 Double-click the name of the A-3-column Layout parent in the Pages panel to display the spread. If necessary, choose View > Fit Spread In Window.

2 Choose File > Place. Open the Links folder in the Lesson03 folder located inside the Lessons folder within the InDesignCIB folder. Click the file named Header-Snippet.idms, and then click Open.

3 Position the loaded snippet icon (⌐) outside the upper-left corner of the spread, where the red bleed guides meet. Click to place the snippet.

The snippet adds to the header at the top of the page. It includes an empty blue graphics frame and a text frame with white placeholder text on both the left and right parent pages.

▶ **Tip:** To create a snippet, select one or more objects on a page or spread. Choose File > Export, and then choose InDesign Snippet from the Save As Type menu (Windows) or the Format menu (macOS). Choose the location of the file, assign a name, and then click Save.

4 Double-click the name of the B-2-column Layout parent in the Pages panel to navigate to that parent page. Notice how the new elements you just applied to the A-3-column Layout parent have been automatically applied to this parent.

5 Navigate back to the A-3-column Layout parent. Click the left blue graphics frame to select it. Open the Swatches panel by clicking the icon (▦) in the panel dock, choose Fill color (🎨), and click the Green-Bright-Medium swatch. Navigate to the B-2-column Layout parent in the Pages panel again, and see that the color of the left header frame is now green as well.

▶ **Tip:** The parent–child relationship structure enables you to quickly apply design changes to common elements, without having to make the same change to those items on several parent pages.

6 Choose File > Save.

Applying parent pages to document pages

Now that you have set up the parent pages, it's time to apply them to the pages in the document. By default, all of the document pages are formatted with the A-3-column Layout parent. You will apply the B-2-column Layout parent to several pages in the newsletter, and then you'll apply the None parent page to the cover page, which doesn't require header or footer information and thus does not require a parent page.

You can apply parent pages to document pages by dragging parent page icons onto document page icons in the Pages panel or by using an option from the Pages panel menu.

►**Tip:** In long documents, you may find it easier to display the page icons horizontally in the Pages panel. To do this, choose View Pages > Horizontally from the Pages panel menu.

1 Double-click the name of the B-2-column Layout parent in the Pages panel. Make sure that all parent pages and document pages are visible in the panel.

2 Drag either the highlighted parent page name or the accompanying spread icon of the B-2-column Layout parent onto the icon of document page 4; then release the mouse button. The page thumbnail changes to display a B, indicating which parent is applied.

3 Select page 5 in the Pages panel. From the Pages panel menu (☰), choose Apply Parent To Pages. From the Apply Parent menu, choose B-2-column Layout. The value 5 will already be entered for To Pages because you selected the page first. Click OK.

4 Double-click the page numbers 4–5 (below the page icons) in the Pages panel to display this spread. Notice that both pages have the two-column layout of the applied parent page, as well as the header and footer elements from the Based On parent page. Also notice that the correct page numbers are displayed on each page as a result of the Current Page Number characters you placed on the A-3-column Layout parent page spread, which was inherited by the B-2-column Layout parent.

5 Double-click the icon for document page 1 in the Pages panel. Because it's based on the A-3-column Layout parent, it includes header and footer elements, which aren't required on the cover of the newsletter.

6 Drag the parent page icon [None] onto the icon of document page 1. All of the parent page objects are no longer visible on page 1.

7 Choose File > Save.

Adding new document pages

You can add new pages to an existing document. Next, you'll add six additional pages to the newsletter. Later in this lesson, you'll use four of these pages for a special section within the newsletter that uses a different page size and separate page numbering.

1 From the Pages panel menu (≡), choose Insert Pages.

2 In the Insert Pages dialog, type **6** in the Pages field, choose After Page from the Insert menu, enter **4** in the accompanying (page number) field, and then choose [None] from the Parent menu.

3 Click OK. Six blank pages are added in the middle of the document. Lengthen the Pages panel so that you can see as many document pages as possible.

Rearranging and deleting document pages

You can use the Pages panel to rearrange the sequence of pages, as well as to delete and add pages.

1 In the Pages panel, click page 12 to select it. Notice that it's based on the A-3-column Layout parent. Drag the page 12 icon upward onto the icon for page 11, which is based on the B-2-column Layout parent. When the small arrow near the hand is pointing to the right, indicating that page 11 will be "pushed" in that direction, release the mouse button.

Notice that page 11 is now based on the A-3-column Layout parent, and the page that was previously page 11 is now page 12 (displays a B because the B parent is applied). Pages 13 and 14 remain unchanged.

2 Click page 5, and then press the Shift key and click page 6.

3 Click the Delete Selected Pages button (🗑) at the bottom of the panel. Pages 5 and 6 are deleted from the document, leaving it with 12 pages.

4 Choose File > Save.

Changing the size of pages within one InDesign document

Next, you'll create an insert within the newsletter by changing the size of four pages that will be a separate section of the publication. This section will be slightly narrower and shorter than the newsletter.

1 Select the Page tool (⬚). Double-click page 5 in the Pages panel, and then press the Shift key and click page 8. The icons for pages 5–8 are highlighted in the panel. These are the pages whose size you will change.

2 In the Control panel, set the reference point to the center-left position (⬚), and enter **7.5** for W (Width) and **10** for H (Height). Choose Edit > Deselect All.

3 Double-click page 8 in the Pages panel, and then choose View > Fit Spread In Window. Notice that the spread now contains pages of unequal size. Close the Pages panel if it obstructs your view of the spread.

Using the Measure tool

Note: Hold down the Shift key as you drag the Measure tool to constrain the direction to horizontal, vertical, or a 45-degree angle.

1 Notice that the outside margins on the smaller page look the same as on the original, larger page. InDesign maintained the original margin and column settings, resulting in narrower columns on the narrower pages. To understand this adjustment, we'll use the Measure tool (✎) to compare column widths.

2 Both pages show three columns within the outer margins. Press K on the keyboard to select the Measure tool (✎), and then press the Shift key and drag the tool from left to right within one column on page 9. The Shift key constrains the direction to exactly horizontal. The Info panel pops up. Note the measurement for W (Width). Next measure a column on page 8. Now you can

see that InDesign has made the columns on page 8 narrower than the original to fit on a narrower page, while keeping the margins the same. Close the Info panel.

Original column width (left) and narrow column width (right).

Note: The Measure tool is also available from the Tools panel. It's grouped with the Color Theme tool and the Eyedropper tool. Press and hold the Color Theme tool to activate the hidden tools menu and choose the Measure tool.

3 Choose File > Save.

Adding sections to change page numbering

The special section you just created will use its own page numbering system. You can use different kinds of page numbering within a document by creating sections. Next, you'll start a new section on the first page of the special section, and then you'll adjust the page numbering of the subsequent newsletter pages that begin again after the insert so that they continue the original numbering.

1 Choose the Selection tool (▶). In the Pages panel, double-click the page 5 icon to select and display it. This is the start of the special section with the smaller pages.

2 From the Pages panel menu (≡), choose Numbering & Section Options, or choose Layout > Numbering & Section Options. In the New Section dialog, make sure that Start Section and Start Page Numbering At are selected and that the Start Page Numbering At value is 1.

3 Choose i, ii, iii, iv… from the Style menu in the Page Numbering area of the dialog. Click OK.

The triangle above the page i thumbnail indicates the start of a section.

4 Examine the page icons in the Pages panel. Starting with the fifth document page, the numbers below the page icons now appear as Roman numerals. This is what we want for the special section, but not what we want for the newsletter pages.

Now you'll learn how to return to original numbering style for the newsletter pages that follow the special section and also continue the numbering from the page prior to the first page of the special section.

● Note: Single-clicking a parent page icon or a document page icon targets the page for editing purposes but does not cause that page to be displayed in the document window. If you want to navigate to a page, double-click its icon in the Pages panel.

1 Select page v in the Pages panel by clicking its icon once. This is the first page that returns to the original page size.

2 Choose Numbering & Section Options from the Pages panel menu.

3 In the New Section dialog, make sure that Start Section is selected.

4 Select Start Page Numbering At and specify a value of **5** in the accompanying field. This resumes the numbering from the document pages that precede the special insert section (1–4).

5 Make sure that 1, 2, 3, 4... is selected in the Style menu, and then click OK.

Now the pages are correctly renumbered. Notice that a small black triangle is displayed above pages 1, i, and 5 in the Pages panel. These triangles indicate the start of a new section.

In this document, we returned to the original page numbering at page 5, but the numbering could be another pattern. The important point to note is that whenever you see the triangle above a page in the Pages panel, it indicates a section change, regardless of the numbering pattern in that document.

6 Choose File > Save.

Adjust Layout

The Adjust Layout feature enables InDesign to do some of the work of scaling and realigning elements automatically when the size of a document is changed.

For example, you might have to publish in different regions of the world where standard page sizes are different. A4 size is the standard in many areas, and it's narrower and taller than an American Letter size. Or, the specifications of a project might change after you have already created many of the pages. Or you might have to make a poster-size version of a magazine advertisement, or different sizes of the same ad for different publications. There are many situations where this feature will save you a lot of time.

Adjust Layout is available in the Document Setup dialog, from the File menu, in the Properties panel, and in the Margins And Columns dialog. When you use Adjust Layout from the Margins And Columns dialog, it affects only the current page or selected pages. When you use Adjust Layout from any of the other locations, it applies to the entire document.

Note that you can choose to prevent InDesign from changing font sizes by keeping the Adjust Font Size option unchecked. When making a small page size change, you probably don't want to change your type styling. But when making a large change, you probably do want the fonts to scale with the rest of the objects.

1 Switch to the 03_End.indd file, or open it.

2 Choose File > Adjust Layout, and explore the options. Try changing the newsletter to A4 size, click OK, and then examine how the objects have changed.

3 Choose File > Document Setup. In the Document Setup dialog, click the Adjust Layout button—and this time make a dramatic change. Choose Tabloid from the Page Size menu, and select Adjust Font Size. Examine the results.

4 Choose File > Revert, or close the document without saving changes.

Overriding parent page items and placing text and graphics

Now that the framework of the 12-page publication is in place (the eight-page main section and four-page narrow insert section), you're ready to lay out document pages. You'll learn more about creating and modifying objects in Lesson 4, "Working with Objects," and about importing text in Lesson 6, "Flowing Text," and graphics in Lesson 11, "Importing and Modifying Graphics," so for this lesson, we've simplified the layout process to minimize your work.

1 Choose File > Save As, name the file **03_Newsletter.indd**, navigate to the Lesson03 folder, and click Save.

▶ **Tip:** Double-clicking the page number label below a page or spread in the Pages panel is another way to navigate to a page or spread. The view magnification is not changed.

2 In the Pages panel, double-click the page numbers 2–3 below the page icons, and choose View > Fit Spread In Window (if necessary).

Notice that because the A-3-column Layout parent is assigned to pages 2 and 3, these pages include the guides, headers and footers, and placeholder frames from the A-3-column Layout parent.

To import text and graphics created with other applications, such as a text file from Microsoft Word or an image from Adobe Photoshop, you use the Place command (File > Place) or the Quick Action from the Properties panel (you'll learn about other ways to import in later lessons).

3 Choose File > Place. If necessary, open the Links folder in the Lesson03 folder, located inside the Lessons folder within the InDesignCIB folder. Click the Article1.txt file, and then Ctrl-click (Windows) or Command-click (macOS) Article2.txt, Graphic_1_HoneyBee-1.jpg, and Graphic_2_GardenTools.jpg to select all four files. Click Open.

The pointer changes to a loaded text icon (📰), with a preview of the first few lines of the Article1.txt text file that you are placing. There's a (4) after the loaded text icon, indicating that you have four items to place.

● **Note:** Parentheses are displayed when InDesign recognizes a preexisting frame beneath the loaded text icon when importing text into a layout. If you click within an existing frame, InDesign uses that frame rather than creating a new text frame. Graphics frames behave the same way but show the graphics icon.

4 Position the loaded text icon over the placeholder text frame on page 2 (not directly on the guides). Click to place the Article1.txt text into the frame.

5 To place the three remaining files, click within the text frame on page 3 to place the Article2.txt text file; then click within the graphics frame on page 2 to place Graphic_1_HoneyBee-1.jpg, and last, click within the graphics frame on page 3 to place Graphic_2_GardenTools.jpg.

6 Choose Edit > Deselect All, and choose View > Fit Spread In Window.

To save time, you'll import a snippet with the remaining objects to complete the layout of the spread.

7 Choose File > Place. Click the Snippet2.idms file, and then click Open.

8 Position the loaded snippet icon (⌷) outside the upper-left corner of the spread, where the red bleed guides meet. Click to place the snippet.

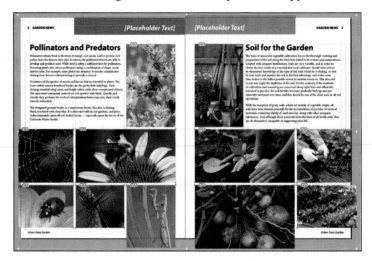

9 Choose Edit > Deselect All, or click an empty area of the page or pasteboard to deselect all objects.

10 Choose File > Save.

Next, you'll override two parent items on your spread—the two text frames that contain the header text—and then replace the placeholder text with new text.

Replacing placeholder text

Graphic designers will often use placeholder text to establish the look of a publication and then replace that text with the actual text when it's available. An advantage of using the parent page to do this is that consistency of those objects is maintained throughout the document. You will replace the placeholder text now.

1 Select the Type tool (**T**). Hold down Shift+Ctrl (Windows) or Shift+Command (macOS), and then click within the placeholder text frame on page 2 that contains "[Placeholder Text]." Replace the placeholder text with **Bees and Bugs**.

2 Repeat step 1 to change the header text on page 3 to **Gardening Tips**.

3 Notice that the frame boundaries of these two text frames are no longer dotted lines but solid, indicating that the frames are no longer parent page objects. Choose Edit > Deselect All.

4 Choose File > Save.

Printing to the edge of the paper: Using the bleed guides

A very important concept to keep in mind when setting up a document is whether any elements will print all the way to the edge of the paper. If so, you need to account for how that is accomplished in commercial printing. The bleed guides that we set up in the newsletter template are there to enable you to do that.

In commercial printing, pages are printed on large paper, rather than on single sheets as on an office printer, and pages are arranged to fold correctly on bindery machines. For example, the pages could be printed two-up on a small digital press or eight-up on a typical large offset press. Throughout the printing process, tolerances are built in to allow for slight variations in the manufacturing process—for example, during the trimming process (cutting the pages to exact size). Adding bleed is a strategy to compensate for these slight variations.

Sheets of printed material are cut while in large stacks, and even with a very sharp industrial blade, it's impossible to cut exactly to the edge of an image hundreds or thousands of times. Therefore, allowance must be made for the slight movement of sheets of paper as the blade cuts through the stack. To get a perfect edge every time while allowing for the mechanics of cutting paper in stacks, you must ensure that any artwork that you want to extend to the edge of the paper in the finished piece extends *past* where the blade will cut the printed sheet. The blade must cut through printed artwork. That extra artwork is in the bleed area.

▶ **Tip:** A best practice is to consider bleed requirements right from the beginning of the design and production process. There might be a photo that has to be enlarged or have the background extended so that it can bleed. These issues are best dealt with early in the process, and not just before a deadline.

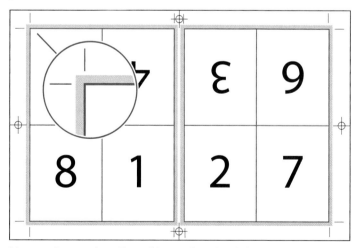

Diagram of a press sheet. The pink line is where the blade will cut the piece to the final size. The blue represents the bleed. Notice that the bleed extends past where the blade will cut.

Bleed guides help you make sure artwork is large enough because they show the minimum distance the items must extend. Bleeding objects past the trim produces a clean edge because the blade cuts through printed image, not unprinted paper.

It's best to add bleed while you are building a file because you may have a photo or other art that is not big enough to extend past the page edge, and it's better to deal with that early in the process, not right before it's due to print. You will now learn how to check that design elements extend sufficiently beyond the page edge and how to fix them if they don't.

1 Using the Selection tool (▶), double-click the page 2 icon in the Pages panel to display it.

2 Choose View > Screen Mode > Normal (if you've changed to a different view) and focus on the red bleed guides.

3 First, look at the bottom photos on the left and right. Notice that the photos on the left of the spider web and the ladybug extend to the red bleed guide, which means there is enough image to get a clean edge when the paper is cut.

4 Scroll right to page 3. Look at the photo of the strawberries on the far right. See that the image ends exactly at the edge of the page. This image needs to be extended at least up to the red bleed guide. Click this photo with the Selection tool, in an area away from the content grabber. Pull the center-right handle of the frame farther to the right to make the graphics frame big enough to meet or pass the red bleed guide.

Close-up of strawberries image with no bleed; image ends at the page edge.

Image extending past the bleed guide.

5 Next, look across the top of the spread. The green graphics frame on the left is lower than the blue graphics frame on the right. It ends at the top trim but actually needs to bleed up.

▶ **Tip:** You can choose View > Screen Mode > Bleed and page through an entire document to check if bleed has been applied throughout a document where needed. This is a best practice during the production cycle and especially before sending a file to a print service provider.

6 Try clicking the green graphics frame with the Selection tool. You won't be able to select it since this item is on a parent spread. Because this is a parent page object that needs to be correct on every page, it's more efficient to fix it on the parent page since you need to fix it only once. Navigate to the A-3-column Layout parent by double-clicking it in the Pages panel. Now you can select the green frame. Pull the center handle upward to make the frame bigger. Stop either at the red bleed guide or slightly past it.

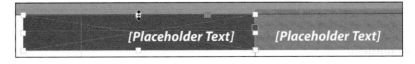

[Placeholder Text] [Placeholder Text]

7 Navigate back to page 2 and notice that the green frame is now big enough to bleed off the top. Every document page that uses this parent page, and the parent pages based on this parent, will now bleed correctly without you having to fix each one. This demonstrates another advantage of using parent pages: make a correction once and it's automatically done on all pages using or based on that parent page. Imagine how much time you'll save if several pages need the same correction or any type of change, especially in long documents.

Bees and Bugs **Gardening Tips**

8 Choose File > Save.

Viewing the completed spread

At this point, you're ready to hide guides and frames and see what the completed spread looks like.

1 Choose View > Fit Spread In Window.

2 Choose View > Screen Mode > Preview to hide the pasteboard and all guides, grids, invisible characters, and frame edges. Press the Tab key to hide any panels so that you have an unobstructed view of the spread. Preview is the closest onscreen view that shows best how the pages will look when printed and trimmed to size.

> ▶ **Tip:** You can't use the Tab key to hide and show the panels when you're working with text using the Type tool.

3 Press the Tab key again to redisplay the panels, and then choose File > Save.

Congratulations! You have finished the lesson.

Rotating spreads

In some cases, you may want to rotate a page or spread to make it easier to view and work on its content. For example, a standard-sized magazine with portrait-oriented pages might require a page with a landscape orientation, such as a calendar. You could lay out such a page by rotating all objects 90 degrees, but then you would have to turn your head or rotate your monitor to modify the layout and edit text. To make editing easier, you can rotate—and unrotate—spreads. This rotation is a view only; it's not changing the page setup.

For an example of this feature, open the 03_End.indd document in the Lesson03 folder (if it's not already open).

1 In the Pages panel, double-click page ii to display it in the document window.

2 Choose View > Fit Page In Window to center the page within the document window.

3 Select the title, June 2023, and try editing the text. It feels awkward to work with the text rotated this way.

4 Choose View > Rotate Spread > 90° CW.

After you rotate the spread (clockwise), it's easier to work with the objects on the page. For example, editing or adding text is much easier. Now try editing the title again and notice that now selecting and editing text feels normal and easy, rather than awkward.

5 Choose View > Rotate Spread > Clear Rotation.

6 Close the document without saving changes.

Exploring on your own

A good way to reinforce the skills you've learned in this lesson is to experiment with them. Try some of the following exercises. They'll give you more practice with InDesign techniques.

▶ **Tip:** Choose View > Screen Mode > Normal to return to your normal display as you explore on your own.

- Create another parent page for the document. Base it on the B-2-column Layout parent, name it **4-column Layout** (InDesign will automatically make the Prefix C), and then modify it so that it contains four columns instead of three. Apply the new parent page to any of the newsletter's full-sized pages that don't contain objects (folios 1, 4 or 5–8, not the smaller insert pages).

- Not all types of printed materials have a spine like the newsletter example in this lesson. Another common type is a trifold (or six-panel), where there are three panels that fold into the size of one panel. The panel that folds behind the cover must actually be slightly narrower so that the paper will lie flat when the trifold is closed. This example is typical of when it's very helpful to use different page sizes within one InDesign document because the design needs to be adjusted on the narrower panel that will fold in behind the cover.

 A sample file of a trifold is included with this lesson. Open the file named 03_Trifold_Template.indd in the Lesson03 folder, located inside the Lessons folder within the InDesignCIB folder on your hard drive. Click the pages with the Pages tool and notice which ones are narrower. Also examine the Pages panel, which shows three pages next to each other and the page numbering in reader order. This layout is also an example of a document setup where Facing Pages is turned off.

- Try making a parent page for the special section in the newsletter. This time, make it an independent parent page (not based on another parent page) because the special section will look different. Make the page size 7.5 × 10 to match the size of the pages in the special section. Add elements, such as a footer, that might be included. Apply this parent page to pages i through iv in the newsletter.

InDesign will display a warning about the parent page size. In this case, the special section is the same size as the new parent, so there really isn't an issue. Select Apply To All and click Use Parent Page Size.

The following example shows a footer added to the new parent page so that the special section will show a separate footer and page numbers from the rest of the newsletter.

Review questions

1 What are the advantages of adding objects to parent pages?

2 How do you change the page-numbering scheme (pattern) within a document?

3 How do you select a parent page item on a document page?

4 What's the advantage of basing a new parent page on an existing parent page?

5 How do you set up InDesign to automatically place page numbers on document pages?

6 How do you handle items that print to the edge of the paper?

Review answers

1 By adding objects such as guides, footers, automatic page numbers, and placeholder frames to parent pages, you can maintain a consistent layout on the pages to which the parent is applied. Also, you can make changes on the parent page once, and that change will be applied to all pages based on that parent page.

2 In the Pages panel, select the page icon where you want new page numbering to begin. Then, choose Numbering & Section Options from the Pages panel menu, or choose Layout > Numbering & Section Options and specify the new page-numbering scheme.

3 Hold down Shift+Ctrl (Windows) or Shift+Command (macOS), and then click the object to override it from the parent page and select it. You can then edit or delete the object.

4 By basing a new parent page on an existing parent page, you create a parent–child relationship between the new parent page and the existing one. Any changes you make to the Based On parent page are automatically applied to the second parent. This makes it much faster to apply global changes.

5 Use the Current Page Number marker character on a parent page. Create a text frame on a parent page and choose Type > Insert Special Character > Markers > Current Page Number.

6 Objects that will print up to the edge of paper must extend past the edge of the page in the file, into the pasteboard area *at least* up to the bleed guides. The bleed guides show the minimum amount that they must extend past the page edge.

4 WORKING WITH OBJECTS

Lesson overview

In this lesson, you'll learn how to do the following:

- Work with layers.
- Create and edit text frames and graphics frames.
- Import graphics into graphics frames.
- Crop, move, and scale graphics.
- Adjust the space between frames.
- Add captions to graphics frames.
- Wrap text around an object or a graphic.
- Change the shape of frames.
- Create complex frame shapes.
- Convert frame shapes to other shapes.
- Modify and align objects.
- Select and modify multiple objects.
- Flow type on a path.
- Add arrowheads to a line.

 This lesson will take about 90 minutes to complete. To get the lesson files used in this chapter, download them from the web page for this book at adobepress.com/InDesignCIB2023. For more information, see "Accessing the lesson files and Web Edition" in the Getting Started section at the beginning of this book.

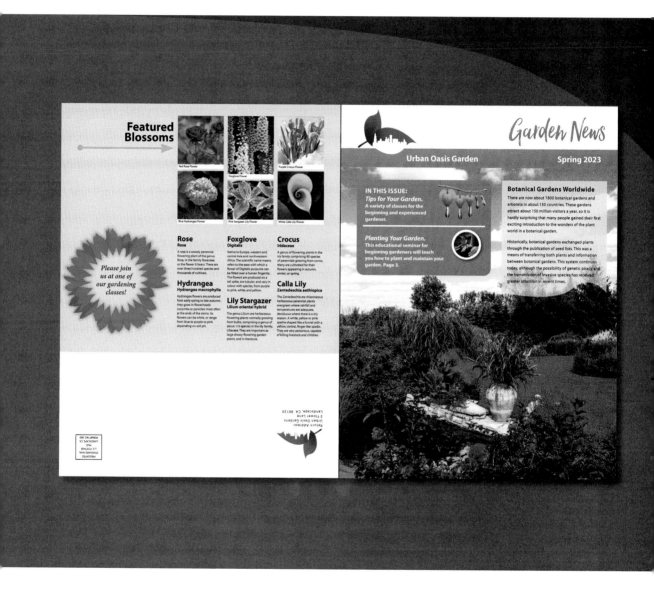

Adobe InDesign frames can contain text, graphics, or color. As you work with frames, you'll discover that InDesign provides you with a great amount of flexibility and control over your design.

Getting started

● **Note:** If you have not already downloaded the project files for this lesson to your computer from your Account page, make sure to do so now. See "Getting Started" at the beginning of the book.

In this lesson, you'll work on a pair of spreads that make up a four-page newsletter. You'll add text and images and make several modifications to the objects on the two spreads.

1 To ensure that the preferences and default settings of your InDesign program match those used in this lesson, move the InDesign Defaults file to a different folder following the procedure in "Saving and restoring the InDesign Defaults file" on pages 3–4.

2 To begin working, you'll open an InDesign document that is already partially completed. Start InDesign. Choose File > Open, and open the 04_Start.indd file in the Lesson04 folder, located inside the Lessons folder within the InDesignCIB folder on your hard drive. (If the Issues With Links message displays, click Update Modified Links.)

● **Note:** As you work through the lesson, move panels or change the zoom level to a magnification that works best for you.

3 To ensure that the panels and menu commands match those used in this lesson, choose Window > Workspace > [Advanced], and then choose Window > Workspace > Reset Advanced.

4 Choose File > Save As, rename the file **04_Objects.indd**, and save it in the Lesson04 folder.

5 To see what the finished document looks like, open the 04_End.indd file in the same folder. You can leave this document open to act as a guide as you work. When you're ready to resume working on the lesson document, choose Window > 04_Objects.indd or click its tab at the top of the document window.

● **Note:** To better view the interface onscreen or in print, the screen captures in this book reflect the Medium Light interface rather than the default setting of Medium Dark. In addition, some screen captures illustrate User Interface Scaling for a closer look at interface elements. You can modify interface settings in Preferences.

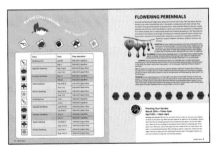

The newsletter that you will work on in this lesson contains two spreads. The spread on the left contains page 4 (the back page on the left) and page 1 (the cover on the right); the spread on the right contains pages 2 and 3 (the center spread). Keep this page arrangement in mind as you navigate from page to page. Here you see the finished newsletter.

Introducing layers

Before you begin creating and modifying objects, it's important to understand how layers work in InDesign. Placing objects on different layers lets you organize them for easy selection and editing. For example, by locking a layer you can easily select and move some objects without accidentally selecting or moving other objects, such as background images, that you want to stay where they are. By default, every new InDesign document contains one layer (named Layer 1). You can rename this layer and add more layers at any time as you work on a document.

Think of layers as transparent sheets stacked on top of each other. Each layer contains its own set of objects.

The Layers panel (Window > Layers) displays a list of a document's layers and lets you create, manage, and delete layers. The Layers panel also lets you display the names of all objects on a layer and select, show, hide, or lock individual objects or the whole layer. Click the triangle to the left of a layer name to alternately display and hide the names of the objects on the layer.

Document page view.

The order displayed in the Layers panel is the stacking order in the file. If each layer is one transparent sheet, all the layers are several sheets in a stack, like a stack of paper.

The topmost layer in the panel is the topmost layer in the file, and so on. The objects within each layer follow the same logic. One way to move an object in front of (above) or behind (below) another object is to move it up or down in the Layers panel.

Think of layer *order* like the floors of a building with several stories, where each floor is a layer. Your view of the page is looking straight down from the top floor with the ability to see through the floors. The objects on

Layers panel view.

Imagine layers as stacked transparent sheets, or the floors of a building.

each layer are like the furniture, which can be moved to any floor. But unlike with a building, whole layers in InDesign can also move up and down. It's as if you could take a lower floor of the building with all of its furniture and move it above the top floor. Then, from your top-down point of view, you'd be able to clearly see the furniture on the floor that you moved up, while your view of the furniture on other floors would be partially blocked. This is the view of the Layers panel.

Now think of that building with transparent floors (the layers) turned on its side while your point of view is looking straight on at the top floor. The top floor is now in front of the next floor and so on, while the bottom floor is now farthest back. The furniture on the top floor is in front of the furniture on all of the other floors. This is the view when you are looking at a document page.

1 To practice a little with layer concepts before starting on the lesson file, choose File > Open, and open the file called 04_Layers_Intro.indd.

2 Click the Layers panel icon (❧) in the panel dock or choose Window > Layers to open the Layers panel.

3 Click the eye icon (👁) in the first column of the panel next to the Type layer. All the objects on the Type layer are hidden, leaving only the objects on the other layers visible. The eye icon lets you hide or display individual layers. When you turn off the visibility of a layer, the eye disappears from the Layers panel. Click the empty box to the far left of the Type layer again to display the layer's contents again. Now click the eye icon of a different layer. All the objects on that layer are hidden. Click the empty box to the far left of that layer to make it visible again. When you're finished experimenting, set all of the layers to be visible (eye icon showing).

Click the eye icon to hide layer contents. Click again to make the layer content visible again.

▶ **Tip:** Use contrasting colors for layers rather than colors that are similar to each other. This makes it easier to understand immediately which layer any selected object is on.

4 Click once on the hollow box in the far-right column of the Type layer in the Layers panel. It turns into a solid magenta box, and the objects on that layer are selected on the page. The frames on that layer are also magenta. The color is an option you choose when setting up the layers. Using different colors for different layers is a visual cue that tells you which layer any selected object is on because the text and graphics frames on the page are the same color as the layer.

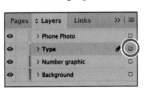

Click the box in the far-right column to select all the objects on a layer.

5 Move your pointer over the blue highlighted area to the right of the layer name, and then click and hold. The pointer turns into a gripping hand icon (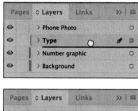), and a thick black line appears below the layer. Drag down until the black line is below the layer named Background and release the mouse button. Notice that most of the objects on the Type layer are no longer visible. This is because you just moved the Type layer below (behind) the Background layer.

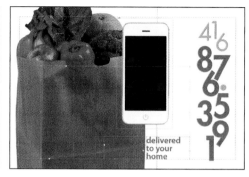

6 Using the Selection tool (▶), click the photo of the bag of groceries. Notice that the Background layer is selected in the Layers panel and that the photo's frame is the same color as the Background layer. In the Layers panel, move your pointer to the solid orange box in the right column of the Background layer. Click and drag this box up to the Phone Photo layer and release the mouse button. The grocery bag is now the topmost object in the Phone Photo layer, so it's in front of the phone, hiding part of it.

▶ **Tip:** To move an item to another layer, select it with the Selection tool, and then select and drag the solid box from the right column in the Layers panel into the destination layer. The solid box indicates that one or more objects in a layer are selected.

7 Close the file without saving. You can return to this file any time to practice moving layers, moving objects between layers, and moving objects within layers, which are all techniques you'll learn in this lesson.

Now that you've practiced with some important layer concepts, you're ready to begin work on the lesson file.

Working with layers

The 04_Objects.indd document has two layers. You'll experiment with these layers to learn how the arrangement of the layers and the placement of objects on layers can affect the design of your document. You'll also add a new layer.

1 Click the Layers panel icon (❧) in the panel dock or choose Window > Layers to open the Layers panel (it may still be open).

2 Click the Text layer in the Layers panel. The layer is highlighted to indicate that it's selected. Notice that a pen icon (✎) appears to the right of the layer name. The pen icon indicates that this layer is the target layer, and while it's selected, anything you import or create is placed on this layer.

▶ **Tip:** When you turn on Paste Remember Layers from the Layers panel menu, pasted items retain their layer structure. They are pasted in layers matching the source layer names, and where the source layer names don't exist in the current document, new layers with the source layer names are added.

3 Click the small triangle to the left of the Text layer name. All objects on this layer are now displayed below the layer name. Use the panel's scroll bar to view the objects' names in the list. Note that you can drag objects within a layer to move them in front of or behind other objects within that layer. Click the triangle again to hide the list.

▶ **Tip:** Frames are also called "containers" and the graphic within "content." You can switch to select the content when you have the container selected, and vice versa: choose Object > Select > Content or Object > Select > Container. You can also toggle between selecting the container or content by double-clicking within the frame using the Selection tool.

4 Use the Zoom tool (🔍) to zoom in on the blue frame on the cover (page 1). Then, using the Selection tool (▶), move the pointer within the pink flower photo. Notice the blue frame edge on the graphics frame. This blue border indicates that the frame is on the Text layer, which has been assigned a blue color. A transparent doughnut shape, the content grabber (◉), is displayed in the center of the frame. When you move the pointer within the content grabber, it changes to a hand, indicating that the content will be selected if you click, instead of the frame.

5 Since the layer color is so similar to the color used on the page, it's a good idea to change it to a color that makes selections easier to see. Double-click the Text layer in the Layers panel, or choose Layer Options for "Text" from the panel menu. From the Color menu, choose Orange. Click OK.

Click when the arrow pointer is displayed to select the frame along with the graphic.

Click when the hand pointer is displayed to select only the graphic within the frame.

6 Move the pointer back outside the content grabber (the arrow pointer is displayed), and then click within the graphics frame to select it. In the Layers panel, notice that the Text layer is selected.

● **Note:** To see the position of the pink flower in the Graphics layer relative to other objects in the layer, expand the Graphics layer by clicking the triangle to the left of the layer name. The topmost item in the list is the topmost item in the layer.

7 In the Layers panel, drag the small orange square from the Text layer up to the Graphics layer, and then release the mouse button. The image is now on the Graphics layer and is now the topmost object on the top layer (new items are topmost by default). Notice that the small square in the Layers panel turns dark green, corresponding to the layer color, and so does the frame of the photo.

Select the image and drag the orange square in the Layers panel up a layer.

The object is now on the Graphics layer, and the frame color changed to dark green.

8 The commands to move objects in front of or behind other objects operate within each layer, and not between layers. To see this in action, choose Object > Arrange > Send To Back. The pink flower does not move behind the blue background as you expect. This is because the pink flower is on the Graphics layer, which is above the layer that contains the blue frame (the Text layer). Now move the dark green square in the Layers panel back to the Text layer and choose Object > Arrange > Send To Back again. Now the pink flower moves behind the blue frame because they are on the same layer. To move the pink flower back to the Graphics layer, choose Edit > Undo twice.

▶ **Tip:** The Object > Arrange command moves objects within a layer above or below each other—that is, in front of or behind each other.

Creating and reordering layers

1 Click the empty layer lock box to the left of the Graphics layer to lock the layer. The lock icon appears in the second column. Notice that the pen icon (✖) now has a diagonal strikethrough, also indicating that no changes or additions can be made to the layer.

 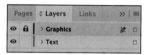

2 Choose View > Fit Spread In Window.

Next, you will make a new layer and move existing content to it.

▶ **Tip:** Press Alt (Windows) or Option (macOS) and click the New Layer button to create a new layer and display the Layer Options dialog automatically.

3 At the bottom of the Layers panel, click the Create New Layer button (⊞). Because the Graphics layer was selected when you created the new layer, the new layer is positioned above the Graphics layer in the Layers panel.

4 Double-click the name of the new layer (Layer 3) to open the Layer Options dialog. Change the name to **Background**. InDesign automatically assigns a color to the layer. Choose Green from the Color menu to change that color, and click OK.

▶ **Tip:** You can also rename a layer by selecting the layer in the Layers panel and then clicking its name.

5 In the Layers panel, drag the Background layer to the bottom of the layer stack.

 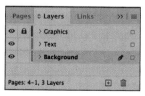

Moving objects to the Background layer

Now you'll move objects to the Background layer and lock that layer so that you can work with objects on the Text and Graphics layers without accidentally selecting or moving the backgrounds.

1 Click with the Selection tool (▶) on the light green background on the left-hand page. Hold down the Shift key and click the large photo on the cover page.

2 In the Layers panel, drag the orange square down from the Text layer to the Background layer. The square next to the Background layer is now green, and the frames for both of these items have changed to green, indicating that they have moved to the Background layer.

3 Navigate to the next spread (pages 2–3) by clicking the Next Spread arrow in the lower left of the document window.

4 Select both the blue frame on the left and the light green frame on the right by dragging across a small area, starting in the pasteboard above where the two frames meet and then moving down and across a small section of each frame. This is a quick way to select multiple items while being careful not to select too many items.

5 In the Layers panel, drag the orange square down to the Background layer, which moves both items to the Background layer at the same time.

6 Click the box to the left of the Background layer to lock this layer.

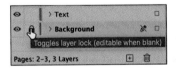

7 Choose File > Save.

Creating and modifying text frames

In most cases, text is placed inside a frame. (You can also use the Type On A Path tool [↘] to flow text along a path.) Text frames can be created with the Type tool and can be modified using a variety of tools—as you'll do in this part of the lesson.

Creating and resizing text frames

Now you'll create a text frame, adjust its size, add and style text, and then resize another frame.

1 Open the Pages panel by clicking its icon (▦) in the panel dock, and double-click the icon for page 4 to center it in the document window.

2 In the Layers panel (✦), click the Text layer to select it. Any content created will be placed on that layer because it is selected.

3 Select the Type tool (T) in the Tools panel. Position the pointer at .5 inch on both the horizontal and vertical rulers, which is the same as the margin guides. Drag to create a frame that snaps to the right edge of the second column and has a height of about an inch.

Note: If you see this icon (), it means that the layer is locked.

4 Press Ctrl+= (Windows) or Command+= (macOS) a few times to zoom in on the text frame. When you use the zoom commands with an object selected, InDesign centers the view on that object.

5 In the new text frame, type **Featured**. Press Shift+Enter (Windows) or Shift+Return (macOS) to create a forced line break (without creating a new paragraph), and then type **Blossoms**.

6 Now you'll apply a paragraph style to the text. Click the Paragraph Styles panel icon () in the panel dock or choose Type > Paragraph Styles to open the panel. Click the style named Right Flush Title to apply it to the paragraph.

Tip: To zoom in, press Ctrl+= (Windows) or Command+= (macOS) to increase the magnification by one preset increment. To zoom out, press Ctrl+– (Windows) or Command+– (macOS) to decrease the magnification by one preset increment.

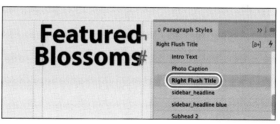

You'll learn more about paragraph styles in Lesson 9, "Working with Styles."

7 Press the Escape key to switch to the Selection tool () and double-click the center-bottom handle of the selected text frame to fit the frame to the text vertically.

Tip: It isn't necessary to highlight an entire paragraph before applying a paragraph style to it. You can select a paragraph by clicking anywhere within it.

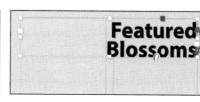

Double-click to fit the frame to its content. Result.

8 Choose View > Fit Spread In Window, and then press Z to temporarily access the Zoom tool and magnify the rightmost column on the cover (page 1) by clicking in that area three times. Use the Selection tool (▶) to select the text frame that contains the headline "Botanical Gardens Worldwide."

The red plus sign (+) at the lower-right corner of the text frame indicates that the frame contains overset text. Overset text is not visible because the frame is too small to display it. You'll fix this by changing the size of the text frame.

9 Drag the center-bottom handle of the selected text frame down to resize the height of the frame until the bottom is at about 5.5 inches on the vertical ruler guide. When the pointer approaches the ruler guide, the arrows change in appearance from black to white, indicating that the frame edge is about to snap to the guide.

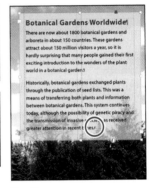

Resize the frame by dragging the center handle.

Result.

10 Note that the red plus sign disappears and that you see a hash tag character at the end of the text. This character indicates that there is no more text in the story. Choose Edit > Deselect All, and then choose File > Save.

Reshaping a text frame

▶ **Tip:** The techniques in this exercise can also be used on graphics frames.

So far, you've resized a text frame with the Selection tool by dragging a handle. Now you'll reshape the frame using the Direct Selection tool to move one of the frame's anchor points. Then you'll change the shape by changing the anchor point with the Pen tool.

1 In the Tools panel, select the Direct Selection tool (▷), and then click within the text frame you just resized. Four small hollow anchor points now appear at the corners of the selected text frame and one at the bottom center. You may have to zoom in to see them.

2 The Direct Selection tool allows you to select the individual points of a frame that define its shape. Select and hold the anchor point at the center-bottom of the text frame, pausing for a moment until the arrow pointer turns black.

Drag straight up until the point aligns with the bottom of the blue frame to the left of this text frame that contains the pink flower image. (the Smart Guide will appear), and then release the mouse button. As you drag, the text reflows simultaneously to give you a real-time view. After you release the mouse button, notice that the overset text indicator (the red plus sign) is displayed again.

● **Note:** Be sure to drag only the anchor point—make sure it is solid, not hollow, before you drag. If you accidentally move the frame, choose Edit > Undo Move and try again.

Unselected anchor point. Selected anchor point.

3 Switch to the Convert Direction Point tool (⬈.) under the Pen tool (✐.) in the Tools panel. Press and hold on the point you just moved and drag up and to the right. The anchor point will be converted from a corner point to a smooth point with handles. Release the mouse button.

4 Press the A key to switch back to the Direct Selection tool (▷), select the same anchor point again, and drag down and to the right until the text is no longer overset.

5 Adjust the shape of the text frame as you wish by dragging a handle up or down or making one or both of the handles shorter or longer by dragging their endpoints toward or away from the center. Press the V key to switch to the Selection tool. Notice the difference between the guides indicating the path and the bounding box of the object.

▶ **Tip:** To resize a text frame and the text characters inside it simultaneously, select the frame and then double-click the Scale tool (⊞.), which is combined with the Free Transform, Rotate, and Shear tools in the Tools panel. You can then specify values in the Scale dialog. You can also use the Selection tool, hold down Ctrl+Shift (Windows) or Shift+Command (macOS), and drag a text frame handle. Including the Shift key ensures that the object and content are scaled proportionally.

Change the shape of the curve by dragging the handles of the curve up or down, or make one of them shorter or longer.

Path

Bounding box

6 Choose Edit > Deselect All, and then choose File > Save.

Using Smart Guides

Smart Guides appear dynamically as you work to provide instant visual feedback. With Smart Guides, you can snap objects to the edges and centers of other objects, to the vertical and horizontal centers of pages, and to the midpoints of columns and gutters. You can align objects precisely without interrupting your creative process to add ruler guides, type in exact measurements, or use the Align buttons.

You can enable four Smart Guide options in the Guides & Pasteboard preferences (Edit > Preferences > Guides & Pasteboard [Windows] or InDesign > Preferences > Guides & Pasteboard [macOS]):

- **Align To Object Center.** Causes object edges to snap to the center of other objects on a page or spread when you create or move an object.

- **Align To Object Edges.** Causes object edges to snap to the edge of other objects on a page or spread when you create or move an object.

- **Smart Dimensions.** Causes the width, height, or rotation of an object to snap to the dimensions of other objects on a page or spread when you create, resize, or rotate an object.

- **Smart Spacing.** Lets you quickly arrange objects so that the space between them is equal.

The Smart Guides command (View > Grids & Guides > Smart Guides) lets you turn Smart Guides on and off. Smart Guides are enabled by default.

To familiarize yourself with Smart Guides, create a new multicolumn one-page document. (In the New Document dialog, specify a value greater than 2 in the Columns Number field.)

1 Select the Rectangle Frame tool (⊠). Drag slowly from the left margin guide to the second column guide. As the pointer moves across the page, notice that a guide is displayed when the pointer reaches the middle of a column, the midpoint within a gutter, and the vertical center of the page. Release the mouse button when a Smart Guide appears in the center of the second gutter.

2 With the Rectangle Frame tool still selected, create a second rectangle within the third column, close to the top margin. Switch to the Selection tool (▶), and drag this rectangle down until a Smart Guide appears showing that the top of this rectangle is aligned with the bottom of the first rectangle.

3 In an empty area of the page, create one more object with the Rectangle Frame tool. Drag the mouse slowly and watch carefully. Smart Guides appear when the pointer reaches the edge or center of any other objects. Also, when the height or width of the new object equals the height or width of either of the other two objects, a vertical or horizontal (or both) line with arrows at both ends appears next to the object you're creating and next to the object with the matching height or width.

4 Close the document without saving changes.

Creating multicolumn text frames

Now you'll convert an existing text frame to a multiple-column text frame.

1 Choose View > Fit Spread In Window, and then use the Selection tool (▶) to select the text frame that begins with "Rose." Press Ctrl+= (Windows) or Command+= (macOS) three times to increase the magnification and center this text frame in your window.

2 Choose Object > Text Frame Options. In the Text Frame Options dialog, enter **3** in the Number field and **.125 in** in the Gutter field if necessary (it may be set as the default). The gutter controls the distance between the columns. Click OK.

3 Choose Type > Show Hidden Characters. (If Hide Hidden Characters is displayed—rather than Show Hidden Characters—at the bottom of the Type menu, hidden characters are already showing.)

4 To begin each column with a heading, select the Type tool (T), insert the cursor before the "F" in "Foxglove," and then choose Type > Insert Break Character > Column Break. This forces "Foxglove" to the top of the second column. Insert another column break before the heading "Crocus."

▶ **Tip:** Hidden Characters show nonprinting formatting characters such as spaces and paragraph returns.

The small orange down-pointing triangles are the Column Break characters.

5 Choose Type > Hide Hidden Characters.

6 In the Layers panel, click the lock icon (🔒) to unlock the Graphics layer, which is where you'll work next.

Adjusting text inset and vertical alignment

You'll now finish the red title bar on the cover by fitting the text nicely into the frame. By adjusting the space between the edge of the frame and the text, you make the text easier to read.

1 Choose View > Fit Spread In Window, and then use the Zoom tool (🔍) to magnify the upper area of the cover (page 1), or scroll to the right to see the cover. Using the Selection tool (▶), select the text frame with a purple fill and white text that says "Urban Oasis Garden Spring 2023."

2 Choose Object > Text Frame Options. If necessary, drag the Text Frame Options dialog aside so that you can still see the selected text frame as you set options.

3 In the Text Frame Options dialog, make sure that the Preview option in the lower-left corner is selected. Then, in the Inset Spacing area, make sure the Make All Settings The Same icon is disabled (▣) so that you can change settings independently. Change the Left value to **2 in** to move the left margin of the text frame 2 inches to the right and away from the left edge of the frame, and then change the Right value to **.625 in**.

4 In the Vertical Justification area of the Text Frame Options dialog, choose Center from the Align menu. Click OK.

5 Select the Type tool (T,), and then click to the left of "Spring 2023" to establish an insertion point. To move the date text so that it aligns with the right inset you specified in step 3, choose Type > Insert Special Character > Other > Right Indent Tab, which aligns the text to the right edge of the frame.

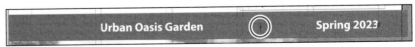

The screen capture shows the invisible character for Right Indent Tab.

6 Choose Edit > Deselect All, and then choose File > Save.

Creating and modifying graphics frames

In this section, you'll focus on different techniques for creating and modifying graphics frames and their contents.

Drawing a new graphics frame

To begin, you'll create a frame for the logo at the top of the cover page (the page on the right in the first spread).

1 If the Layers panel is not visible, click the Layers panel icon (❧) in the panel dock, or choose Window > Layers.

2 In the Layers panel, lock the Text layer by clicking the box to the left of the layer name. Select the Graphics layer by clicking the name of the layer so that the new elements are assigned to this layer.

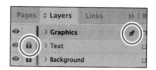

3 Use the Zoom tool (🔍) to zoom in on the upper-left corner of the cover, just to the left of the words "Urban Oasis Garden" in the purple text frame you just changed.

▶ **Tip:** Press the Z key to use the Zoom tool temporarily. After you click to zoom, InDesign returns to the tool you were using before you pressed the Z key.

4 In the Tools panel, select the Rectangle Frame tool (⊠). Move the pointer to the upper-left corner area of the page aligned with the left margin; drag down until the pointer crosses over the red text frame, about to the baseline of the words "Urban Oasis Garden"; and then drag across to the second margin guide.

Drag to create a graphics frame.

5 Switch to the Selection tool (▶) and make sure that the graphics frame is still selected.

Placing a graphic within an existing frame

Now you'll place the logo graphic file within the selected frame.

1 Choose File > Place, navigate to the Links folder in the Lesson04 folder, and then double-click urban-oasis-logo.ai. The image appears in the graphics frame.

2 To ensure that the graphic is displayed at the highest possible resolution, choose Object > Display Performance > High Quality Display.

Note: If a graphics frame isn't selected when you choose File > Place, the pointer changes to the loaded graphics icon (🖼). In this case, you could click within the graphics frame to place the image within the frame.

Resizing a graphics frame to crop or show a graphic

The graphics frame you created isn't quite wide enough to show the entire logo, so you'll widen it to reveal the hidden portion.

▶ **Tip:** You can also reveal the cropped portion of the graphic by choosing Object > Fitting > Fit Frame To Content.

1 Using the Selection tool (▶), drag the center-right handle to the right until the entire logo is visible. If you pause just after you start to drag, you'll see the cropped portion of the image as you drag—a feature called Dynamic Preview— and you can easily see when the frame edge is beyond the edge of the logo.

▶ **Tip:** You can also hide part of an image by making the frame smaller than the image.

2 Choose Edit > Deselect All, and then choose File > Save.

Placing a graphic without an existing frame

The newsletter uses another instance of the logo on the back cover. This time you'll import the logo graphic without first creating a graphics frame.

1 Choose View > Fit Spread In Window, and then use the Zoom tool (🔍) to display the lower-right quarter of the back cover (page 4), near the return address.

2 Choose File > Place, and then double-click the file urban-oasis-logo.ai in the Links folder in the Lesson04 folder. The pointer changes to a thumbnail of the graphic you have chosen with a loaded graphics icon in the upper-left corner. (The icon changes depending on the file format of the graphic.)

▶ **Tip:** If you click— rather than click and drag—an empty area of the page when you place an image, the image is placed at 100 percent of its original size. The upper-left corner of the image is placed where you click.

3 Position the loaded graphics icon at the left edge of the rightmost column slightly below the rotated text frame that contains the return address. Drag until the pointer reaches the right edge of the column, and then release the mouse button. Notice that as you drag, a rectangle is displayed. This rectangle is proportional to the logo image, and the graphic within the frame is scaled to fit the frame.

You don't need to resize the frame as you did earlier because the frame already shows the entire image. The graphic still needs to be rotated, but you'll do that later in the lesson.

4 Choose Edit > Deselect All, and then choose File > Save.

Placing multiple graphics in a grid of frames

The back cover of the newsletter will show six photos in a grid. You could place the photos one by one and then position each one individually, but it's possible to place all the photos and arrange them in a grid at the same time.

1 Choose View > Fit Spread In Window. Depending on your screen size, you might want to zoom into the top half of the right-hand page (the back cover).

2 Choose File > Place. Navigate to the Links folder in the Lesson04 folder, click the graphic file named 01Rose.jpg to select it, and then press Shift and click the file named 06CallaLily.jpg to select all six photos. Click Open.

3 Position the loaded graphics icon (⊡) at the intersection of the horizontal ruler guide at the top margin and the left edge of the third column.

4 Drag down and toward the right margin. As you drag, press the Up Arrow key once and the Right Arrow key twice. As you press the arrow keys, the proxy image changes to a grid of rectangles with dotted lines to indicate the layout of the grid.

▶ **Tip:** When using any of the frame creation tools (Rectangle, Polygon, Type, and so on), you can create multiple and equally spaced frames by using the same arrow key gestures as you drag with the tool.

5 Continue dragging until the pointer snaps to the right margin guide, and then release the mouse button. A grid of six graphics frames displays the six photos you placed. Your grid may be slightly taller or shorter than the examples shown.

 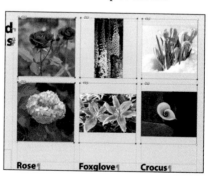

6 With all six frames still selected, move them slightly above the top margin by pressing the Up Arrow key six times.

7 Choose Edit > Deselect All, and then choose File > Save.

Resizing and moving images within frames

Now that you've placed the six photos, you need to resize and reposition them so that they fill the graphics frames and are cropped correctly.

A graphics frame and its content can be manipulated independently. Each has its own bounding box (the outer edges of the area occupied by the object). To resize the image (without resizing the frame), select the content by choosing Object > Select > Content, or click the content grabber (⊚), which displays as you hover over the graphic. You can see the different bounding boxes when either the content or the frame is selected because they are different colors and sizes.

● **Note:** If you want, you can use the Zoom tool to magnify the area you're working on as you perform the tasks in this lesson.

1 Zoom in to the area showing the six photos you just placed. Using the Selection tool (▶), position the pointer over the content grabber within the image of the crocus (the top-right photo). When the pointer is within the content grabber, a hand icon (✋) is displayed. Click to select the frame's contents (the image itself). Notice that the color of the frame and handles are orange even though the layer color is dark green. When you select content, InDesign automatically uses a color that contrasts with the layer color. In this case, the layer color is dark green and so the frame is dark green, but when you select the contents of the frame, those handles and the image bounding box are orange. This color change is a visual cue that you've selected the content.

2 To make the photo large enough to fill the frame, hold down the Shift key and drag the center-bottom handle slightly past the bottom edge of the graphics frame. Do the same with the center-top handle and drag it past the top edge of the frame. The Shift key maintains the proportions of the graphic so that it is not distorted as you scale. Remember that if you pause briefly just after you start dragging, you'll see the dynamic preview of the cropped graphic contents (the parts that extend outside the frame). Notice that the bounding box of the content (the photo) becomes larger than the frame. This tells you that the image is bigger than the frame.

▶ **Tip:** To constrain the movement to horizontal, vertical, or 45-degree angles, press the Shift key while dragging.

3 The image now fills the frame. To change how the image is cropped, position the pointer over the content grabber within the image and drag to the left until the crocus is more centered in the frame. You may also want to scale again until the image is pleasing to you.

4 The image in the middle frame on the top row is too narrow to fill the frame. Click the content grabber with the Selection tool to select the image. While holding down the Shift key, drag the center-left handle to the left edge of the graphics frame. Do the same with the center-right handle and drag to the right edge of the frame. Make sure that the image entirely fills the graphics frame. Notice that the handles of the image bounding box extend beyond the frame's bounding box only at the top and bottom.

▶ **Tip:** When resizing an image with the Selection tool, press Alt+Shift (Windows) or Shift+Option (macOS) to size the image proportionately from the center outward.

5 Use the same technique on the remaining photo in the top row to fill the frame with the image.

You'll use a different method to resize the other three photos.

6 Use the Selection tool to select the graphic on the left of the second row. You can select either the frame or its content.

7 Choose Object > Fitting > Fill Frame Proportionally. This increases the scale of the image so that the frame is filled. Small portions of the graphic are now cropped by the left and right edges of the frame.

8 Repeat steps 6 and 7 for the remaining two photos in the bottom row.

▶ **Tip:** You can also access the frame-fitting commands in the Control and Properties panels and from the context menu by right-clicking (called Fitting in the context menu).

▶ **Tip:** If you enable the Auto-Fit option for a graphics frame, the image within will automatically resize when you resize the frame. To enable Auto-Fit for a selected graphics frame, choose Object > Fitting > Frame Fitting Options and then select Auto-Fit, or select Auto-Fit in the Control panel.

9 Choose Edit > Deselect All, and then choose File > Save.

Next, you'll adjust the space between some of the photos to give the grid arrangement a visual tweak.

Adjusting the space between frames

The Gap tool (⊢⊣) lets you select and adjust the space between frames. You'll use it to adjust the space between two of the photos in the top row and then two of the photos in the bottom row.

1 Select the Gap tool (⊢⊣), and then move the pointer into the horizontal gap between the two center pictures. The gap is highlighted—all the way across the row of photos. Hold down the Shift key and notice that the highlighted area now includes only the gap between the top-center photos.

2 Drag the gap down to about the top of the pink flower below, making the graphics frame on the top longer than the rest of the grid and the one on the bottom shorter than the grid. (Holding down Shift while dragging selects the gap between those two photos only; otherwise, you'll move the gap between all the photos in the row.)

The Gap tool enables you to change a design by working with the space between objects. With this technique, the size of the area between frames is maintained while you change the size of a frame. You can also change the size of the gap instead of moving it by using Ctrl-drag (Windows) or Command-drag (macOS).

▶ **Tip:** The entry fields of many settings let you perform operations such as addition (+), subtraction (–), multiplication (*), and division (/), as well as figure a percentage (%). Taking advantage of this feature will make you much more efficient when making changes. Refer to the second exercise in the "Exploring on your own" section for more information and practice.

3 Choose View > Fit Page In Window.

4 Using the Selection tool (▶), drag across the pictures in the top row to select them. Set the reference point in the Control panel to the lower left (⊞). Click after the number in the Y entry, type **–.0625**, and then press Enter (Windows) or Return (macOS). The photos move up by one-sixteenth of an inch. By selecting the reference point, you control the direction of the move, and InDesign does the subtraction for you. Using math in the Control panel is a powerful and efficient way to move and/or scale objects precisely in InDesign.

X: 3.55 in
Y: :92 in–.0625

5 Choose Edit > Deselect All and then File > Save. You've completed the grid of images on the back cover (page 4).

Adding metadata captions to graphics frames

You can automatically generate captions for placed graphics based on metadata information stored in the original graphic files. Next, you'll use the Captions feature to automatically add captions to the pictures using metadata information.

InDesign lets you create either static captions, which generate caption text from a graphic's metadata but don't maintain a link to that metadata, or live captions, which are variables that retain links to a graphic's metadata and can be automatically updated if the metadata is changed.

1 With the Selection tool (), select the six graphics frames of the flowers by dragging across a portion of all six photos (you don't have to select all the way around them). Press Ctrl+= (Windows) or Command+= (macOS) a couple of times for a better view of the six images.

2 Click the Links panel icon () in the panel dock to display the Links panel, and then choose Captions > Caption Setup from the panel menu.

3 In the Caption Setup dialog, specify the following settings:

 • In the Text Before field, delete any text that might be there by default.

 • Choose Description from the Metadata menu (you may have to scroll up the list from the default selection).

 • In the Text After field, type **Flower**. Enter a space character before the word Flower. Don't add a period.

 • Choose Below Image from the Alignment menu.

 • In the Offset field, enter **.02 in**.

 • Choose Photo Caption from the Paragraph Style menu.

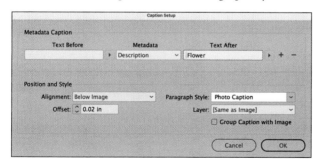

4 Click OK to save the settings and close the Caption Setup dialog.

5 With the photos still selected, return to the Links panel menu, and choose Captions > Generate Static Captions.

Each of the graphic files contains a metadata element named "Description," which stores the name of the flower. InDesign pulls this metadata information from the graphic file when the caption is generated.

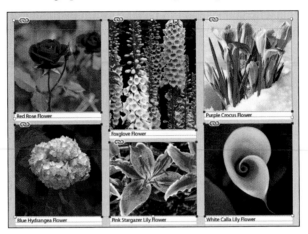

6 Choose Edit > Deselect All, and then choose File > Save.

Wrapping text around a graphic

With InDesign, you can wrap text around graphics in several ways: around the rectangular bounding box of any object, around objects of any shape, and around the contours of imported images. As you wrap text around a graphic in this exercise, you'll see the difference between wrapping around its bounding box and wrapping around the shape of the graphic.

1 Open the Links panel, and click the word "Name" in the title bar. This sorts the links in the panel by name. Click the name of the graphic BleedingHeart.psd, click the 1 (indicates page 1) to navigate to this graphic, and then press the Esc key to select the graphic's frame rather than the content.

2 Choose Edit > Copy. Navigate to page 3 by clicking the Next Page button (▸) in the lower left of the window twice. Press Ctrl+= (Windows) or Command+= (macOS) two times to zoom in to the upper half the page.

3 Press Ctrl+V (Windows) or Command+V (macOS) to paste a copy of the bleeding heart photo on this page. Position it so that it begins to the left of the text frame and overlaps the last two lines of the first paragraph.

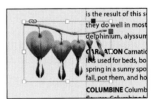

Notice that the graphic is covering up part of the text. You'll change this by applying a text wrap.

4 Use the Zoom tool to zoom in on the frame you just moved so that you see the whole graphic and the text around it. Before applying a text wrap, you'll enlarge the flower graphic. Press Ctrl+Shift (Windows) or Shift+Command (macOS), select the bottom-right handle, and drag down and to the right. Watch the Control panel values and release the mouse button when the graphic is scaled to about 175%. Using this key combination scales the graphic and its frame at the same time and keeps them proportional.

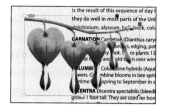

Note: If you don't hold down the Shift key, the graphic will be distorted—that is, stretched horizontally or vertically.

5 Choose Window > Text Wrap. In the Text Wrap panel, select Wrap Around Bounding Box () to wrap the text around the bounding box. If necessary, choose Show Options from the panel menu to display all the controls in the Text Wrap panel.

 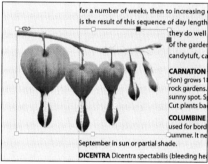

Wrap text around a bounding box. Result.

This option is not the desired design, so you'll try another Text Wrap option.

6 In the Text Wrap panel, select Wrap Around Object Shape (). In the Contour Options area, choose Detect Edges from the Type menu. In the Wrap Options area, choose Right Side from the Wrap To menu. Enter **.125 in** in the Top Offset field to add more space between the edge of the graphic and the text, or click the up arrow twice. This also creates a gentler text wrap.

Note: You may see an animation demonstrating the Select Subject text wrap feature, and the contour options may be set to Select Subject by default. You'll learn about this feature, subject-aware text wrapping, in Lesson 11, "Importing and Modifying Graphics." Click OK to close the animation.

Wrap text around an object shape. Result.

7 Press Esc to select the frame and use the arrow keys to nudge the position of the graphic to adjust how the text flows, using your judgment.

8 Click a blank area to deselect all, or choose Edit > Deselect All. Close the Text Wrap panel, and choose File > Save.

Transforming the shape of frames

InDesign has many features that let you change the shape of frames. To begin learning these capabilities, you'll subtract the area of one shape from another. After that, you'll create a compound frame, convert a frame from one shape to another, repeat shapes, and distribute the space between shapes. You'll then add rounded corners to a frame.

Changing shapes with other shapes

You can change the shape of an existing frame by adding shapes together or by subtracting one shape from another. The shape of a frame can be changed even if the frame already contains text or graphics. In this exercise, you'll subtract a shape from the light green background on page 3 to create a white background for the article at the bottom of the page.

1 Choose View > Fit Page In Window to fit and center page 3 in the document window. Open the Layers panel and unlock the Background layer. Click the Background layer so that the next object will be on that layer.

2 Using the Rectangle tool (▢), draw a frame around the story in the lower right. Start at the margin guide that bisects the circular photo and the guide above it. Drag down and to the right past the intersection of the bleed guides that meet outside the lower-right corner of the page.

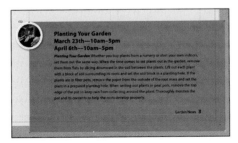

3 Switch to the Selection tool (▶), hold down the Shift key, and click the light green background shape that covers page 3 to simultaneously select the new rectangle and the background frame. Two frames are now selected.

4 Choose Window > Object & Layout > Pathfinder to display the panel. Choose the second option under the Pathfinder area, Subtract, to subtract the top shape

(the new rectangle) from the background shape. The shape of the light green frame is changed to exclude the area where the overlapping rectangle used to be.

● **Note:** The Pathfinder tools are also available in the Properties panel.

Both rectangles selected; Pathfinder panel. Subtract the front object.

5 Open the Layers panel and lock the Background layer again to avoid accidental repositioning of the frame.

6 Close the Pathfinder panel and choose File > Save.

Working with compound shapes

Compound paths combine two or more paths into one object. This is commonly used to create a cutout of one shape with another where you can see through the cutout so that other objects behind become visible.

1 Navigate to page 4, the back cover, and zoom in on the area to the left of the flower descriptions.

2 With the Selection tool (▶), click the spiked purple circle on top of the yellow flower photo; then press the Shift key and select the photo as well. Choose Object > Paths > Make Compound Path.

The circle shape cut through the photo, revealing the text frame behind.

3 Drag the compound shape to the right over the text frame. Notice that the photo and the cutout shape where the spiked purple circle used to be are now one object. Choose Edit > Undo.

Tip: Alt-click (Windows) or Option-click (macOS) an anchor point or path segment with the Direct Selection tool to select nested shapes within compound paths or object groups.

4 Choose Edit > Deselect All and zoom in to the cutout shape. To edit a compound shape, choose the Direct Selection tool () in the Tools panel or press the A key. Move the Direct Selection tool over the shape's path. The points along the path become visible. Press Alt (Windows) or Option (macOS), and click an anchor point of the cutout shape path. Now all of the points are solid, indicating that the whole path is selected.

5 Drag the path or nudge it with the arrow keys to slightly change its position. The path that defines the cutout moves without moving the whole frame. If you'd like, you can also edit the shape of the cutout by selecting individual points and moving them, by selecting handles and changing their angle, or by changing corner points to smooth points using the Convert Direction Point tool, which is grouped with the Pen tool. When you are satisfied with your changes, choose File > Save.

Converting shapes

You can change the shape of an existing frame, without having to draw a new shape. You'll try this out by creating a square and then converting it to a circle in one step.

1 Navigate to page 3, and choose View > Fit Page In Window. Depending on your screen size, you might want to zoom into the lower half of the left-hand page.

2 Click the Layers panel icon () in the panel dock or choose Window > Layers to open the Layers panel, if you closed it after the previous exercise. If necessary, click the Graphics layer to select it, and then select the Rectangle frame tool ().

3 Click in the light green area between the stories on page 3, aligning with the upper horizontal guide. Hold down the Shift key and drag down and to the right until the Width and Height values are about .625 in. Holding down the Shift key constrains the rectangle to a square.

4 Choose File > Place, and from the Lesson 4 Links folder, click bee-on-flower.psd to select it, and click Open. Choose Object > Fitting > Center Content.

5 Select the image, not the frame, by switching to the Selection tool () and clicking the content grabber (). Set the reference point in the Control panel to the center position () and choose **50%** from the Scale field. Then nudge the image up within the frame so that the bee is approximately centered.

Tip: The Convert Shape options are also available in the Pathfinder and Properties panels.

6 Press Esc to select the frame and choose Object > Convert Shape > Ellipse. You now have a circle. Check this by looking at the measurements in the Control panel. They are still .625 in for both Width and Height.

Repeating and distributing shapes

A common need in design is to evenly space a number of objects across a page. InDesign has tools that make this task quick and easy, even when you have to change the number of shapes after they've been created the first time.

1 With the circle from the previous exercise still selected, choose Edit > Step And Repeat.

2 Under Offset, enter **0 in** for Vertical, set Horizontal to **.75 in**, and enter **12** for Count. (Enter the Offset number first because the default value may be too large to have enough room for 12 repeats.) Click OK.

3 The shape has been repeated with an exact amount of space between them. Choose Edit > Deselect All, and then use the Selection tool to delete any two circles. Next you'll learn how easy it is to even out the space when the number of required objects changes.

4 Drag across all the circles to select them (make sure you locked the Background layer so that you select only the circles).

5 Choose Distribute Horizontal Centers () from the Align area of the Control panel or from the Align panel (Window > Object & Layout > Align).

▶ **Tip:** The Distribute Space options are also available in the Properties panel. Click the more options button (⋯) in the Align area to reveal them.

The circles are evenly distributed once again, with equal space between them.

6 With the row of circles still selected, choose Window > Properties to open the Properties panel. Under Quick Actions, click the Convert Shape button and select one of the other options, such as Polygon. All of the shapes are converted at the same time. Choose Edit > Deselect All and then File > Save. Close the Layers panel and the Align or Properties panel.

Adding rounded corners to frames

Next, you'll modify a frame by rounding its corners.

1 Navigate to page 1 by choosing 1 from the page field at the bottom of the document window. Choose View > Fit Page In Window.

2 Select the Selection tool (▶) and hold down the Z key to temporarily access the Zoom tool (🔍). Zoom in on the blue text frame with the pink flower by clicking the Zoom tool four or five times, and then release the Z key to return to the Selection tool.

● **Note:** If the yellow square is not visible when selecting the frame, choose View > Extras > Show Live Corners. Also ensure that Screen Mode is set to Normal (View > Screen Mode > Normal). For rotated or transformed frames, the yellow Live Corners square could appear near other corners of the frame.

3 Open the Layers panel and unlock the Text layer. Select the blue text frame, and then click the small yellow square that's slightly below the resizing handle at the upper-right corner of the frame. Four small yellow diamonds replace the four resizing handles at the corners of the frame. This is Live Corner Editing mode.

Click the yellow square. The corner handle changes to a yellow diamond.

4 Drag the diamond at the upper-right corner of the frame to the left and release the mouse button when the live radius (R:) value is approximately .2 in. As you drag, the other three corners change, too. (If you hold down the Shift key when dragging, only the corner you are working on changes.)

Note that you can also set corner options by choosing Object > Corner Options. You can change the size of the effect, apply different settings to each corner, and change to a different corner effect. Experiment as you wish; then choose Edit > Undo.

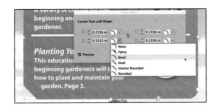

▶ **Tip:** After you create rounded corners, you can Alt-click (Windows) or Option-click (macOS) any of the diamonds to cycle through several different corner effects.

5 Choose Edit > Deselect All to exit Live Corner Editing mode, and then choose File > Save.

Transforming and aligning objects

Various tools and commands in InDesign let you modify an object's size or shape and change its orientation on the page. All transformations—rotating, scaling, shearing, and flipping—are available in the Transform, Control, and Properties panels, where you can precisely specify transformations. You can also align or distribute objects horizontally or vertically along the selection, margins, page, or spread.

You'll experiment with some of these features now.

Rotating an object

InDesign offers several methods for rotating objects. In this exercise, you'll use a couple of those methods to rotate one of the logos you imported earlier in the lesson.

1 Use either the page field at the bottom of the document window or the Pages panel to display page 4 (the first page of the document; the back page of the newsletter). Scroll to the bottom of the page so that you can see the return address and the logo.

2 Using the Selection tool (▶), select the logo you imported earlier in the lesson. (Make sure you select the graphics frame and not the graphic within.)

3 Move the pointer outside the frame near one of the corners. It changes to a curved double arrow (↱). Now you can rotate the frame by dragging.

4 Drag up a bit and watch how the preview of the frame shows the angle of rotation. Release the mouse button. This technique is called Free Rotation.

5 Press Ctrl+Z (Windows) or Command+Z (macOS) to undo this rotation. In this case, we need to rotate an exact amount.

6 In the Transform area of the Properties panel, make sure that the center point is selected on the reference point locator (▦) so that the object rotates around its center. Click the three dots (⋯) in the Transform area to show more options. Choose 180° from the Rotation Angle menu.

7 Click the content grabber and press the Up Arrow key several times to move the logo closer to the return address. Notice once again the difference in frame colors when you select the frame (dark green) and when you select the content (orange).

Rotating an image within its frame

You can also rotate the content of a graphics frame without rotating the frame.

Tip: Another way to rotate a selected object is by choosing Object > Transform > Rotate and entering a value in the Angle field of the Rotate dialog.

1 Scroll up to the top half of page 4. Using the Selection tool (▶), select the image of the calla lily (second row, right) by clicking within the content grabber. The arrow pointer changes to a hand when it's within the doughnut shape.

2 Move the pointer slightly outside the resizing handle at the upper-right corner of the picture. The rotate pointer (↰) is displayed.

Tip: The angle of the rotation is also displayed in the Control and Properties panels.

3 Drag clockwise to rotate the image until the tip of the flower is pointing toward the lower-right corner of the frame (about −35°). As you drag, the angle of rotation is displayed. Release the mouse button.

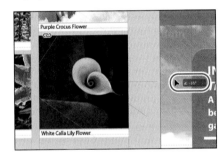

4 In the Control panel, select the center point in the reference point locator (✥).

Note: The reference point locator is tilted 45 degrees from the normal position to indicate that the selected object container or content is rotated at an angle other than 0, 90, or 180 degrees.

5 After being rotated, the image no longer fills the frame. To fix this, first make sure that the Constrain Proportions For Scaling icon (🔗) to the right of the Scale X and Scale Y Percentage fields in the Control panel is selected, and then enter **100** in the Scale X Percentage field and press Enter or Return.

6 Using either the Direct Selection tool or the content grabber, make sure the hand icon (✋) is displayed and drag the image to center the flower in the frame. Choose Edit > Deselect All, and then choose File > Save.

Aligning multiple objects

Precise alignment is made easy when you use the Align tools. Next, you'll learn to horizontally center multiple objects on a page, and then you'll align multiple images.

1 Choose View > Fit Page In Window, and then choose page 2 in the page field at the bottom of the document window.

2 Using the Selection tool (▶), click the text frame at the top of the page containing the "Partial Class Calendar" text and Shift-click the logo above it. (Unlike the two logos you imported earlier, this logo is a group of InDesign objects, not a placed graphic. You'll work with this group later in the lesson.)

3 Choose Window > Object & Layout > Align to open the Align panel.

4 In the Align panel, choose Align To Page from the Align To menu, and then click the Align Horizontal Centers button (♣). Both objects are now aligned to the center of the page.

▶ **Tip:** The Align options are also available in the Properties panel. You can complete this exercise using those controls.

Align panel.

Result.

5 Click a blank area or choose Edit > Deselect All.

Now you'll align a different set of objects using the concept of a key object. The object you select as the key object stays in its original position. The other objects you select move in relation to that key object.

6 Use the scroll bar at the bottom of the document window to show more of the pasteboard on the left of page 2, if necessary. You'll see nine icons.

7 Using the Selection tool (▶), drag-select the nine graphics frames in the pasteboard. Press the Shift key and select the graphics frame with the tomato that is on the page. Release the Shift key.

8 Click the tomato graphic again. Notice that it now has a thick dark green border (the color of the layer), indicating that it's the key object.

9 Click the Align Right Edges button (◀|) in the Control, Align, or Properties panel. All of the

▶ **Tip:** InDesign automatically assigns the object you selected first as the key object. To change the key object once you've selected all objects to be aligned, click the object that you want to be the key object. A thicker selection border will then appear around that object.

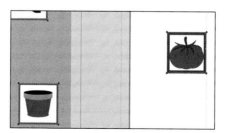

The key object displays a thicker border.

objects that were scattered in the pasteboard are now precisely aligned to the right edge of the tomato graphic.

Control panel.

Align panel.

Properties panel.

10 Choose Edit > Deselect All, and then choose File > Save.

Scaling multiple objects

InDesign lets you scale multiple selected objects at the same time. Next you'll select two of the icons and resize both of them at once.

1 Use the Zoom tool (Q) to zoom in on the two icons that are smaller than the rest of the icons in the column.

2 Using the Selection tool (▶), click the first of the icons to select it, and then Shift-click the second icon to select both.

● **Note:** If you press only the Shift key, the frames will scale proportionally, but the graphics within will not scale. You may have to repeat the scaling more than once to get the size correct.

3 Press Ctrl+Shift (Windows) or Shift+Command (macOS), and then drag the handle at the upper-left corner up and to the left to make the two icons the same width as the trowel icon above or the tree icon below the selected icons. A Smart Guide is displayed when the left edges of the selected frames align with the frame above. Release the mouse button and choose Edit > Deselect All.

Drag to resize the selected icons.

Smart Guide showing when left edges align.

Result.

Smart Guides showing the space between objects.

4 Drag each icon down one at a time to adjust the vertical position, again watching how the Smart Guides show you when the space between adjacent objects is equal. You will need to move them individually and more than once to end up with equal space between them. Choose Edit > Deselect All when you are satisfied.

Transforming multiple objects at once

InDesign lets you apply a transformation, and even transformations with multiple steps, to multiple selected objects all at the same time. This feature saves you from having to perform tedious, repetitive tasks.

1 Choose View > Fit Page In Window. Using the Selection tool (▶), select the trowel icon and press Alt-Shift (Windows) or Option-Shift (macOS) while dragging it up to the area between the table and the calendar headline. This technique makes a copy of the object. Adding the Shift key constrains the movement so that the copy of the object will move straight up.

● **Note:** The Shift key constrains movement to multiples of 45 degrees.

2 Press Alt (Windows) or Option (macOS), and drag each of the graphics (tomato, pot, tree, and sun icons) to the same area and to the right of the trowel. Notice how the Smart Guides show you when the objects are aligned.

3 Move the sun icon to the right and align it with the red guide on the right of the page. Then drag across all five icons to select them and select Align To Selection from the Align, Control, or Properties panel (because the Background layer is locked, you won't select the background frame). Then click the Distribute Horizontal Centers button. The icons are now spread evenly across the top of the table.

▶ **Tip:** Making a copy by pressing Alt (Windows) or Option (macOS) while you drag an object is a very useful technique to quickly copy an object and leave the original in place. The Selection Tool arrow symbol changes to a double arrow (▶) when a copy is being made while dragging.

4 Choose Edit > Deselect All; then select the trowel icon again. Using the Control or the Properties panel, set the reference point to the center position. Choose 125% for the scale and 30° for the angle.

5 Drag across the other four icons. Then choose Object > Transform Again > Transform Sequence Again Individually. InDesign applies the same scale and angle that you applied to the trowel icon to the other four icons without you having to apply them one at a time to each object. A sequence of many transformations can be applied to other objects using this feature.

6 Select all five icons and nudge them up or down using the keyboard arrow keys so that they are approximately centered between the table and the calendar headline, if necessary.

7 Close the Align panel, choose Edit > Deselect All, and then choose File > Save.

Selecting and modifying grouped objects

Earlier you aligned the logo at the top of page 2 to the center of the page. Now you'll change the fill color of some of the logo's shapes, which are InDesign vector objects in a group. You can apply modifications to a group as a unit, but you can also select individual objects within a group. You'll now change the fill color of just a few of the shapes without ungrouping or changing the other objects of the group.

The Direct Selection tool, the set of Select Content buttons, or a set of commands in the Object menu (Object > Select) let you select objects within a grouped object.

1 With the Selection tool (▶), click the logo at the top of page 2. Press Ctrl+= (Windows) or Command+= (macOS) five times to zoom in to the area you're working on. Notice that the bounding box is a dotted line rather than a solid line, indicating that the selected object is a group.

▶ **Tip:** You can also select an object in a group by double-clicking the object with the Selection tool, by selecting the group and choosing Object > Select > Content, or by right-clicking the group and choosing Select > Content from the context menu.

2 Click the Select Content button (✥) in the Control panel to select one object in the group without ungrouping.

Select the group with the Selection tool.

Click Select Content.

First object in the group selected.

3 Click the Select Next Object button (⊞▸) in the Control panel to select the first vertical leaf in the logo. Change the fill color of this object to Green-Bright-Medium in the Swatches, Control, or Properties panel.

Click Select Next Object.

Note that the Select Previous Object button (◂⊞) selects in the opposite direction so that you can move back to the previous object if needed. Using these two buttons enables you to move back and forth through the objects in a group to make changes without ungrouping.

4 Click the Next Object button () again and change this object to Green-Medium. Click the Next Object button two more times to select the third large leaf object and change its fill color to Green-Brightest.

5 Choose Edit > Deselect All, and then choose File > Save.

Flowing type along a path

Now we'll change the design of the headline on page 2, flowing text along a curve rather than inside a frame, using the Type On A Path feature.

1 First, drag to select both the logo and the text frame with the class calendar headline, and drag them to the right and up to temporarily move them out of the way. Zoom out if needed.

2 Scroll to the left until you see the two black curved lines in the pasteboard. Select both lines and then drag these objects onto the page.

3 With the Type tool, select the headline "Partial Class Calendar" and press Ctrl+C (Windows) or Command+C (macOS) to copy this text.

4 Select the Type On A Path tool (), which is grouped with the Type tool (**T**) in the Tools panel. Move the pointer over the top line until you see a plus sign appear. Click and press Ctrl+V (Windows) or Command+V (macOS) to paste the text onto the path.

Note: If you click before the plus sign appears, the path is not selected, and text will not flow along it. If you paste before the plus sign appears, the text will be pasted into a new text frame in the middle of the screen.

5 Press the Esc key to return to the Selection tool, and then choose Type > Type On A Path > Options. In the Type On A Path Options dialog, select the Flip option,

which moves the text above the line and makes it flow forward in normal reading order. Select Preview, and feel free to experiment with the available choices in this dialog. Then enter the settings as shown and click OK.

6 Double-click the text frame (double-clicking while using the Selection tool switches to the Type tool) or switch to the Type tool (T,), and triple-click to select the whole line. Change the font to Myriad Pro Bold and the size to **24 pt** using the Control, Character, or Properties panel. Press the Esc key to return to the Selection tool.

● **Note:** It may be helpful during this exercise to toggle back and forth between Normal view and Preview to see your work without the guides and invisible characters.

7 Now select the other curved line and drag it to the right to position it so that it loosely continues the curve of the first line.

8 With the Type tool, select the subhead "April–August 2023" and press Ctrl+C or Command+C to copy this text.

9 Select the Type On A Path tool (↖.) again, and this time move the pointer over the second line until you see the plus sign appear. Click and press Ctrl+V or Command+V to paste the text onto the path.

10 Press Ctrl+A (Windows) or Command+A (macOS) to select all the text, and change the font size to **20 pt** using the Control, Character, or Properties panel. Press the Esc key to return to the Selection tool.

11 Drag to select both curved paths that now have type flowing along them. Open the Swatches panel (▦), and choose Select Stroke Color (▨), or use the Stroke button on the Control or Properties panel. Change the stroke to [None].

12 Adjust the position of the paths to approximate what's shown here:

13 Finish up this new headline design by moving the logo back to the left and under the main headline. Delete the original text frame with the headline by selecting it with the Selection tool and pressing Delete on the keyboard, or choose Edit > Clear. Finally, choose Edit > Deselect All and then File > Save.

Drawing lines and modifying arrowheads

InDesign has the ability to add many styles of arrowheads or other shapes to the beginning and/or end of a line, and they can be scaled independently of line size. Next, you'll use this feature to complete the design of the newsletter.

1 Navigate to page 4 and zoom in near the "Featured Blossoms" headline. Select the Line tool (✏). Position the pointer on the left margin guide, slightly below the text frame with the "Featured Blossoms" text. (See the figure in step 3.)

2 With the Line tool selected, open the Swatches panel (▦) and change the fill color to None (▨) and the stroke color to Purple-Warm (▨). Change the tint on the stroke to **60%**.

3 While pressing the Shift key, drag horizontally from the left margin guide to the vertical column guide at the right of the second column. The Shift key constrains the line to be perfectly horizontal.

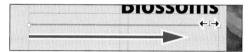

4 Click the Stroke panel icon (☰) in the panel dock or choose Window > Stroke to open the Stroke panel. Choose 4 from the Weight menu, CircleSolid from the Start Arrowhead menu, and Triangle from the End Arrowhead menu.

5 Make sure Link Start And End Arrowhead Scales is not selected (⬚) so that you can independently scale the start and end arrowheads. Enter **75** in the Scale Factor For Start Arrowhead field, enter **200** in the Scale Factor For End Arrowhead field, and press Enter or Return.

► **Tip:** In addition to adding arrowheads to straight lines created with the Line tool, you can add arrowheads to curved lines created with the Pen tool.

Default arrowhead scales.

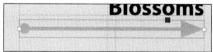

Start and End scaled independently.

6 Notice the difference between the ends when you use the default scale and when they are independently scaled. This independence gives you a lot of flexibility in designing arrows. Nudge the arrow down if needed. Close the Stroke panel, and choose File > Save.

Finishing up

Now it's time to admire your work.

1 Choose Edit > Deselect All.

2 Choose View > Fit Spread In Window.

▶ **Tip:** To quickly check how the area you're working on will look when finished, press the W key to toggle between Preview mode and Normal mode. Press the W key again to return to Normal mode. If you are editing text, press the Esc key first so that you don't inadvertently type a W in your text.

3 At the bottom of the Tools panel, hold down the Current Screen Mode button (▣) and choose Preview from the menu that appears. Preview mode is an ideal way to see what a document will look like when it's printed or exported to PDF or other formats. Preview mode displays artwork as if it were printed and trimmed, with all nonprinting elements suppressed (grids, guides, frame edges, nonprinting objects). The pasteboard is set to the preview color defined in Preferences.

4 Press the Tab key to close all the panels at the same time. Press the Tab key again when you are ready to show all the panels.

5 Navigate to the next spread to view those results as well. Choose File > Save.

Congratulations! You have finished the lesson.

Exploring on your own

One of the best ways to learn about objects is to experiment on your own.

First, you'll experiment with more Pathfinder features. You'll see that using the Pathfinder functions enables you to cleanly create many custom shapes without drawing them from scratch.

1 Create a new document using the default settings in the New Document dialog. Open the Properties panel.

2 Select the Ellipse tool (◯). Hold down the Shift key while you drag to create a circle. Set the fill to Magenta (one of the default colors: C=0 M=100 Y=0 K=0) and the stroke to [None].

3 Switch to the Selection tool (▶), press Alt+Shift (Windows) or Option+Shift (macOS), and drag down and to the right to make a copy of the circle moved along a 45-degree angle from the first circle.

4 Convert the second circle to a square by choosing Object > Convert Shape > Rectangle or by using the Pathfinder or the Properties panel. Drag to select both frames.

5 Press Alt+Shift (Windows) or Option+Shift (macOS), and drag a second copy of these two frames to use later. Then drag to select the first two objects again. Choose Window > Object & Layout > Pathfinder to display the panel. Click the Add button. Notice that the two objects are now one.

● **Note:** The Add, Subtract, Intersect, Exclude Overlap, and Minus Back Pathfinder buttons are also available in the Properties panel, and appear when you select both frames.

6 Make three more copies of the original set of frames and spread them out on the page. Now you'll try each of the other Pathfinder functions. Select one set of two frames and click the Subtract button. The front object is used to subtract the area of overlap from the back object.

7 Next, select another set of two frames and click the Intersect button. This creates a new object that includes only the area of overlap.

8 Select another set of two frames and click the Exclude button. This keeps only the areas that don't overlap.

9 Select the last set of two frames and click the Minus Back button. This is the opposite of the Subtract button, cutting out from the front object, the area where the back object overlaps it.

When you need to transform objects, letting InDesign do the calculation is faster than looking at the current values, doing the math on your own, and entering the new value you calculated. You can use addition (+), subtraction (−), multiplication (*), division (/), or percent (%).

1 Choose any object in the lesson file and practice moving it horizontally by using + (moves right) or − (moves left) in the X Location field in the Control, Transform, or Properties panel. Type the math symbol after the number in the field; then type the amount you want to move and press Enter or Return. Try the same concept to move vertically using the Y Location field, entering + (moves down) or − (moves up). You will often need to move objects an exact amount.

2 Next we'll try division. Navigate to page 4 and select the arrow you made in the upper left of the page. Let's say you have to make the arrow half as long, and it needs to stay under the headline. In the Transform, Control, or Properties panel, set the reference point to the far-right center position (⊞). This will keep the end of the arrowhead in its current location. In the Line Length field, after 2.925 in, type a forward slash (/) and **2** and press Enter or Return. The arrow is now half as long as it was.

▶**Tip:** You can use a key object to control which object remains in place and which object moves.

3 Another situation you'll often face is the requirement to have an exact amount of space between objects. InDesign can do this math for you in the Distribute Spacing area of the Align or Properties panel. Select two objects, and then click the field next to Use Spacing and enter a number. Click the Distribute Vertical Space (⊟) button, and the space between the objects changes to the amount you specified. Then set an exact amount for the horizontal space between two objects and click the Distribute Horizontal Space (⊪) button.

Next, you'll examine the document structure of the Lesson 4 exercise file.

1 Open the file 04_End.indd in the Lesson04 folder.

2 Open the Pages panel. Notice the page order on the first spread is 4, 1. This is because the first document page (page 4) is the outside back cover, which when a booklet is printed and stitched is on the same spread as the outside front cover. The document setup shows this, and it's often advantageous to work this way when design elements flow across both covers.

Note that both pages in the first spread have a black triangle above, indicating the start of a section.

▶**Tip:** You can also double-click the black triangle icon above the page icon to open the Numbering & Section Options dialog.

3 Click to select the first page in the panel (page 4), and choose Layout > Numbering & Section Options. Note that Start Page Numbering is set to 4. Click Cancel to close the panel.

4 Click to select the second page in the panel (page 1), and choose Layout > Numbering & Section Options. Note that Start Section is turned on and that Start Page Numbering is set to 1. Click Cancel to close the panel.

Review questions

1 When should you use the Selection tool to select an object, and when should you use the Direct Selection tool to select an object?

2 How do you move an object from one layer to another?

3 When you select an object and choose Object > Arrange > Bring To Front, but the object is still not in front of some objects, why does that happen?

4 Without ungrouping objects, how do you select an object within a group?

5 How do you align objects to another specific object?

Review answers

1 Use the Selection tool for general layout tasks, such as positioning, rotating, and resizing objects. Use the Direct Selection tool for tasks involving editing paths or frames, such as moving an anchor point on a path or selecting an object within a group and then changing the object's fill or stroke color. Use the Direct Selection tool to select the content of the frame to make changes without changing the frame, such as rotating or scaling an image inside a frame while the frame remains unchanged.

2 When the object is selected, a solid square displays in the right column of the Layers panel. Drag this square to a different layer. The object will now be on the new layer. You'll be able to see that it's now behind or in front of objects on other layers, depending on whether you moved it to a higher or lower layer.

3 The arrange commands operate within each layer, and not between layers. That object is not on the top or frontmost layer.

4 To select an object within a group, use the Selection tool (▶) to select the group, and then click the Select Content button (✛) in the Control panel to select one object in the group. You can then click the Select Previous Object or Select Next Object button to select different objects in the group. You can also select an object in a group by clicking the object with the Direct Selection tool (▷) or double-clicking it with the Selection tool.

5 Select all of the objects you want to align. Then click the object to which you want all of the other objects to align again. This becomes the key object, which is indicated by a thicker highlight around that object. Then choose Align To Key Object from the Align, Control, or Properties panel. Click the alignment you want, such as Align Top Edges or Align Horizontal Centers, or any of the other choices.

5 WORKING WITH COLOR

Lesson overview

In this lesson, you'll learn how to do the following:

- Set up color management.

- Specify output requirements.

- Create color swatches.

- Apply colors to objects, strokes, and text.

- Search and replace colors.

- Create and apply a tint.

- Create and apply a gradient swatch.

- Work with color groups.

- Create color themes and add them to CC Libraries.

 This lesson will take about 60 minutes to complete. To get the lesson files used in this chapter, download them from the web page for this book at adobepress.com/InDesignCIB2023. For more information, see "Accessing the lesson files and Web Edition" in the Getting Started section at the beginning of this book.

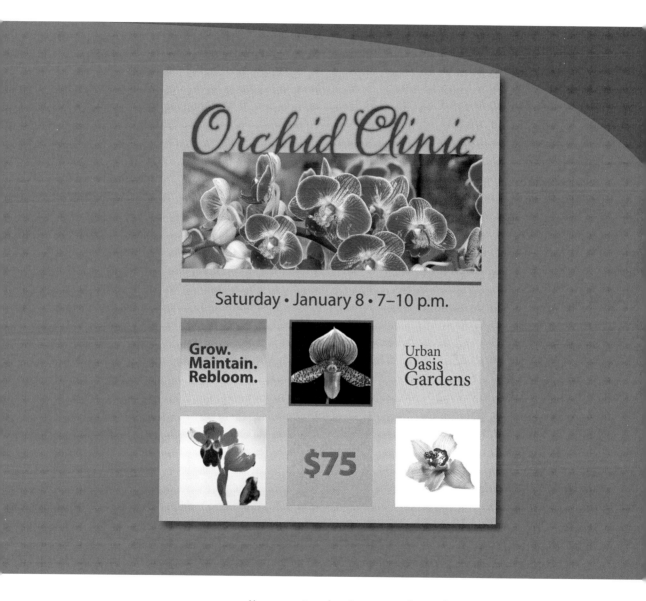

You can create and apply process and spot color swatches to objects, strokes, and text. Color themes make it easy to achieve color harmony in layouts. For consistent color usage across projects and workgroups, you can add color themes to CC Libraries. Using a preflight profile helps ensure that colors output properly.

Getting started

In this lesson, you'll add colors, tints, and gradients to a full-page flyer for a gardening clinic. The flyer consists of CMYK colors and a spot metallic color along with imported CMYK images. (You'll learn more about CMYK later in this lesson.) Before you get started, however, you will do two things to ensure that the document looks as good in print as it does onscreen: You will review color management settings and use a preflight profile to review the color modes of the imported images. When the flyer is finished, you will organize the colors into a color group.

● **Note:** If you have not already downloaded the project files for this lesson to your computer from your Account page, make sure to do so now. See "Getting Started" at the beginning of the book.

1 To ensure that the preferences and default settings of your Adobe InDesign program match those used in this lesson, move the InDesign Defaults file to a different folder following the procedure in "Saving and restoring the InDesign Defaults file" on pages 3–4.

2 Start InDesign.

3 The InDesign Home screen displays. Click Open at the left. (If the Home screen does not display, choose File > Open from the InDesign menu bar.)

4 Open the 05_Start.indd file in the Lesson05 folder, located inside the Lessons folder in the InDesignCIB folder on your hard drive.

5 If an alert informs you that the document contains links to sources that have been modified, click Update Modified Links.

6 Choose File > Save As, rename the file **05_Color.indd**, and save it in the Lesson05 folder.

● **Note:** To better view the interface onscreen or in print, the screen captures in this book reflect the Medium Light interface rather than the default setting of Medium Dark. In addition, some screen captures illustrate User Interface Scaling for a closer look at interface elements. You can modify interface settings in Preferences.

7 To ensure that the panels and menu commands match those used in this lesson, choose Window > Workspace > [Advanced], and then choose Window > Workspace > Reset Advanced.

8 If you want to see what the finished document looks like, open the 05_End.indd file located in the same folder. You can leave this document open to act as a guide as you work.

9 When you're ready to resume working on the lesson document, click its tab in the upper-left corner of the document window.

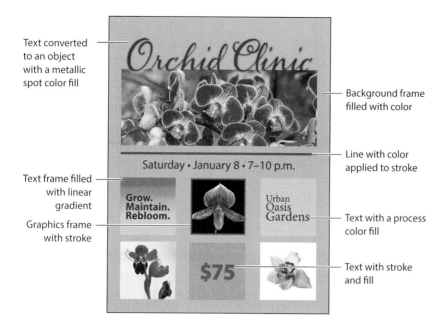

Text converted to an object with a metallic spot color fill

Background frame filled with color

Line with color applied to stroke

Text frame filled with linear gradient

Graphics frame with stroke

Text with a process color fill

Text with stroke and fill

Managing color

Color management works to reproduce colors consistently across a range of output devices, such as monitors, laptops, tablets, smartphones, color printers, and high-resolution printing presses. InDesign gives you easy-to-use color management features that help you achieve good, consistent color without needing to become a color management expert. With color management enabled out of the box, you'll be able to view colors consistently while ensuring more accurate colors from edit to proof to final output (print or digital).

Translating colors across devices

No screen, film, printer, copier, or printing press can produce the full range of color visible to the human eye. Each device has specific capabilities and makes different kinds of compromises in reproducing color images. The unique color-rendering abilities of a specific output device are known collectively as its "gamut." InDesign and other graphics applications, such as Adobe Photoshop and Adobe Illustrator, use color numbers to describe the color for each pixel. The color numbers correspond to the color model, such as the RGB values for red, green, and blue, or the CMYK values for cyan, magenta, yellow, and black.

Color management is simply a way of translating the color numbers for each pixel from the source (the document or image) to the output device (such as a smartphone or color printer). Because each source and output device has its own specific gamut (or range) of colors that it is capable of reproducing, the aim of the color translation is color accuracy across devices.

▶ **Tip:** Consider a red sweater you spot in a store's app on your smartphone, in a printed catalog, and in a web browser on a laptop. You don't really know what shade of red that sweater is unless you see the real thing. Many factors impact the color displayed, including the quality and lighting of the original picture, any retouching done on the photo, the paper and print quality, the screen resolution, and more. This is why graphic designers use color management.

Creating a viewing environment for color management

▶ **Tip:** You can find additional information about color management in the InDesign Help file, online at adobe.com (search for "manage color in InDesign"), and in videos such as Peachpit's *Color Management for Photographers and Designers: Learn by Video*.

Your work environment influences how you see color on your monitor and on printed output. For best results, control the colors and light in your work environment by doing the following:

- View your documents in an environment that provides a consistent light level and color temperature. For example, the color characteristics of sunlight change throughout the day and alter the way colors appear onscreen, so keep shades closed or work in a windowless room.

- To eliminate the blue-green cast from fluorescent lighting, you can install D50 (5000° Kelvin) lighting. You can also view printed documents using a D50 light box.

- View your document in a room with neutral-colored walls and ceiling. A room's color can affect the perception of both monitor color and printed color. Neutral gray is the best color for a viewing room.

- The color of your clothing reflecting off your monitor may affect the appearance of colors onscreen.

- Remove colorful background patterns on your monitor desktop. Busy or bright patterns surrounding a document interfere with accurate color perception. Set your desktop to display a neutral gray.

- View document proofs in the real-world conditions under which your audience will see the final piece. For example, you might want to see how a housewares catalog looks under the typical light bulbs used in homes, or view an office furniture catalog under the LED or fluorescent lighting used in offices.

- For print, always make final color judgments under the lighting conditions specified by the legal requirements for contract proofs in your country.

—From Adobe Help

Displaying images at full resolution

In a color management workflow, even using default color settings, you should display images at high quality for the best possible color representation that your monitor is capable of showing.

To see the difference in one of your documents, experiment with the options in the View > Display Performance menu.

- Fast Display: Ideal for quick text editing because images do not display.

- Typical Display: Displays images more quickly, but colors are less precise; the default for most computers.

- High Quality Display: Displays images at high resolution.

For this lesson, be sure View > Display Performance > High Quality Display is selected.

You can specify Display Performance defaults in the Preferences dialog, and you can change the display of an individual object using the Object > Display Performance menu.

Specifying color settings in InDesign

For consistent color in InDesign, you can specify a color settings file (CSF) with preset color management policies and default profiles. The default setting is North America General Purpose 2, which is the best option for beginners.

In this section, we review some of the preset color settings in InDesign that you can use to help achieve consistent color in your projects. However, you will not change any color settings.

1 Choose Edit > Color Settings. These settings apply to the InDesign application rather than to individual documents.

2 Click the various options in the Color Settings dialog to see what is available.

3 Point at the Working Spaces title to see a description of this feature in the Description box at the bottom of the dialog.

4 Point at various other features to see their descriptions.

▶ **Tip:** According to Adobe, only those who are knowledgeable about color management should change color settings. The preset color settings have been tested by Adobe Systems. A graphic design firm or ad agency may have a color-managed workflow and provide specifications for you.

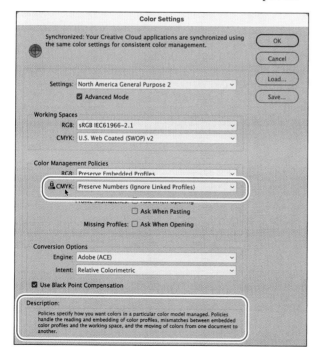

5 Click Cancel to close the Color Settings dialog without making changes.

Proofing colors onscreen

▶ **Tip:** To be sure that your screen is displaying colors to the best of its ability, calibrate it according to information supplied with your monitor.

When you proof colors onscreen, also known as "soft proofing," InDesign attempts to display colors according to specific output conditions. The accuracy of the simulation depends on various factors, including the lighting conditions of the room and whether your monitor is calibrated. To experiment with soft proofing, do the following:

1 Choose Window > Arrange > New Window for 05_Color.indd to open a second window for your lesson document.

2 If necessary, click the 05_Color.indd:2 window to activate it.

▶ **Tip:** The Proof Setup default is Document CMYK - U.S. Web Coated SWOP V2, which reflects the typical output method for print documents in the United States. SWOP stands for Specifications for Web Offset Publications.

3 Choose View > Proof Colors. This displays a soft proof of the colors according to the current settings under View > Proof Setup. Notice the minor differences between the original view of the document and the soft proof view.

4 To customize the soft proof, choose View > Proof Setup > Custom.

5 In the Customize Proof Condition dialog, click the Device To Simulate menu and review the available presses, desktop printers, and output devices such as monitors and HDTV.

6 Scroll down in the menu and select Dot Gain 20% from the Device To Simulate menu, and click OK.

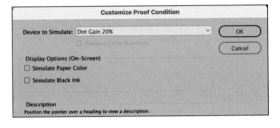

Grayscale profiles such as Dot Gain 20% let you preview how a document will print in black and white. Notice that the InDesign document's title bar shows which device is being simulated, such as (Dot Gain 20%) or (Document CMYK).

7 Try different soft-proofing options. When you're finished reviewing the various soft-proofing options, click 05_Color.indd:2's close box to close the second window.

Defining printing requirements

Whether you are working on a document for delivery in a print or a digital format, it's a good idea to know the output requirements before you start working. For example, for a print document, meet with your printer and discuss your document's design and use of color—particularly if you plan to use a special paper or metallic ink. Because printers understand the capabilities of their equipment, they may suggest ways for you to save time and money, increase quality, and avoid potentially costly printing or color problems. The flyer used in this lesson was designed to be printed by a commercial printer using CMYK colors and a metallic spot color. (Color modes are described in more detail later in this lesson.)

▶ **Tip:** Your commercial printer may provide a preflight profile with all the necessary specifications for output. You can import the profile and use it to check your work against these criteria.

To confirm that your document matches the printing requirements, you can check it against a preflight profile, which contains a set of rules regarding the document's size, fonts, colors, images, bleeds, and more. The Preflight panel can alert you to anything in the document that does not follow the rules set in the profile. In this exercise, you will import a preflight profile, select it in the Preflight panel, and resolve an issue with the document.

Loading a preflight profile

First, you will load a preflight profile provided by the printer.

1 Choose Window > Output > Preflight.

2 Choose Define Profiles from the Preflight panel menu (≡).

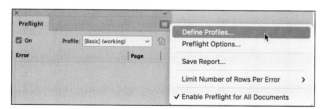

3 In the Preflight Profiles dialog, click the Preflight Profile Menu button (≡) below the list of preflight profiles at the left. Choose Load Profile.

4 Select the Flyer Profile.idpp file in the Lesson05 folder, located inside the Lessons folder within the InDesignCIB folder on your hard drive. Click Open.

5 With Flyer Profile selected, look through the settings specified for the output of this flyer. Click the arrows next to a few different categories to see the options you can include in a preflight profile.

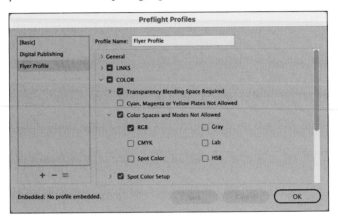

InDesign will flag violations for the checked options. For example, under Color > Color Spaces And Modes Not Allowed, RGB is selected. As a result, all uses of RGB colors will be reported as errors.

6 Click OK to close the Preflight Profiles dialog.

Selecting a preflight profile

Now, you will select the Flyer Profile and review any errors that it flags.

1 From the Profile menu in the Preflight panel, choose Flyer Profile. Notice that the profile detects one issue with the colors that currently exist in the document.

2 To view the error, click the triangle next to COLOR (1).

3 Click the triangle next to Color Space Not Allowed (1).

4 Double-click Line to select the line on the page that is triggering the error.

5 If necessary, click the triangle next to Info to see details of the problem. Leave this panel open for the next exercise.

Because this document is destined for CMYK printing, colors in the RGB color mode are not allowed. The stroke color of the line is in the RGB color model. You will resolve this in the next exercise.

▶ **Tip:** The lower-left corner of the document window displays the number of preflight errors in a document (provided that On is selected in the upper-left corner of the Preflight panel). If you start to see a lot of errors, open the Preflight panel to see more information.

Converting a color mode for a swatch

Now, you will resolve the preflight error by converting the color mode of the swatch applied to the line.

1 Choose Window > Color > Swatches to display the Swatches panel.

2 In the list of colors in the Swatches panel, double-click the Green-Dark swatch to open the Swatch Options dialog.

3 Select CMYK from the Color Mode menu, and then click OK. (If necessary, scroll up in the menu to see CMYK.)

▶ **Tip:** When you package a document for final output (File > Package), InDesign may flag issues with color models. You will change the color mode in the same way as shown here.

4 Notice that the error no longer displays in the Preflight panel.

5 Close the Preflight panel, and choose File > Save.

Creating colors

For maximum design flexibility, InDesign provides a variety of methods for creating colors. Once you create colors and color swatches, you can apply them to objects, strokes, and text in the layout. For consistent color usage, you can share colors among documents and users. You can create colors in the following ways:

● **Note:** As you work through the lesson, you can move panels around and change the zoom level to a setting that works best for you. For more information, see "Working with panels" and "Changing the magnification of a document" in Lesson 1.

* Create colors on the fly using the Color panel.

* Create named color swatches for repeated and consistent usage with the Swatches panel.

* Select a color from an image using the Eyedropper tool.

* Use the Color Theme tool or Object > Extract From Image > Color Themes command to choose among color themes generated from images or objects.

* Create and select themes from Adobe Color (color.adobe.com).

* Use the CC Libraries feature to share colors with Photoshop and Illustrator, with other members of your workgroup, and with other documents.

You can define colors in a variety of color modes, including RGB, CMYK, HSB, and "spot color" modes such as PANTONE. The difference between spot and process (CMYK) colors is discussed later in this exercise.

This flyer will be printed by a commercial printer using CMYK color, which requires four separate plates for printing—one each for cyan, magenta, yellow, and black. However, the CMYK color mode has a limited range of colors, which is where spot colors are useful. Spot colors are used to add colors beyond the range of CMYK (for example, metallic inks) and to ensure consistent color (for example, the color used in a company logo).

In this exercise, you will use the Swatches panel to create a PANTONE metallic spot color for a headline. You will then use the Eyedropper tool, Color panel, and Swatches panel to create a CMYK color swatch for the flyer's background color.

Creating a PANTONE color swatch

In this flyer, the "Orchid Clinic" headline calls for a metallic ink for an eye-catching and elegant look. You'll now add a metallic spot color from a color library. Note that the metallic color looks like any other color onscreen. You would see the difference in the metallic ink on the press, particularly with high-quality paper. Be sure to consult a printer about their capabilities and the extra costs of using metallic inks.

1 Using the Selection tool (▶), click the pasteboard surrounding the page to make sure nothing is selected.

2 If necessary, choose Window > Color > Swatches to display the Swatches panel.

3 Choose New Color Swatch from the Swatches panel menu (≡).

4 In the New Color Swatch dialog, choose Spot from the Color Type menu.

5 Select PANTONE+ Metallic Coated from the Color Mode menu.

6 In the PANTONE C field, type **8483** to automatically scroll the list of Pantone swatches to the color you want for this project, which is PANTONE 8483 C.

7 Click OK. The spot color is added to your Swatches panel.

The icon (⬛) to the right of the color name in the Swatches panel indicates that it is a spot color. New colors added to the Swatches panel are stored with the document in which they are created.

8 Choose File > Save.

You'll apply the newly added spot color to the "Orchid Clinic" headline later in this lesson.

▶ **Tip:** When selecting PANTONE colors for print, it's a good idea to select them from a printed PANTONE color guide, available from pantone.com. Selecting PANTONE colors from the screen may not be reliable.

Creating CMYK color swatches

To create a CMYK color swatch from scratch, you need an understanding of color mixing and color values. Alternatively, you can experiment with defining colors in the Colors panel and add the color as a color swatch. You can also use the Eyedropper tool to "pick up" a color from an image. In this exercise, you will use the Eyedropper tool to get a head start on creating a CMYK color swatch. Then, you will create three additional colors by entering color values.

1 Zoom as necessary to view the yellow flower in the lower-left corner of the page.

2 Choose Edit > Deselect All to be sure nothing is selected on the page.

3 Choose Window > Color > Color to display the Color panel.

4 Press I on the keyboard to select the Eyedropper tool (🖊.).

5 Click the Eyedropper tool on a lighter area of the yellow flower in the lower-left corner of the page as shown.

The color picked up from the image displays in the Color panel. The color values may differ depending on precisely where you clicked. To create the intended color, you will fine-tune the color values.

▶ **Tip:** Using the Swatches panel to name colors makes it easy to apply, edit, and update colors for objects in a document. Although you can also use the Color panel to apply colors to objects, there is no quick way to update these colors, which are considered "unnamed colors." Instead, if you want to change an unnamed color on multiple objects, you need to change each one individually.

6 In the Color panel, enter the values shown below in the C, M, Y, and K fields. You can tab between fields, and when you're finished entering values, press Enter (Windows) or Return (macOS).

- C (Cyan): **10**
- M (Magenta): **0**
- Y (Yellow): **40**
- K (Black): **0**

7 Choose Add To Swatches from the Color panel menu (≡).

A color swatch is added to the bottom of the list in the Swatches panel, and it is automatically selected. Close the Color panel.

8 Click the New Swatch icon (⊞) at the bottom of the Swatches panel. This makes a copy of the currently selected swatch; you can use this swatch as a starting place for a new swatch.

● **Note:** To see all the swatches, drag the lower-right corner of the Swatches panel to expand it.

9 Double-click the new swatch added to the bottom of the Swatches panel. This opens the Swatch Options dialog so that you can edit the swatch.

10 Make sure Color Type is set to Process and Color Mode is set to CMYK. Adjust the color by typing values in the following fields; you can tab from field to field.

- Cyan: **25**
- Magenta: **75**
- Yellow: **0**
- Black: **0**

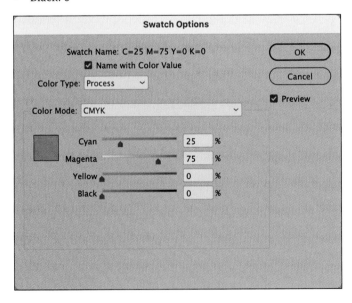

11 Click OK to close the Swatch Options dialog and add the new swatch.

12 Press Alt (Windows) or Option (macOS) while you click the New Swatch icon (⊞) at the bottom of the Swatches panel. This creates a new swatch and automatically opens the New Color Swatch dialog.

13 Make sure that Color Type is set to Process and that Color Mode is set to CMYK.

14 Enter the following values in the fields, tabbing between fields:

- Cyan: **90**

- Magenta: **70**

- Yellow: **30**

- Black: **0**

Click OK to update the color.

15 Choose New Color Swatch from the Swatches panel menu (≡).

16 Make sure that Color Type is set to Process and Color Mode is set to CMYK.

17 Enter the following values in the fields, tabbing between fields:

- Cyan: **65**

- Magenta: **25**

- Yellow: **100**

- Black: **0**

18 Click OK to update the color, and then choose File > Save.

You have now created a spot color swatch (metallic blue) and three CMYK color swatches (pink, blue, and green) in addition to the yellow swatch created with the Eyedropper tool. In the next exercise, you will apply colors to objects on the page.

▶ **Tip:** If you want to give a color a recognizable name, such as Aqua or Forest Green, deselect Name With Color Value in the Swatch Options dialog. You can then enter a name in the Swatch Name field.

About spot and process colors

You can designate colors as either spot or process color types, which correspond to the two main ink types used in commercial printing. In the Swatches panel, you can identify a color's type by the icon that displays next to its name. When applying colors in InDesign, keep in mind the final output (print or digital) so that you create and apply colors with the appropriate color model.

A spot color is a special premixed ink used instead of, or in addition to, CMYK process inks. Each spot color requires its own printing plate on a printing press, so use spot colors when few colors are specified and color accuracy is critical. Spot color inks can accurately reproduce colors outside the gamut of process colors. However, the exact appearance of the printed spot color is determined by the combination of the ink as mixed by the commercial printer and the paper it's printed on, not by color values you specify or by color management.

A process color is printed using a combination of the four standard process inks: cyan, magenta, yellow, and black (CMYK). Use process colors when a job requires so many colors that using individual spot inks would be expensive or impractical, as when printing color photographs.

- For best results in a high-quality printed document, specify process colors using CMYK values printed in process color reference charts, such as those available from a commercial printer.

- The final color values of a process color are its values in CMYK, so if you specify a process color using RGB, those color values are converted to CMYK when you print color separations. These conversions differ based on your color-management settings and document profile.

- Don't specify a process color based on how it looks on your monitor, unless you are sure you have set up a color-management system properly and you understand its limitations for previewing color.

- Avoid using process colors in documents intended for onscreen viewing because CMYK has a smaller color gamut than that of a typical screen.

Sometimes, you will use process and spot inks in the same job. For example, you might use one spot ink to print the exact color of a company logo on the same pages of an annual report where you need process colors to reproduce photos. You can also use a spot-color printing plate to apply a varnish over areas of a process color job. In both cases, your print job would use a total of five inks—four process inks and one spot ink or varnish.

Each spot color you create generates an additional spot-color plate for the press. In general, commercial printers produce either two-color (using black and one spot color) or four-color CMYK work, with the possibility of adding one or more spot colors. Using spot colors typically increases printing costs. It is a good idea to consult with your printer before using spot colors in a document.

—Condensed from InDesign Help

► **Tip:** In addition to spot and process colors, InDesign provides Mixed Ink colors to expand the color palette of a publication that uses multiple spot colors. To use this feature, select New Mixed Ink Swatch from the Swatches panel menu. You can then mix a spot color and black (or two spot colors) to create an additional color, offering the tonal range you would see in a duotone image. If the New Mixed Ink Swatch option is not available, make sure that the document includes a spot color swatch.

Applying colors

Once you create color swatches, you can apply them to objects, text, and more. The Swatches panel, Control panel, Properties panel, and CC Libraries panel offer the primary tools for applying colors. There are three general steps to applying a color:

1 Select the text or object.

2 Select the stroke (edge) or fill (background) option, depending on what you want to change.

3 Select a swatch.

You use the Stroke/Fill box (⬚) to specify whether you want to apply color to a selection's stroke (outline) or fill (background). You can find the Stroke/Fill box on the Tools panel, the Swatches panel, and the Color panel. Whenever you apply colors, keep an eye on this box, as it's easy to apply color to the wrong part of an object.

▶ **Tip:** The Control and Properties panels provide separate Fill and Stroke menus, which can make it easier to apply colors.

InDesign provides many other options for applying colors, including dragging swatches onto objects, copying color from an object with the Eyedropper tool, and specifying colors in styles. As you work with InDesign, you will discover which methods work best for you.

In this exercise, you will apply color swatches to strokes, fills, and text using various panels and techniques.

Applying fill colors to objects

In this task, you will apply fill colors to various objects on the page by using the Swatches panel, dragging a swatch, and using the Eyedropper tool.

1 If necessary, choose View > Fit Page In Window, and choose Window > Color > Swatches.

2 Choose View > Screen Mode > Normal to see the frame edges.

3 Using the Selection tool (▶), click anywhere in the margin of the page (outside the margin guides) to select the large background frame.

▶ **Tip:** Clicking the small arrow on the Fill/ Stroke box (⬚) swaps the stroke and fill colors of a selected object.

Click in the margins of the page to select the large text frame as shown here. The square resizing handles show that the frame is selected.

4 Click the Fill box (⬚) on the Swatches panel.

5 Click the green color swatch named C=65 M=25 Y=100 K=0.

6 At the top of the Swatches panel, drag the Tint slider to 40.

7 Using the Selection tool, select the text frame at the lower right containing the words "Urban Oasis Gardens."

8 With the Fill box still selected, click the yellow color swatch named C=10 M=0 Y=40 K=0.

9 Click the pasteboard to make sure nothing is selected on the page.

10 In the Swatches panel, drag the pink color swatch (C=25 M=75 Y=0 K=0) to the text frame centered at the bottom of the page containing "$75."

11 Click the pasteboard to make sure nothing is selected.

12 Using the Selection tool, click "Orchid Clinic" at the top of the page.

13 With the Fill box still selected, click the PANTONE 8483 C spot color swatch.

▶ **Tip:** The "Orchid Clinic" text at the top of the page is an object created by choosing Type > Create Outlines for a selected text frame. This creates a frame (shaped like the text) that may be filled with a graphic or otherwise manipulated.

14 Choose File > Save. To prepare for the next exercise, click the pasteboard to make sure nothing is selected, and choose View > Fit Page In Window.

Applying colors to strokes

The Stroke panel (Window > Stroke) lets you apply a border to lines, frames, and text. Here, you will apply color to an existing line and a graphics frame stroke using options on the Control panel.

1 Using the Selection tool (▶), click the horizontal line above the date in the middle of the page.

2 Click the Stroke menu on the Control panel.

3 Resize the Swatches panel as necessary (or scroll down) and select the Green-Dark swatch.

● **Note:** If you apply color to the wrong object or the wrong part of an object, you can always choose Edit > Undo and try again.

4 Using the Selection tool, click the graphics frame containing the orchid bud. Be sure to click outside the content grabber to select the frame.

5 Click the Stroke box () on the Swatches panel.

6 Scroll down and click the Green-Dark color swatch.

7 Choose File > Save.

Applying colors to text

▶ **Tip:** To create reverse type, which is lighter text on a dark background, you apply a lighter color to text and a darker color to the paragraph shading or text frame.

You will now select text with the Type tool and apply a fill color to it using the Swatches panel and the Control panel.

1 Using the Type tool (**T**), click in the text frame containing the date "Saturday • January 8 • 7–10 p.m." Drag to select all the text.

On the Swatches panel, notice that the Fill box has changed to indicate that text is selected: (**T**).

2 With the Fill box still selected, click the Green-Dark swatch.

3 Using the Type tool, click in the frame at the left containing the words "Grow. Maintain. Rebloom." Press Ctrl+A (Windows) or Command+A (macOS) to select all the text in the paragraph.

4 With the Fill box still selected, click the Green-Dark swatch.

5 Using the Type tool, click in the frame at the right containing the words "Urban Oasis Gardens." Click four times to select all the text.

▶ **Tip:** As you're creating and applying colors, be sure you are staying within your client's or company's branding guidelines. Ask for a style guide or branding guide, which will typically spell out approved colors, fonts, logo usage rules, and more.

6 Locate the text Fill button (**T**) on the Control panel. Click the Fill button, and select the Green-Dark swatch.

7 Choose Edit > Deselect All to see your progress in applying colors.

If the Swatches panel is taking up too much space onscreen, you may close it.

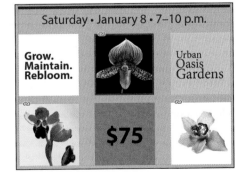

8 Choose Window > Properties to display the Properties panel.

9 Using the Type tool, click in the text frame centered at the bottom of the page containing "$75." Choose Edit > Select All to select all the text.

10 In the Properties panel, click the Fill button, and then select the lighter green color swatch named C=65 M=25 Y=100 K=0.

11 Type **1 pt** in the Weight field (next to the Stroke button). Press Enter or Return.

12 Click the Stroke button, and then select the blue color swatch named C=90 M=70 Y=30 K=0.

Click the pasteboard to deselect the text, and then zoom as necessary to see how the formatting looks. Choose Window > Properties to close the Properties panel.

13 Choose Edit > Deselect All, and then choose File > Save.

Finding and changing color swatches

If you need to selectively make changes to color usage in a document, you can do so through a search-and-replace operation. For example, you may decide to change the color of the rules on the chapter opening pages in a book without changing the rules on the other pages.

▶ **Tip:** If you no longer want to use a color in a document, you can delete it from the Swatches panel and replace it with another color.

The Find This Color option in the Swatches panel menu lets you selectively search and replace colors. In this exercise, you will experiment with this feature by finding where the Green-Dark color swatch is applied and then change two instances to a different color. You will see that this feature can save time and ensure consistency in a longer document.

1 Using the Selection tool (▶), click the horizontal line above the date in the middle of the page.

2 On the Swatches panel, note the Green-Dark color swatch is applied to the line.

3 With the Green-Dark color swatch still selected, choose Find This Color from the Swatches panel menu.

4 The Find/Change dialog displays with the Color tab selected. Leave Find Color set to Green-Dark. In the Change Color area, select the blue color swatch: C=90 M=70 Y=30 K=0.

● **Note:** Drag the Find/ Change dialog out of the way as necessary to see the page.

5 Click Find Next to highlight text or objects where the color is used. When the text is selected, click Find Next to skip those instances.

6 When the stroke on the flower image is selected, click Change. When the horizontal line above the date is selected, click Change.

7 After you change the two instances of the stroke color, click Done to close the Find/Change dialog.

8 Choose File > Save.

Working with tint swatches

A tint swatch is a screened (lighter) version of a color that you can apply quickly and consistently. The tint swatch is available on the Swatches panel and in other color menus, such as in the Control panel. You can share tint swatches with other documents by using the Load Swatches command on the Swatches panel menu. You will now create a light green tint swatch and apply it to the yellow text frame.

Creating a tint swatch

You create a tint swatch from an existing color swatch.

1 Choose View > Fit Page In Window to center the page in the document window.

2 Using the Selection tool (▶), click the pasteboard surrounding the page to make sure nothing is selected.

3 In the Swatches panel, select the pink color swatch named C=25 M=75 Y=0 K=0.

4 Choose New Tint Swatch from the Swatches panel menu (≡).

5 In the New Tint Swatch dialog, the Tint option at the bottom is the only option you can modify. Type **65** in the Tint field, and then click OK.

● **Note:** To see all the swatches, drag the lower-right corner of the Swatches panel to expand it.

The new tint swatch appears at the bottom of the list of swatches. The Tint field at the top of the Swatches panel displays information about the selected swatch.

Applying a tint swatch

You will apply the tint swatch as a fill color.

1 Using the Selection tool (▶), click the text frame at the bottom containing "$75."

2 Click the Fill box (▣) on the Swatches panel.

3 Click the new tint you just created in the Swatches panel. Its tint swatch name will be C=25 M=75 Y=0 K=0 65%. Notice how the color changes.

4 Choose File > Save.

▶ **Tip:** Tint swatches are helpful because InDesign maintains the relationship between a tint and its parent color. So if you change the parent color swatch to a different color, the tint swatch becomes a lighter version of the new color.

Working with gradients

▶**Tip:** It's a good idea to test gradients on the intended output device, whether it's digital or print.

A gradient is a graduated blend between two or more colors or between tints of the same color. You can create either a linear or a radial gradient. In this exercise, you will create a linear gradient swatch with the Swatches panel, apply it to an object, and adjust the gradient with the Gradient Swatch tool.

Linear gradient.

Radial gradient.

Creating a gradient swatch

When you create a gradient in the New Gradient Swatch dialog, the gradient is defined by a series of color stops in the gradient ramp. A stop is the point at which each color is at full intensity between the transitions; it is identified by a square below the gradient ramp. Every InDesign gradient has at least two color stops. By editing the color of each stop and adding color stops, you can create custom gradients.

1 Choose Edit > Deselect All to make sure no objects are selected.

2 Choose New Gradient Swatch from the Swatches panel menu (≡).

3 For Swatch Name, type **Pink/Yellow**. Leave the Type menu set to Linear.

4 Click the left stop marker (🏠) on the gradient ramp.

▶**Tip:** To create a gradient that uses a tint of a color, first create a tint swatch in the Swatches panel.

5 From the Stop Color menu, select Swatches, and then scroll down the list and select the pink color swatch named C=25 M=75 Y=0 K=0.

Notice that the left side of the gradient ramp is now pink.

6 With the left stop marker still selected, type **5** in the Location field.

7 Click the right stop marker (🏠), and select the yellow color swatch named C=10 M=0 Y=40 K=0. Type **70** in the Location field.

The gradient ramp shows a color blend between pink and yellow.

8 Click OK. The new gradient swatch appears at the bottom of the list in the Swatches panel.

9 Choose File > Save.

Applying a gradient swatch

Now you'll replace the fill in one of the text frames with the gradient.

1 Using the Selection tool (▶), click the text frame at the left containing the words "Grow. Maintain. Rebloom."

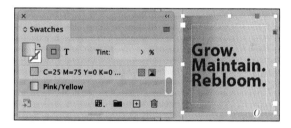

2 Click the Fill box (◰) on the Swatches panel.

3 Click the new gradient you just created in the Swatches panel: Pink/Yellow.

4 Choose File > Save.

Adjusting the direction of the gradient blend

Once you have filled an object with a gradient, you can modify the gradient by using the Gradient Swatch tool to "repaint" the gradient along an imaginary line that you draw. This tool lets you change the direction of a gradient and change its beginning point and end point. When using the Gradient Swatch tool, the farther away you start from the outer edges of the object, the more gradual the gradient blend will be. You'll now change the direction of the gradient.

1 Make sure the "Grow. Maintain. Rebloom." text frame is still selected, and then press G on the keyboard to select the Gradient Swatch tool () in the Tools panel.

2 To create a less gradual gradient effect, position the cursor close to the left edge of the selected text frame, and drag to the right as shown.

Tip: To constrain gradient angles to horizontal, vertical, or 45-degree angles, press the Shift key while dragging with the Gradient tool.

When you release the mouse button, you'll notice that the transition between pink and yellow is less gradual than it was previously.

Tip: The farther you drag the Gradient Swatch tool, the more gradual the resulting gradient will be.

3 To create a diagonal gradient, drag from the upper-left corner to the lower-right corner using the Gradient Swatch tool. Continue to experiment with the Gradient Swatch tool so that you understand how it works.

4 When you are finished experimenting, drag from the top to the bottom of the text frame to form a gradient from top to bottom. That's how you'll leave the gradient for the "Grow. Maintain. Rebloom." text frame.

 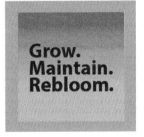

5 Choose File > Save.

Working with color groups

If a document contains many color swatches intended for specific purposes (such as chapter openers or divider pages), you can group the swatches in the Swatches panel. You can then easily share the color group with other documents and with other designers working on the marketing campaign.

Adding colors to a color group

You will organize the colors in this document into a new color group.

1 Press V on the keyboard to switch to the Selection tool (▶).

2 Click the pasteboard to make sure no objects are selected.

3 To create a new color group, choose New Color Group from the Swatches panel menu (≡). Click None in the Swatches panel.

4 In the New Color Group dialog, type **Orchid Clinic Flyer**. Click OK.

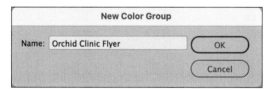

Now, you will drag the color swatches, tint swatch, and gradient swatch created for the flyer into the new color group.

5 To select the swatches, Shift-click the first swatch and last swatch you want to move. Be sure that [None], [Registration], [Paper], and [Black] are not selected.

6 Click in the blue highlighted area to the left of the selected swatches, and drag them below the Orchid Clinic Flyer folder until a line displays.

7 Choose File > Save.

▶ **Tip:** As you design a document, you often create more color swatches than you use. When you settle on a final design and color palette, you will want to delete any unused colors to make sure they aren't applied accidentally. To do this, choose Select All Unused from the Swatches panel menu (≡). Then, click the Delete Selected Swatch/Groups button (🗑) at the bottom of the panel.

Previewing the final document

As a final step, you'll preview the document in its finished state.

1 Choose View > Screen Mode > Preview.

2 Choose View > Fit Page In Window.

3 Press Tab to hide all the panels and review the results of your work.

4 Press Tab again to restore your panels.

Congratulations! You have now completed this lesson.

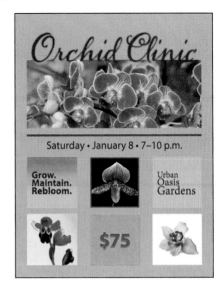

Exploring on your own

Follow these steps to learn more about working with color themes.

Creating a color theme

To create colors that complement an image in a document, you can use the InDesign Color Theme tool. The tool analyzes an image or object, selects representative colors, and generates five different themes. You can select and apply swatches from a color theme, add a color theme's swatches to the Swatches panel, and share the color themes through CC Libraries. To use the Color Theme tool:

• Click an image or object with the Color Theme tool to create a color theme from a small area.

• Drag the Color Theme tool to marquee images and/or objects on a page from which to create a color theme.

• Alt-click (Windows) or Option-click (macOS) the Color Theme tool to clear the existing color theme and create a new one.

Viewing color themes

First, you will view the possible color themes from the orchid bud image. Then, you will select the color theme you want to use.

1 On the Tools panel, click the Eyedropper tool (✏.). Hold down the mouse button to view the pop-out menu, and then select the Color Theme tool (✎.).

2 Locate the orchid bud image in the center of the page.

3 Click the Color Theme tool anywhere on the image.

Notice that the Color Theme panel appears with a color theme picked up from the image.

4 On the Color Theme panel, click the Current Theme menu. Select the Muted theme.

You can select and use any of the swatches shown here, but instead you will add the entire color theme to the Swatches panel.

▶ **Tip:** To select the Color Theme tool from the keyboard, press Shift+i.

Adding a theme to the Swatches panel

You can add a single color from a color theme to the Swatches panel in addition to adding an entire theme. To add a single swatch, select it on the Color Theme panel, and then Alt-click (Windows) or Option-click (macOS) the Add To Swatches button.

The Muted color theme will work best for the flyer in progress. First, you will add the color theme to the Swatches panel. Then, you will share this color theme with others in your workgroup who are working on other pieces in the marketing campaign.

1 With the Muted theme selected on the Color Theme tool's panel, click the Add This Theme To Swatches button (⊞).

2 If necessary, choose Window > Color > Swatches to open the Swatches panel.

● **Note:** The CMYK color values in the Muted theme's colors may vary slightly. This will not affect your ability to explore these features.

3 Scroll down as necessary to see the Muted theme added to the Swatches panel as a color group (organized in a folder).

4 Choose File > Save.

Adding a color theme to your CC Library

The InDesign Creative Cloud Libraries feature makes it easy to share assets, such as color swatches and themes, with a workgroup. If multiple designers are working on a magazine or marketing campaign, this ensures that everyone on the creative team has easy access to the same content. Here, you will add two color themes to your Creative Cloud library. For more information about CC Libraries, see Lesson 11, "Importing and Modifying Graphics."

1 On the Color Theme tool's panel, with the Muted theme still showing, click the Add This Theme To My Current CC Library button ().

● **Note:** To use the Creative Cloud Libraries features, make sure the Adobe Creative Cloud application is running on your system.

Another way to create and add color themes is with the Extract panel. You will try this now.

2 Using the Selection tool (), click the image of the orchids at the top of the page under the headline "Orchid Clinic."

▶ **Tip:** If you choose an option from Object > Extract From Image with no image selected, you can import a graphics file from your computer.

3 Choose Object > Extract From Image > Color Themes.

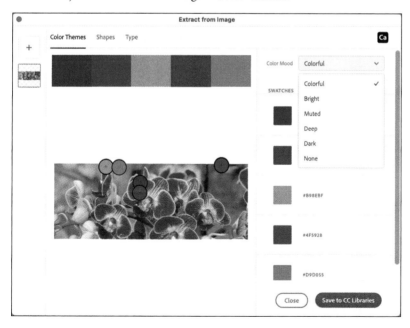

4 Click the Color Mood menu to see the various color themes extracted from the image.

5 Choose one of the themes from the menu, and then click Save To CC Libraries. Click the Extract From Image panel's close button.

6 To view the themes in your CC Libraries panel, choose Window > CC Libraries.

7 If necessary, click Sort Options (≡↓) and select Group By Type to view the color themes.

8 Click the CC Libraries panel menu to see the collaboration options: Invite People and Get Link.

9 Choose File > Save.

Managing color themes

InDesign users have many options for creating and managing color themes. These tools help you synchronize colors across your applications and projects and collaborate with other users.

- The Adobe Capture app for iPad, iPhone, and Android lets you create color themes from anything you point at with your device's camera.

- The Adobe Color website at color.adobe.com lets you create your own color themes, explore other users' themes, and review your themes.

- The CC Libraries panel (Window > CC Libraries) allows you to share color themes with a workgroup and manage color themes by copying, moving, or deleting them.

For more information about any of these features, consult InDesign Help.

Review questions

1 What is the advantage of creating colors in the Swatches panel instead of the Color panel?

2 What are the three general steps involved in applying a swatch of color?

3 What are the pros and cons of using spot colors versus process colors?

4 After you create a gradient and apply it to an object, how do you adjust the direction of the gradient blend?

Review answers

1 If you use the Swatches panel to apply a color to text and objects and then decide you want to use a different color, you don't need to update each use of the color individually. Instead, change the color's definition in the Swatches panel, and the color changes automatically throughout the layout.

2 The three general steps to applying a color swatch are: (1) selecting the text or object, (2) selecting the stroke or fill box, depending on what you want to change, and (3) selecting the color. You can access color swatches in various panels, including Swatches, Control, Properties, and Tools.

3 By using a spot color, you can ensure color accuracy. However, each spot color requires its own plate on the press, so using spot colors can be more costly. Use process colors when a job requires so many colors that using individual spot inks would be expensive or impractical, such as when printing color photographs.

4 To adjust the direction of the gradient blend, use the Gradient Swatch tool to repaint the fill along an imaginary line in the direction you want.

6 FLOWING TEXT

Lesson overview

In this lesson, you'll learn how to do the following:

- Import and flow text into existing text frames.

- Resize text frames automatically.

- Link text frames to flow text across columns and pages.

- Create linked frames automatically.

- Add pages and linked frames automatically while flowing text.

- Clean up text by deleting extra paragraph returns.

- Apply paragraph styles to text.

- Control column breaks.

- Align text to the baseline grid.

- Make a jump line to indicate where an article continues.

This lesson will take about 60 minutes to complete. To get the lesson files used in this chapter, download them from the web page for this book at adobepress.com/InDesignCIB2023. For more information, see "Accessing the lesson files and Web Edition" in the Getting Started section at the beginning of this book.

How to grow
peas, please!

PEAS, PLEASE
Plant: May
Soil: Moist
Fertilizer: Dairy dressing
Sow: 5" deep
Thin: 1" apart
Pick: August

Peas grow well in heavy, moist soil that is not suitable for some other vegetables. However, the land for peas, as for all vegetable plants, should be drained and free from standing water. Nothing is quite so good as dairy dressing for peas, and it is worthwhile to get it if possible.

Fertilizing

When dairy dressing is at hand, be sure the ground is soft and fine; then open furrows about eight inches deep. These should be three feet apart for the Nott's Excelsior type, and four feet for the climbing types. Into these furrows throw a liberal layer of dairy dressing to cover the bottom of the furrow. If you can spare it, put in a wheelbarrow load to twenty feet since peas are great feeders and need nourishment during the hot days of July when the crop is ripening.

Here is one case where dairy dressing may be used that is rather fresh, as peas seem to do well with dairy dressing at any stage. Stable dressing, which contains straw and horse manure, is more likely to develop heat, which will hurt the seed;

Peas continued on 2

Adobe InDesign provides methods for flowing text into existing text frames, creating frames while flowing text, and adding frames and pages while flowing text. This makes it easy to flow copy for anything from a catalog to a magazine article to an ebook.

Getting started

In this lesson, you'll work on a booklet in progress. The design of the opening spread of the article is almost finished, and several pages are ready for text. While working on this article, you will experiment with various text-flow methods and create a "jump line" to indicate the page on which an article continues.

● **Note:** If you have not already downloaded the project files for this lesson to your computer from your Account page, make sure to do so now. See "Getting Started" at the beginning of the book.

1 To ensure that the preferences and default settings of your InDesign program match those used in this lesson, move the InDesign Defaults file to a different folder following the procedure in "Saving and restoring the InDesign Defaults file" on pages 3–4.

2 Start InDesign.

3 The InDesign Home screen displays. Click Open at the left. (If the Home screen does not display, choose File > Open from the InDesign menu bar.)

4 Open the 06_Start.indd file in the Lesson06 folder, located inside the Lessons folder within the InDesignCIB folder on your hard drive.

5 If an alert informs you that the document contains links to sources that have been modified, click Update Modified Links.

6 Choose File > Save As, rename the file **06_FlowText.indd**, and save it in the Lesson06 folder.

● **Note:** To better view the interface onscreen or in print, the screen captures in this book reflect the Medium Light interface rather than the default setting of Medium Dark. In addition, some screen captures illustrate User Interface Scaling for a closer look at interface elements. You can modify interface settings in Preferences.

7 To ensure that the panels and menu commands match those used in this lesson, choose Window > Workspace > [Essentials], and then choose Window > Workspace > Reset Essentials.

8 If you want to see what the finished document looks like, open the 06_End.indd file in the same folder. You can leave this document open to act as a guide as you work.

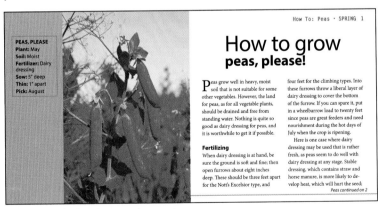

9 When you're ready to resume working on the lesson document, display it by clicking its tab in the upper-left corner of the document window.

Flowing text into an existing frame

When you import text, you can flow it into a new frame or an existing frame. If the frame is empty, you can click the loaded text icon in the frame to flow the text. On the left page of the opening spread of this booklet, an empty sidebar box is ready for text to be inserted. You will import a Microsoft Word document into this frame, apply a paragraph style, and automatically adjust the height of the text frame.

Importing text into an existing text frame

1 Choose Type > Show Hidden Characters to see paragraph returns, spaces, tabs, and other hidden characters onscreen. This helps you place and format text.

2 Zoom in to comfortably view the sidebar text frame on the left page of the opening spread. The frame is about 1 inch wide and has a stroke.

3 Choose Edit > Deselect All to make sure no objects are selected.

4 Choose File > Place. At the bottom of the Place dialog, make sure the three options are deselected: Show Import Options, Replace Selected Item, and Create Static Captions. (If necessary, click Options in macOS to see the options.)

▶ **Tip:** You edit text with the Type tool and thread (link) text frames with the Selection tool, but it does not matter what tool is selected when you import text.

5 Locate 06_Highlights.docx, in the Lesson06 folder, and then double-click it.

 The pointer becomes a loaded text icon (⬛), previewing the first few lines of text in the article you are placing. When you move the loaded text icon over an empty text frame, parentheses enclose the icon (⬛).

6 Position the loaded text icon over the placeholder text frame.

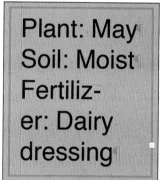

7 Click to place the text.

8 Choose File > Save.

The text does not fit in the text frame and is considered "overset." Overset text is indicated by a red plus sign (+) in the out port, which is in the lower-right corner of the text frame. You will resolve the overset text later in this exercise.

Applying a paragraph style

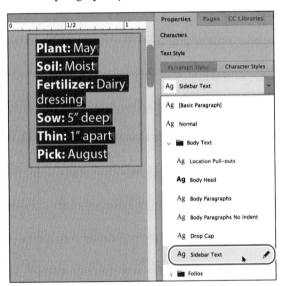

Tip: As you work, you can tear off panels, resize them, and move them to suit your needs. The configuration of your panels is largely dependent on the amount of screen space available. Some InDesign users have a second monitor for managing panels.

Now you will apply a paragraph style to the sidebar text. The paragraph style includes a nested style that automatically applies bold to the beginning of a paragraph until InDesign encounters the first colon.

1 Using the Type tool (T), click in the sidebar text frame so that you can format the text.

2 Choose Edit > Select All to select all the text in the frame (even the text you cannot see).

3 In the Text Styles area of the Properties panel, click the Paragraph Styles tab and then click the menu to see the styles.

4 Click the triangle to the left of the Body Text style group to open it.

5 Click the paragraph style Sidebar Text.

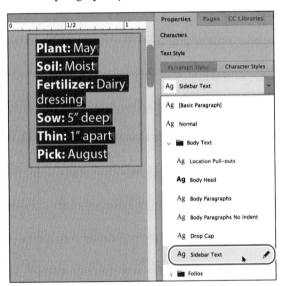

6 Click in the pasteboard to deselect the text. Choose File > Save.

Resizing text frames automatically

While adding, deleting, and editing text, you often end up resizing text frames. With the Auto-Size feature, you can specify that a text frame resize itself automatically according to your specifications. You will now use the Auto-Size feature to automatically adjust the height of the sidebar text frame based on the length of the text.

1 Using the Type tool (T), click in the sidebar immediately before the word "Plant."

2 Press the Caps Lock key on your keyboard, and then type the headline **PEAS, PLEASE**. (The headline does not include the period.)

3 Press Enter (Windows) or Return (macOS), and then press Caps Lock again to turn it off.

After adding the heading, the sidebar text no longer fits in the text frame. This overset text is indicated by the red plus sign (+) in the lower-right corner of the text frame.

4 With the sidebar text frame still selected, choose Object > Text Frame Options. In the Text Frame Options dialog, click Auto-Size in the list at the left.

5 Select Preview in the lower-left corner to see changes as you make them.

6 Choose Height Only from the Auto-Sizing menu.

7 If necessary, click the center icon in the top row (⬍) to indicate that you want the text frame to "grow down" as if you were manually dragging down the bottom handle of the text frame.

▶ **Tip:** The Auto-Size feature is ideal for text frames with a stroke and/or fill providing a boundary for the text (for example, a sidebar or coupon). If the text is shortened, the frame becomes smaller as well. If the text is lengthened, the frame becomes bigger so that text is not overset. Note that Auto-Size works only on an individual text frame or on the last frame in a series of threaded text frames.

8 Click OK.

9 Click the pasteboard to deselect objects on the page, and then choose View > Screen Mode > Preview to see how the sidebar looks.

PEAS, PLEASE
Plant: May
Soil: Moist
Fertilizer: Dairy dressing
Sow: 5" deep
Thin: 1" apart
Pick: August

10 Choose View > Screen Mode > Normal to restore the layout aids, such as guides and hidden characters.

11 Choose File > Save.

Flowing text manually

The process of taking an imported text file and flowing it across several connected text frames is called "threading text." InDesign lets you flow text manually for greater control, flow text automatically to save time, and flow text while automatically adding enough pages to hold all the text.

In this exercise, you will flow the feature article text into the two columns on the right-hand page. First, you will select a Word file to import into the existing text frame in the first column. Second, you will thread the first text frame to the second text frame. Finally, you will create new text frames on the third page of the document to contain more text.

1 Choose View > Fit Spread In Window to locate the two text frames at the right under the "How to grow peas, please!" headline.

2 Zoom in as necessary to view these text frames.

▶ **Tip:** To prepare to import text, you can pre-thread empty text frames. Using the Selection tool, click a frame's out port, and then click anywhere in the next frame. Repeat this process until all the frames are threaded.

3 Using the Type tool (**T**), click in the text frame at the left, as shown here.

4 Choose File > Place.

5 Locate and select 06_Peas.docx in the Lesson06 folder.

6 Select Replace Selected Item at the bottom of the Place dialog. (If necessary, click Options in macOS to see this option.) Click Open.

The text flows into the existing frame in the left column. Notice that the text frame includes an out port in the lower-right corner. The red plus sign (+)

indicates that some of the text you imported is overset, meaning that not all of the text fits into the existing text frame. You will now flow the additional text into another text frame in the second column.

7 Using the Selection tool (▶), click in the text frame's out port to load the text icon. (If necessary, first click the frame to select it, and then click the out port.)

▶ **Tip:** As you flow text, the Selection tool's cursor changes to various loaded text icons.

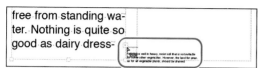

8 Move the loaded cursor over the text frame to the right, and click once in the frame, as shown.

9 The text flows into the second column. The out port in the text frame at the right contains a red plus sign (+), indicating that there is still overset text.

▶ **Tip:** If you change your mind and decide you don't want to flow overset text, you can press Esc or click any tool in the Tools panel to cancel the loaded text icon. No text will be deleted.

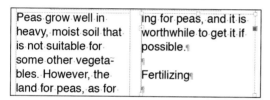

10 Choose File > Save. Leave the page in this position for the next exercise.

Loading the Type tool with multiple text files

In the Place dialog, you can "load" the Type tool with multiple text files and then place them individually. Loading the Type tool works as follows:

▶ **Tip:** You can "load" the Type tool with graphic files and text files at the same time.

- First, choose File > Place or click Import File on the Properties panel.

- In the Place dialog, Ctrl-click (Windows) or Command-click (macOS) to select multiple noncontiguous files. Shift-click to select a contiguous range of files.

- When you click Open, the loaded text icon shows in parentheses how many files are loaded, such as (4).

- Press the arrow keys on the keyboard to change which text file is loaded for placement, and press Esc to remove a text file from the loaded text icon.

- Click to place the text files one at a time.

Creating text frames while flowing text

▶Tip: The loaded text icon changes slightly in appearance, depending on whether you are threading text manually or using semi-autoflow or autoflow.

Now, you will try two different text flow methods. First, you will use semi-autoflow to place text into a column. Semi-autoflow lets you create threaded text frames one at a time. The pointer becomes a loaded text icon that automatically reloads after each column of text is placed. After that, you will use the loaded text icon to manually create a text frame.

Note that the success of these exercises relies on holding the correct modifier keys on the keyboard and clicking in the correct place. Therefore, it may help to read all the steps in each exercise before you perform them. If anything goes wrong, be sure to choose Edit > Undo, and then repeat the step.

1 Using the Selection tool (▶), click the out port of the text frame in the second column on the right page (page 1). This loads the text icon with the overset text.

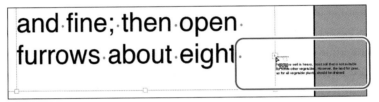

You will create new text frames on page 2 to contain more of the text. Guides indicate where to place the text frames.

2 Choose Layout > Next Spread to display pages 2 and 3, and then choose View > Fit Spread In Window.

When the loaded text icon is active, you can still navigate to different document pages or add new pages.

3 On the page at the left, position the loaded text icon (🖼) in the upper-left corner where the guides intersect. For proper placement, watch for the black arrow in the loaded text icon to turn white.

▶Tip: When the loaded text icon is over an empty text frame, a chain icon indicates that you can thread to that frame. You can also flow overset text into an empty graphics frame; the graphics frame is automatically converted to a text frame.

4 Hold down the Alt (Windows) or Option (macOS) key and click.

The text flows into the first column. Because you held down Alt or Option, the pointer is still a loaded text icon, ready for you to flow text into another frame.

5 Release the Alt or Option key, and position the loaded text icon (⬚) in the second column indicated by the guides.

6 Click to create a frame within the column guides in the right column.

inches·deep.·These·
should·be·three·feet·
apart·for·the·Nott's·

Clicking the loaded text icon creates text frames within the column guides and flows the text.

inches·deep.·These·
should·be·three·feet·
apart·for·the·Nott's·

July·when·the·crop·is·
ripening.·¶

▶ **Tip:** When you create a text frame by clicking with the loaded text icon, InDesign creates the new text frame as wide as the column where you click. Although these frames are placed within the column guides, you can move, resize, and reshape these text frames as necessary.

Text remains overset, as indicated by the red plus sign (+) in the lower-right corner of the second text frame. You will fix this later.

7 Choose File > Save. Leave the page in this position for the next exercise.

Creating threaded frames automatically

To speed up the creation of column-width linked text frames, InDesign provides a shortcut. If you press the right arrow key as you drag the Type tool to create a new text frame, InDesign automatically divides the text frame into multiple threaded frames. For example, if you press the right arrow key once while creating a text frame, the text frame is divided into two text frames of equal width. If you press the right arrow key five times, the text frame is divided five times, resulting in six columns of equal width.

▶ **Tip:** You can create columns by threading individual text frames or by dividing text frames into multiple columns using the General tab of the Text Frame Options dialog (Object menu). Some designers prefer separate text frames for more layout flexibility.

You will now create a two-column text frame on page 3. You can then thread the text frames to help contain the overset text.

1 Choose View > Fit Spread In Window to center pages 2 and 3 in the window.

2 Select the Type tool (T), and position it in the first column on the page at the right, where the column guide (purple) and margin guide (pink) intersect.

3 Drag the Type tool down and to the right to create a text frame that spans the width of both columns. As you drag, tap the right arrow key once.

InDesign automatically subdivides the text frame into two threaded text frames of equal width.

4 Continue to drag down and to the right to position the text frame within the column and margin guides. If necessary, use the Selection tool (▶) to adjust the text frames to fit within the guides, as shown.

5 Using the Selection tool, click the text frame in the second column on page 2. Click the frame's out port in the lower-right corner to load the text icon with overset text.

6 Click the loaded text icon () in the new text frame on page 3.

The text flows through the two columns.

7 Choose File > Save. Leave the page in this position for the next exercise.

Wait, the images are figures, not navigation. Let me not tag them.

Flowing text automatically

You will now autoflow the remaining text into the booklet. When you autoflow text, InDesign automatically creates new text frames within column guides on subsequent pages until all of the overset text is placed. This feature is ideal for longer projects, such as books. For this sample project, it will end up obscuring some of the images that are already placed. You can fix that easily by deleting the text frames; the text flow is automatically rerouted through the remaining frames in the thread.

1 Using the Selection tool (), click the out port in the lower-right corner of the text frame in the second column on page 3.

This loads the text icon with the overset text. (If necessary, first click the frame to select it, and then click the out port.)

2 Choose Layout > Next Spread to display pages 4 and 5.

3 Position the loaded text icon () in the first column on page 4, precisely where the column and margin guides intersect.

Tip: A thin vertical rule (line) between columns can add style and enhance readability. You can add rules between columns automatically in the Column Rules tab of the Text Frame Options dialog (Object menu).

▶ **Tip:** Shift-clicking the loaded text icon creates and flows text into automatically created text frames, adding pages as necessary to flow all the text into the document.

4 Hold down the Shift key and click.

Notice that new text frames are added to the remaining pages in the document, even on top of the photos. This is because you held down the Shift key to autoflow text.

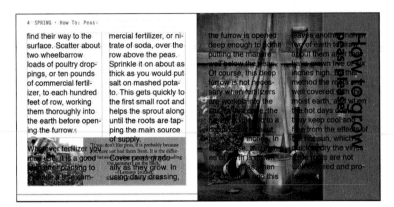

5 Using the Selection tool, Shift-click to select the two new text frames added to page 5 (the frame on top of the image of the gardening tools).

6 Choose Edit > Clear to delete the text frames.

● **Note:** Because the new text frames are placed within the page margins, the text partially obscures existing sidebar boxes on the pages. You will resolve this later in the lesson.

7 Choose Layout > Next Spread to display pages 6 and 7. As you can see, the text is flowing from page 4 to page 6 to page 7.

8 Using the Selection tool, Shift-click the two new text frames added to page 7 (the frames on top of the image of peas).

9 Choose Edit > Clear to delete the text frames.

Text is still overset, but you will resolve that in two ways. First, you will delete extra paragraph returns in the text, and then you will format the text so that it fits within the frames.

10 Choose File > Save.

Adding pages while flowing text

In addition to threading text frames on existing pages, you can add pages while flowing text. This feature, called Smart Text Reflow, is ideal for flowing long passages of text such as book chapters. With Smart Text Reflow, flowing text or typing into a primary text frame automatically adds pages and threaded text frames to contain all the text. If text becomes shorter through editing or reformatting, any extra pages can be automatically deleted as well. To experiment with Smart Text Reflow in a new document, follow these steps:

1 Choose File > New > Document. On the New Document screen:

 • Click Print across the top.

 • Click the Letter - Half icon.

 • Click the Landscape icon for Orientation.

 • Select Primary Text Frame.

> **Primary Text Frame**
> ☑

2 Click Create.

3 Choose Edit > Preferences > Type (Windows) or InDesign > Preferences > Type (macOS) to open the Type preferences. The Smart Text Reflow controls are at the bottom of the Type preferences. The options let you specify how pages are handled when you use Smart Text Reflow. Options include:

 • Where pages are added (to the end of a story, section, or document)

 • Whether Smart Text Reflow applies only to primary text frames or to other text frames in a document

 • How pages are inserted into facing-page spreads

 • Whether empty pages are deleted as text becomes shorter

4 Smart Text Reflow is selected by default, but confirm that it is selected. Click OK.

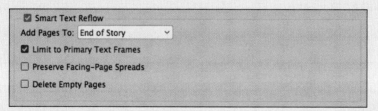

5 Choose File > Place. In the Place dialog, locate and select 06_Peas.docx in the Lesson06 folder, and click Open.

6 On the first page of the new document, click the loaded text icon within the page margins to flow all the text into the primary text frame, adding pages as necessary. Note the number of pages in the Pages panel (Window menu).

7 Close the file without saving it.

Using Find/Change to delete extra paragraph returns

▶ **Tip:** To add space between paragraphs, whether in Microsoft Word or InDesign, use the paragraph formatting controls to specify the amount of space before and after paragraphs. This provides space for comfortable writing and editing without leaving extra paragraph returns.

When writers and editors type in Microsoft Word, they often press the Enter or Return key every time they want space between paragraphs. This helps them read onscreen, but it is not helpful to graphic designers. Many publications indicate a new paragraph with an indent rather than space between paragraphs. Even if a publication does use space to indicate a new paragraph, an entire paragraph return is generally too much space. As a result, graphic designers are in the habit of stripping documents of extra paragraph returns. Fortunately, you can search for two paragraph returns and replace them with one fairly quickly. You will now delete extra paragraph returns in the imported story.

1 Double-click the page 1 icon on the Pages panel to center page 1 in the document window.

2 Be sure that Type > Show Hidden Characters is selected so that you can see the extra paragraph returns.

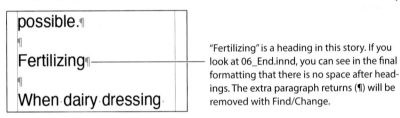

"Fertilizing" is a heading in this story. If you look at 06_End.innd, you can see in the final formatting that there is no space after headings. The extra paragraph returns (¶) will be removed with Find/Change.

3 Using the Type tool (**T**), click at the beginning of the story before "Peas grow well" (on the right-facing page in the far-left column).

4 Choose Edit > Find/Change, and click the Text tab across the top.

5 Click Forward for the search direction.

6 Select Story from the Search menu, which defines the scope of the search.

 Using the Search menu in the Find/Change dialog, you can choose the scope of the search such as Story or All Documents.

7 In the Find What area, click the Special Characters For Search (@) menu. Select End Of Paragraph from the menu. This places the code for a paragraph return (^p) in the Find What field.

8 With the text insertion bar still in the Find What field, select End Of Paragraph from the Special Characters For Search (@) menu again.

 You have set up the Find What field to locate two paragraph returns in a row within text as you see in the above image. Now, you will set up Change To to replace the two paragraph returns with one.

9 Press Tab to navigate to the Change To field. Select End Of Paragraph from the Special Characters For Replace (@) menu.

▶ **Tip:** Find/Change is helpful for replacing two spaces after a period with one space. In professional publishing, two spaces after a period results in too much space. Writers and editors who learned to type on typewriters may still submit stories with extra spaces, and these spaces need to be removed.

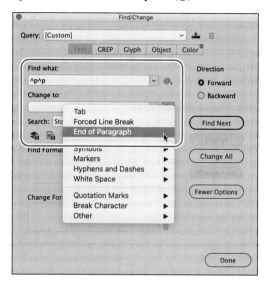

The Find/Change query will appear as Find What: ^p^p and Change To: ^p.

10 Click Find Next. When the first instance of two paragraph returns is highlighted, click Change All.

11 When the alert indicates that 18 replacements were made, click OK.

● **Note:** If something goes wrong in the text, select Edit > Undo. Then recheck the query setup.

possible.¶
Fertilizing¶
When·dairy·dressing·

12 Click Done to close the Find/Change dialog.

13 Choose Layout > Next Spread to look through the pages and notice the lack of space between paragraphs. You will resolve this by applying paragraph styles.

14 Choose File > Save.

Applying paragraph styles to text

Now that all the threaded text frames are in place and the text is flowing through them, you can format the text. This formatting gives you a clear view of how the text fits and how it looks with the layout. Here, you will format the entire article with the Body Paragraphs style, and then you will format the opening paragraph and subheads.

1 Double-click the page 1 icon on the Pages panel.

2 Using the Type tool (**T.**), click anywhere in the text frame containing the main article you just imported. Zoom as necessary to see the text during the exercise.

3 Choose Edit > Select All to select all the text in the story (the text in the series of threaded frames).

4 In the Text Styles area of the Properties panel, click Paragraph Styles, and then click the menu to see the styles.

5 If necessary, click the triangle to the left of the Body Text style group to open it.

6 Click the paragraph style Body Paragraphs; this applies the paragraph style to the entire story. Scroll through the pages to see the formatted text.

▶ **Tip:** Style groups help you organize styles in panels such as the Paragraph Styles and Swatches panels. When the group is expanded, you can select options in the group.

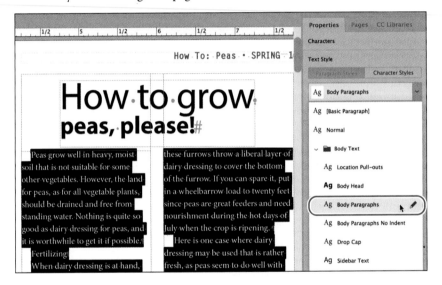

7 Choose Layout > Go To Page. Enter **1** in the Page field, and click OK. If it's helpful for your screen size, choose View > Fit Page In Window.

8 On page 1, click in the first paragraph of the article, starting with "Peas grow well in heavy." Click the Drop Cap paragraph style in the Paragraph Styles panel.

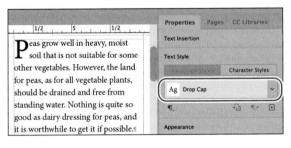

Now you will format the six subheads in the article.

9 Using the Type tool, click in the subhead that reads "Fertilizing" in the left column of page 1. This targets the paragraph for paragraph formatting.

10 Click the Body Head paragraph style in the Paragraph Styles panel.

11 Click in the next paragraph, starting with "When dairy dressing," and then click the Body Paragraphs No Indent paragraph style in the Paragraph Styles panel.

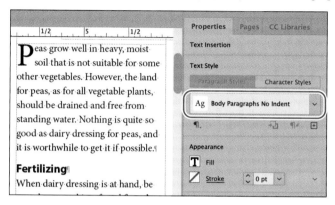

12 Follow steps 9–11 to apply the Body Head paragraph style to the remaining subheads in the story. Apply Body Paragraphs No Indent to the paragraph following each subhead as well.

- Page 2, left column: "Sowing"
- Page 3, left column: "Thinning Out"
- Page 3, right column: "Protection from Birds"
- Page 3, right column: "Caring for the Vines"
- Page 4, left column: "Picking Peas"
- Page 4, right column: "Follow Crops"

13 Choose File > Save. Remain on this page for the next exercise.

Adjusting columns

InDesign provides many methods for adjusting the length of columns of text. You might do this to suit the layout or to keep specific topics together. One way to do this is to resize the text frame with the Selection tool. Another method is to manually "bump" text to the next column with the Column Break character. Here, you will adjust the size of the text frames to suit the layout.

1 Double-click the page 4 icon on the Pages panel to center page 4 in the document window.

2 Using the Selection tool (▶), click the text frame on the left containing the main article.

● **Note:** If necessary, type **2.1 in** in the Height field on the Control panel and press Enter or Return to resize the frame.

3 Drag the bottom of the text frame up so that the height of the frame shows approximately 2.1 in.

4 Select the text frame at the right, which contains the second column of text. Drag the bottom of the frame up to match the height of the text frame at the left.

Resizing these text frames keeps the article text from obscuring the shaded sidebar box.

▶ **Tip:** To adjust how text flows within frames, you can enter break characters such as Column Break and Frame Break (Type > Insert Break Character).

5 Choose Layout > Next Spread to see pages 6 and 7. The bottom of page 6 contains a box with a quote from E.M. Forster.

6 Using the Selection tool, click the text frame at the left on page 6. Drag the bottom of the text frame up so that the height of the frame shows 2.5 in.

7 Select the text frame at the right, which contains the second column of text. Drag the bottom of the frame up to match the height of the text frame at the left.

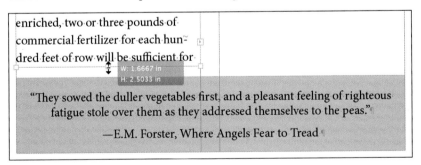

8 Click the pasteboard to deselect all objects on the page, and choose File > Save.

Using the baseline grid to align text

An aspect of vertical spacing is aligning lines of text horizontally across columns. You can do this using a baseline grid (also called a "leading grid") for the entire document. The baseline grid represents the leading (line spacing) for your document's body text and is used to align the baseline of type in one column of text with the baseline of type in neighboring columns and pages. First, you set up the grid, and then you set a paragraph format that aligns paragraphs to the grid.

▶ **Tip:** You can set up a baseline grid at the text frame level, which is ideal for situations in which different stories have different leading values. Choose Object > Text Frame Options, and then click the Baseline Options tab.

Peas grow well in heavy, moist soil that is not suitable for some other vegetables. However, the land for peas, as for all vegetable plants, should be drained and free from standing water. Nothing is quite so good as dairy dressing for peas, and it is worthwhile to get it if possible.¶

Fertilizing¶
When dairy dressing is at hand, be sure the ground is soft and fine; then open furrows about eight inches deep. These should be three feet apart for the Nott's Excelsior type, and four feet for the climbing types. Into these furrows throw a liberal layer of dairy dressing to cover the bottom of the furrow. If you can spare it, put in a wheelbarrow load to twenty feet since peas are great feeders and need nourishment during the hot days of July when the crop is ripening.¶

Here is one case where dairy dressing may be used that is rather fresh, as peas seem to do well with dairy dressing at any stage. Stable dressing, which contains straw and horse manure, is more likely to develop heat, which will hurt the seed;

When paragraphs are aligned with the baseline grid, lines of type are aligned across columns.

Before you set up the baseline grid, you need to check the leading value for the body text.

1 Choose Layout > Go To Page, enter **1** in the field, and click OK.

2 Select the Type tool (T.) in the Tools panel.

3 Click to place an insertion point in the first full paragraph of the story, which starts with "Peas grow well." Look at the leading value (⌃A) in the Properties panel. The leading is set to 11 pt (11 points).

4 Choose Edit > Preferences > Grids (Windows) or InDesign > Preferences > Grids (macOS) to set the baseline grid options.

5 In the Baseline Grid section, type **0** in the Start field and select Top Of Page from the Relative To menu.

This option sets the location of the first grid line for the document. If you use the default value of 0.5 in, the first grid line would appear above the top margin.

6 Confirm the Increment Every field is set to 11 pt to match the leading. Leave the View Threshold value at 75%.

7 Click OK.

8 Choose Edit > Deselect All, and choose File > Save.

Viewing the baseline grid

Now you'll make the new grid visible onscreen.

1 To view the baseline grid in the document window, choose View > Grids & Guides > Show Baseline Grid, and then choose View > Actual Size.

Notice how the text does not align horizontally across the columns.

Fertilizing

When dairy dressing is at hand, be sure the ground is soft and fine; then open furrows about eight inches deep. These should be three feet apart for the Nott's Excelsior type, and

Here is one case where dairy dressing may be used that is rather fresh, as peas seem to do well with dairy dressing at any stage. Stable dressing, which contains straw and horse manure, is more likely to develop heat, which will hurt the seed;

▶**Tip:** The View Threshold menu sets the minimum zoom level at which you can see the grid onscreen. When this setting is 100%, the grid appears in the document window only at magnifications of 100% or higher.

You can align one paragraph, selected paragraphs, or all the paragraphs in a story to the baseline grid. (A story is all the text in a series of threaded text frames.) In the following steps, you will use the Paragraph panel to align the main story to the baseline grid.

2 Using the Type tool (**T**), click to place an insertion point anywhere in the first paragraph on the spread, and then choose Edit > Select All to select all the text in the main story.

3 Choose Type > Paragraph to open the Paragraph panel.

If necessary, choose Show Options from the Paragraph panel menu (≡) to see all the options.

4 In the Paragraph panel, click Align To Baseline Grid (≡≡). The text shifts so that the baselines of the characters rest on the grid lines.

▶ **Tip:** As with most other paragraph-formatting controls, the baseline grid controls are available in the Control panel as well.

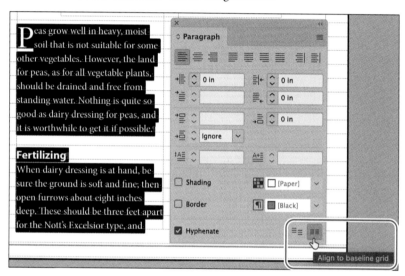

5 Click the Paragraph panel close box, and then click the pasteboard to deselect the text. Choose View > Grids & Guides > Hide Baseline Grid.

6 Scroll through the entire document to see how the text flows now.

7 Choose File > Save.

Updating paragraph styles to align to the baseline grid

The formatting in the story no longer matches the formatting specified in the paragraph styles applied to the various paragraphs. This occurs when you apply additional formatting after applying styles. Continuing to fine-tune formatting is common and is fine for single-purpose documents. However, many times styles are used throughout an entire project, such as a book or magazine. To ensure that the styles match any agreed-upon formatting, you will quickly update the styles.

1. Choose Layout > Go To Page, enter **1** in the field, and click OK.

2. Choose Type > Paragraph Styles to open the Paragraph Styles panel. Drag the panel off the dock so that you can reposition it as necessary.

3. Using the Type tool (**T**), click in the first paragraph of the story, starting with "Peas grow well." (Choose View > Fit Page In Window if you need help finding the story.)

 The Drop Cap style is highlighted in the Paragraph Styles panel because it is applied to the paragraph. The plus sign (+) next to the style name indicates that the paragraph formatting no longer matches the style.

▶ **Tip:** The Paragraph Styles panel provides two options for finding out how the selected text differs from the style (the overrides). You can click Override Highlighter ([a+]) at the top of the Paragraph styles panel or point at Clear Overrides (¶⁄) at the bottom.

4. Choose Redefine Style from the Paragraph Styles panel menu (≡).

 The Drop Cap paragraph style now reflects the change you made (to align text to the baseline grid). The plus sign will no longer display next to the style name.

5. To update the remaining paragraph styles, click in one paragraph with the style applied and select Redefine Style. The paragraph styles used to format the text are Body Head, Body Paragraphs, and Body Paragraphs No Indent.

6. Choose Type > Paragraph Styles to close the Paragraph Styles panel, and choose File > Save.

Adding a jump line page number

When an article continues onto other pages, forcing readers to turn pages, it helps to add a jump line, such as "(Continued on page x)." You can create jump lines in InDesign that automatically reflect the number of the page where the story continues.

1. Double-click the page 1 icon in the Pages panel to center the page in the document window. Scroll down to view a portion of the pasteboard. Zoom in as necessary to see the text.

2. Using the Type tool (**T**) and working on the pasteboard, drag to create a text frame approximately 1.7 inches by 0.25 inches.

3 Using the Selection tool (▶), drag the new text frame to the bottom of the second column on page 1. Be sure the top of the new text frame touches the bottom of the existing text frame; the frames must touch for the feature to work.

4 Using the Type tool, click to place an insertion point in the new frame. Type **Peas continued on** followed by a space. Do not worry if the text is overlapping the story right now.

5 Right-click to display a context menu, and then choose Insert Special Character > Markers > Next Page Number. The jump line now reads "Peas continued on 2."

● **Note:** For the Next Page Number character to work properly, the text frame containing the jump line must touch or overlap the threaded frame.

6 Choose Type > Paragraph Styles to open the Paragraph Styles panel. If necessary, click the arrow next to the Folios style group to open it.

7 With the text insertion point still in the jump line, click the Continued From/To Line paragraph style (in the Folios style group) to format the text according to the template.

8 Choose Type > Paragraph Styles to close the Paragraph Styles panel, and choose File > Save.

9 Choose View > Fit Spread In Window.

10 Choose View > Screen Mode > Preview. Scroll through the document to see all the pages.

Congratulations, you have finished the lesson.

Exploring on your own

In this lesson, you learned how to create a jump line that indicates the page number on which an article continues. You can also create a jump line that indicates the page number from which a continued article originated.

1 Choose View > Screen Mode > Normal to see the frame edges. Double-click the page 1 icon in the Pages panel.

2 Using the Selection tool (▶), select the text frame containing the jump line on page 1. Choose Edit > Copy.

3 Choose Layout > Next Spread, and then choose Edit > Paste to paste the jump line's text frame on page 2.

4 Drag the jump line's text frame so that it touches the top of the text frame in the first column at the left. (Drag the top of the main text frame down as necessary so that the jump line isn't touching the page header.)

5 Using the Type tool (T), change the words in the text frame from "Peas continued on" to "Peas continued from" and delete the number 2.

At this point, you need to replace the Next Page Number character with the Previous Page Number character.

6 Choose Type > Insert Special Character > Markers > Previous Page Number.

The jump line now reads "Peas continued from 1."

7 Choose File > Save.

Review questions

1 Which tool lets you thread text frames?

2 How do you load the text icon?

3 What happens when you click the loaded text icon between column guides?

4 Which key do you press to automatically divide a text frame into multiple threaded frames?

5 What is the name of the feature that automatically adds pages and threaded text frames to contain all the text in an imported text file?

6 What feature automatically adjusts the size of a text frame based on the length of the text?

7 What do you need to do to ensure that the Next Page Number and Previous Page Number characters work in a jump line?

8 How do you update a paragraph style to match formatted text?

Review answers

1 The Selection tool.

2 Choose File > Place and select a text file, or click in an out port that contains overset text. You can also drag text files from the desktop onto a page.

3 InDesign creates a text frame where you click; the frame fits within the vertical column guides.

4 Press the right arrow key as you drag with the Type tool. (You can also press the left arrow key to decrease the number of threaded text frames.)

5 Smart Text Reflow.

6 The Auto-Size feature, found in the Text Frame Options dialog (Object menu).

7 The text frame containing the jump line must touch or overlap the threaded text frame containing the story.

8 Click in the formatted text and then choose Redefine Style from the Paragraph Styles panel menu.

7 EDITING TEXT

Lesson overview

In this lesson, you'll learn how to do the following:

- Enter and import text.

- Find and change text and formatting.

- Check the spelling in a document.

- Edit a spelling dictionary.

- Automatically correct misspelled words.

- Use the Story Editor.

- Move text by dragging and dropping.

- Track changes.

- Review the Adobe Fonts service.

 This lesson will take about 45 minutes to complete. To get the lesson files used in this chapter, download them from the web page for this book at adobepress.com/InDesignCIB2023. For more information, see "Accessing the lesson files and Web Edition" in the Getting Started section at the beginning of this book.

Protect Your Peas

HIGH-PROTEIN, LOW-CALORIE, VITAMIN-RICH PEAS ARE
EASY TO GROW AND DELICIOUS TO EAT.

Peas are easy to grow, but once they pop up they need a little protection. A little daily attention will ensure an awesome crop and a supply of nutritious side dishes and snacks. Enjoy the fresh air and satisfaction of gardening during the day, and peruse your cookbooks for ideas at night. Next month, we'll have plenty of great recipes for you to try.

Cover. Cover peas gradually as they grow. In using dairy dressing, the furrow is opened deep enough to admit putting the manure well below the peas. Of course this deep furrow is not necessary when fertilizers are worked into the soil. In that case, the furrow is opened to a depth of only about four or five inches. In either case, two inches of earth is drawn over the peas when first planted, and this leaves another inch or two of earth to draw about them after they have grown five or six inches high.

Thinning Out. When the peas are up an inch or so, it is time to thin them out. Crowding is responsible for many poor crops of peas. Thin out the dwarf peas so that they stand about an inch apart, and the tall ones so that they stand about an inch and a half apart. Pull out the weaker sprouts first. TIP: It may take some courage to thin them out, but it pays in the end.

Protection from Blackbirds. Blackbirds are fond of pea vines when they are young and tender. Sometimes they will nip off the sprouts and spoil a long row in one early breakfast. A white string, stretched above the row, with white rags tied here and there, will usually keep them away. Small flags, made by tying a strip of white cotton cloth to a stick will serve well also. TIP: If there are many blackbirds about, it is a wise gardener who takes this easy precaution. It is a little too late after the blackbirds have been there.

Caring for the Vines. The dwarf peas need no further care, except cultivation to keep the earth soft and free from weeds. The blossoms form in about four weeks, and the peas ripen quickly after that. The season for peas begins early in May, and they are picked in August along the northern belt. Because of its fondness for cool climates and moist earth, the pea is most delicious and profitable in those states where the summer days are not extremely hot.

Picking Peas. It does not pay to pick peas before they are fairly well filled out, as they are wasted in that way. You can soon learn to tell, by a gentle pressure of the thumb near the lower end of the pod, whether the peas are large enough to pick. On the other hand, it is unwise to leave them on the vines to dry, as that will tend to check the growth of the peas forming at the top of the vine. In taking the pod from the vines, be careful to use both hands. Hold the vine with one hand just above the pea, to save the tender branches from being torn. TIP: Remember the new peas which are coming above those you are picking, and give them a free chance to mature.

Follow Crops. As soon as the crop of peas is harvested, pull out the vines, put away the supports you wish to save for the next season, and dig over the ground for a crop of something else. Bush string beans, turnips, cabbage, winter beets, lettuce, and other quick growing plants may be put in the same rows.

Recipes. Next month look for recipes for Soupe Aux Pois (Pea Soup), Balsamic Pea Salad, Lemon Orzo with Peas, Fregola with Peas and Ricotta, and Peas with Pancetta.

Source. "Protecting Your Peas" excerpted from Garden Steps: A Manual for the Amateur in Vegetable Gardening, by Ernest Cobb, 1917.

peas

Adobe InDesign offers many of the text-editing features you find in dedicated word-processing software, including the ability to search and replace text and formatting, check spelling, automatically correct spelling as you type, and track changes as you edit.

Getting started

In this lesson, you will perform editorial tasks commonly expected of a graphic designer. These include importing a Microsoft Word file containing an article and using the editorial features in InDesign to search and replace text and formatting, check spelling, enter and track text changes, and more.

● **Note:** If you have not already downloaded the project files for this lesson to your computer from your Account page, make sure to do so now. See "Getting Started" at the beginning of the book.

1 To ensure that the preferences and default settings of your InDesign program match those used in this lesson, move the InDesign Defaults file to a different folder following the procedure in "Saving and restoring the InDesign Defaults file" on pages 3–4. Following this step is particularly important to ensure that the check spelling exercises work as expected.

2 Start InDesign.

3 The InDesign Home screen displays. Click Open at the left. (If the Home screen does not display, choose File > Open from the InDesign menu bar.)

4 If possible, log in to the Creative Cloud desktop application to access a font.

- This document uses a font from the Adobe Fonts service called Urbana Light.

- If your system is connected to the internet and Creative Cloud, the font is automatically activated.

- If connecting through Creative Cloud is not possible, the "Protecting Your Peas" headline will be highlighted in pink in Normal screen mode. In that case, you may apply a different font, such as Myriad Regular, to this headline.

- For more information on the Adobe Fonts service, see the end of this lesson.

● **Note:** To better view the interface onscreen or in print, the screen captures in this book reflect the Medium Light interface rather than the default setting of Medium Dark. In addition, some screen captures illustrate User Interface Scaling for a closer look at interface elements. You can modify interface settings in Preferences.

5 Open the 07_Start.indd file in the Lesson07 folder, located inside the Lessons folder within the InDesignCIB folder on your hard drive.

6 Choose File > Save As, rename the file **07_Text.indd**, and save it in the Lesson07 folder.

7 To ensure that the panels and menu commands match those used in this lesson, choose Window > Workspace > [Essentials], and then choose Window > Workspace > Reset Essentials.

8 To see what the finished document looks like, open the 07_End.indd file in the same folder. If you are logged into a Creative Cloud account when you open the document, the Minion Pro Bold font is activated automatically. You can leave this document open to act as a guide as you work.

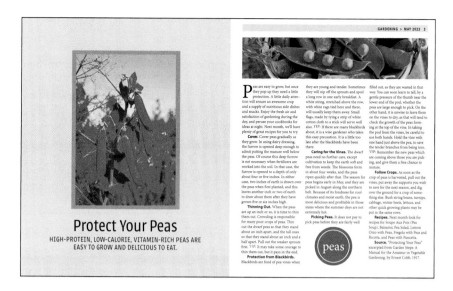

9 When you're ready to resume working on the lesson document, 07_Text.indd, display it by clicking its tab in the upper-left corner of the document window.

Entering and importing text

You can enter text directly into your InDesign documents, and you can import text prepared in other applications, such as word-processing software. To type text, you need to use the Type tool and select a text frame, text path, or table cell. Options for importing text include dragging files from the desktop, "loading" the cursor with one or more text files to import, or importing text into a selected text frame.

Entering text

Generally, graphic designers are not responsible for the text in all their layouts, but they often enter edits from a marked-up hard copy or Adobe PDF. In this exercise, you will use the Type tool to revise the headline.

1 Choose View > Screen Mode > Normal so that you can see layout aids such as guides, frame edges, and hidden characters.

 Because View > Extras > Show Frame Edges was already selected, the text frames are outlined in gold so that you can see them. Locate the text frame on the left-facing page containing the headline "Protecting Your Peas." You will change "Protecting" to "Protect" in the headline.

2 Using the Type tool (**T**,), click in the text frame immediately to the right of the word "Protecting."

3 Press Backspace (Windows) or Delete (macOS) three times to delete the "ing."

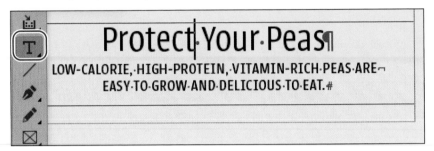

4 Choose File > Save.

Importing text

When working with a template for a project such as a magazine, designers generally import article text into existing text frames. In this exercise, you will import a Microsoft Word file and apply body-copy formatting to it.

1 Using the Type tool (**T**,), click in the first column of the text frame on the right-facing page.

Click the Type tool in the text frame to place a text insertion bar.

▶ **Tip:** In the Place dialog, you can Shift-click to select multiple text files. When you do this, the cursor is "loaded" with those files. You can then click in text frames or click on the page to import the text from each file. This works well with content such as photo captions that are saved in different text files.

2 Choose File > Place. In the lower-left corner of the Place dialog, make sure Show Import Options is not selected.

3 Navigate to and select the 07_Gardening.docx file in the Lesson07 folder, located inside the Lessons folder within the InDesignCIB folder on your hard drive.

4 Click Open. If the Missing Fonts dialog displays, click Close to dismiss it. You will apply a different font through a paragraph style.

The text flows from column to column, filling the first two columns and part of the third.

5 Choose Edit > Select All to select all the text in the story.

6 Locate the Properties panel at the right. In the Text Style area, click the Paragraph Styles tab. Click the menu below and select the Body Paragraph style.

7 Click in the first body paragraph starting with "Peas are easy to grow." Select First Body Paragraph from the Paragraph Styles menu in the Properties panel, as shown.

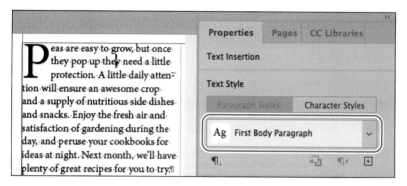

Now that you have changed the formatting, the story may no longer fit. In the lower-right corner of the text frame on the right-facing page, a red plus sign (+) will indicate overset text (additional text). Later, you will use the Story Editor to resolve this.

● **Note:** The Find/Change and Spell Check features in the following sections still work on overset text.

8 If necessary, choose Edit > Deselect All to deselect the text.

9 Choose File > Save.

Finding and changing text and formatting

Like most popular word-processing software, InDesign lets you search and replace text and formatting. While graphic designers are working on layouts, the copy is still being revised in most cases. When editors request global changes, Find/Change helps ensure accurate and consistent changes.

Finding and changing text

For this article, an editor decided to change all instances of "bird" to "blackbird." You will set up a search-and-replace to change all instances of "bird" in the document.

1 Using the Type tool (**T**), click at the beginning of the story before "Peas are easy to grow" (on the right-facing page in the far-left column).

● **Note:** Adjust the view scale as necessary to see the text.

2 Choose Edit > Find/Change.

3 Click the menu in the Query field to see the built-in Find/Change options. Click each tab across the top to view other options: Text, GREP, Glyph, Object, and Color.

4 Click the Text tab for a simple search-and-replace of text.

▶ **Tip:** You can toggle the search direction by pressing Ctrl+Alt+ Enter (Windows) or Command+Option+ Return (macOS).

5 Click Forward for the search direction.

6 Type **bird** in the Find What field.

Press Tab to navigate to the Change To field. Type **blackbird**.

Using the Search menu in the Find/Change dialog, you can choose the scope of the search such as Story or Document.

7 Select Story from the Search menu.

Point at each icon in the row below the Search menu to view its tool tip and see how it affects the Find/Change operation. For example, clicking the Whole Word icon (≣) ensures that instances of the Find What text within another word will not be found or changed. (In this case, a search for "bird" will find the text within "birds" if Whole Word is *not* selected.)

▶ **Tip:** When the Find/Change dialog is open, you can still click in the text and make edits with the Type tool. The Find/ Change dialog remains open so that you can resume your search after editing the text.

8 Make sure that Case Sensitive (Aa) and Whole Word (≣) are not selected.

9 Click Find Next. When the first instance of "bird" is highlighted, click Change All.

10 When the alert indicates that four additional replacements were made, click OK.

11 Leave the Find/Change dialog open for the next exercise.

Finding and changing formatting

The editors request one more global edit to this article; this one concerns formatting rather than word choice. The gardening tips in the article are preceded by the word "Tip," which should be in purple, bold, and all capital letters.

1 Using the Type tool (T.), click at the beginning of the story before "Peas are easy to grow" (on the right-facing page in the far-left column).

2 Type **Tip:** in the Find What field.

3 Press Tab to select the text in the Change To field and press Backspace or Delete.

4 Type **TIP:** (in all capital letters) in the Change To field.

5 Click Case Sensitive (Aa) below the Search menu.

▶ **Tip:** Another way to achieve the change from "Tip:" to "TIP:" through Find/Change would be to apply the All Caps type style. Depending on how often this effect is used, you might create a character style that specifies All Caps and the purple color. You can then apply the character style as you edit and format text or through Find/Change.

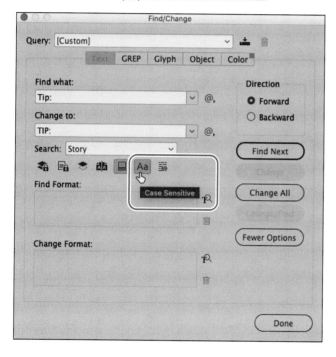

6 In the Change Format section at the bottom of the Find/Change dialog, click the Specify Attributes To Change icon (🔍). This displays the Change Format Settings dialog.

7 In the Change Format Settings dialog, select Basic Character Formats at the left.

8 Type **Bold** in the Font Style field. If you cannot activate Minion Pro Bold, you may skip this step.

9 Select Character Color in the list at the left.

● **Note:** If necessary, click the More Options button to display formatting options for the found text.

10 In the Character Color area, click Purple-Cool to select it.

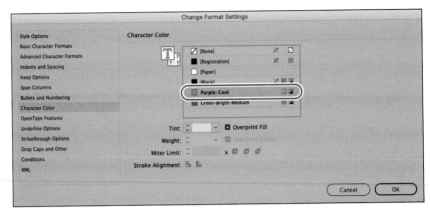

11 Click OK to return to the Find/Change dialog.

Notice the alert icon (🛈) that appears above the Change To field. This icon indicates that InDesign will change the found text to the specified formatting.

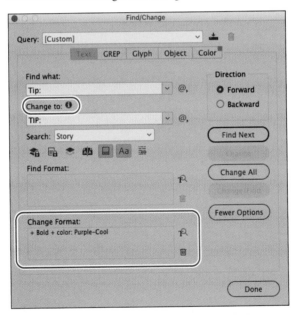

12 Test your settings by clicking Find Next and then clicking Change. Once you confirm that "Tip:" changes to "TIP:" in purple, click Change All.

13 When the alert indicates that two changes were made, click OK.

14 Click Done to close the Find/Change dialog, and select Edit > Deselect All to see the changes.

15 Choose File > Save.

Checking spelling

InDesign has features for checking spelling similar to the options in word-processing programs. You can check the spelling in selected text, an entire story, all the stories in a document, or all the stories in several open documents at once. To customize which words are flagged as possible misspellings, you can add words to your document's dictionary. In addition, you can have InDesign flag possible spelling issues and correct spelling as you type.

The Check Spelling dialog provides the following buttons to handle the words shown in the Not In Dictionary field (otherwise known as suspect words):

▶ **Tip:** Be sure to discuss with your client or editor whether you should be the one checking spelling in InDesign. Many editors prefer to check spelling themselves.

- **Skip:** Click Skip when you are confident of the spelling of the current suspect word but would like to review any other instances of the spelling in context.

- **Change:** Click Change to change the spelling of the current instance of the suspect word to the spelling in the Change To field.

- **Ignore All:** Click Ignore All when you are confident that the spelling of the suspect word is appropriate for use throughout the selection, story, or document. If you relaunch InDesign, words that were previously ignored will be flagged again during the next spell check.

- **Change All:** Click Change All when you are confident that changing the spelling of the suspect word is appropriate for the entire selection, story, or document.

Checking spelling in the document

Before a document is ready for print or electronic distribution, it's a good idea to check spelling. In this case, we suspect the newly imported story may be a little sloppy, so you will check the spelling now.

1 Using the Type tool (T), click before the first word of the article you've been working on: "Peas are easy to grow."

2 Choose Edit > Spelling > Check Spelling. InDesign automatically begins to check the spelling.

 Although the spell-check has started, you can use the Search menu to change the scope. For example, you may prefer to check only a new story and not an entire document. You can choose to check All Documents, Document, Story, To End Of Story, or Selection (if text is selected).

3 Select Story from the Search menu at the bottom of the dialog.

4 InDesign highlights various words that do not match the spelling dictionary.

Handle the flagged words as follows:

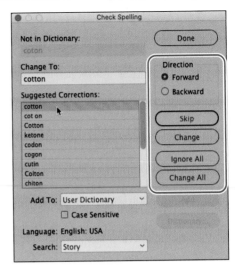

- coton: Select "cotton" in the Suggested Corrections list and click Change.

- gardner: Type **gardener** in the Change To field and click Change.

- Soupe, Pois: Click Ignore All.

- Orzo: Click Add to add this fairly common word to your user dictionary.

- Fregola, Ricotta, Pancetta: Click Ignore All.

5 Click Done.

6 Choose Edit > Deselect All.

7 Choose File > Save.

Adding words to a document-specific dictionary

With InDesign, you can add words to your user dictionary or to a document-specific dictionary. If you work with multiple clients who may have different spelling preferences, for example, it is better to add words to a document-specific dictionary. In this case, you will add "pancetta" to your user dictionary.

1 Choose Edit > Spelling > User Dictionary to display the User Dictionary dialog.

2 If necessary, select User Dictionary from the Target menu.

3 Type **pancetta** in the Word field.

4 Click Add, and then click Done.

5 Choose Edit > Deselect All.

6 Choose File > Save.

Checking spelling dynamically

It's not necessary for you to wait until a document is finished before checking the spelling. Enabling dynamic spelling allows you to see misspelled words in text. To see how this works:

1 Choose Edit > Preferences > Spelling (Windows) or InDesign > Preferences > Spelling (macOS) to display Spelling preferences.

2 In the Find section, you can customize what the Check Spelling dialog flags as possible errors: Misspelled Words, Repeated Words, Uncapitalized Words, and Uncapitalized Sentences. For example, if you're working on a directory with hundreds of names, you might want to deselect Misspelled Words.

3 If necessary, select Enable Dynamic Spelling.

4 In the Underline Color section, use the menus to customize how possible errors are signified.

▶ **Tip:** To quickly enable or disable dynamic spelling, choose Edit > Spelling > Dynamic Spelling.

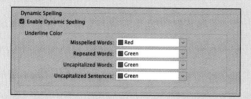

5 Click OK to close the Preferences dialog and return to your document.

Words that may be misspelled (according to the default user dictionary) are now underlined.

6 Right-click a word flagged by dynamic spelling to display a context menu from which you can select an option to change the spelling.

Automatically correcting misspelled words

Autocorrect takes the concept of dynamically checking spelling to the next level. With Autocorrect activated, InDesign automatically corrects misspelled words as you type them. Changes are made based on an internal list of commonly misspelled words. You can add other commonly misspelled words, including words in other languages, to this list if you like.

▶ **Tip:** You can use Autocorrect to quickly convert abbreviations into their spelled-out equivalents as you type. For example, you can quickly convert "WV" to "West Virginia."

1 Choose Edit > Preferences > Autocorrect (Windows) or InDesign > Preferences > Autocorrect (macOS) to display Autocorrect preferences.

2 Select the Enable Autocorrect option. By default, the list of commonly misspelled words is for English: USA.

The editors have realized that "gardener" is frequently typed as "gardner," missing an "e" in the middle. You will prevent this mistake by adding the misspelling and correct spelling to the Autocorrect list.

3 Click Add. In the Add To Autocorrect List dialog, type **gardner** in the Misspelled Word field and **gardener** in the Correction field.

4 Click OK to add the word. To close the Preferences dialog, click OK in the lower-right corner.

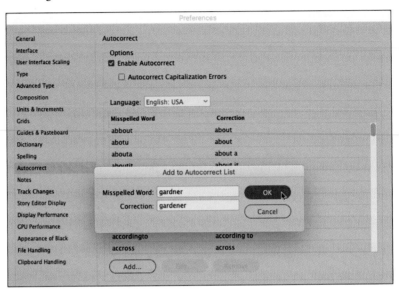

5 Make sure that Edit > Spelling > Autocorrect is selected.

▶Tip: A word is autocorrected once you finish typing it, as indicated by typing a space, period, comma, forward slash, or greater than/less than symbol.

6 Using the Type tool (**T,**), type the word **gardner** followed by a space anywhere in the text.

7 Notice that Autocorrect changes the spelling from "gardner" to "gardener." Choose Edit > Undo until the word you added is deleted.

8 Choose File > Save.

Editing text by dragging and dropping

▶Tip: When you drag and drop text, by default InDesign automatically adds and deletes spaces before and after words as necessary. If you need to turn off this feature, deselect Adjust Spacing Automatically When Cutting And Pasting Words in Type preferences.

To quickly cut and paste words in your document, InDesign allows you to drag and drop text within the same story, between frames, and between documents. You'll now use drag and drop to move text from one paragraph to another in the magazine layout.

1 Choose Edit > Preferences > Type (Windows) or InDesign > Preferences > Type (macOS) to display Type preferences.

2 In the Drag And Drop Text Editing section, select Enable In Layout View. This option lets you drag and drop text in Layout view. Click OK.

> **Drag and Drop Text Editing**
> ☑ Enable in Layout View
> ☑ Enable in Story Editor

3 Locate the subhead below the "Protect Your Peas" headline on the left-facing page. Adjust the zoom level as necessary so that you can read the subhead text.

4 Using the Type tool (T.), drag to select the words "LOW-CALORIE" along with the comma and the space after the comma.

5 Position the I-bar pointer over the selected word until the pointer changes to the drag and drop icon (▸).

6 Drag the pointer to the correct location for the words, immediately before "VITAMIN."

▶ **Tip:** If you want to copy a selected word instead of moving it, hold down the Alt (Windows) or Option (macOS) key after you start dragging.

7 Click the pasteboard to deselect the text, and then choose File > Save.

Using the Story Editor

If you need to enter many text edits, rewrite a story, or reduce a story's length, you can isolate the text with the Story Editor. The Story Editor window works as follows:

• Text displays without formatting with the exception of the following type styles: bold, italic, and bold italic. Any graphics and other nontext elements are omitted to make editing easier.

• The column to the left of the text displays a vertical depth ruler and the name of the paragraph style applied to each paragraph.

• Dynamic spelling (if enabled) highlights misspelled words, just like in the document window.

• If the Enable In Story Editor option is selected in Type preferences, you can also drag and drop text in the Story Editor, just as you did in the previous exercise.

- In Story Editor Display preferences, you can customize the font, size, background color, and more for the Story Editor window.

The article on the right-facing page is too long to fit in the text frame. After you delete a sentence in the Story Editor, the story will fit.

1 Choose View > Fit Spread In Window.

2 Using the Type tool (T), click in the first full paragraph in the third column of the article, starting with "Follow Crops."

● **Note:** If the Story Editor window goes behind the document window, you can bring it to the front by choosing its name from the bottom of the Window menu.

3 Choose Edit > Edit In Story Editor. Position the Story Editor window next to the far-right column on the spread. Zoom as necessary for comfortable reading.

4 Drag the vertical scroll bar in the Story Editor to the end of the story. Note the red vertical line that indicates the overset text.

5 In the Story Editor, scroll to the paragraph starting with "Follow Crops." Locate and select the last sentence in the paragraph: "If the peas have been well enriched, two or three pounds of commercial fertilizer for each hundred feet of row will be sufficient for the second crop." Be sure to select the final period but not the paragraph return (¶).

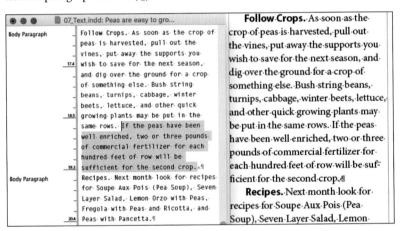

6 Press Backspace or Delete. If necessary, type a paragraph return before "Recipes" so that it remains in a separate paragraph.

7 Choose File > Save. Leave the Story Editor open for the next set of steps.

Tracking changes

For some projects, it's important to see what changes are made to the text throughout the design and review process. In addition, reviewers may suggest changes that another user can accept or reject. As with a word-processing program, you can track text that is added, deleted, or moved using the Story Editor.

Now, you will change the name of a recipe and see how the changes are tracked.

1 Choose Type > Track Changes > Track Changes In Current Story.

2 In the Story Editor, locate the paragraph starting with "Recipes."

3 Using the Type tool (T) in the Story Editor, select "Seven Layer" and type **Balsamic Pea** over it.

Notice how the changes are marked in the Story Editor window.

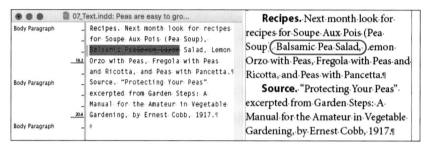

▶ **Tip:** InDesign provides a Notes panel and a Track Changes panel for reviewing and collaborating on documents (Window > Editorial, Type > Notes, and Type > Track Changes). Many of the controls are in panel menus.

4 With the Story Editor window still open, choose Type > Track Changes, and review the options for accepting and rejecting changes. Once you have reviewed the possibilities, choose Accept All Changes > In This Story.

5 When the alert dialog displays, click OK.

6 Click the Story Editor window's close box. If necessary, choose Edit > Spelling > Dynamic Spelling to disable this feature, and then choose Edit > Deselect All.

7 Choose View > Fit Spread In Window, View > Screen Mode > Preview, and then choose File > Save.

Congratulations. You have finished the lesson.

Exploring on your own

Now that you have tried the basic text-editing tools in InDesign, experiment with them more to edit and format this document.

1 Proofread the story and edit it as you like using the Story Editor and Track Changes. See how the different changes are marked and experiment with accepting and rejecting the changes.

2 Using the Type tool (T), change the formatting of the text with options in the Properties panel. You can experiment with fonts, sizes, indents, spacing, and more to achieve different looks.

3 If you have additional text files on your system, try dragging them from the desktop to the layout to see how they're imported. Choose Edit > Undo if you don't want to keep them in the document.

▶ **Tip:** In Track Changes preferences, you can customize which changes are tracked and how the changes display in the Story Editor.

Adobe Fonts service

▶ **Tip:** Pink highlight on text indicates that a missing font is applied. The highlight displays in Normal mode when Substituted Fonts is selected in Preferences > Composition > Highlight.

To understand the Adobe Fonts service, it's first important to understand that fonts are separate files that are not part of your documents. Fonts are activated on your system and accessed via applications to format text. Many applications do provide a basic suite of fonts, but in higher-end graphic design you will need access to a significant library of fonts. Fortunately, Creative Cloud members have access to thousands of already licensed fonts at no extra charge.

When you open a document, any missing fonts available in the Adobe Fonts service are automatically activated—provided that your computer is connected to the internet and logged in to Creative Cloud. To explore fonts available through Adobe Fonts, visit fonts.adobe.com and click Manage Fonts in the upper-right corner. In addition to providing access to fonts, the service helps you manage fonts on your system. Near the top of the Adobe Fonts browser screen, select Active Fonts, Previously Active, Web Projects, and Favorites to see the options.

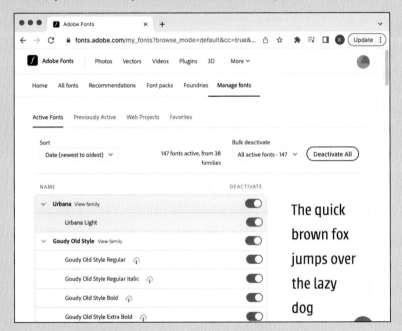

If you open a document that uses a font that is not available in the Adobe Fonts service, the Missing Fonts dialog displays. You can use the Missing Fonts dialog to see how the font is used and decide if you want to replace it with another font. You can choose Type > Find/Replace Font at any time to review the fonts used in a document as well.

In general, it's best to continue using the precise fonts with which a document was designed. Therefore, if you receive a document and do not have the font, you should attempt to acquire it through the typeface vendor. Once you have the font, you can use font management software to activate it, or you can add the font files to your InDesign Fonts folder.

Review questions

1 Which tool lets you edit text?

2 Where are most of the commands for editing text?

3 What is the InDesign search-and-replace feature called?

4 While checking the spelling in a document, InDesign flags words that are not in the dictionary as spelling errors—but they are spelled correctly. How can you ensure these words are not flagged as misspelled every time you check spelling?

5 If you seem to continually type a word incorrectly, what can you do?

6 What happens when you open a document that uses a font that is not available on your system?

Review answers

1 The Type tool allows you to edit text.

2 Most commands for editing text are in the Edit menu and the Type menu.

3 InDesign uses the term Find/Change (Edit menu) for search and replace.

4 Add words that InDesign does not recognize (but are spelled correctly) to the document's or InDesign's default spelling dictionary for the languages of your choice (Edit > Spelling > User Dictionary).

5 If a word is easy to type incorrectly, add the word and preferred spelling to your Autocorrect preferences.

6 When you open documents, any fonts used in the document that are available through the Adobe Fonts service are activated automatically. If you are not connected to the internet or logged in to Creative Cloud—or, if the font is not available through the Adobe Fonts service—the Missing Fonts dialog displays so that you can resolve the problem by acquiring and activating the font or replacing it.

8 WORKING WITH TYPOGRAPHY

Lesson overview

In this lesson, you'll learn how to do the following:

- Adjust vertical and horizontal text spacing.

- Change fonts and type styles.

- Insert special characters.

- Create a headline that spans multiple columns.

- Adjust line and column breaks.

- Hang punctuation outside a margin.

- Add and format a drop cap.

- Adjust line breaks.

- Specify a tab with a leader and create a hanging indent.

- Add a rule and shading to a paragraph.

 This lesson will take about 60 minutes to complete. To get the lesson files used in this chapter, download them from the web page for this book at adobepress.com/InDesignCIB2023. For more information, see "Accessing the lesson files and Web Edition" in the Getting Started section at the beginning of this book.

Strawberries

Heart-shaped fruit that's good for your heart? Check. Fruit that can boost your immunity, lower your cholesterol, protect your vision, prevent cancer (and wrinkles!) and help with weight management? Check. Vitamin C and vitamin K? Check, check. And on top of all that, strawberries are easy to grow.

Plant your strawberries in the full sun, 12 to 18 inches apart. Cover the roots, keep the central growing bud at soil level, and use a balanced fertilizer. In the spring, add compost and fertilizer, and then in fall mulch with straw. As your strawberries grow, keep them moist and weeded. As strawberries begin to ripen, cover them with lightweight netting to keep the birds at bay.

Pick strawberries when they're cool and refrigerate them immediately. Wash before use and enjoy! Your yogurt, pancakes, shortcakes and more are waiting.

"You stand out like a strawberry in a bowl of peas."

Chocolate-Covered Strawberries

½ lb strawberries with stems
½ cup chocolate chips
¼ cup sprinkles

1. Wash the strawberries.
2. Melt chocolate in the microwave in 30-second bursts; stir in between.
3. Dip the strawberries in the chocolate, and then in the sprinkles.
4. Place on wax paper to set, about 30 minutes.

Nutritional Facts

Serving Size	6
Calories	280
Calories from Fat	35%
Protein	0g

The Adobe InDesign typography features make it easy to find just the right font to help convey a document's message; fine-tune character, word, line, and paragraph spacing for a professional look; and add special touches such as fractions and drop caps.

Getting started

In this lesson, you'll fine-tune the typography in a magazine layout for a botanic gardens cafe. For the rich look of the magazine, the typography includes precision formatting and spacing along with decorative touches.

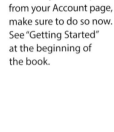● **Note:** If you have not already downloaded the project files for this lesson to your computer from your Account page, make sure to do so now. See "Getting Started" at the beginning of the book.

1 To ensure that the preferences and default settings of your InDesign program match those used in this lesson, move the InDesign Defaults file to a different folder following the procedure in "Saving and restoring the InDesign Defaults file" on pages 3–4.

2 If possible, confirm that Adobe Caslon Pro is not active on the Windows or macOS system.

3 Start InDesign.

4 The InDesign Home screen displays. Click Open at the left. (If the Home screen does not display, choose File > Open from the InDesign menu bar.)

5 Open the 08_Start.indd file in the Lesson08 folder, located inside the Lessons folder within the InDesignCIB folder on your hard drive.

6 Choose File > Save As, rename the file **08_Type.indd**, and save it in the Lesson08 folder.

7 To ensure that the panels and menu commands match those used in this lesson, choose Window > Workspace > [Essentials], and then choose Window > Workspace > Reset Essentials.

8 If you want to see what the finished document looks like, navigate to the Lesson08 folder on your system. Double-click 08_End.pdf to open it.

This lesson previews a PDF of the final document because the necessary fonts are embedded in the PDF file. If you were to open the final InDesign document now, the necessary fonts would be activated automatically. You would be able to complete the lesson, but you would not be able to practice activating the font family.

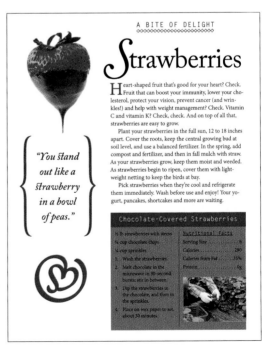

In this lesson, you will work intensively with text. You can use the character- and paragraph-formatting controls in the Properties panel for convenience, and you can use the Character panel and the Paragraph panel when you need more power.

● **Note:** Drag the Paragraph panel tab into the Character panel tab to create a panel group, if you prefer.

9 Choose Type > Character and Type > Paragraph to open the two primary text-formatting panels. Leave these panels open until you finish this lesson.

10 Choose Type > Show Hidden Characters so that you can see spaces, paragraph returns, tabs, and the like while you work on this lesson.

Adjusting vertical spacing

InDesign provides several options for customizing and adjusting the vertical spacing of text in a frame. You can do the following:

- Set the space between lines of paragraphs using a baseline grid (covered in Lesson 6).

- Set the space between lines using the Leading menu in the Character panel.

- Set the space between paragraphs using the Space Before and Space After options in the Paragraph panel. To prevent awkward spacing, the Space Before value is not applied at the top of a column, and the Space After value is not applied at the bottom of a column.

- Use the Vertical Justification and Balance Columns options in the Text Frame Options dialog to position text within a frame.

- Control how paragraphs flow from one column to the next using the Keep With Previous, Keep With Next, and Keep Lines Together settings available in the Keep Options dialog (choose Keep Options from the Paragraph panel menu).

● **Note:** To better view the interface onscreen or in print, the screen captures in this book reflect the Medium Light interface rather than the default setting of Medium Dark. In addition, some screen captures illustrate User Interface Scaling for a closer look at interface elements. You can modify interface settings in Preferences.

In this lesson, you will adjust the space between paragraphs and the line spacing within a paragraph.

Changing the spacing between paragraphs

▶ **Tip:** Specifying Space Before and/ or Space After values for paragraphs is preferable to typing extra paragraph returns between paragraphs. A full paragraph return is often too much space, and it can end up at the top of a page or column, leaving undesirable space.

To adjust space between paragraphs, you select the paragraphs and specify a Space Before and/or Space After value. (The amount of space between paragraphs ends up being the sum of the space after one paragraph and the space before the next paragraph. Therefore, it's generally best to use one or the other—space before or space after—to prevent confusion.) The Space Before and Space After values can be saved in paragraph styles and applied consistently across a document.

Here, you'll add more space between paragraphs in the Chocolate-Covered Strawberries recipe at the bottom of the page.

1 Scroll and zoom as necessary to view the recipe in the green box.

2 Using the Type tool (**T.**), click immediately in front of the first line of the recipe, "1/2 lb strawberries with stems."

3 Drag to select all the recipe text from "1/2 lb strawberries with stems" to "Protein 0g."

4 In the Paragraph panel, click the up arrow once next to Space After (⟱).

This adds .0625 inches (or 4.5 points) of space between paragraphs. The text will overset the frame, but this will be resolved later with the addition of columns.

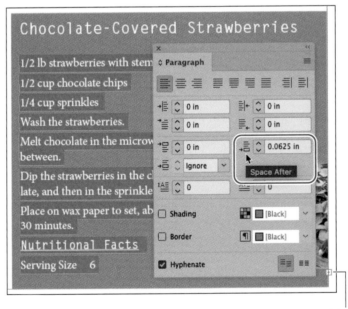

The red plus sign + in the lower-right corner of the text frame indicates overset text (more text than can fit in the frame). This is resolved later in the lesson.

5 Choose Edit > Deselect All.

6 Choose File > Save.

Working with fonts, type styles, and glyphs

Changing the fonts and type styles of text can make a dramatic difference in the appearance of your document. InDesign automatically installs a few fonts, and Creative Suite members have access to thousands of already licensed fonts at no extra charge through Adobe Fonts. Once a font is installed, you can apply it to text and change its size, select a style (such as bold or italic), and more. In addition, you can access all the glyphs (every form of each character) in the font. For example, fonts have variations of special characters such as these: % % $ $ # #.

Adding a font from Adobe Fonts

This exercise uses Adobe Caslon Pro, which is available for free from Adobe Fonts. If the font is already installed on your system, follow the steps to see how you can add another font.

● **Note:** Activating fonts from the Adobe Fonts service requires access to the internet.

1 In the Character panel, click the arrow to the right of Font to display the menu.

2 Click Find More at the top of the menu.

3 Scroll down in the list to locate Adobe Caslon Pro.

4 Click the Activate button (⌂) to the right of the font family folder, and then click OK to confirm.

▶ **Tip:** A font family is a collection of styles of the same font. For example, the Adobe Caslon Pro family includes the following fonts: Regular, Italic, Semibold, Semibold Italic, Bold, and Bold Italic. You can activate the entire family or an individual style within the font.

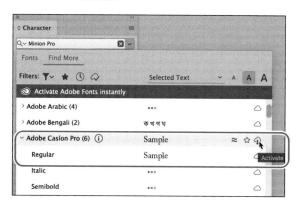

Note: A longtime font format, Type 1, was retired by Adobe in January 2023. When opening documents that require Type 1 fonts, you may encounter an alert. You may be able to replace Type 1 fonts with an OpenType font of the same name.

OpenType fonts

OpenType fonts, such as Adobe Caslon Pro, may display many more glyphs than you are accustomed to seeing. (Glyphs are representations of characters within a font.) OpenType fonts can contain many more characters and glyph alternates than other font formats. InDesign supports a new OpenType font format called Variable Font as well. This format provides convenient slider controls for adjusting weight, width, slant, optical size, and more. For more information on OpenType fonts, visit www.adobe.com/products/type/opentype.html.

Applying a font, style, size, and leading

First, you'll apply a different font to the headline and then to the first character of the headline. Next, you'll change the font family, style, size, and leading for the text in the quote on the left side of the page.

1 Scroll and zoom as necessary to view the headline.

2 Using the Type tool (T), select the story headline, "Strawberries," at the top of the page.

Tip: For a little more control, use the arrow keys on your keyboard to move up and down in the Font menu.

3 Click the Font menu in the Character panel. Scroll through the list to see how "Strawberries" looks in various fonts.

4 In the list, find the font family you just activated, Adobe Caslon Pro, which may be alphabetized under "C."

5 Click the arrow to the right of Adobe Caslon Pro to open the font family, and select Regular from the menu.

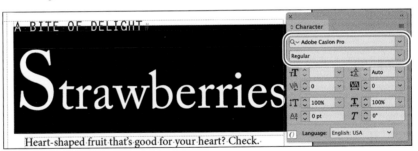

6 Using the Type tool, click immediately to the left of the first "S" in the "Strawberries" headline. Drag to select the "S."

7 In the Character panel, select Italic from the Style menu below the Font menu.

Now you will work on the quote on the left side of the page: "You stand out like a strawberry in a bowl of peas." Scroll and zoom as necessary to view the quote.

8 Using the Type tool (**T**), click inside the quote's text frame. To select the entire paragraph, quadruple-click (click four times rapidly).

9 In the Character panel, set the following options:

- Font: Adobe Caslon Pro

- Style: Semibold Italic

- Size: **25 pt**

- Leading: **35 pt**

▶ **Tip:** To quickly select a font, you can type the first few letters in the Font field until it is recognized.

10 Click the Character panel menu, and select OpenType. Notice that Swash is already selected, indicating that some glyphs have already been replaced with more ornate glyphs.

▶ **Tip:** In the OpenType menu, the options in brackets are not available for the selected font.

11 Select Swash to deactivate this feature, and notice the changes (such as the Y vs. *Y* in Adobe Caslon Pro Semibold Italic). Select Swash from the OpenType menu again to reactivate the feature.

12 If the OpenType badge ([O]) is not displayed somewhere on the paragraph, click in the quote's paragraph four times to reselect it.

13 Click the OpenType badge, which offers another way to access Open-Type features available in the font.

▶ **Tip:** Ligatures combine two or three glyphs into a single glyph to achieve a more harmonious look. Common ligatures include the "fi" and "fl" letter pairs.

14 Check Discretionary Ligatures along with Swash, and note how the two "st" glyph pairs are replaced with an "st" ligature: ſt.

15 Choose Edit > Deselect All.

16 Choose File > Save.

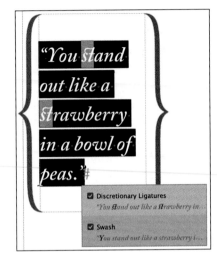

Adding a special character

Many types of special characters—such as bullets, checkboxes, accented characters, and ornamental curlicues—are used in documents for useful and decorative purposes. Now you'll add a decorative character in the lower-left corner of the page.

▶ **Tip:** You can access some of the more commonly used glyphs (such as the copyright and trademark symbols, bullets, and dashes) in the Type menu (Insert Special Character) and the context menu. To access the context menu, right-click at the insertion point.

1 If necessary, scroll down to see the text frame below the quote about peas.

2 Using the Type tool (T), click to place an insertion point in the text frame.

3 Choose Type > Glyphs. You can use the Glyphs panel to view and insert OpenType attributes, such as ornaments, swashes, fractions, and ligatures.

4 In the Glyphs panel, choose Ornaments from the Show menu.

5 Locate the heart-shaped character (♡), and double-click it.

6 Choose Type > Glyphs to close the Glyphs panel, and then choose File > Save.

Finding fonts in the Font menu

InDesign provides multiple ways to quickly find fonts in the Font menus that are available in the Control, Character, and Properties panels.

- **Name Search:** A quick way to find a font is to start typing the font name in the Font field. For example, as you type "Cas" for Adobe Caslon Pro, all fonts with those three characters in it are listed. By default, InDesign searches by the entire font name. You can click the search icon (🔍) to the left of the font name to search by first word only. In that case, you would need to type "Adobe Cas" for the same result.

- **Filter by Class:** Select a font classification from the Filter menu (▼), such as Serif or Script.

- **Favorites:** For quick access to fonts you use frequently, click the star to the right of a font name in any Font menu. Then, click Show Favorite Fonts (★) at the top of the menu.

- **Font Similarity:** Click Show Similar Fonts (≈) to the right of a font to display visually similar fonts in the menu.

▶ **Tip:** When logged into Creative Cloud, you also can activate fonts through fonts. adobe.com and the Manage Fonts link in the left column of the Creative Cloud app.

Icons in the Filter menu indicate the visual characteristics of each font classification.

Applying a stroke and fill to text

Next, you'll add a fill color and stroke to the glyph you just added.

1 With the Type tool (T) still selected, select the heart-shaped glyph.

2 In the Character area of the Properties panel, type **122 pt** in the Font Size field. Press Enter (Windows) or Return (macOS).

3 In the Appearance area of the Properties panel, do the following:

 • Select the Fill box (T), and click the Strawberry Red swatch.

 • Click the up arrow next to the Stroke Weight field to apply a 1 pt stroke.

 • Select the Stroke box (T), and click the Stem Green swatch.

4 Click next to the character so that you can view the stroke effect.

5 Press Ctrl+Shift+A (Windows) or Shift+Command+A (macOS) to deselect anything on the page. Choose File > Save.

Inserting fraction characters

The recipes in this article do not use actual fraction characters—rather, the 1/2 is built with a numeral 1, a slash, and a numeral 2. Most fonts contain individual characters for common fractions such as ½, ¼, and ¾. When available, these elegant fractions look much more professional than using numerals and slashes. You will try several methods for inserting fractions here.

1 Scroll and zoom as necessary to view the recipe.

2 Using the Type tool (T), drag to select the "1/2" in the first line, "1/2 lb strawberries with stems."

3 Choose Type > Glyphs to open the Glyphs panel.

4 Choose Numbers from the Show menu. (If necessary, scroll up in the menu to locate the Numbers option.)

5 Locate the ½ fraction. If necessary, resize the panel and scroll to see more characters.

6 Double-click the ½ fraction to replace the selected 1/2 in the text.

Notice that the ½ fraction is stored in the Recently Used boxes at the top of the Glyphs panel. Now you'll replace the "1/2" in the second line of the recipe.

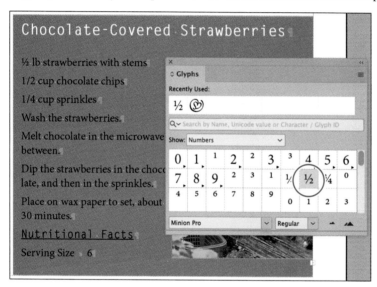

7 Drag to select the "1/2" in "1/2 cup chocolate chips" in the next line of the recipe.

8 Double-click the ½ fraction in the Recently Used box at the top of the Glyphs panel.

9 Drag to select the "1/4" in "1/4 cup sprinkles" in the third line of the recipe.

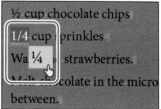

10 Point at the blue underline that displays under "1/4" and click the fraction to replace the 1/4 with ¼.

11 Close the Glyphs panel, and choose Edit > Deselect All.

12 Choose File > Save.

► **Tip:** If you are working on a cookbook or other document that requires a variety of fractions, the fractions built into most fonts will not cover all the values you need. You will need to research numerator and denominator formatting options, which are available in some OpenType fonts, or purchase a specific fraction font.

● **Note:** Only OpenType fonts offer convenient inline access to glyph variations.

Working with columns

▶ **Tip:** Attractive and readable type relies on many factors that work together, including the font choice and size, line length (column width), leading (space between lines), alignment (such as justified), and more. As you design pages, you may experiment with all these options, keeping readability in mind.

You can specify the number of columns in a text frame, the width of the columns, and the space between them. Once a text frame is divided into columns, you can create a heading that spans multiple columns (also known as a "straddle head"). In this section, you will add columns and a straddle head to a text frame.

Specifying columns for a text frame

The recipe in the green text frame will look better and be more legible if it's divided into two columns with a rule between the columns.

1 Using the Selection tool (▶), click the recipe's text frame to select it.

2 Choose Object > Text Frame Options, and then click the General tab. Check Preview to see the changes.

3 In the Columns area, enter **2** in the Number field.

4 Press Tab to select the Gutter field, and then type **.25 in**.

5 Click the Column Rules tab at left, and then check Insert Column Rules.

6 Under the Stroke area, enter **1** in the Weight field and select Strawberry Red from the Color menu. Drag the dialog out of the way to see the changes.

7 Click OK, and choose File > Save.

Creating a straddle head

The heading for the recipe needs to span the two columns. You can do this with a paragraph format rather than by placing the heading in its own text frame.

1 Using the Type tool (T,), click in the "Chocolate-Covered Strawberries" heading. This selects the paragraph for formatting.

2 Select Span Columns from the Paragraph panel menu (☰).

3 In the Span Columns dialog, select Span Columns from the Paragraph Layout menu.

4 Choose All from the Span menu, and select Preview to confirm the change.

5 Click OK.

6 Choose File > Save.

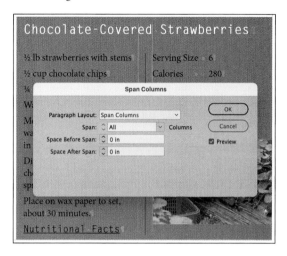

▶ **Tip:** You can also access the Span Columns controls in the Control panel.

Adjusting columns

Now that the heading is positioned, you can complete the fine-tuning of the recipe sidebar by balancing the amount of text in each column. You can do this automatically by selecting Balance Columns in the General tab of the Text Frame Options dialog (Object menu) or by inserting a "break character" that shifts text to the next column, frame, or page.

1 Using the Type tool (T,), click immediately before "Nutritional Facts" in the recipe.

2 Choose Type > Insert Break Character > Column Break.

3 Choose File > Save.

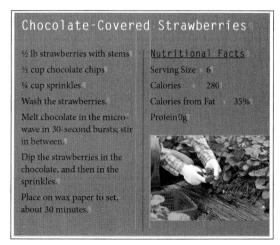

▶ **Tip:** Designers often use Insert Break Character because it's quick. However, if text reflows due to edits, the character remains and can force text to the wrong column or into overflow. Therefore, you should use this technique when editing and design are close to final.

Changing paragraph alignment

You can easily manipulate how a paragraph fits within its text frame by changing the horizontal alignment. You can align text with one or both edges of a text frame, or you can apply inset spacing. In this exercise, you'll use different methods to apply paragraph alignments.

1 Choose View > Fit Page In Window to view the entire page.

2 Using the Type tool (**T**), click to place an insertion point in the tagline at the top of the page: "A BITE OF DELIGHT." Zoom as necessary to see the text.

3 In the Paragraph panel, click Align Center (≣).

4 Click in the first paragraph of the story below the "Strawberries" headline (starting with "Heart-shaped fruit").

5 Choose Edit > Select All, and then click Justify With Last Line Aligned Left (≣) in the Properties panel.

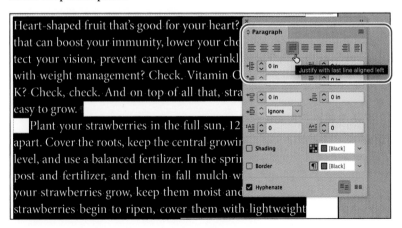

6 Click in the "Chocolate-Covered Strawberries" recipe heading. Press Ctrl+Shift+C (Windows) or Shift+Command+C (macOS) to center the one-line paragraph.

7 Click in the pea quote at the left to select the paragraph. Click Align Center (≣) in the Properties panel.

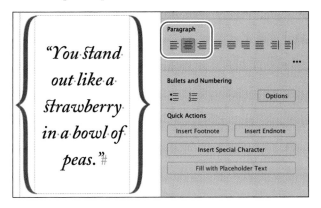

8 Choose Edit > Deselect All.

9 Choose File > Save.

Hanging punctuation outside the margin

Sometimes, particularly with punctuation at the beginning and end of lines, margins that are in fact even may appear uneven. To fix this visual discrepancy, designers use optical margin alignment to "hang" punctuation and swashes on characters slightly outside the text frame.

"I can't get enough strawberries," she said, "especially with chocolate!" The waiter rushed off with her order, returning with a plate of fresh berries and a fondue pot of melted chocolate. "Oh, I didn't know if was fondue—even better," she added.	"I can't get enough strawberries," she said, "especially with chocolate!" The waiter rushed off with her order, returning with a plate of fresh berries and a fondue pot of melted chocolate. "Oh, I didn't know if was fondue—even better," she added.

Without (left) and with (right) optical margin alignment. Notice the alignment of the quotation marks, hyphens, and em dashes. The text looks more visually aligned on the right.

● **Note:** When you select Optical Margin Alignment, it applies to all the text in a story—defined as all the text in a frame or a series of threaded text frames. If you have paragraphs that should not hang outside the margin, you can select the paragraphs and select Ignore Optical Margin from the Paragraph panel menu.

In this exercise, you will apply optical margin alignment to the main story.

1 Using the Selection tool (▶), click to select the text frame containing the main story, starting with "Heart-shaped fruit that's good for your heart?"

2 Choose Type > Story to open the Story panel.

3 Select Optical Margin Alignment. Enter **14 pt** in the field and press Enter or Return.

Note how the hyphen extends slightly beyond the edge of the text frame. Overall, this creates the appearance of a smoother edge.

4 Click the Story panel's close box, and then choose File > Save.

Creating a drop cap

You can add creative touches to your document using InDesign typographic features. For example, you can make the first character or word in a paragraph a drop cap and then apply additional formatting to the drop-cap character. Here, you'll create a drop cap out of the first character in the first paragraph of the story.

1 Using the Type tool (T), click to place an insertion point anywhere in the paragraph of the story starting with "Heart-shaped fruit that's good for your heart?"

2 In the Paragraph panel, type **2** in the Drop Cap Number Of Lines field (⌶≣) to make the letter drop down two lines. Press Enter or Return.

3 Note the 1 in the Drop Cap One Or More Characters field (A≣) to see how you would increase the number of characters that drop.

4 Using the Type tool, select the drop-cap character.

Now, you can apply any character formatting you want.

5 Select Stem Green from the Fill menu in the Properties panel.

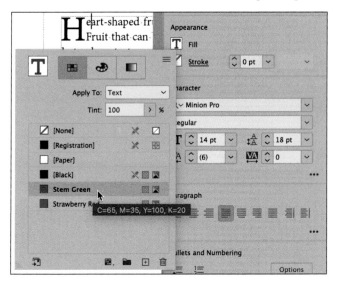

▶ **Tip:** You can create a drop cap and apply a character style in one step using the Drop Caps And Nested Styles dialog (Paragraph panel menu). You can then save that formatting in a paragraph style.

6 Click the pasteboard to deselect the text and view the drop cap.

7 Choose File > Save.

Adjusting letter and word spacing

To change the spacing between letters and words, you use the kerning and tracking controls. You can also control the overall spacing of text in a paragraph by using the Adobe Single-Line Composer and the Adobe Paragraph Composer. This type of fine-tuning is the hallmark of professional typography.

Adjusting the tracking and kerning

Tracking increases or decreases spacing across a range of selected letters. By adjusting kerning, you can add or subtract space between specific letter pairs. You can use both kerning and tracking on the same text.

Here, you'll track out the "A BITE OF DELIGHT" heading for effect and then track in the "Strawberries" heading. Finally, you will manually kern the space between the swash "S" and the remainder of the "Strawberries" headline.

1 To see the results of the tracking and kerning more clearly, scroll and zoom as necessary to view the top quarter of the page.

2 Using the Type tool ($T_{.}$), click in the "A BITE OF DELIGHT" heading at the top of the page. Click three times to select the entire heading.

3 In the Character panel, choose 100 from the Tracking menu (VA).

4 Click in the "Strawberries" heading and click two times to select the entire heading.

5 Type −**20** in the Tracking field in the Character panel.

6 Click to place an insertion point between the "S" and the "t" in "Strawberries."

7 Press Alt+Left Arrow (Windows) or Option+Left Arrow (macOS) on the keyboard three times to decrease the amount of space between the two characters.

The Kerning field (VA) in the Character panel and the Control panel lets you see and adjust the amount of space between characters.

8 Click the pasteboard to deselect the text. Choose View > Fit Page In Window to see the results.

9 Choose File > Save.

Adjusting line breaks

Hyphenation and line breaks at the end of each line affect readability and impact. For example, when paragraphs are aligned left, the right edge remains ragged. Too much "rag" can make the text easier or harder to read based on many factors, including the font, size, leading, column width, and more. Three other paragraph formats affect the readability of the text:

▶ **Tip:** For justified text, Justification settings combine with the Paragraph Composer and Hyphenation Settings to control how dense paragraphs look. To adjust these settings for a selected paragraph, choose Justification from the Paragraph panel menu.

- The Adobe Single-Line Composer and Adobe Paragraph Composer, which automatically determine line breaks

- Hyphenation settings, such as whether to hyphenate capitalized words

- The Balance Ragged Lines feature

Typically, a graphic designer will experiment with a combination of settings until a few paragraphs of sample text look just right. Then, all these options can be saved in paragraph styles and applied with one click.

Adobe Single-Line Composer	Adobe Paragraph Composer	Adobe Paragraph Composer with Balance Ragged Lines
A perusal of the menu, while munching fresh bread and savoring a glass of wine, tempts you with its carefully planned variety. "The menu is all designed to teach cooking methods," says Kleinman. "It covers 80 to 85 percent of what students have been learning in class—saute, grill, braise, make vinaigrettes, cook vegetables, bake and make desserts." In a twist on "You have to know the rules to break them," Kleinman insists that students need to first learn the basics before they can go on to create their own dishes.	A perusal of the menu, while munching fresh bread and savoring a glass of wine, tempts you with its carefully planned variety. "The menu is all designed to teach cooking methods," says Kleinman. "It covers 80 to 85 percent of what students have been learning in class—saute, grill, braise, make vinaigrettes, cook vegetables, bake and make desserts." In a twist on "You have to know the rules to break them," Kleinman insists that students need to first learn the basics before they can go on to create their own dishes.	A perusal of the menu, while munching fresh bread and savoring a glass of wine, tempts you with its carefully planned variety. "The menu is all designed to teach cooking methods," says Kleinman. "It covers 80 to 85 percent of what students have been learning in class—saute, grill, braise, make vinaigrettes, cook vegetables, bake and make desserts." In a twist on "You have to know the rules to break them," Kleinman insists that students need to first learn the basics before they can go on to create their own dishes.

Note the difference in line breaks with successive applications of line break methods. The first column shows a paragraph with the Adobe Single-Line Composer applied. The middle column shows the same paragraph with the Adobe Paragraph Composer applied. As you can see, the right edge is much less ragged. The column on the right shows the paragraph with both Adobe Paragraph Composer and Balance Ragged Lines applied, which helps balance the length of lines in the paragraph.

Hyphenation settings

Whether and how words are hyphenated at the ends of lines is a paragraph format. In general, Hyphenation Settings are editorial decisions, not design decisions. A publication's style guide, for example, may specify that capitalized words should not be hyphenated.

Tip: When you're editing text, you can use the Hyphenate option in the Control panel or the Paragraph panel to quickly enable and disable hyphenation for selected paragraphs.

1 Using the Type tool (**T.**), click to place an insertion point in the main story, starting with "Heart-shaped fruit that's good for your heart?"

2 Choose Edit > Select All to select all the paragraphs in the story.

3 From the Paragraph panel menu, select Hyphenation. Make sure Preview is selected so that you can see the changes.

4 Deselect Hyphenate to see how the text looks with no hyphenation.

5 Select Hyphenate again, and then type **2** in the Hyphen Limit field to prevent more than two lines in a row ending with a hyphen.

6 Click OK to close the dialog, but keep the text selected.

The hyphenation helps prevent gaps in the justified lines of text. However, the justified text is not suited to this casual magazine.

7 With the text still selected, press Ctrl+Shift+L (Windows) or Shift+Command+L (macOS) to align the text with the left margin.

8 Choose Edit > Deselect All, and then choose File > Save.

Inserting manual line breaks

Tip: Another way to control how text flows is to use a nonbreaking space between two words. For example, you might use a nonbreaking space to "glue" two words together so that they cannot split at the end of a line (such as "et al."). To do this, delete the existing space and choose Type > Insert White Space > Nonbreaking Space.

Once a layout is nearly complete, you may want to fine-tune line breaks for aesthetic or contextual reasons. Here, you will add two line breaks to the quote on the left side of the page.

1 Using the Type tool (**T.**), click in the fourth line of the quote, immediately before the word "of."

2 Enter a forced line break character by choosing Type > Insert Break Character > Forced Line Break, or pressing Shift+Enter (Windows) or Shift+Return (macOS).

3 Choose Edit > Deselect All, and then choose File > Save.

A forced line break character

Understanding the Adobe Paragraph and Single-Line Composers

The density of a paragraph (sometimes called its "color") is determined by the composition method used. InDesign's composition methods consider the word spacing, letter spacing, glyph scaling, and hyphenation options you've selected and then determine the best line breaks. InDesign provides two options for composing text: the Adobe Paragraph Composer, which examines all the lines in a paragraph before composing each line, and the Adobe Single-Line Composer, which composes text one line at a time starting with the first line.

● **Note:** The Adobe World-Ready Single-Line Composer and the Adobe World-Ready Paragraph Composer are intended for use with Middle Eastern languages. With these composers, you can enter text in a combination of Arabic, Hebrew, English, French, German, Russian, and other Latin languages.

- When you use the Paragraph Composer, InDesign composes a line while considering the impact on other lines in the paragraph to set the best overall arrangement of the paragraph. As you change type in a given line, previous and subsequent lines in the same paragraph may break differently, making the overall paragraph appear more evenly spaced. When you use the Single-Line Composer, which is the standard for other layout and word-processing software, InDesign recomposes only the lines following the edited text.

- The Single-Line Composer handles each line individually. As a result, some lines in a paragraph appear denser or sparser than others. Because the Paragraph Composer looks at multiple lines at once, it makes the density of the lines in a paragraph more consistent. Using the Single-Line Composer is helpful if you are adjusting all line breaks by hand in a design such as a wedding invitation.

The Adobe Paragraph Composer and Adobe Single-Line Composer—along with other hyphenation and justification controls—are available in the Paragraph panel menu.

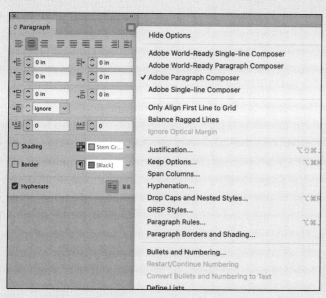

Setting tabs

▶ **Tip:** Tabs are paragraph formats, so to organize a column of text with tabs, each line needs to be its own paragraph.

As you're typing or formatting text, pressing the Tab key lets you quickly and consistently place text across a column or frame. The default tab stops are placed at every .5 inch, often resulting in too much space. To fine-tune the tab spacing, you can specify the location of each tab stop and how the text aligns to it. The Tabs panel provides all the controls for adding and changing tabs.

▶ **Tip:** See Lesson 6 for details on using Find/Change to quickly delete extra characters such as tabs and spaces.

When you're working with tabs, it helps to view the tab characters by choosing Type > Show Hidden Characters. It is common to receive word-processing files in which the writer or editor has entered multiple tabs to align the text onscreen—or worse, entered spaces rather than tabs. The only way to see what you're dealing with (and to fix it) is to view hidden characters.

Nutritional·Facts ¶
Serving·Size → → ····6 ¶
Calories → → 280 ¶
Calories·from·Fat → 35% ¶
Protein → → ····0g ¶

A writer, working in Microsoft Word, entered multiple tabs and spaces to align the text onscreen. The tabbed alignment works only for the font and size in use at the time, and the spaces are an imprecise way to align the numbers. These extra tabs and spaces need to be removed in InDesign.

Aligning text to tabs and adding tab leaders

Here, you'll format the tabbed Nutritional Facts list in the Chocolate-Covered Strawberries recipe. The tab markers have already been entered in the text, so you will specify the final location of the text. In addition, you will enter a leader character to fill the space between the text and the tab stop.

1 Scroll and zoom as necessary to view the recipe.

2 To view the tab markers in the text, make sure that hidden characters are showing (Type > Show Hidden Characters) and that Normal Mode (🖻) is selected in the Tools panel.

3 Using the Type tool (T), click immediately before "Serving Size" after the "Nutritional Facts" heading. Drag to select the text through the last line, "Protein 0g."

4 Choose Type > Tabs to open the Tabs panel.

When a text frame has an insertion point and enough space at the top, the Tabs panel snaps to the top of the frame so that the measurements in the panel's ruler exactly match the text. Regardless of the position of the Tabs panel, you can enter values to set tabs with precision.

5 In the Tabs panel, click Right-Justified Tab (↓). This specifies that text aligns to the left of the tab stop.

6 Type **2 in** in the X (tab stop) field, and press Tab to jump to the Leader field.

You will now create a tab leader, such as the periods that lead your eye across the page in a table of contents. In this case, you will use a space between periods to create a more open dot sequence in the tab leader.

7 Type a period (.) and a space in the Leader field. Press Enter or Return to complete the tabs.

The information following each tab marker in the selected text now aligns to the new tab stop, and a dotted line (of periods and spaces) helps lead the eye across the line.

8 Choose Type > Tabs to close the Tabs panel, and then choose Edit > Deselect All.

9 Choose File > Save.

Working with tabs

The controls for creating and customizing tabs in InDesign are similar to those in a word processor. You can precisely position tabs, repeat tabs across a column, create leaders for tabs, specify how text aligns with tabs, and easily modify the tabs you've created. Tabs are paragraph formats, so they apply to the paragraph containing an insertion point or any selected paragraphs. All the controls are in the Tabs panel, which you open by choosing Type > Tabs. Here's how the tabs controls work:

- **Enter tabs:** To enter a tab in text, press the Tab key.

- **Specify tab alignment:** To specify how text aligns with a tab stop—for example, to the left of the tab stop (the traditional setting) or on a decimal point—click one of the tab buttons in the upper-left corner of the Tabs panel: Left-Justified Tab, Center-Justified Tab, Right-Justified Tab, or Align To Decimal (Or Other Specified Character) Tab.

- **Position tabs:** To position a tab stop, click one of the tab buttons, type a value in the X field, and press Enter or Return. You can also click a tab button and then click just above the ruler.

- **Repeat tabs:** To create multiple tab stops the same distance apart, select a tab on the ruler. Choose Repeat Tab from the Tabs panel menu. This creates tab stops across the column based on the distance between the selected tab stop and the previous tab stop (or the paragraph's left indent).

- **Specify a character on which to align text:** To align text on a specific character—for example, a decimal point—click the Align To Decimal (Or Other Specified Character) Tab button at the left, and then type or paste the character into the Align On field. (If the text does not contain that character, the text will align to the left of the tab stop.)

- **Create a tab leader:** To fill the white space between text and tabs—for example, to add periods between text and page numbers in a table of contents—enter up to eight characters to repeat in the Leader field.

- **Move tabs:** To change the position of a tab stop, select the tab on the ruler, type a new position in the X field, and press Enter or Return. Or, drag the tab on the ruler to a new location.

- **Delete tabs:** To delete a tab, drag it off the tab ruler. Or, select the tab on the ruler and choose Delete Tab from the Tabs panel menu.

- **Reset default tabs:** To return to the default tab stops, choose Clear All from the Tabs panel menu. The default tab stops are placed at every half-inch.

- **Change tab alignment:** To change a tab stop's alignment, select it on the ruler and then click a different tab button. Or, press the Alt (Windows) or Option (macOS) key while clicking the tab on the ruler to cycle through the four alignment options.

Creating a numbered list with a hanging indent

InDesign makes it easy to create bulleted lists and numbered lists to clearly delineate information. Lists generally feature a "hanging indent" so that the text hangs to the right of the tab. Here, you will add step numbers to the recipe instructions.

1 Scroll and zoom as necessary to see the recipe at the bottom of the page.

2 Using the Type tool (**T**), click immediately before the first step in the recipe, "Wash the strawberries." Drag to select all four paragraphs through the word "minutes."

3 Click the Numbered List button () in the Properties panel.

▶ **Tip:** Click the Options button next to the Bullets And Numbering buttons to fine-tune the numbering, bullet characters, spacing, and more.

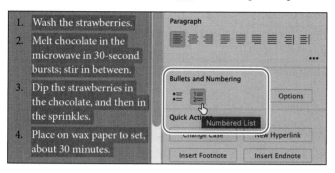

4 Deselect the text, and view the numbered list with the hanging indent.

5 Choose File > Save.

Hanging indents and bulleted lists

You can adjust paragraph indents—including the Left Indent, Right Indent, First Line Left Indent, and Last Line Right Indent—by entering values in the Control panel and the Paragraph panel (Type > Paragraph). In addition to specifying values, you can create hanging indents in the following ways:

• **Drag the indent markers on the tab ruler:** Drag the indent markers to the right, and then press the Shift key while dragging the top indent marker to the left. The Shift key lets you drag the indent markers independently.

• **Insert an Indent To Here character:** Set the text insertion point in the first line of the paragraph, and then press Ctrl+\ (Windows) or Command+\ (macOS). Or, you can choose Type > Insert Special Character > Other > Indent To Here. The Indent To Here character hangs all the subsequent lines in the paragraph to the right of the character.

You can use a combination of hanging indents and bullet characters or numerals to create bulleted or numbered lists. A quicker way to do this, however, is to use the Bullets And Numbering feature in the Properties panel or the Bulleted & Numbered Lists submenu of the Type menu. You can save bulleted list and numbered list formatting as part of a paragraph style.

Working with paragraph shading and rules

To call attention to text within a story—such as a new subhead, a quote, or an author's biography—you can apply a border around a paragraph, shade a paragraph, or place a rule (line) above or below a paragraph. InDesign offers many options for fine-tuning the color, placement, and look of these paragraph formats.

While you can achieve the look of paragraph borders, shading, and rules with various objects, applying them as paragraph formats offers advantages. These formats will travel with paragraphs as text reflows, and they can be included in paragraph styles for quick and consistent application across a document.

Here, you will apply paragraph shading and a rule below a paragraph. Applying a border to a paragraph is similar to applying shading or a rule above/below.

Applying shading to a paragraph

The final touch in this layout is using shading to create a reverse type effect for the recipe heading.

▶ **Tip:** The paragraph-shading controls are available in the Control panel as well. To fine-tune the shading, choose Paragraph Borders And Shading from the Paragraph panel menu, and click the Shading tab at the top. You can also open the Paragraph Borders And Shading dialog by Alt-clicking (Windows) or Option-clicking (macOS) the Shading Color button in the Control panel or the Paragraph panel.

1 Using the Type tool (T.), click in the "Chocolate-Covered Strawberries" recipe heading. This targets the paragraph for formatting.

2 Select Shading in the lower-left corner of the Paragraph panel.

3 To select the color of the shading, click the Shading Color menu to the right of the Shading option. Select the Strawberry Red swatch.

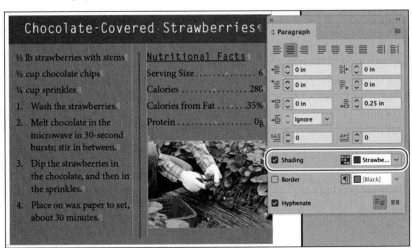

4 Choose Edit > Deselect All.

5 Choose File > Save.

Applying a rule to a paragraph

Here you'll add a rule below "A BITE OF DELIGHT" at the top of the page.

1 Choose View > Fit Page In Window.

2 Using the Type tool (T), click to place an insertion point in the "A BITE OF DELIGHT" tagline.

A · BITE · OF · DELIGHT #

3 Choose Paragraph Rules from the Paragraph panel menu.

4 At the top of the Paragraph Rules dialog, choose Rule Below from the menu, and select Rule On to activate the rule.

5 Select the Preview option. Move the dialog so that you can see the paragraph.

6 In the Paragraph Rules dialog, set these options:

 • Weight: 8 pt

 • Color: Stem Green

 • Width: Text

 • Type: White Diamond

 • Offset: .0625 in (one click of the up arrow)

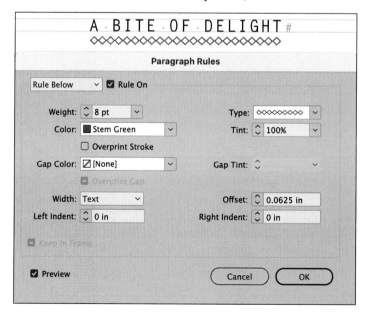

7 Click OK to apply the changes. A rule now appears below the tagline.

▶ **Tip:** To learn more about typography and definitions of terms such as "widow," see *InDesign Type: Professional Typography with Adobe InDesign* (Adobe Press, 4th Edition, 2018).

8 Choose File > Save.

9 To view your results at full screen, choose View > Screen Mode > Presentation.

10 When you're finished viewing the document, press Esc.

Congratulations, you have finished the lesson. To finalize this article, you would likely spend time with an editor or a proofreader to fix any tight or loose lines, awkward line breaks, runts, widows, and orphans.

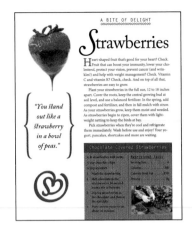

Exploring on your own

● **Note:** To use the Extract From Image features, you need to be logged into a Creative Cloud account.

InDesign provides a feature for extracting inspiration from the digital images you find around you. Place any picture in a document to extract color themes, shapes, and fonts from the image. To try this feature:

1 Create a new document of any size.

2 Choose File > Place. Locate MenuFontIdea.jpg, in the Lesson08 folder, and then double-click it. Click the page to place the graphics file.

● **Note:** Once InDesign finds fonts, the Find Similar Fonts button becomes the Save To CC Libraries button.

3 Choose Object > Extract From Image > Type. Position the blue box around type on the image, and then click Find Similar Fonts.

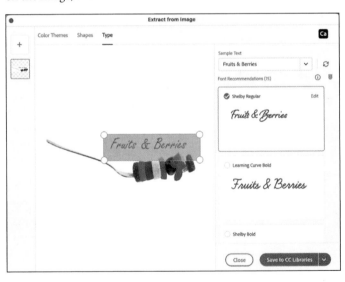

4 Click the other two options at the top of the Extract From Image dialog, Color Themes and Shapes, to extract colors and shapes from the image.

Review questions

1 What is the advantage of specifying a Space Before/Space After value for paragraphs rather than entering extra paragraph returns to add space?

2 What are glyphs? How do you insert them into text?

3 A drop cap affects a character, so why is it specified as a paragraph format?

4 What is a tab leader?

5 What is the difference between kerning and tracking?

6 What is the difference between the Adobe Paragraph Composer and the Adobe Single-Line Composer?

Review answers

1 Using Space Before/Space After values allows for precision spacing that can be applied consistently through paragraph styles. Paragraph returns often result in too much space between paragraphs, and they can end up leaving space at the bottom or top of a column as text flows.

2 A glyph is a representation of a character within a single font. For example, a font may provide two different options for a dollar sign, such as the two dollar sign symbols ($ and $) available in Warnock Pro. The Glyphs panel (Type menu) provides access to all the glyphs in a font.

3 Drop caps are paragraph formats because they are not specific to selected text. If a drop cap is applied to a paragraph, it remains even if the text is edited. In addition, drop cap formatting can be applied consistently through paragraph styles.

4 A tab leader is a character (or multiple characters) that fills the space between text and a tab marker.

5 Kerning adjusts the space between two characters; tracking adjusts the space between a range of selected characters. Kerning controls are available when the text insertion point is flashing; tracking controls are available when a range of text is selected. The controls are available in the Control panel and the Character panel.

6 The Paragraph Composer evaluates all lines in a paragraph when determining the best possible line breaks. The Single-Line Composer evaluates only one line at a time when determining line breaks.

9 WORKING WITH STYLES

Lesson overview

In this lesson, you'll learn how to do the following:

- Create and apply paragraph styles.

- Create and apply character styles.

- Nest character styles inside paragraph styles.

- Create and apply object styles.

- Create and apply cell styles.

- Create and apply table styles.

- Globally update styles.

- Import and apply styles from other InDesign documents.

- Experiment with style packs.

 This lesson will take about 60 minutes to complete. To get the lesson files used in this chapter, download them from the web page for this book at adobepress.com/InDesignCIB2023. For more information, see "Accessing the lesson files and Web Edition" in the Getting Started section at the beginning of this book.

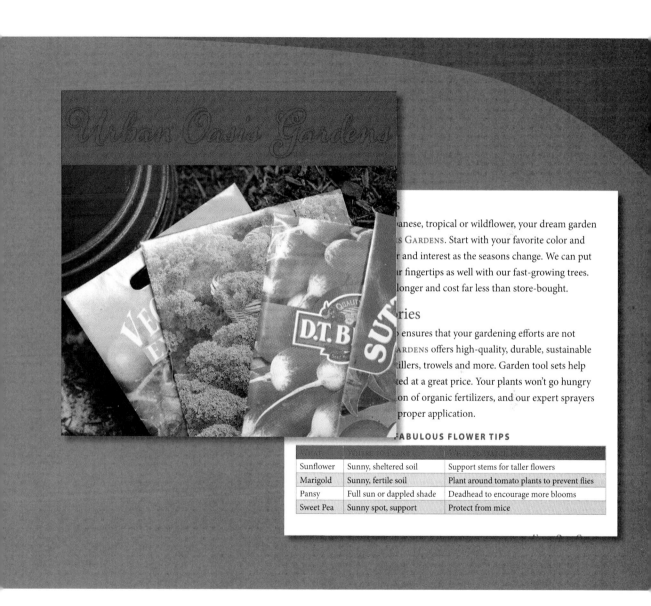

anese, tropical or wildflower, your dream garden
...S GARDENS. Start with your favorite color and
...r and interest as the seasons change. We can put
...r fingertips as well with our fast-growing trees.
...longer and cost far less than store-bought.

...ries

...p ensures that your gardening efforts are not
...ARDENS offers high-quality, durable, sustainable
...tillers, trowels and more. Garden tool sets help
...ted at a great price. Your plants won't go hungry
...on of organic fertilizers, and our expert sprayers
...proper application.

FABULOUS FLOWER TIPS

WHAT	WHERE TO PLANT	WHAT TO WATCH FOR
Sunflower	Sunny, sheltered soil	Support stems for taller flowers
Marigold	Sunny, fertile soil	Plant around tomato plants to prevent flies
Pansy	Full sun or dappled shade	Deadhead to encourage more blooms
Sweet Pea	Sunny spot, support	Protect from mice

With Adobe InDesign, you can create styles—sets
of formatting attributes—and apply them in one
step to text, objects, tables, and table cells. Any
changes to a style automatically affect all the text
or objects to which the style is applied. Styles offer
a quick, consistent method for formatting layouts.

Getting started

In this lesson, you'll create and apply styles for a few pages of a catalog for the Urban Oasis Gardens. Styles are collections of attributes that allow you to quickly and consistently apply formatting to text, tables, and objects throughout a document. (For example, a Body Text paragraph style specifies attributes such as font, size, leading, and alignment.) The catalog pages here contain text, tables, and objects that you will manually format and then use as the basis for creating styles. Later, if you were to place more catalog content, you could use styles to format the new text, tables, and objects with one click.

● **Note:** If you have not already downloaded the project files for this lesson to your computer from your Account page, make sure to do so now. See "Getting Started" at the beginning of the book.

1 To ensure that the preferences and default settings of your InDesign program match those used in this lesson, move the InDesign Defaults file to a different folder following the procedure in "Saving and restoring the InDesign Defaults file" on pages 3–4.

2 Start InDesign.

3 The InDesign Home screen displays. Click Open at the left. (If the Home screen does not display, choose File > Open from the InDesign menu bar.)

4 Open the 09_Start.indd file in the Lesson09 folder, located inside the Lessons folder within the InDesignCIB folder on your hard disk.

5 Choose File > Save As, rename the file **09_Styles.indd**, and save it in the Lesson09 folder.

6 Confirm that Window > Workspace > Essentials is selected, and then choose Window > Workspace > Reset Essentials.

7 If you want to see what the finished document will look like, open the 09_End.indd file in the same folder. Choose Layout > Next Spread and Layout > Previous Spread to explore all the pages. You can leave this document open to act as a guide as you work.

When you're ready to resume working on the lesson document, click its tab in the upper-left corner of the document window.

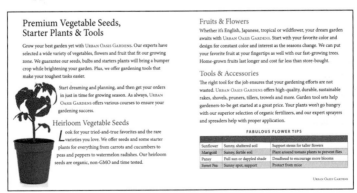

Understanding styles

InDesign provides styles for automating nearly all text, table, and object formatting. Creating, applying, modifying, and sharing styles works the same way for all types of styles: paragraph, character, object, table, and cell styles. You can open any Styles panel from the Styles submenu of the Window menu. The panel icons and panel menu options are similar for all the Styles panels.

Icons across the bottom of each Styles panel let you create a new style group, clear overrides, create a new style, and delete the selected style. Point at each icon to see its tool tip. Some Styles panels have additional, feature-specific icons as well.

Basic styles

The default formatting of everything in a new InDesign document is determined by its respective "basic" style. For example, when you create a new text frame, its formatting is determined by the [Basic Text Frame] object style. Therefore, if you wanted to specify that all new text frames have a 1-pt stroke, you would modify [Basic Text Frame]. To create a new default for all new InDesign documents, modify the "basic" style when no documents are open. Whenever you find yourself repeating a formatting task, stop and think about whether it makes sense to modify the relevant basic style or create a new style.

Creating styles

The various styles panels all include a New Style command on the panel menu and a Create New Style icon (+) at the bottom of the panel. Three different strategies work for specifying the formatting for the style.

- The most visual and flexible way to create a style is to format a sample of the text, table, table cells, or object. Then, you can create a new style based on the selected sample. This approach lets you use any controls you prefer, such as the Swatches panel and the Character panel.

- The Options dialog for creating each type of style has a Preview option. First, select Preview, and then change options until you are happy with the style. Because the Options dialog are large, you may need to drag them out of the way to see the changes.

- You also can create styles from scratch with no text, table, table cells, or object selected in the document. This method relies on you to visualize how the formatting might look.

continues on next page

Once you have a rough idea of how you want text, objects, and tables to look, you can start creating styles and applying them. Then, as you experiment with a design and make changes, you can simply modify styles to update the formatting.

Applying styles

Applying a style is as simple as making a selection and then clicking a style name in the relevant Styles panel. For example, to format a table, you select the table and then click a style name in the Table Styles panel. You can set up keyboard shortcuts for applying styles as well. Paragraph and character styles also may be applied during a search-and-replace operation (Edit > Find/Change).

Using Quick Apply

An easy way to apply styles without lifting your hands from the keyboard is by using Quick Apply. To use it, press Ctrl+Enter (Windows) or Command+Return (macOS). In the Quick Apply dialog, start typing the name of the style until it's recognized. Use the arrow keys to select it in the list, and then press Enter (Windows) or Return (macOS). Other ways to display the Quick Apply dialog include choosing Edit > Quick Apply or clicking the Quick Apply (⚡) button in the Control panel.

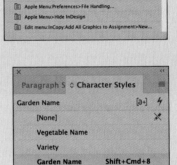

Assigning keyboard shortcuts to apply styles

You can assign keyboard shortcuts to all styles to expedite formatting. Here are a few tips for creating keyboard shortcuts:

- If you have an extended keyboard, create keyboard shortcuts that use the numbers on the number pad. This will give you less chance of creating keyboard shortcuts that conflict with other InDesign shortcuts or system shortcuts.

- Keyboard shortcuts are especially handy for formatting text. A quick way to remember shortcuts is to include a hierarchical number in the style name. For example, if you create a paragraph style named "1 Headline" with the shortcut Ctrl+Shift+1, it's easy to remember the shortcut because it's often the first style you apply.

Modifying and redefining styles

A primary benefit of using styles is the ability to apply formatting consistently and make global changes quickly. To modify a style, double-click its name in its respective Styles panel; this displays its Options dialog so that you can make changes. You can also modify the formatting of text, a table, or an object with a style applied and then choose Redefine Style from the respective Styles panel menu.

Creating and applying paragraph styles

Paragraph styles let you apply and globally update text formatting to speed up formatting and create a more consistent overall design. Paragraph styles incorporate all elements of text formatting, including character attributes such as font, size, style, and color, along with paragraph attributes such as indents, alignment, tabs, and hyphenation. Paragraph styles differ from character styles in that they are applied to entire paragraphs, not just to selected characters.

Creating a paragraph style

In this exercise, you'll create a paragraph style and apply it to selected paragraphs. First, you will manually format the text in the document locally (that is, not based on a style). Then, you will have InDesign pick up this formatting and build it into a new paragraph style.

1 Navigate to page 2 in the 09_Styles.indd document. Adjust the view scale and scroll as necessary so that you can easily see the text.

2 Using the Type tool (T), drag to select the "Heirloom Vegetable Seeds" subhead, which follows the introductory paragraph on page 2.

3 In the Appearance area of the Properties panel at the right, click the character Fill box (T) and click the Red-Tomato swatch.

4 In the Character area, enter **18 pt** in the Font Size field.

5 In the Paragraph area of the Properties panel, click the More Options (⋯) button. Increase the Space Before (⁺≡) to **.05 in**, and decrease the Space After (₊≡) to **.025 in**.

 Now you'll create a paragraph style using this formatting so that you can use it to format the other subheads in the document.

▶ **Tip:** When working on longer documents, such as books and catalogs, using styles can save hours of time in manual formatting. A common way to get started is to select all the text in a document and apply a "body text" paragraph style with one click. You can then go through the text and apply heading paragraph styles and character styles with keyboard shortcuts. You also can automate text formatting to some degree with style packs, which are discussed later in this lesson.

● **Note:** To better view the interface onscreen or in print, the screen captures in this book reflect the Medium Light interface rather than the default setting of Medium Dark. In addition, some screen captures illustrate User Interface Scaling for a closer look at interface elements. You can modify interface settings in Preferences.

6 Make sure that the "Heirloom Vegetable Seeds" subhead is still selected. Open the Paragraph Styles panel by choosing Type > Paragraph Styles. Tear the Paragraph Styles panel off the dock for easier access to it.

● **Note:** In this document, the Paragraph Styles panel already has a few styles provided for you, including the default, [Basic Paragraph].

7 In the Paragraph Styles panel, create a new paragraph style by choosing New Paragraph Style from the panel menu. The New Paragraph Style dialog opens, displaying the formatting you just applied to the subhead in the Style Settings section.

8 In the Style Name field at the top of the dialog, type **Head 2** to name this style as the second largest headline.

Below the Style Name field, notice that the new style is based on the Intro Body style. Since Intro Body was applied to the subhead when you created the style, the new style is automatically based on Intro Body. By using the Based On option in the General section of the New Paragraph Style dialog, you can use an existing style as a starting point for a new style. In this case, the Intro Body formatting is unrelated to the heading style, so you will change the Based On style to No Style.

9 Select [No Paragraph Style] from the Based On menu.

To speed up text formatting while typing in InDesign, you can specify a Next Style for a paragraph style. Each time you press Enter or Return, InDesign automatically applies the Next Style. For example, your headline style might be followed by your body paragraph style.

10 Select Intro Body from the Next Style menu, because this is the style used for the text following each Head 2 headline.

You can also create keyboard shortcuts for easily applying styles in InDesign.

11 Click in the Shortcut field, hold down Shift (Windows) or Command (macOS), and press 9 on your keyboard. (InDesign requires the use of a modifier key for style shortcuts.)

12 Select Apply Style To Selection to apply this new style to the text you just formatted.

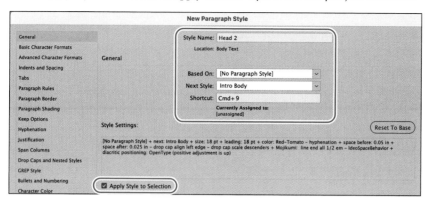

● **Note:** If you don't select Apply Style To Selection, the new style appears in your Paragraph Styles panel but is not automatically applied to the selected text you used to create the style.

13 Click OK to close the New Paragraph Style dialog.

The new Head 2 style appears in the Paragraph Styles panel and is highlighted to indicate that it's applied to the selected paragraph.

14 In the Paragraph Styles panel, click the triangle next to the Heads style group to open it. Then, drag the Head 2 style up between Head 1 and Head 3.

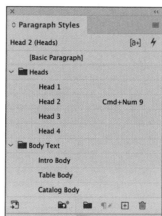

15 Choose Edit > Deselect All, and then choose File > Save.

Applying a paragraph style

Now you'll apply your paragraph style to other paragraphs in the document.

1 If necessary, scroll to the right to see the right page of the spread.

2 Using the Type tool (T), click to place an insertion point anywhere within "Fruits & Flowers."

● **Note:** You can use the keyboard shortcut you defined earlier (Shift+9 or Command+9) to apply the Head 2 style as well. To apply styles in Windows, be sure the Num Lock key on the keypad is down.

3 Click the Head 2 style in the Paragraph Styles panel to apply the style to the paragraph. The text attributes change to reflect the paragraph style.

4 Repeat steps 2 and 3 to apply the Head 2 style to "Tools & Accessories" on page 3.

▶**Tip:** When you are formatting text with styles and something doesn't look quite right, local overrides often are the culprit. See the "Best practices when working with styles" sidebar later in this lesson for more information.

When a paragraph style is applied to text, you can continue to change the text formatting. These formats are referred to as "local overrides." In some cases, local overrides are acceptable, and in other cases you will want to remove them so that the formatting exactly matches the style definition. In the next steps, you will apply, view, and remove local overrides.

5 Using the Type tool, triple-click to select "Tools & Accessories."

6 In the Appearance area of the Properties panel at the right, click the character Fill box (T) and click the Green-Medium swatch.

7 Click once in the "Tools & Accessories" paragraph to keep the paragraph selected and see the type color.

8 In the Paragraph Styles panel, note the plus sign (+) next to the style name, indicating local overrides. Point at the style name to see how the selected text deviates from the paragraph style definition.

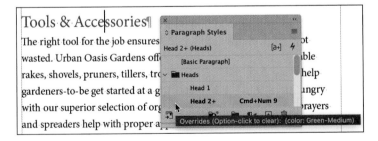

9 Click Clear Overrides In Selection (¶⁄) at the bottom of the Paragraph Styles panel. The text reverts to the style definition.

10 Choose Edit > Deselect All, and then choose File > Save.

Creating and applying character styles

In the previous exercise, paragraph styles allowed you to apply character and paragraph formatting to text with a single click or a keystroke. Similarly, character styles are a way to apply multiple attributes—such as font, size, and color—to text using a single action. Unlike paragraph styles, which format the entire paragraph, character styles apply formatting only to selected characters such as a word or phrase.

Character styles include only differences, such as italic, from the attributes specified in the paragraph style. The benefit of this is that you can use the same character style with different paragraph styles. For example, say that a newsletter's style is to italicize the names of books and movies. The newsletter has a body text style in Minion Pro and a sidebar body text style in Myriad Pro. You need only one character style that specifies Italic for use with both paragraph styles. InDesign will know to use the italic version of the correct font.

▶**Tip:** Character styles are helpful for lead-in characters such as bullet characters, numbers in numbered lists, and drop caps. They are also useful for emphasizing text within body copy—for example, stock symbols (investments) are often formatted in bold and small caps.

Character Style Options		
General	Style Name: Garden Name	
Basic Character Formats	Location:	
Advanced Character Formats	General	
Character Color		
OpenType Features	Based On: [None]	
Underline Options	Shortcut: Shift+Cmd+8	
Strikethrough Options		
Export Tagging	Style Settings:	Reset To Base
	[None] + color: Green–Medium + small caps	

The Character Style Options dialog provides easy access to all character formatting controls. In the General tab shown here, the Style Settings area summarizes the character style definition.

Creating a character style

Now you will create and apply a character style to selected text in the document. In this exercise, you can see how using character styles ensures more efficient and consistent formatting.

1 Scroll to view the first paragraph on page 2 at the left.

2 If it's not already visible, open the Character Styles panel by choosing Type > Character Styles. Tear the Character Styles panel off the dock for easier access to it. If you prefer, you can dock it with the Paragraph Styles panel.

The only style listed in this panel is the default, [None]. As you did with the paragraph style in the previous section, you'll build a character style based on existing text formatting. This approach lets you see the formatting before you create the style. In this case, you'll format the Urban Oasis Gardens name and build it into a character style so that it can be reused efficiently throughout the document.

3 Using the Type tool (**T.**), select the first instance of the words "Urban Oasis Gardens" in the first paragraph on page 2.

4 In the Appearance area of the Properties panel at the right, click the character Fill box (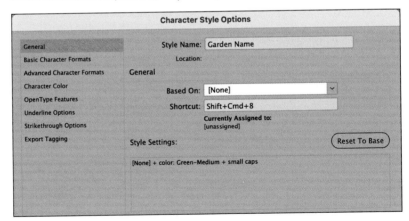T) and click the Green-Medium swatch.

5 In the Character area of the Properties panel, click the More Options (...) button to see additional character formatting controls. Click Small Caps (Tᴛ).

Now that the text is formatted, you'll create a new character style.

6 Click Create New Style (⊞) at the bottom of the Character Styles panel.

7 Double-click the new Character Style 1 that displays in the Character Styles panel. The Character Style Options dialog opens.

8 In the Style Name field at the top of the dialog, type **Garden Name** to define the style's purpose.

As you did for the paragraph style you created, now you'll create a keyboard shortcut to easily apply this character style.

▶ **Tip:** If you have an extended keyboard, create keyboard shortcuts that use the numbers on the number pad. That way, you will have less chance of creating keyboard shortcuts that conflict with other InDesign shortcuts or system shortcuts.

9 Click in the Shortcut field, and press Alt+Shift+8 (Windows) or Shift+Command+8 (macOS) on your keyboard.

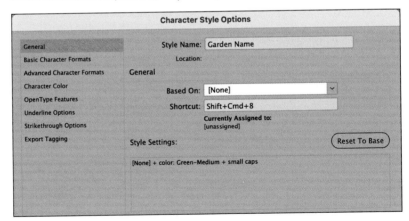

10 Notice the character style formatting listed in the Style Settings box.

11 Click OK to close the Character Style Options dialog. The new Garden Name style appears in the Character Styles panel and is now applied to the text.

12 Choose Edit > Deselect All, and then choose File > Save.

Applying a character style

You're ready to apply your character style to selected text in the document. As with paragraph styles, using character styles prevents you from having to manually apply multiple type attributes to each instance of text.

▶ **Tip:** You can use Find/Change (Edit menu) to search for all instances of a word or phrase and then apply a character style to it.

1 Using the Type tool (T), select the words "Urban Oasis Gardens" in the second paragraph of body text on the left page of the spread.

 To maintain a consistent look for the company name, you'll apply the Garden Name character style.

2 In the Character Styles panel, click the Garden Name style to apply it to this text. You should see the text change to reflect the character style you created.

3 Scroll to the right to view the right page of the first spread.

4 Using the Type tool, select the words "Urban Oasis Gardens" in the first paragraph of body text on the right page of the spread.

5 In the Character Styles panel, click the Garden Name style to apply it to this text.

6 In the second body paragraph, select the words "Urban Oasis Gardens." Press Alt+Shift+8 (Windows) or Shift+Command+8 (macOS) to apply the Garden Name character style.

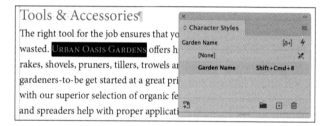

 Leave the Character Styles panel open for the next exercise.

7 Choose Edit > Deselect All, and then choose File > Save.

Nesting character styles inside paragraph styles

To make the use of styles more convenient and powerful, InDesign lets you nest character styles within paragraph styles. These nested styles allow you to apply distinct character formatting to specific portions of a paragraph—such as the first character, the second word, or the first line—at the same time you apply a paragraph style. This makes nested styles ideal for creating run-in headings, where the first portion of a line or paragraph is styled differently from the rest of the line or para-graph. In fact, whenever you can define a pattern of formatting within a paragraph, such as applying an italic type style until reaching the first period, you can automate the formatting with a nested style.

Creating character styles for nesting

▶ Tip: You can use the powerful nested styles feature to automatically apply different formatting within a paragraph according to a specific set of rules. For example, in a table of contents, you can automatically apply bold to the text, change the tracking in the tab leader (the dots that lead to the page number), and change the font and color of the page number.

To create a nested style, you need to first create both a character style and a paragraph style in which to nest it. In this section, you'll create two character styles for nesting and then nest them within the paragraph style Catalog Body, which already exists.

1 Double-click page 4 in the Pages panel, and then choose View > Fit Page In Window. If the body copy is too small to view, zoom in to the first paragraph under the "Beans" heading, beginning with "Green: Black Valentine."

2 Review the text and punctuation.

In this exercise, you'll create two nested styles to distinguish the vegetable's variety from its name.

* A colon (:) separates the vegetable's variety and name.

* A period appears after the name and before the description.

These characters will be important when creating your nested styles later in this section.

> BEANS¶
> Green: Black Valentine. Tasty snap beans, hardy and productive plants, flat pods. ¶

3 Using the Type tool (T,), select the first instance of "Green" and the colon following it.

4 In the Character Styles panel, choose New Character Style from the panel menu.

5 In the Style Name field at the top of the dialog, type **Variety** to define the text to which the style will be applied. Select Apply Style To Selection.

To make the name of each vegetable variety stand out more, you will change the font, style, and color.

6 From the categories on the left side of the dialog, click Basic Character Formats.

7 From the Font Family menu, select Myriad Pro. From the Font Style menu, select Bold.

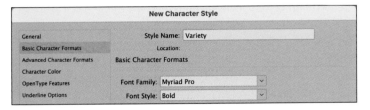

New Character Style		
General	Style Name:	Variety
Basic Character Formats	Location:	
Advanced Character Formats	**Basic Character Formats**	
Character Color		
OpenType Features	Font Family:	Myriad Pro
Underline Options	Font Style:	Bold

8 From the categories on the left side of the dialog, click Character Color.

9 In the Character Color settings that appear on the right side of the dialog,
 select the Green-Medium swatch.

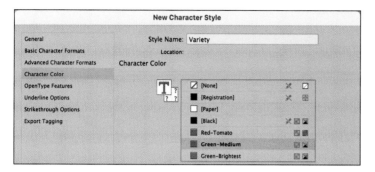

10 Click OK to close the New Character Style dialog. The new Variety style appears
 in the Character Styles panel.

 Now you'll create a second character style for nesting.

11 Select the text "Black Valentine" and the period after it. Using the Type menu
 in the Appearance area of the Properties panel, change the font to Myriad Pro
 and the font style to Italic.

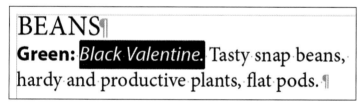

12 With "Black Valentine." still selected, choose New Character Style from the
 Character Styles panel menu.

13 Type **Vegetable Name** in the Style Name field.

14 Select Apply Style To Selection.

15 Click OK to create the character style based on the formatting applied in step 11.

16 Choose Edit > Deselect All, and then choose File > Save.

You have created two new character styles.
Using these along with the existing Catalog Body
paragraph style, you are ready to create and
apply the nested style.

Creating a nested style

▶ **Tip:** In addition to nested styles, InDesign provides nested line styles. These let you specify formatting for individual lines in a paragraph—such as a drop cap followed by small caps, which are common in the lead (first) paragraphs of magazine articles. If the text is edited, InDesign adjusts the formatting to encompass only the specified lines. The controls for creating nested line styles are in the Drop Caps And Nested Styles panel of the Paragraph Style Options dialog.

When you create a nested style within an existing paragraph style, you're basically specifying a secondary set of rules for InDesign to follow while formatting a paragraph. In this exercise, you'll build a nested style into the Catalog Body style using the character styles you created in the previous exercise.

1 If necessary, double-click page 4 in the Pages panel to center the page in the document window.

2 If the Paragraph Styles panel is not visible, choose Type > Paragraph Styles.

3 In the Paragraph Styles panel, double-click the Catalog Body style to open the Paragraph Style Options dialog.

4 From the categories on the left side of the dialog, select Drop Caps And Nested Styles.

5 In the Nested Styles section, click the New Nested Style button to create a new nested style.

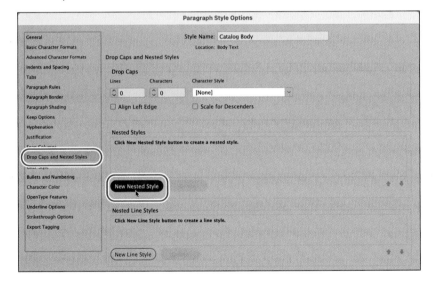

A nested style that applies the [None] character style through 1 Words appears.

6 Click [None] to display a menu of character styles. Select the Variety character style; this is the first nested style in the sequence.

7 Click the word "through" to reveal another menu. This menu contains only two choices: Through and Up To. The Variety character style needs to be applied through the first colon (:) after Green, so select Through. Leave the third option at the default setting (1).

8 Click Words to reveal a text field and menu. Click the menu button to the right of the field to view elements to which the style can be applied, including sentences, characters, and spaces. Double-click Words to select it, and press Backspace (Windows) or Delete (macOS). Type a colon (:) in the field.

▶ **Tip:** Using nested styles can automate some very tedious formatting. When making style decisions for longer documents, think about establishing a pattern that will enable automatic formatting through nested styles.

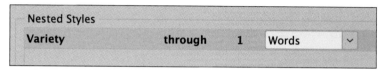

9 In the lower-left corner, select Preview. Move the Paragraph Style Options dialog so that you can see the columns of text.

Now you'll add another nested style to format the vegetable names.

10 Click the New Nested Style button.

11 Repeat steps 6 through 8 to set up an additional nested style with the following formatting:

- First option: Choose Vegetable Name.
- Second option: Choose Up To.
- Third option: Leave at the default setting (1).
- Fourth option: Select Sentences to apply the formatting up to a period.

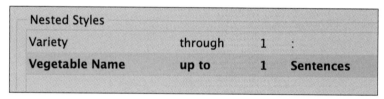

12 Review the changes in the text, and then click OK.

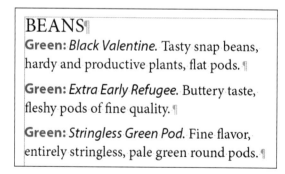

13 Choose Edit > Deselect All, and then choose File > Save. Close the Paragraph Styles and Character Styles panels if they are in your way.

Best practices when working with styles

InDesign styles offer many sophisticated features for streamlining formatting by organizing styles, sharing styles among documents, and ensuring styles are applied properly.

Basing styles on existing styles

All styles can be based on an existing style; the existing style serves as a starting place for the new style. If you change the style on which other styles are based—for example, by changing the font in a paragraph style—the changes update all styles based on that style. Basing styles on other styles is helpful when you're creating a series of related styles, such as Body Copy, Body Copy Indent, Bulleted Body Copy, and so on. If the font of the Body Copy style changes, InDesign updates the font in all related styles as well. Unique characteristics of styles based on other styles are maintained.

Breaking the link to a style

If you have a specific instance of text, tables, table cells, or objects that you no longer want associated with a style, you can break its link to the style. You might do this for a highly designed headline for a magazine article, for example. Each Styles panel has a Break Link To Style command in the panel menu.

Sharing styles among documents

Styles are shared among documents frequently to ensure a consistent look across an organization's media. On all the Styles panels, the panel menu provides a Load command for importing styles from other InDesign documents. You can also share paragraph styles and character styles with a workgroup through InDesign CC Libraries. To do this, select a style in the Paragraph Styles panel or Character Styles panel and click Add Selected Style To My Current CC Library at the bottom of the panel. To use this style in another document, apply it to selected text from the CC Library. The style is automatically added to the document's Paragraph Styles or Character Styles panel.

Organizing styles in style groups

All of the InDesign Styles panels let you group similar styles in folders called "style groups." To create a style group, click the Create New Style Group button at the bottom of the panel. Click in the group's folder to name it. You can drag styles into the folder to organize them, and you can drag styles up and down in the list to organize them.

Overriding manual formatting

In most cases, you will want text, tables, table cells, and objects to precisely match the applied style's specifications. To achieve this, sometimes you need to override any manual formatting. If a selection does not precisely match its style, a plus sign appears next to the style name. This is referred to as a "style override." For example, if a paragraph style specifies left-aligned paragraphs but you decide to center a paragraph, the centering is a style override. To see and manage style overrides:

- To see how the formatting in the selection varies from the style, point at the style name in the Styles panel; a tool tip describes the overrides applied.

- Most Styles panels have a Clear Overrides control at the bottom, indicated by an icon and a plus sign. Move your mouse over the icon to learn how to clear overrides in the selection.

- Note that if you are having trouble clearing overrides while applying a paragraph style, check to see whether a character style is applied to the text.

- InDesign indicates style overrides to alert you to inconsistent formatting. In some cases, however, manual overrides are necessary, and you may leave the style overrides as is.

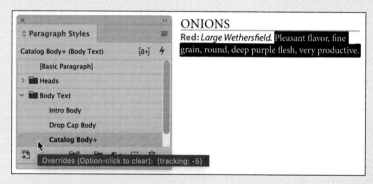

The Overrides tool tip shows how the formatting of the selected text varies from the formatting specified in the paragraph style. In this case, the tracking of the text is different. Small amounts of tracking often are used for copyfitting purposes, so this is an override you may leave alone.

Understanding paragraph styles and character styles

A paragraph style includes all text formatting attributes—such as font, size, and alignment—and applies to all the text in a paragraph. You can select a paragraph for formatting by clicking in it, highlighting any part of it, or highlighting all of it. A character style includes only character attributes—such as font style (bold, italic, condensed, etc.) and color—and applies only to selected text within a paragraph. Character styles typically are applied to call attention to specific text within a paragraph. In general, you will apply paragraph styles to most text and then apply character styles to variations.

A common strategy for applying styles is to select all the text in the document and then apply the most commonly used paragraph style. For example, if you were designing a book, you might have a body text paragraph style that applies to most of the paragraphs. Then, you go through the pages and apply chapter heads, subheads, captions, character styles, and more. You also can automate text formatting to some degree with style packs, which are discussed later in this lesson.

Creating and applying object styles

Object styles let you apply and globally update formatting to objects, such as frames. Combining formatting attributes—including fill, stroke, transparency, and text wrap options—into object styles helps create a more consistent overall design and speeds up tedious production tasks.

Formatting an object for a style

In this section, you will create an object style that quickly applies a drop shadow to objects. In this catalog design, the decorative headlines are actually objects created by selecting text and choosing Type > Create Outlines. With outlines, you no longer need the font active on your system, and you have more flexibility, such as importing images into the shape.

1 Double-click page 1 in the Pages panel to center the page in the document window.

2 Using the Selection tool (▶), click "Urban Oasis Gardens" to select the text-shaped object.

3 Choose Object > Effects > Drop Shadow.

4 Notice that Drop Shadow is selected in the list at the left. Leave the other options at their default settings.

5 Select Preview to see the changes, and click OK.

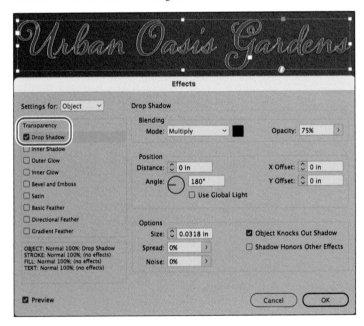

6 Choose Edit > Deselect All to see the effect, and choose File > Save.

Creating an object style

Now that the object is formatted properly, you are ready to create the object style from its formatting.

1 Using the Selection tool (▶), click "Urban Oasis Gardens" with the drop shadow effect.

2 Choose Window > Styles > Object Styles to open the Object Styles panel.

3 In the Object Styles panel, hold down the Alt (Windows) or Option (macOS) key while you click Create New Style in the lower-right corner.

▶ **Tip:** Just as with paragraph and character styles, you can base an object style on another object style. Changes made to the Based On style update all object styles based on that style. (Unique characteristics of styles based on other styles are maintained.) The controls for basing a style on another are in the General panel of the New Object Style dialog.

When you Alt-click or Option-click the Create New Style button, the New Object Style dialog opens automatically. The selected boxes on the left side of this dialog indicate which attributes will be applied when this style is used.

4 In the Style Name field at the top of the New Object Style dialog, type **Drop Shadow** to describe the purpose of the style.

In the list at the left, click through the options you can set for an object style. In addition to basic formatting attributes such as stroke and fill, object styles can include size (width, height) and position options (X, Y).

5 Select Apply Style To Selection at the bottom, and click OK.

Applying an object style

Now you'll apply your new object style to the headline on the back page of the catalog. Remember, the advantage to using styles is that when you modify a style, the text, table, or objects to which the style is applied will update automatically.

1 Double-click the page 6 icon on the Pages panel to display the last page in the document window.

2 If necessary, choose View > Fit Page In Window.

3 Using the Selection tool (▶), select the "How to Grow" text-shaped object.

 As with the previous headline, this text has been converted to curves using Type > Create Outlines.

4 Click Drop Shadow in the Object Styles panel.

5 If the formatting does not match the new style, choose Clear Overrides from the Object Styles panel menu.

6 Choose Edit > Deselect All, and then choose File > Save.

Creating and applying table and cell styles

Table and cell styles let you format tables with the same convenience and consistency you get from formatting text with paragraph and character styles. Table styles let you control the visual attributes of the table, including the table border, space before and after the table, row and column strokes, and alternating fill patterns. Cell styles let you control cell inset spacing, vertical justification, individual cell strokes and fills, and diagonal lines. You'll learn more about creating tables in Lesson 10, "Creating Tables."

In this exercise, you'll create and apply a table style and two cell styles to tables in the catalog document to help distinguish the tips on planting each flower.

Creating cell styles

You'll begin by creating a cell style for the header row of the table at the bottom of page 3. Later, you'll nest this style inside the table style, a process similar to how you nested character styles inside a paragraph style earlier in this lesson. You'll now create a cell style.

1 Double-click page 3 in the Pages panel.

2 Using the Zoom tool (🔍), zoom in on the table at the bottom of the page to make it easily visible.

3 Using the Type tool (T.), point at the left edge of the first row of the table, starting with "What." When the horizontal arrow (→) displays, click to select the entire row.

4 Choose Table > Cell Options > Strokes And Fills. For Cell Fill, select the Green-Brightest swatch. Click OK.

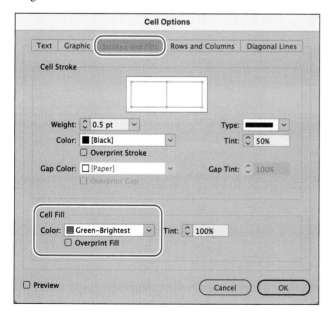

5 With the cells still selected, open the Cell Styles panel by choosing Window > Styles > Cell Styles.

6 From the Cell Styles panel menu, choose New Cell Style.

The cell formatting you applied to the selected cells is displayed in the Style Settings box. You'll also notice additional cell formatting options on the left side of the dialog. In this exercise, you will specify the desired paragraph style to use for the text within the header row.

7 In the Style Name field at the top of the New Cell Style dialog, type **Table Head**.

8 From the Paragraph Style menu, choose Head 4. This paragraph style was already created in the document. Click OK.

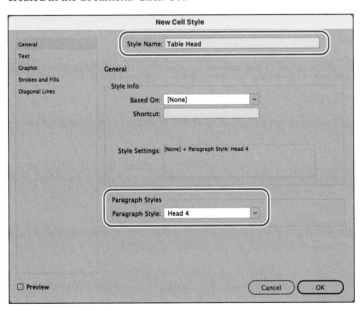

The new cell style appears in the Cell Styles panel.

9 With the header row still selected, click Table Head in the Cell Styles panel to apply it.

10 If a plus sign (+) displays next to the Table Head style (indicating that the formatting does not exactly match the style), select the entire header row, and choose Clear Overrides from the Cell Styles panel menu.

11 Choose Edit > Deselect All to see the results.

FABULOUS FLOWER TIPS¶		
#	#	#
Sunflower#	Sunny, sheltered soil#	Support stems for taller flowers#
Marigold#	Sunny, fertile soil#	Plant around tomato plants to prevent flies#
Pansy#	Full sun or dappled shade#	Deadhead to encourage more blooms#
Sweet Pea#	Sunny spot, support#	Protect from mice#

12 Choose File > Save.

Creating a table style

Now you'll create a table style that formats the overall look of the table and applies the cell style you just created to the header row.

1 Using the Type tool (T.), click anywhere in the table to select it.

2 Click the Table Styles tab in the Cell Styles panel group or choose Window > Styles > Table Styles. From the Table Styles panel menu, choose New Table Style.

3 In the Style Name field, type **Garden Table**.

4 In the Cell Styles section, select Table Head from the Header Rows menu.

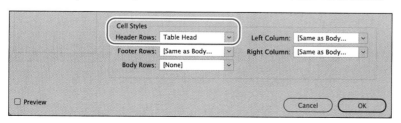

You'll now set up the table style to apply alternating rows of color to the body rows.

5 Select the Fills category on the left side of the New Table Style dialog.

6 Choose Every Other Row from the Alternating Pattern menu. The options for alternating rows appear.

7 Specify the following Alternating options in the list at the left:

- First Rows: 1
- Color: Paper

8 Specify the following Alternating options in the list at the right:

- Next Rows: 1
- Color: Green-Brightest
- Tint: 30%

9 Click OK. The new table style, Garden Table, appears in the Table Styles panel.

10 Choose Edit > Deselect All, and then choose File > Save.

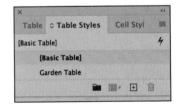

Applying a table style

▶ **Tip:** You can apply a table style when creating a new table using the Table > Create Table or Table > Convert Text To Table command.

Now you'll apply the table style you just created to the two tables in the document.

1 With the table still easily visible onscreen, select the Type tool (**T**).

2 Click to place an insertion point anywhere in the table, and choose Table > Select > Table.

3 In the Table Styles panel, click the Garden Table style. Click once in the table to see the formatting, which matches the table and cell styles you created.

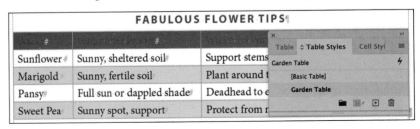

4 Double-click page 6 in the Pages panel, and then choose View > Fit Page In Window. Click to place an insertion point anywhere in the "Drop-In Gardening Clinics" table, and then choose Table > Select > Table.

5 In the Table Styles panel, click the Garden Table style. The table is reformatted with the table and cell styles you created.

6 If a plus sign (+) displays next to the Garden Table style (indicating that the formatting does not exactly match the style), choose Clear Overrides from the Table Styles panel menu. Click once in the table to see the final formatting.

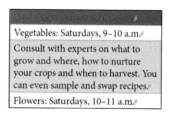

7 Choose Edit > Deselect All, and then choose File > Save.

Globally updating styles

InDesign features two ways to update paragraph, character, object, table, and cell styles. The first way is to open a style options dialog and make changes to the formatting options. The other way to update a style is to use local formatting to modify some formatting and then redefine the style based on the updated formatting. In either case, formatting is updated wherever the style is applied. In this exercise, you'll make a change to the Head 3 style to include a paragraph rule below it.

1 Double-click page 4 in the Pages panel, and then choose View > Fit Page In Window.

2 Using the Type tool (T), double-click in the "Beans" subhead at the top of the first column.

3 Choose Type > Paragraph to display the Paragraph panel. Choose Paragraph Rules from the panel menu.

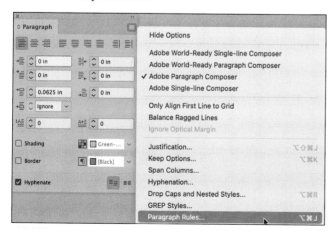

4 In the Paragraph Rules dialog, choose Rule Below from the menu at the top of the dialog, and select Rule On. Make sure that Preview is selected, and move the dialog so that you can see "Beans" on your screen.

5 Format the rule using the following settings:

 * Weight: **.5 pt**

 * Color: Red-Tomato

 * Offset: **.025 in**

Leave all other settings at their defaults.

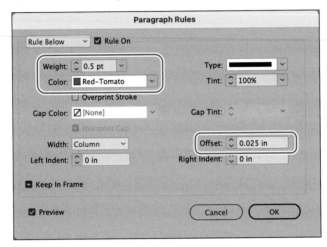

6 Click OK. A thin red line now appears below "Beans."

7 If it's not already visible, choose Type > Paragraph Styles to view the Paragraph Styles panel.

In the Paragraph Styles panel, notice that the Head 3 style is selected, indicating that it is applied to the selected text. You will also see a plus sign (+) next to the Head 3 style name. This indicates that the selected text has local formatting applied to it, which is overriding the applied style.

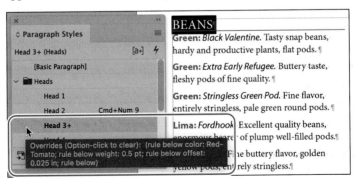

Now you'll redefine the paragraph style so that the local changes are incorporated in the paragraph style definition and automatically applied to all the headings previously formatted with the Head 3 style.

8 In the Paragraph Styles panel menu, choose Redefine Style.

The + should no longer appear next to the Head 3 style name. All headlines in the document that have been styled with Head 3 should globally update to reflect the changes you made.

9 Choose View > Fit Spread In Window to see the changes.

10 Choose Edit > Deselect All, and then choose File > Save.

Loading styles from another document

Styles are available in the document in which you create them. For consistency among documents for the same client or campaign, you can share styles between InDesign documents. In this exercise, you'll import a paragraph style and character style from the finished document 09_End.indd and apply the style to the first body paragraph on page 2.

1 Double-click page 2 in the Pages panel, and then choose View > Fit Page In Window.

2 If it's not already visible, choose Type > Paragraph Styles to view the Paragraph Styles panel.

3 Choose Load All Text Styles from the Paragraph Styles panel menu.

4 In the Open A File dialog, double-click 09_End.indd in the Lesson09 folder. The Load Styles dialog displays.

5 Click Uncheck All; you do not need to import all the styles because most already exist in this document.

▶ **Tip:** In addition to loading styles from another document, you can share paragraph and character styles among multiple documents through CC Libraries. To do this, select a style in the Paragraph Styles panel, and click Add Selected Style To My Current CC Library at the bottom of the panel. To use this style in another document, apply it from the CC Library. It is then automatically added to the document's Paragraph Styles panel.

Note: The style group name displays in front of the paragraph style name in the Load Style dialog. In this case, look for Body Text: Drop Cap Body.

6 Check the box to the left of the paragraph style Body Text: Drop Cap Body to select it. Scroll down and note that the character style that Drop Cap Body uses (Drop Cap) is automatically selected.

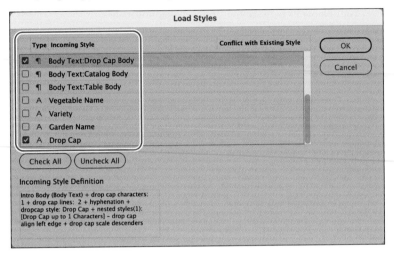

Because the selected paragraph style uses the Drop Caps And Nested Style feature to automatically apply the Drop Cap character style, this style is also selected.

7 Click OK to import the two styles.

8 Using the Type tool (**T.**), place an insertion point in the third body paragraph, which starts with "Look for your tried-and-true favorites."

9 Click the new Drop Cap Body style in the Paragraph Styles panel.

The initial "L" in "Look" becomes a light green drop cap in Myriad Pro Italic.

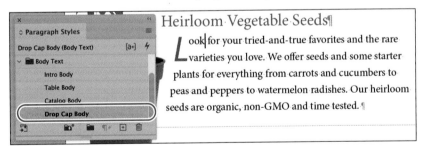

10 Choose Edit > Deselect All, and then choose File > Save.

Finishing up

As a final step, you'll preview the document in its finished state.

1 At the bottom of the Tools panel, select Preview.

2 Choose View > Fit Spread In Window.

3 Press Tab to hide all the panels and review the results of your work.

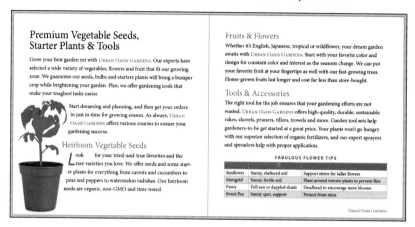

4 Press Tab again to restore the panels.

Congratulations! You have now completed this lesson.

Exploring on your own

InDesign styles are designed to streamline formatting and ensure consistency. This lesson focuses on creating styles, but you can acquire premade styles in many ways, including in InDesign templates and from CC Libraries. Once you have styles in a document, spend a few minutes fine-tuning and organizing styles so you—and users of the document—can easily find and use the styles. For longer documents, formatting text can be one of the more tedious tasks. InDesign now provides the Style Packs panel to expedite this process.

Downloading free templates with styles

Adobe provides free InDesign document templates that you can download and modify or use as is. Many of these templates include styles. If you are logged into your Creative Cloud account, visit stock.adobe.com, click Royalty-Free Templates, and download a template to explore.

Fine-tuning styles for a template

When you're creating a long document or a template to use as the basis for other documents, you want to take full advantage of all features related to styles. To fine-tune the styles further, try the following:

- Rearrange styles in the Paragraph Styles panel. For example, drag the new Drop Cap Body style into the Body Text group.

- Add keyboard shortcuts to the existing styles.

Applying styles automatically

To simplify the process of formatting text, InDesign provides paragraph-style themes in the Style Packs panel. The Style Packs feature analyzes any selected text and applies paragraph styles to headings, body paragraphs, and bulleted lists.

1 Choose File > New > Document.

2 In the New Document dialog, click Print across the top, and then click Letter.

3 Click Create.

4 Choose File > Place.

5 In the Place dialog, select 09_Gardening.docx and click Open.

6 Position the loaded text icon (⌷) in the upper-left corner where the guides intersect. For proper placement, watch for the black arrow in the loaded text icon to turn white.

7 Click to create a text frame within the page margins; the text flows into it.

8 Choose Window > Styles > Style Packs.

● **Note:** If you are logged into Creative Cloud, InDesign automatically activates any fonts needed in the paragraph styles. If the fonts are not activated, the text is highlighted in pink.

9 Click an option in the Style Packs panel to see how InDesign automatically formats the text.

10 Choose Type > Paragraph Styles to see how the paragraph styles from the selected style pack are added to the document.

11 Experiment with other style packs to see the different text formatting.

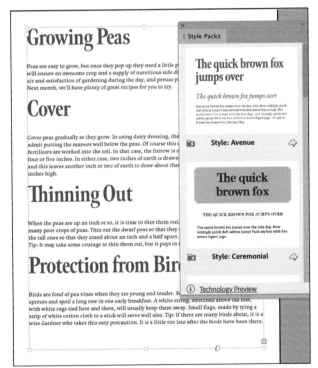

Once the base paragraph styles are applied, you can modify text formatting and update the styles.

Review questions

1 How can using object styles speed up your workflow?

2 What must you create before you can create a nested style?

3 What are the two ways to globally update a style you've applied in an InDesign document?

4 How would you import styles from another InDesign document?

5 What are the primary ways to apply styles?

Review answers

1 Object styles save time by allowing you to group formatting attributes and quickly apply them to frames and lines. If you need to update the formatting, you don't have to change each object formatted with the style individually. Instead, you can simply modify the object style to automatically update all the objects to which it is applied.

2 The two prerequisites for creating a nested style are that (1) you have first created a character style and (2) you have built a paragraph style in which to nest it.

3 InDesign offers two ways to update styles. The first is to edit the style itself by making changes to the formatting options. The other is to use local formatting to change an instance and then redefine the style based on that instance.

4 From any Styles panel (Paragraph, Object, Cell, etc.), choose Load Styles from the panel menu. Locate the InDesign document from which you want to load the styles. You can then select the styles to load.

5 To apply styles, first make a selection in the document (paragraphs, characters, objects, table cells, tables). You can then click the style name on the associated Styles panel, use the Quick Apply feature, or use a keyboard shortcut assigned to the style. Paragraph and character styles can be applied during a search-and-replace operation as well (Edit > Find/Change).

10 CREATING TABLES

Lesson overview

In this lesson, you'll learn how to do the following:

- Convert text to a table, import tables from other applications, and create tables from scratch.

- Change the number of rows and columns in a table.

- Rearrange rows and columns.

- Adjust row and column sizes.

- Format tables with strokes and fills.

- Specify repeating header rows for long tables.

- Place graphics in table cells.

- Create and apply table and cell styles.

This lesson will take about 45 minutes to complete. To get the lesson files used in this chapter, download them from the web page for this book at adobepress.com/InDesignCIB2023. For more information, see "Accessing the lesson files and Web Edition" in the Getting Started section at the beginning of this book.

Urban Oasis Gardens Summer Schedule

DAILY DROP-IN ACTIVITIES

Activity	Day	Time	Fee	
Attracting Butterflies	Su	8–10 a.m.	$10	
Illustrating Botanicals 🖋	M	noon–2 p.m.	$25	
Creating Garden Flags	T	10 a.m.–2 p.m.	$25	
Making Hummingbird Feeders	W	2–5 p.m.	$50	
Tending Flowers	Th	9–11 a.m.	$10	
Growing Edible Flowers	F	1–3 p.m.	$10	
Making and Flying Kites 🖋	Sa	8–11 a.m.	Free	

🖋 Indicates off-site activity.

With Adobe InDesign, you can easily create tables, convert text to tables, and import tables from other applications. Rich formatting options—including headers, footers, and alternating row and column patterns—can be saved as table styles and cell styles.

Getting started

In this lesson, you'll work on a fictional botanic gardens activity flyer designed to be attractive, easy to use, and easy to revise. You'll convert text to a table and then format the table using options in the Table menu and various panels. The table will include header rows that repeat when the table flows across multiple pages. Finally, you will create a table style and a cell style so that you can apply formatting quickly and consistently to other tables.

● **Note:** If you have not already downloaded the project files for this lesson to your computer from your Account page, make sure to do so now. See "Getting Started" at the beginning of the book.

1 To ensure that the preferences and default settings of your InDesign program match those used in this lesson, move the InDesign Defaults file to a different folder following the procedure in "Saving and restoring the InDesign Defaults file" on pages 3–4.

2 Start InDesign.

3 The InDesign Start screen displays. Click Open at the left. (If the Start screen does not display, choose File > Open from the InDesign menu bar.)

4 Open the 10_Start.indd file in the Lesson10 folder, located inside the Lessons folder within the InDesignCIB folder on your hard drive.

5 Choose File > Save As, rename the file **10_Tables.indd**, and save it in the Lesson10 folder.

6 To ensure that the panels and menu commands match those used in this lesson, choose Window > Workspace > [Advanced], and then choose Window > Workspace > Reset Advanced.

● **Note:** To better view the interface onscreen or in print, the screen captures in this book reflect the Medium Light interface rather than the default setting of Medium Dark. In addition, some screen captures illustrate User Interface Scaling for a closer look at interface elements. You can modify interface settings in Preferences.

7 If you want to see what the finished document looks like, open the 10_End.indd file in the same folder. You can leave this document open to act as a guide as you work.

Working with tables

InDesign tables are grids of individual cells set in vertical columns and horizontal rows. To create a table, you can convert existing text into a table, insert a new table at an insertion point in text (which anchors the table in the text), create a new freestanding table, or import a table from another application (such as Microsoft Excel).

You will use the Type tool to edit and format tables. Controls for formatting tables are in the Tables menu, Tables panel, Properties panel, and Control panel. Throughout this lesson, you will experiment with different options for selecting table elements and modifying tables. Once you become accustomed to working with tables, you can use the options that work best for you.

Converting text to a table

Often, the text for a table already exists in the form of tab-delimited text, in which the columns of information are separated by tab characters and the rows of information are separated by paragraph returns. In this case, the InDesign document was received from the botanic gardens in its current tab-delimited state. You will select this text and convert it to a table.

1 Choose View > Actual Size and scroll as necessary to better see the text.

2 Using the Type tool (**T**.), click in the text frame starting with the words "DAILY DROP-IN ACTIVITIES." Choose Edit > Select All.

Note: As you work through this lesson, change the zoom level to suit your screen size and vision.

DAILY DROP-IN ACTIVITIES
Attracting Butterflies Su » 8–10 a.m. » $10
Illustrating Botanicals M » noon–2 p.m. » $25
Creating Garden Flags » T » 10 a.m.–2 p.m. $25
Making Hummingbird Feeders » W » 2–5 p.m. » $50
Tending Flowers » Th » 9–11 a.m. » $10
Making and Flying Kites » Sa » 8–11 a.m. » Free
Growing Edible Flowers » F » 1–3 p.m. » $10

3 Choose Table > Convert Text To Table.

In the Convert Text To Table dialog, you will indicate how the selected text is currently separated. Because Hidden Characters (Type menu) is selected, you can see that the columns of information are separated by tabs (》) and that the rows are separated by paragraph returns (¶).

4 From the Column Separator menu, choose Tab. From the Row Separator menu, choose Paragraph.

Note: If you do not see the paragraph returns, tabs, and spaces, choose Type > Show Hidden Characters.

▶ Tip: Microsoft Word users often align columns onscreen with tabs, including entering multiple tabs between columns of data. While this may visually align the text in the Word document, it will result in extra columns and data in the wrong place. Take a look at the tab-delimited text before converting it to a table. If you spot instances of two tabs (» ») in a row, you can delete the second tab or use Find/Change to search for two instances of a tab and replace them with one tab.

5　Confirm that Table Style is set to [No Table Style], and then click OK.

The new table is automatically anchored in the frame that contained the text.

DAILY DROP-IN ACTIVITIES#	#	#	#
Attracting Butterflies#	Su#	8–10 a.m.#	$10#
Illustrating Botanicals#	M#	noon–2 p.m.#	$25#
Creating Garden Flags#	T#	10 a.m.–2 p.m.#	$25#
Making Hummingbird Feeders#	W#	2–5 p.m.#	$50#
Tending Flowers#	Th#	9–11 a.m.#	$10#
Making and Flying Kites#	Sa#	8–11 a.m.#	Free#
Growing Edible Flowers#	F#	1–3 p.m.#	$10#
#	#	#	#

6　Choose File > Save.

Changing rows and columns

Even when you start with source data from a client, you will often need to make changes such as adding a few rows, rearranging text, and editing content to complete the table. Once a table is created, you can easily add rows and columns, delete rows and columns, merge cells, rearrange rows, adjust row height and column width, and specify text inset for cells. In this section, you will complete the table content so that you know its size before you start formatting it.

Adding and deleting rows

You can add rows above or below a selected row. The controls for adding and deleting columns work the same as for adding and deleting rows. Here, you will add a row to the top of the table to contain the column descriptions.

1　Using the Type tool (**T**), click in the first row of the table, which starts with "DAILY," to activate a cell. You can click in any cell.

2　Choose Table > Insert > Row.

3 In the Insert Row(s) dialog, type **1** in the Number field, and click Below. Click OK to add the row.

4 Click in the first new cell and type **Activity**. To add column heads to the remaining cells, click with the Type tool in each empty cell, or press the Tab key to navigate from cell to cell. Type the following text in each cell, as shown:

- Second cell: **Day**
- Third cell: **Time**
- Fourth cell: **Fee**

DAILY DROP-IN ACTIVITIES#	#	#	#
Activity#	**Day**#	**Time**#	**Fee**#
Attracting Butterflies#	Su#	8–10 a.m.#	$10#
Illustrating Botanicals#	M#	noon–2 p.m.#	$25#
Creating Garden Flags#	T#	10 a.m.–2 p.m.#	$25#
Making Hummingbird Feeders#	W#	2–5 p.m.#	$50#
Tending Flowers#	Th#	9–11 a.m.#	$10#
Making and Flying Kites#	Sa#	8–11 a.m.#	Free#
Growing Edible Flowers#	F#	1–3 p.m.#	$10#
#	#	#	#

5 Using the Type tool, click in the first cell of the second row, and then drag to the right to select all cells in the row with the new column headings.

6 Choose Type > Paragraph Styles. If necessary, click the arrow next to the Table Styles group to open it.

7 Click Table Column Heads in the Paragraph Styles panel. Choose Type > Paragraph Styles to close the panel.

8 Click in the cell containing the word "Fee" to activate the cell.

You will insert a column to the right of this column to contain images.

9 Choose Table > Insert > Column.

10 In the Insert Column(s) dialog, type **1** in the Number field, and click Right. Click OK to add the column.

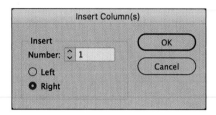

The table is now wider than the frame and the page; you will resolve that later.

DAILY DROP-IN ACTIVITIES	#		#		#		#	
Activity	**Day**		**Time**		**Fee**			
Attracting Butterflies	Su		8–10 a.m.		$10			
Illustrating Botanicals	M		noon–2 p.m.		$25			
Creating Garden Flags	T		10 a.m.–2 p.m.		$25			
Making Hummingbird Feeders	W		2–5 p.m.		$50			
Tending Flowers	Th		9–11 a.m.		$10			
Making and Flying Kites	Sa		8–11 a.m.		Free			
Growing Edible Flowers	F		1–3 p.m.		$10			
#	#		#		#			

11 Choose File > Save.

Deleting rows

You can delete selected rows and columns. Here, you will delete the blank row at the bottom of the table.

1 Using the Type tool (**T**), move the pointer over the left edge of the last row of the table until it appears as a horizontal arrow (→). Click to select the row.

Making and Flying Kites	Sa	8–11 a.m.	Free	#	
Growing Edible Flowers	F	1–3 p.m.	$10		
→		#	#		

2 Choose Table > Delete > Row.

3 Choose Edit > Deselect All, and then choose File > Save.

► **Tip:** To activate a row or column to delete, click in it. To select multiple rows to delete, position the Type tool on the left edge of the table until the arrow displays; then drag to select the rows. To select multiple columns to delete, position the Type tool on the top edge of the table until the arrow displays; then drag to select the columns.

Rearranging rows and columns

While working on a table, you may find that information works better in a different order, or you may discover a mistake. In that case, you can select and drag rows or columns to a new location. The rows in this table are in day-of-the-week order, but the Friday row is in the wrong location.

1 Locate the last row of the table, which starts with the word "Growing".

2 Using the Type tool (T.), move the pointer over the left edge of the "Growing" row until it appears as a horizontal arrow (➡).

3 Click to select the row, and then release the mouse button.

 The row is selected so that you can drag it up or down within the table.

4 Click and hold in the selected row, and then drag the "Growing Edible Flowers" row up and drop it just under the "Tending Flowers" row. A bold blue line indicates where the row will be inserted.

Making Hummingbird Feeders	W	2–5 p.m.	$50		
Tending Flowers	Th	9–11 a.m.	$10		
Making and Flying Kites	Sa	8–11 a.m.	Free		
Growing Edible Flowers	F	1–3 p.m.	$10		

5 Choose Edit > Deselect All, and then choose File > Save.

Adjusting column widths, row heights, and text placement

Columns and rows, and the way text fits within them, often need fine-tuning according to the content and the design. By default, table cells expand vertically to fit their content—so if you keep typing within a cell, it gets taller. You can, however, specify a fixed row height or column width. Or you can have InDesign create columns or rows of equal size within the table.

In this exercise, you will manually adjust the column widths, and then you will modify how the text fits within the cells.

1 Adjust the zoom as necessary to view the table.

2 Using the Type tool (T.), point at a vertical divider between any two columns. When the double-arrow icon (↔) displays, drag to the left or right to resize the column.

3 Choose Edit > Undo. Experiment with resizing columns and rows a few more times to get a feel for the tool. Choose Edit > Undo after each move. As you drag, keep an eye on the horizontal and vertical rulers on the document window.

▶ **Tip:** To drag and drop rows or columns, you must select the entire row or column. To drag a copy of a row or column to a new position, press Alt (Windows) or Option (macOS) while dragging.

4 Place the final columns by dragging the right edge of each column, using the horizontal ruler at the top of the window as a guide.

- Activity column: 3.5"

- Day column: 4.25"

- Time column: 5.5"

- Fee column: 6.25"

- Blank image column: 7.75"

A guide on the horizontal ruler indicates the placement of the right edge of the column.

DAILY DROP-IN ACTIVITIES	Activity	Day	Time	Fee
Attracting Butterflies	Su	8–10 a.m.	$10	
Illustrating Botanicals	M	noon–2 p.m.	$25	
Creating Garden Flags	T	10 a.m.–2 p.m.	$25	
Making Hummingbird Feeders	W	2–5 p.m.	$50	
Tending Flowers	Th	9–11 a.m.	$10	
Growing Edible Flowers	F	1–3 p.m.	$10	
Making and Flying Kites	Sa	8–11 a.m.	Free	

DAILY DROP-IN ACTIVITIES	Activity	Day	Time	Fee
Attracting Butterflies	Su	8–10 a.m.	$10	
Illustrating Botanicals	M	noon–2 p.m.	$25	
Creating Garden Flags	T	10 a.m.–2 p.m.	$25	
Making Hummingbird Feeders	W	2–5 p.m.	$50	
Tending Flowers	Th	9–11 a.m.	$10	
Growing Edible Flowers	F	1–3 p.m.	$10	
Making and Flying Kites	Sa	8–11 a.m.	Free	

Now that the column widths better fit the text, you will add a little space around the text in the cells. In this case, you will change the entire table, but you can modify selected cells only.

5 Choose Window > Type & Tables > Table to open the Table panel.

6 Click anywhere in the table, and choose Table > Select > Table.

7 Confirm that Make All Settings The Same (![icon]) is selected to increase the inset on all four edges of each cell. Type **.125 in** inside the Top Cell Inset field (![icon]), and press Enter (Windows) or Return (macOS).

▶**Tip:** You can click the arrows (![icon]) next to any field to increase or decrease its value.

8 With the table still selected, click Align Center (![icon]) in the Table panel.

This centers the text vertically within each cell.

See the three cell alignment options at right: Align Top, Align Center, and Align Bottom.

9 Click anywhere in the table to deselect the cells. Drag the Table panel to the dock so you can see more of the page.

10 Choose File > Save.

Merging cells

You can merge adjacent selected cells to produce a single cell. Here, you will merge the cells in the top row so that the header "DAILY DROP-IN ACTIVITIES" spans the table.

1 Choose View > Fit Page In Window or adjust the zoom level for comfortable viewing.

2 Using the Type tool (T.), click in the first cell of the first row, and then drag to select all the cells in the row.

3 Choose Table > Merge Cells. Click the pasteboard to deselect the table.

▶**Tip:** The Properties and Control panels both have a Merge Cells icon (![icon]) for easy access.

4 Choose File > Save.

DAILY DROP-IN ACTIVITIES#				
Activity#	**Day**#	**Time**#	**Fee**#	#
Attracting Butterflies#	Su#	8–10 a.m.#	$10#	#
Illustrating Botanicals#	M#	noon–2 p.m.#	$25#	#

Importing tables

Placing tables from Word or Excel

● **Note:** Importing a table is not part of completing the lesson document. If you want to experiment with importing a table, you can try it with your own Excel or Word file.

InDesign can import tables from other applications, including Microsoft Word and Microsoft Excel. To import a table, follow these steps:

1 Using the Type tool (T), click to place an insertion point in a text frame.

2 Choose File > Place.

3 In the lower-left corner of the Place dialog, select Show Import Options.

4 Select a Word file (.doc or .docx) that contains a table, or select an Excel file (.xls or .xlsx).

5 Click Open.

6 Use the Import Options dialog to specify how to handle the formatting in Word tables. For Excel files, you can specify what worksheet and cell range to import along with how to handle the formatting.

The Import Options dialog for specifying the spreadsheet, cells, and formatting to import.

Linking to tables

● **Note:** For tables to retain their InDesign-applied formatting when an imported file is updated, all cells in the InDesign table must be formatted with table and cell styles. Header and footer rows must be reapplied when updating a link.

When you place a table, you can create a link to the external file. Then, if you update the Word or Excel file, you can easily update that information in the InDesign document. To link to imported tables, follow these steps:

1 Choose Edit > Preferences > File Handling (Windows) or InDesign > Preferences > File Handling (macOS).

2 In the Links section, select Create Links When Placing Text And Spreadsheet Files, and then click OK.

3 If the data in the source file changes, use the Links panel to update the table in the InDesign document.

Formatting a table

Formatting a table with a border and cell strokes helps separate the information. The border is a stroke that lies outside the entire table. Cell strokes are lines within the table that set the individual cells apart from each other. InDesign includes many easy-to-use formatting options for tables. You can use these options to make tables attractive and help them convey information to readers. In this section, you will specify fills and strokes for the table.

Adding a fill pattern

To achieve effects such as shading every other row, InDesign provides fill patterns for both rows and columns. You can specify where the pattern starts, which allows you to exclude any header rows. As you add, delete, and move rows and columns, the pattern updates automatically. You will add a fill to every other row in this table.

1 Using the Type tool (T.), click anywhere in the table to activate it.

2 Choose Table > Table Options > Alternating Fills.

3 From the Alternating Pattern menu, choose Every Other Row. Leave the default settings for the remaining options.

4 Click OK. Every other row now has a gray background.

DAILY DROP-IN ACTIVITIES				
Activity	Day	Time	Fee	
Attracting Butterflies	Su	8–10 a.m.	$10	
Illustrating Botanicals	M	noon–2 p.m.	$25	
Creating Garden Flags	T	10 a.m.–2 p.m.	$25	

5 Choose File > Save.

Applying a fill color to cells

An entire table can have a fill color, and each cell can have its own fill color. Using the Type tool, you can drag to select any contiguous cells to apply a fill color. In this section, you will apply a fill color to the header row.

1 Using the Type tool (**T**), move the pointer over the left edge of the "DAILY DROP-IN ACTIVITIES" row until it appears as a horizontal arrow (➜). Click to select the row.

2 Choose Window > Color > Swatches.

► **Tip:** You can use the Fill box on the Control panel to apply color to cells as well.

3 Select the Fill box (▨) in the Swatches panel, and then click the Purple-Cool swatch.

4 Drag the Tint slider to 50%, and then choose Edit > Deselect All to view the colors.

5 Choose Window > Color > Swatches to close the Swatches panel, and then choose File > Save.

Editing cell strokes

Cell strokes are the lines around individual cells. You can remove or change the stroke for selected cells or for the entire table. In this section, you will remove the horizontal strokes because the alternating pattern provides enough delineation.

1 Using the Type tool (**T**), click anywhere in the table, and then choose Table > Select > Table.

2 Locate the proxy preview (▦) in the center of the Control panel (at the top of the screen).

Each horizontal and vertical line in the proxy represents a row stroke, column stroke, or border stroke. You can click the lines to toggle the selection on (blue) or off (black). Toggling a line to the on position selects that particular stroke for formatting.

3 Click all three horizontal lines in the proxy to select them. Ensure that all horizontal lines (and no vertical lines) are selected (toggled on) on the proxy. The selected lines are blue.

4 Type **0** in the Control panel's Stroke field. Press Enter or Return.

5 Click all three vertical lines in the proxy to select them. Deselect the horizontal lines.

6 Select 0.5 pt from the Stroke menu on the Control panel.

Specifying no (0) stroke for the horizontal lines (left) and 0.5 pt stroke for vertical lines (right). Note the selected strokes on the proxy are blue.

7 Choose Edit > Deselect All to see the results.

DAILY DROP-IN ACTIVITIES				
Activity	**Day**	**Time**	**Fee**	
Attracting Butterflies	Su	8–10 a.m.	$10	
Illustrating Botanicals	M	noon–2 p.m.	$25	
Creating Garden Flags	T	10 a.m.–2 p.m.	$25	
Making Hummingbird Feeders	W	2–5 p.m.	$50	
Tending Flowers	Th	9–11 a.m.	$10	
Growing Edible Flowers	F	1–3 p.m.	$10	
Making and Flying Kites	Sa	8–11 a.m.	Free	

8 Choose File > Save.

Adding table borders

A table border is a stroke around the entire table. As with other strokes, you can customize the border's width, style, color, and more. In this section, you will apply a border to the table.

1 Using the Type tool (T), click anywhere in the table.

2 Choose Table > Select > Table.

3 Choose Table > Table Options > Table Setup. This opens the Table Options dialog and displays the Table Setup tab.

4 On the Table Setup tab, in the Table Border section, choose 0.5 pt from the Weight menu.

5 Click OK, and then choose Edit > Deselect All.

6 Choose View > Screen Mode > Preview to see the results of your formatting.

7 Choose View > Screen Mode > Normal, and then choose File > Save.

Adding graphics to table cells

▶ **Tip:** To format a cell or convert a cell's content, you must first select the cell. To select a graphic cell with the Type tool, drag across the graphic cell.

You can use InDesign to create effective tables that combine text, photographs, and illustrations. By default, table cells are essentially small text frames, but you can convert a text cell to a graphic cell. At that point, the cell essentially functions as a graphics frame whose dimensions are governed by the table. In this exercise, you will add photos to some of the course descriptions.

Converting cells to graphic cells

First, you will convert a selected cell to a graphic cell using the Table menu and the Table panel. Later, you will see how to automatically convert a cell to a graphic cell by placing an image.

1 Using the Type tool (T), click inside the far-right cell of the table's first body row (the "Attracting Butterflies" row).

2 Choose Table > Select > Cell to select the cell.

3 With the cell selected, choose Table > Convert Cell To Graphic Cell.

A graphic cell selected with the Selection tool

4 Click inside the far-right cell in the third body row (the row describing "Creating Garden Flags") to select it.

5 If necessary, choose Window > Type & Tables > Table to display the Table panel.

6 Choose Convert Cell To Graphic Cell from the Table panel menu.

▶ **Tip:** You can convert a text cell to a graphic cell simply by placing an image in it. However, if you are creating a template that indicates where images should be placed, it would be helpful to the template users to convert the cells to graphic cells.

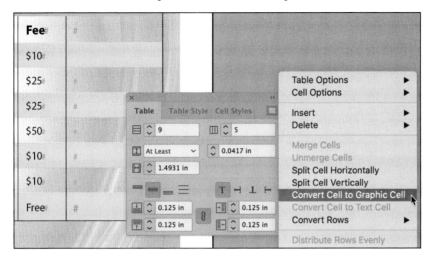

Placing images in graphic cells

Now, you will place images in the two cells converted to graphic cells. You will then automatically convert two text cells to graphic cells as you place images.

1 Using the Selection tool (▶), select the new graphic cell in the "Attracting Butterflies" row.

2 Choose File > Place. In the lower-left corner of the Place dialog, select Replace Selected Item if necessary.

3 Navigate to the Lesson10 folder, select the Butterfly.jpg file, and then click Open.

4 To fit the cell to the image, choose Object > Fitting > Fit Frame To Content.

● **Note:** If necessary, select Show Import Options in the Place dialog.

▶ **Tip:** Use options in the Object > Fitting menu, such as Fit Content Proportionally, to adjust the image size and placement within the cell.

DAILY DROP-IN ACTIVITIES

Activity	Day	Time	Fee	
Attracting Butterflies	Su	8–10 a.m.	$10	

5 Select the new graphic cell in the "Creating Garden Flags" row.

6 Choose File > Place. In the Place dialog, select the GardenFlag.jpg file in the Lesson10 folder, and click Open.

7 To fit the cell to the image, use the keyboard shortcut for Fit Frame To Content: Ctrl+Alt+C (Windows) or Command+Option+C (macOS).

8 Choose File > Place. In the Place dialog, select the WateringCan.jpg file. Then, Ctrl-click (Windows) or Command-click (macOS) the Kite.jpg file to load the pointer with both the WateringCan.jpg and Kite.jpg files. Click Open.

● **Note:** If you place the wrong image in a cell, choose Edit > Undo and try again.

9 Click the loaded graphics icon (🖼) in the last cell of the "Making and Flying Kites" row.

10 Click the loaded graphics icon in the last cell of the "Tending Flowers" row.

11 Using the Selection tool, click the image of the watering can and fit the cell to the image using the keyboard shortcut in step 7 or the Object > Fitting > Fit Frame To Content command. Repeat the process for the kite image.

Tending Flowers	Th	9–11 a.m.	$10	
Growing Edible Flowers	F	1–3 p.m.	$10	
Making and Flying Kites	Sa	8–11 a.m.	Free	

12 Choose Edit > Deselect All, and then choose File > Save.

Adjusting the row heights

The images are 1 inch in height, so you will now make all the table body rows 1 inch high.

● **Note:** As you work through this exercise, remember to change the zoom level to suit your screen size and vision.

1 If necessary, choose Window > Type & Tables > Table to open the Table panel.

2 Using the Type tool (T), move the pointer over the left edge of the first body row (starting with "Attracting Butterflies") until it appears as a horizontal arrow (➜).

3 Drag from the first table body row, starting with "Attracting Butterflies," to the last table row, ending with "Free".

4 With the table body rows selected, choose Exactly from the Row Height menu in the Table panel. Then, type **1 in** inside the Row Height field to the right of the menu. Press Enter or Return.

5 Choose Edit > Deselect All to see the results.

6 Choose File > Save.

DAILY DROP-IN ACTIVITIES				
Activity	Day	Time	Fee	
Attracting Butterflies	Su	8–10 a.m.	$10	
Illustrating Botanicals	M	noon–2 p.m.	$25	
Creating Garden Flags	T	10 a.m.–2 p.m.	$25	
Making Hummingbird Feeders	W	2–5 p.m.	$50	
Tending Flowers	Th	9–11 a.m.	$10	
Growing Edible Flowers	F	1–3 p.m.	$10	
Making and Flying Kites	Sa	8–11 a.m.	Free	

Anchoring graphics in table cells

You can have both text and graphics in a cell by anchoring images in the text. In this exercise, you will place a leaf icon next to the classes that are held off-campus.

1 Zoom to see the leaf icon in the left margin of the left page.

2 Using the Selection tool (▶), select the leaf icon immediately to the left of the header row.

3 Choose Edit > Cut.

4 Select the Type tool (T), or double-click inside the table to automatically switch to the Type tool.

▶ **Tip:** Objects that are anchored in text will flow with the text as it's edited and reformatted.

5 In the second body row of the table, click immediately after "Illustrating Botanicals" and type a space.

6 Choose Edit > Paste.

7 Click the Type tool after "Making and Flying Kites," type a space, and then choose Edit > Paste.

8 Choose File > Save.

Creating a header row

▶ **Tip:** When you edit text in a header row, the text is automatically updated in other instances of the header row. You can edit the text in the table's original header row only; other instances of the header are locked.

A table's name and the column headings are often formatted to stand out from the rest of the table. To do this, you can select and format the cells that contain the header information. This header information may need to repeat if the table flows across multiple pages. With InDesign, you can specify header and footer rows that repeat when a table continues to the next column, frame, or page. Here, you will select the first two rows of the table and specify them as header rows that repeat.

1 Choose View > Fit Page In Window or adjust the zoom to your comfort level.

2 Using the Type tool (T), move the pointer over the left edge of the first row until it appears as a horizontal arrow (→).

3 Click to select the entire first row, and then drag to include the second row. You will have selected "DAILY" through "Fee."

DAILY DROP-IN ACTIVITIES				
Activity	Day	Time	Fee	
Attracting Butterflies	Su	8–10 a.m.	$10	

4 With the two rows still selected, choose Table > Convert Rows > To Header.

5 Click the Type tool in the last row of the table.

6 Choose Table > Insert > Row.

7 In the Insert Row(s) dialog, type **4** in the Number field, and click Below. Click OK to add the rows.

8 Choose Layout > Next Page to view the table on page 2. Notice that the continuation of the table has the same header rows.

● **Note:** You can use these new blank rows to practice typing text in cells. Remember to use the Type tool, press Tab to jump to the next cell, and press Shift+Tab to go back to the previous cell.

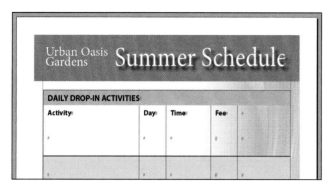

9 Choose Layout > Previous Page to return to page 1, and then choose File > Save.

Creating and applying table and cell styles

To quickly and consistently apply formatting to tables, you can create table styles and cell styles. A table style applies to the entire table, whereas cell styles can be applied to selected cells, rows, and columns. Here, you will create a table style and a cell style so that you can quickly apply the formatting in other tables.

Creating table and cell styles

In this exercise, you will create a table style for the basic table formatting and a cell style for the header rows. Rather than specify formatting for the styles, you will simply create styles based on the formatting of the table.

1 Using the Type tool (**T**), click anywhere in the table on page 1.

2 Choose Window > Styles > Table Styles, and then choose New Table Style from the panel menu.

▶ **Tip:** The Table panel is grouped with the Table Styles and Cell Styles panels by default.

3 Name the style **Activity Table** in the Style Name field. Notice that all the table formatting you applied is listed in the Style Settings area.

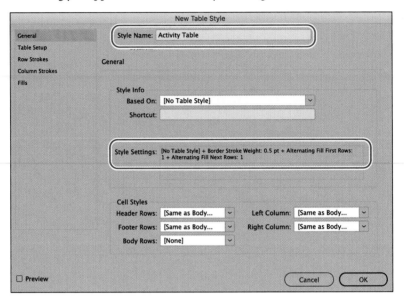

4 Click OK. The new style appears in the Table Styles panel.

5 Using the Type tool, click in the first row of the table, which says "DAILY DROP-IN ACTIVITIES."

6 Choose Window > Styles > Cell Styles, and then click Create New Style (⊞) at the bottom of the panel.

7 Double-click the new Cell Style 1 to open the Cell Style Options dialog. Name the style **Table Header** in the Style Name field.

You will now specify a different paragraph style for the text in cells with the Table Header style applied.

8 From the Paragraph Style menu, select Table Head. This is the paragraph style already applied to the text in the header rows.

▶ **Tip:** To automate formatting, you can specify a paragraph style for header rows within a table style.

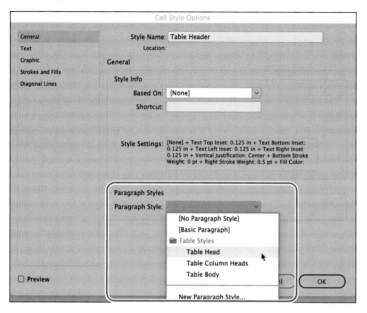

9 Click OK.

10 Choose File > Save.

Applying table and cell styles

Now, you will apply the styles to the table. To make global changes to table formatting later, you can simply edit the table or cell styles.

1 Using the Type tool (T), click anywhere in the table.

2 Click the Activity Table style in the Table Styles panel.

3 Using the Type tool, click in the first header row of the table. Choose Table > Select > Row to select the row.

4 In the Cell Styles panel, note that the Table Header style is applied. To apply a style, you simply click its name.

As a final step, you'll preview the flyer in its current state. If you were going to complete this flyer, you might enter data into the table cells in the blank rows on page 2 and add more rows as necessary.

5 Choose Edit > Deselect All, and then choose View > Fit Page In Window.

6 Select Preview from the Screen Mode button at the bottom of the Tools panel, and then press Tab to close all panels.

7 Choose File > Save.

Congratulations! You have now completed this lesson.

Exploring on your own

Now that you're skilled in the basics of working with tables in InDesign, you can experiment with creating a new, freestanding table.

▶ **Tip:** If you click the table creation pointer between column guides on the page, the new table will span the width of the column.

1 Navigate to the bottom of page 2.

2 Choose Table > Create Table, and enter the number of rows and columns you want. Select an option from the Table Style menu, if you prefer. Click OK.

3 Drag the table creation pointer (⊞) anywhere on the page. When you release the mouse button, InDesign creates a table that matches the dimensions of the rectangle you draw.

4 Using the Type tool (T), click the insertion point in the first cell and then type. Use the arrow keys on the keyboard to navigate among the cells.

5 To convert the table back to text, select it and choose Table > Convert Table To Text. By default, tabs separate what were previously columns and paragraph breaks into separate rows; you can also modify these options.

Review questions

1 What are the advantages of creating InDesign tables rather than creating the look with rules, frames, tabs, and the like?

2 How can you ensure that a table's title and column headings repeat if a table continues on multiple pages?

3 What tool is used most frequently when you work with tables?

4 How can you put graphics in table cells?

Review answers

1 Tables give you much more flexibility and are far easier to format. In a table, text can wrap within a cell, so you don't have to add extra lines to accommodate cells that contain a lot of text. Also, you can assign styles to selected cells, rows, and columns—including character styles and even paragraph styles—because each cell functions like a separate text frame.

2 Select the heading rows you want to repeat and then choose Table > Convert Rows > To Header. You can also repeat footer rows using Table > Convert Rows > To Footer.

3 The Type tool must be selected to work with a table. You can use other tools to work with the graphics within table cells, but to work with the table itself, such as selecting rows or columns, inserting text or graphics, adjusting table dimensions, and so forth, you use the Type tool.

4 You can select a cell with the Type tool, select Table > Convert Cell To Graphic Cell, and then use File > Place to import a graphic. If you simply select a cell and import a graphic through File > Place, the cell is converted automatically to a graphic cell. Another way to add a graphic to a cell is to anchor one in the text inside the cell.

11 IMPORTING AND MODIFYING GRAPHICS

Lesson overview

In this lesson, you'll learn how to do the following:

- Distinguish between vector and bitmap graphics.

- Manage imported graphic files using the Links panel.

- Adjust the display quality of graphics.

- Import Adobe Photoshop and Adobe Illustrator graphics using different techniques.

- Use various sizing and fitting techniques.

- Work with different types of dropped backgrounds.

- Adjust the appearance of graphics by manipulating paths and layers.

- Create an anchored graphics frame that flows with text.

- Wrap text around graphics.

- Fill type with a graphic.

- Create and use libraries of objects.

This lesson will take about 75 minutes to complete. To get the lesson files used in this chapter, download them from the web page for this book at adobepress.com/InDesignCIB2023. For more information, see "Accessing the lesson files and Web Edition" in the Getting Started section at the beginning of this book.

Adobe InDesign makes it easy to enhance your document with photographs and artwork imported from Adobe Photoshop, Adobe Illustrator, and other graphics applications. If these imported graphics change, InDesign can notify you that a newer version of a graphic is available. You can update or replace imported graphics at any time.

Getting started

In this lesson, you'll work on a three-panel folding brochure for a CD by importing, manipulating, and managing graphics from Photoshop and Illustrator. The insert is designed so that after printing and folding, it fits into a CD case.

This lesson includes steps that you can perform using Photoshop if you have it installed on your computer.

● **Note:** If you have not already downloaded the project files for this lesson to your computer from your Account page, make sure to do so now. See "Getting Started" at the beginning of the book.

1 To ensure that the preferences and default settings of your InDesign program match those used in this lesson, move the InDesign Defaults file to a different folder following the procedure in "Saving and restoring the InDesign Defaults file" on pages 3–4.

2 Start InDesign. Choose File > Open, and open the 11_Start.indd file in the Lesson11 folder, located inside the Lessons folder within the InDesignCIB folder on your hard drive. A message appears saying that the document contains links to sources that have been modified.

3 Click Don't Update Links. You will fix the modified links later in the lesson.

4 If necessary, close the Links panel so that it doesn't obscure your view of the page. (The Links panel opens automatically whenever you open an InDesign document that contains missing or modified links.)

● **Note:** To better view the interface onscreen or in print, the screen captures in this book reflect the Medium Light interface rather than the default setting of Medium Dark. In addition, some screen captures illustrate User Interface Scaling for a closer look at interface elements. You can modify interface settings in Preferences.

5 To ensure that the panels and menu commands match those used in this lesson, choose Window > Workspace > [Advanced], and then choose Window > Workspace > Reset Advanced.

6 To see what the finished document looks like, open the 11_End.indd file in the same folder. If you prefer, you can leave the document open as you work to act as a guide. If you leave it open, choose 11_Start.indd from the Window menu or click the 11_Start.indd document tab to return to that document.

7 Choose File > Save As, rename the file **11_cdinsert.indd**, and save it in the Lesson11 folder.

Adding graphics from other programs

InDesign supports many common graphic file formats. While this means that you can use graphics that were created using a wide range of applications, InDesign works best with other Adobe professional graphics applications, such as Photoshop, Illustrator, and Acrobat. For example, some features of InDesign are available with these file formats that are not available with others.

By default, imported graphics are linked to an InDesign document rather than embedded, which means that InDesign displays a preview of the graphic file in your layout without actually copying the entire graphic file into the InDesign document. Updating a linked file that has been modified maintains the current location and settings for the graphic file and replaces the preview image in InDesign with the updated graphic's preview.

There are four major advantages to linking graphic files. First, it reduces the size of InDesign documents because they don't need to include the data for embedded images. Second, you can edit a linked graphic in the application you used to create it and then simply update the link in the InDesign Links panel. Third, it enables everyone using a graphic to be alerted when that graphic has changed. Fourth, it saves disk space.

All linked graphics and text files are listed in the Links panel (Window > Links), which provides buttons and commands for managing links. When you print an InDesign document or export a document as an Adobe Portable Document Format (PDF) file, InDesign uses the links to produce the highest level of quality available from the original, externally stored versions of the placed graphics.

● **Note:** As you work through the lesson, move panels around or change the magnification to a level that works best for you. For more information, see "Changing the magnification of a document" in Lesson 1, "Introducing the Workspace."

Comparing vector and pixel-based graphics

The drawing tools in Adobe InDesign and Adobe Illustrator create vector graphics, which are made up of shapes based on mathematical expressions, like plotting points on a graph. Vector graphics consist of smooth lines that retain their clarity when resized. They are appropriate for illustrations, charts and graphs, type, and graphics such as logos. Vector graphics can be scaled to any size with no loss of quality.

Pixel-based images (also called "bitmap" or "raster" graphics) are made up of a grid of pixels and are typically created with digital cameras and then modified using an image-editing application, such as Photoshop, or created directly in Photoshop. In working with pixel-based images, you edit pixels rather than objects, points, or shapes. Pixel-based graphics are appropriate for continuous-tone images, such as photographs and artwork created in painting applications. Typically, raster images are larger in file size than a vector graphic of similar dimensions. A disadvantage of

pixel-based graphics is that they lose definition and appear "jagged" when enlarged. In other words, pixel-based graphics *do* lose quality when enlarged.

Logo drawn as vector art (left) and rasterized as 300 dpi bitmap art (right).

In general, use vector-drawing tools to create art or type with clean lines, such as a logo, which might be used small on a business card and very large on a poster. You can create vector artwork using the InDesign drawing tools, or you may prefer to take advantage of the wider range of vector-drawing tools available in Illustrator. Use Photoshop to create images that have the soft edges of painted or photographic art, to retouch or alter photographs, and to apply special effects to artwork.

Managing links to imported files

● **Note:** By default, InDesign does not create links to imported text files and spreadsheet files. You can change this behavior in the File Handling area of the Preferences dialog by selecting Create Links When Placing Text And Spreadsheet Files.

When you opened the lesson file, you saw an alert message about problems with the linked files. You'll resolve those issues using the Links panel, which provides complete information about the status of all linked text and graphic files in a document.

You can use the Links panel to manage placed graphics and text files in many ways. For example, you can update graphic and text files that have been modified since they were placed, and you can replace graphic and text files with different files.

Identifying imported images

To identify some of the graphics that have already been imported into the document, you'll use two different techniques involving the Links panel. Later in this lesson, you'll also use the Links panel to edit and update imported graphics.

● **Note:** The page order of this file is set up to show how the pages will fold. The pattern is the same as the trifold template in Lesson 3's "Exploring on your own" ss.

1 Center page 1 in the document window by choosing it from the page field at the lower-left corner of the document window.

2 If the Links panel is not visible, choose Window > Links or click the Links panel icon (∞) in the panel dock.

3 Using the Selection tool (▶), select the Songs of the Garden logo type on page 1. Notice that the graphic's filename, Title.ai, becomes selected in the Links panel when you select the graphic in the layout.

A. Filename column

B. Status column

C. Page column

D. Show/Hide Link Information button

E. Relink From CC Libraries button

F. Relink button

G. Go To Link button

H. Edit Original button

I. Select Next Link In The List button

J. Select Previous Link In The List button

K. Update Link button

Now you'll use the Links panel to locate another graphic in the layout.

4 In the Links panel, select RR-logo.ai, and then click the Go To Link button (⟲).
The graphic becomes selected and centered on the screen. This is a quick way to
find a graphic in a document.

These techniques for identifying and locating linked graphics are useful throughout
this lesson and whenever you work with a large number of imported files.

▶ **Tip:** You can also
click the page number
to the right of a
filename in the Links
panel to jump to that
link and center it in the
document window.

Viewing information about linked files

The Links panel makes it easy to work with linked graphics and text files and to
display additional information about linked files.

1 In the Links panel, select the graphic named Sunflower_2.psd. If you cannot see
the names of all the linked files without scrolling, drag the horizontal divider
bar in the Links panel downward to enlarge the top half of the panel so that all
the links are visible. The Link Info area at the bottom half of the panel displays
detailed information about the selected link.

2 In the Links panel, click the Select Next Link In The List button (▸) to view the
Link Info about the next file in the Links panel list, RR-logo.ai. You can examine
all the links in the list this way, one at a time. Currently, most links display an
alert icon (⚠) in the Status column. This icon indicates a linking problem,
which you'll address later. After you've examined the link information for
various images, choose Edit > Deselect All, and then click the Show/Hide Link
Information button (⌄) above Link Info to hide the Link Info area.

By default, files are sorted in the Links panel by page number but with files
used multiple times in a document listed at the top. You can sort the file
list in different ways by clicking the column headings. Next, we'll add more
column headings to make additional information available at a glance.

Tip: You can detach
the Links panel from
its group of panels by
dragging its tab. Once
you've detached the
panel, you can resize it
by dragging an edge or
lower corner.

● **Note:** In this
document the page
numbering follows the
folding pattern, making
the first spread pages 5,
6, and 1 because it's the
outside covers and the
flap that folds in. The
second spread is the
inside, pages 2, 3, and 4.
The Links panel shows
this order.

3 A faster way to view important link information is to customize the information
displayed in the Links panel columns. Open the menu in the Links panel and
choose Panel Options (at the bottom of the menu). Under Show Column,
click Color Space, Actual PPI, Effective PPI, and Transparency. Click OK. (The
important information in your workflow may vary from this example.)

4 Pull out the panel to the left to see the new columns. The Links panel now has
additional columns showing information for the options you turned on. Drag the
first column divider to the right to make the first column wide enough to see the
filenames. This customized view is a fast way to see important information about
linked graphics, such as whether something has been scaled up so much that it
will look bad when printed (jagged edges, blurry, or pixelated).

Each option turned on under Show Column
in Panel Options will display in an additional
column in the Links panel. You can adjust the
width of each column in the same way you
adjusted the first column. You can also drag
the columns to change the order. (Note that
some of the images used for the exercise
are low resolution, which you can now see
at a glance.)

Showing files in Explorer (Windows) or Finder (macOS)

Although the Links panel gives you information about the attributes and location
in the document of a specific linked graphic file, it does not let you make changes to
the file or change the name of the file. One way you can access the original file of an
imported graphic file is by using the Reveal In Explorer (Windows) or Reveal In
Finder (macOS) option.

1 Select Sunflower_2.psd. From the
Links panel menu, choose Reveal
In Explorer (Windows) or Reveal In
Finder (macOS). The folder where the
linked file is currently stored on your
computer opens, and the file is selected.
This feature is useful for locating files
on your hard drive.

2 Close the window and return to InDesign.

Updating revised graphics

Even after you place text or graphic files in your InDesign document, you can still use other applications to modify those files. The Links panel indicates which files have been modified outside of InDesign and gives you the choice of updating your document with the latest versions of those files.

In the Links panel, the file Title.ai displays an alert icon (▲) in the Status column, indicating that the original file has been modified. This is one of the files that caused the alert message to appear when you first opened this document. You'll update the link for this file so that the InDesign document uses the current version.

▶ **Tip:** You can update multiple instances of a graphic at the same time by updating when the triangle is closed.

1 If necessary, click the triangle (›) in the Links panel to the left of the file Title.ai to reveal two instances of the imported file (it may already be open). Select the instance of the Title.ai file that's on page 1, and click the Go To Link button (⬏) to view the graphic. Notice that the modified link icon (▲) is also displayed in the upper left of the graphic's frame on the page. You don't have to go to the link and view it before you update, but it's a quick way to double-check which imported file you are about to update and see the results.

● **Note:** If you don't see the modified link alert icon in the upper left of the graphic, choose View > Extras > Show Link Badge and ensure View > Screen Mode is set to Normal.

2 Click the Update Link button (↻). The appearance of the image in the document changes to represent its newer version, the modified link icon is no longer displayed in the Links panel, and the modified link badge near the upper-left corner of the graphics frame changes from Modified (▲) to OK (∞).

▶ **Tip:** You can also double-click the modified link icon in the Links panel to update links.

3 Click Cover-Butterfly.psd, the image behind the title. Look in the upper left of the graphic's frame where the modified link badge is displayed, the same icon as in the Links panel. You may need to scroll up to see the badge. Using the Selection tool (▶), click the modified link badge once to update the image.

4 To update the rest of the modified links, choose Update All Links from the Links panel menu.

Now you'll replace the image of the butterfly on the first spread with a different image. You'll use the Relink button to reassign the link to another graphic.

1 Choose View > Fit Spread In Window.

2 Use the Selection tool (▶) to select the Cover-Butterfly.psd image on page 1 again (if necessary). If you click the content grabber, you'll select the graphic rather than the frame, but for this task, you can select either. You can tell when you've selected the right image because the filename becomes selected in the Links panel.

3 Click the Relink button (⊖) in the Links panel.

4 Browse to find the Cover-RedFlower.psd file in the Lesson11 folder, and then click Open. The new image replaces the original image, and the Links panel is updated accordingly.

5 Click a blank area of the pasteboard to deselect all the objects on the spread.

6 Choose File > Save to save your work.

Link status icons in the Links panel

The status of a linked file can appear in the Links panel in any of the following ways:

- In the Status column, an up-to-date graphic displays only the filename and the page on which it's used.

- A modified file displays a yellow triangle with an exclamation point (▲). This icon means that the file on disk has changed since it was placed into your document. For example, this icon appears if you place a Photoshop graphic in InDesign and then you or someone else edits and saves the graphic in Photoshop. To update a modified graphic, select it in the Links panel, and then choose Update Link from the panel menu, or double-click the modified alert icon in the panel or on the graphic's frame, or click the Update Link button (↻).

- A missing file displays a red hexagon with a question mark (❓). This icon means the graphic is no longer in the location from which it was placed, although it may still exist somewhere. Missing links can happen if someone renames a file, deletes the original file, or moves it to a different folder or server after it's been placed in the document. You can't know whether a missing file is up to date until its original is located. If you print or export a document when this icon is displayed, the file will not print or export at full resolution.

- A graphic that has been embedded in the InDesign document (done by selecting the filename in the Links panel and choosing Embed Link from the panel menu) displays an embedded icon (▣). Embedding the contents of a linked file suspends management operations for that link. Unembedding the file restores management operations to the link.

Display performance and GPUs

InDesign provides support for computers with video cards that include a graphics processing unit (GPU). If your computer has a compatible GPU card, InDesign automatically displays documents using the GPU and sets the default Display Performance to High Quality. If your computer does not have a compatible GPU card, the default Display Performance setting is Typical. This book presumes that readers are using computers without a GPU. If your computer has a compatible GPU, you can ignore steps that ask you to switch to High Quality Display. For more information about GPU support in InDesign, go to https://helpx.adobe.com/indesign/using/gpu_performance.html.

Adjusting display quality

Now that you've resolved all the links, you're ready to start adding more graphics. First, however, you will adjust the view quality of the Illustrator file (Title.ai) that you updated earlier in this lesson.

When you place an image in a document, InDesign automatically creates a low-resolution (proxy) preview of it, corresponding to the current settings in the Display Performance area of the Preferences dialog. The images in this document are currently low-resolution proxies, which is why they appear to have jagged edges. Reducing the onscreen quality of placed graphics doesn't affect the quality of the final output but enables pages to display faster. You can control this setting on individual images or for a whole document.

Tip: You can change the default display setting InDesign uses when you open any file by choosing a setting when no documents are open.

1 In the Links panel, select the Title.ai file you updated in the previous exercise (the instance on page 1). Click the Go To Link button (⤴) to center the graphic in your window.

2 Right-click the Songs of the Garden graphic, and then choose Display Performance > High Quality Display from the context menu. The image appears at full resolution. You can use this process to confirm the clarity, appearance, and exact position of a placed graphic in your InDesign layout. Choose Edit > Deselect All.

 Onscreen appearance using Typical Display.

 Onscreen appearance using High Quality Display.

Tip: On older computers and for designs with many imported graphics, High Quality Display can sometimes result in slower screen redraw. In many cases, it is advisable to set your Display Performance to Typical Display and then change the display quality of individual graphics as needed.

3 To change the display performance for the entire document, choose View > Display Performance > High Quality Display. All graphics are displayed at the highest quality. Change back to Typical Display if InDesign slows down.

Importing and sizing graphics

The most basic way to import a graphic into InDesign is to use File > Place. There are several other ways to import graphics, which you'll try next.

Importing, sizing, and cropping

1 Navigate to page 5. Open the Layers panel by clicking the Layers panel icon () in the panel dock, and then click the Photos layer so that the imported images will be placed on that layer. Choose File > Place and navigate to the Lesson11 folder. Select the file Blue-Hydrangea.psd and click Open.

2 Move the loaded raster graphics icon (⟨⟩) into the pasteboard area just above the page and click once. This places the graphic independently of any existing frame. InDesign automatically creates a frame around the graphic and scales it to actual size (100%).

● **Note:** Many of the steps in this lesson refer to the Control panel. You can use the Properties panel if you prefer, but it is not part of the default [Advanced] workspace. To open it, choose Window > Properties. To save screen space, dock it with the rest of panel dock, drag the tab to the bottom of the panel dock, and then click to open and close it as needed.

3 This photo is much too large at actual size, so you'll need to resize it. In this case, it needs to be scaled down. One way to do this is to type a percentage or measurements in the Control panel and InDesign will scale the graphic to those numbers, in the direction of the selected reference point (⊞). Or you can scale the graphic visually. Choose the Selection tool (▶) and hold down Shift+Ctrl (Windows) or Shift+Command (macOS). Drag the lower-right handle up and to the left. Watch the Control panel's Size and Scale (or the numbers in the gray box next to the Selection tool) until the image is about 2 inches high. Holding down the Ctrl or Command key while dragging scales both the frame and the content within (in this case an image). Adding the Shift key keeps the image proportions so that the image is not distorted while it's changing size.

4 Drag the image down and to the right of the empty frame at the upper left of the page until you see the green Smart Guides appear that show the top of this frame aligned with the empty frame.

5 Now we want to crop out most of the leaves. To do this, you change the size of the frame without changing the size of the graphic inside. Drag the lower-right corner handle in toward the flower so that most of the leaves are no longer visible. Then click the content grabber (◎) and notice that the image bounding box (shown in a contrasting color to the layer color) is now much larger than the

frame, indicating that part of the image is being cropped by the frame. Drag the image up and to the left so that the flower is centered in the frame.

The green smart guides appear when the top of the objects are aligned.

After positioning the picture inside the smaller frame, notice that the handles are now outside the picture frame and are a contrasting color to the layer color.

Placing a graphic into an existing frame and using frame fitting options

The next way to use File > Place is to place a graphic into an existing frame.

1 Click the empty frame to the left of the Blue-Hydrangea.psd image. Choose File > Place, select Butterfly-on-flower.psd, and click Open. This time the image is imported into the frame. Once again, it's at actual size (100%), and that's too large since only part of the butterfly is visible in the frame.

2 Choose Object > Fitting > Fit Content To Frame, which seems like the right choice. But examine the result: the image is indeed within the frame, but the butterfly is distorted (stretched vertically). Confirm this by clicking the content grabber (⊚) in the center of the frame (so that you are viewing data about the image rather than the frame), and then look at the scale values in the Control panel or the Properties panel. The horizontal and vertical numbers are very different, showing the distortion.

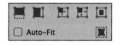

▶ **Tip:** All frame fitting options are also available as buttons on the Control panel:

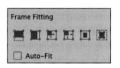

and the Properties panel:

Frame Fitting

3 To scale the image without distortion, choose Object > Fitting > Fit Content Proportionally. The image is not distorted, but now it's too small, leaving the bottom half of the frame empty. Choose Object > Fitting > Fill Frame Proportionally. This option

sizes the image within the frame without distortion, and it crops part of the image if it's a different shape than the frame (as in this case). However, this is still not what we want because the butterfly is too far to the right of the frame.

4 Choose Object > Fitting > Content-Aware Fit. This feature intelligently fits the image in the frame by evaluating various parts of the image. The butterfly and flower are now nearly centered in the frame automatically. You can nudge the content over if you'd like.

● **Note:** You can choose fitting options for a frame before you place a graphic. You'll do this in a later exercise.

5 Select the circular picture frame in the lower left and place the image Calla-Lilly.psd. This frame was set up to center the image at 100% size. The photo is centered within the frame, but the subject of the photo (the flower) is not centered in the original image. Select either the circular frame or the image within and choose Object > Fitting > Content-Aware Fit. The flower now fits much better in the circle because Content-Aware Fit attempts to find the subject of an image. Notice that InDesign scaled as well as moved the image.

Placing a graphic into an existing frame by dropping from the desktop

1 Another way to import graphics is to drop them onto a page from your desktop. Switch to File Explorer (Windows) or the Finder (macOS), and open the Lesson11 folder, which contains the Starflower.jpg file.

Resize and arrange your File Explorer window (Windows) or Finder window (macOS) and your InDesign window, as needed, so that you can simultaneously see the list of files in the Lesson11 folder and the InDesign document window. Make sure that the right side of page 5 in your document is visible.

2 Choose Edit > Deselect All. Drag the Starflower.jpg file over the empty frame to the right of the circular frame and release the mouse button. You do not have to select the empty picture frame before dropping the image.

3 Click the content grabber (◎) and notice that the image bounding box (blue) is smaller than the placeholder frame (orange). Select the frame and choose Object > Fitting > Fit Frame To Content. Then switch to the Selection tool (▶) and move the picture to a pleasing position in the group as you wish. Choose Edit > Deselect All when you're done.

Using Adobe Bridge to import graphics

Adobe Bridge is a separate application available to Creative Cloud users with an All Apps subscription. Bridge lets you browse local and networked computers for graphics and then place them into an InDesign layout. Importing files is just one of many features the application provides. If you don't have Bridge available, you can complete this exercise by dropping the graphic files from the desktop again, but this time change your folder view to icons.

1 Navigate to page 1. Then choose File > Browse In Bridge to launch Bridge. Bridge automatically opens the folder in which the InDesign document is saved or in which a selected graphic is stored. If you don't see this folder, click the Folder panel at the top of the left panel to navigate to the Lesson11 folder.

● **Note:** If you do not already have Bridge installed, Creative Cloud will install it when you choose Browse In Bridge. On first launch of Bridge from within InDesign, an alert appears asking you to enable the Bridge extension. Click Yes to enable this extension.

Use the slider at the bottom of the window to make the previews larger or smaller.

Adobe Bridge can help you preview, organize, edit, and publish multiple creative assets quickly and easily. It can display very detailed information about each asset.

2 Scroll down until you see the maple leaf images. Click the graphic maple-leaf-.psd once, and then click the filename to make it editable. Rename the file **maple-leaf-yellow**, and press Enter (Windows) or Return (macOS) to commit the change.

3 If necessary, make the Bridge window smaller by dragging the lower-right corner and position it so that you can also see page 1 (the cover) of the InDesign document. Drag the maple-leaf-yellow.psd file into your InDesign document onto an open area of the pasteboard above the page and near the dark blue square. Scroll to make the pasteboard above visible if necessary. Pause for a moment while pressing the mouse button to return to InDesign. Click the pasteboard to place the image at full size.

▶ **Tip:** To learn more about what you can do with Bridge, start at the Bridge page on the Adobe website: https://helpx.adobe.com/bridge/get-started.html.

4 Use the Selection tool (▶) to position the leaf graphic in the upper-left corner of the page, on top of the empty Blue-Dark frame. Press Shift+Ctrl (Windows) or Shift+Command (macOS) and drag a corner of the frame to scale both the frame and its contents. Scale to a size just a bit larger than the empty Blue-Dark frame. Then align the top and right edges of the graphics frame with the top and right edges of the Blue-Dark frame.

▶ **Tip:** You can also replace an image by dragging it from Explorer or the Finder and dropping it over another image. If this doesn't work, check that the layer in which the graphic appears isn't locked.

A very useful feature of dragging photos from Bridge is that you can quickly change pictures in a frame while seeing the new image in Bridge and then the result in InDesign. This technique is very useful in projects where the layout repeats but you need to import different pictures. You'll try this now.

5 With the yellow maple leaf still selected, bring the Bridge window to the front again (if needed) and choose the file maple-leaf-red.psd. Drag and drop it right over the yellow maple leaf. InDesign retains the scaling, and now you've switched out the image with the new one, in position, in just a few seconds. Try it again with maple-leaf-orange.psd. Select the image with the content grabber and set the reference point to the center position (▦) using the Control, Transform, or Properties panel. Then rotate the image within the frame by typing **20** in the Rotation Angle field in any of the above panels. Drag and drop the red leaf again. The image is switched while both the scaling and rotation are retained.

6 To see how the reference point affects the center of rotation and how this changes the results, experiment with rotating the image again using different reference points, such as the upper left or lower right. In different situations using a different reference point will get the result you're looking for quicker than if you always leave the reference point on the default setting.

7 Choose File > Save to save your work.

Relinking multiple files at the same time

In many workflows, the situation arises where the linked files for a project are moved to a new location. When you open the InDesign document linked to those files, the missing icon () appears in the Links panel for several or all images. InDesign can handle that situation in two ways.

One, when you relink one image, InDesign looks for all other missing images in the new folder to which you just relinked that one image. This is controlled by an option called Search For Missing Links In This Folder, which is turned on by default. (If you want to turn it off, it's a checkbox at the bottom of the relink window.)

Two, select the missing images in the Links panel and select the Relink To Folder option from the panel menu. Navigate to the folder where the links are now, select the folder, and click Choose. You can repeat this procedure and choose other folders if some of the linked images have been moved to more than one new folder.

▶ **Tip:** You can sort the Links panel by status so that you can see all the missing links at the top of the list and more easily select them all. To do so, click the Status column heading.

Editing placed pictures

The quickest way to make a change to an imported graphic while you're working in InDesign is to use the Edit Original feature. This opens the graphic in the corresponding image program (usually Illustrator or Photoshop). You can make the desired changes and save the file, and it will be automatically updated in InDesign.

1 If the Links panel is not already open, choose Window > Links, or click the Links panel icon (∞) in the panel dock.

2 Select Blue-Hydrangea.psd and click the page number following the name to center it in your window.

3 At the bottom right of the Links panel, click the Edit Original button (✐). This opens the image in an application that can view or edit it. This image was saved in Photoshop, so if Photoshop is installed on your computer, InDesign starts Photoshop and opens the selected file. Click OK in the Embedded Profile Mismatch dialog if it appears.

4 In Photoshop, make a change to the image, such as applying a filter or making a dramatic change with an adjustment layer. Save the file and return to InDesign, and the image is automatically updated in InDesign. In the example you see in the 11_End.indd file, a filter was applied to blur the background.

● **Note:** The Edit Original button may open an image in an application other than Photoshop or the application in which it was created. When you install software, some installer utilities change your operating system's settings that associate file types with applications. The Edit Original command uses these settings for associating files with applications. To change these settings, see the documentation for your operating system.

Working with dropped backgrounds

There are two basic types of images with white, or "dropped," backgrounds, both of which are widely used. The difference is whether the edge between the foreground and background is a crisp, sharp edge or a soft, blending edge. The type of edge used depends on what is appropriate for the image content.

▶ **Tip:** A mask is a shape that's used to contain and crop an image. The portion of the image within the mask shape is visible; any areas outside the mask shape are not visible.

Images with sharp edges between the foreground and background can use a vector path to separate the foreground from the background. This is called a "clipping path." When Photoshop files with vector paths are placed in InDesign, you can turn on the path in InDesign, and you can choose different paths saved within the same image. InDesign can automatically detect the edge between the subject and the background and create a clipping path if an image has a relatively light or white background (or a relatively dark background if the subject is light). However, this technique works best for simple shapes or for creating a path to use for Text Wrap, as we did in Lesson 4, "Working with Objects."

Images with a soft, blending edge between the foreground and background use transparency and soft brushes to delete the background in Photoshop.

Working with clipping paths from Photoshop in InDesign

1 Navigate to page 4 of the document by double-clicking page 4 in the Pages panel, and choose View > Fit Page In Window.

2 In the Layers panel, make sure that the Photos layer is selected so that the imported image is placed on that layer. You can lock the Background photos layer to be sure you don't accidentally click into the blue square's or background photo's frame. Choose File > Place, and double-click the file Pears.psd in the Lesson11 folder.

▶ **Tip:** If you accidentally click within the existing frame, choose Edit > Undo Place and try again.

3 Position the loaded raster graphics icon () outside the blue square in the center of page 4—to the left and slightly below the top edge (make sure you are not placing the pointer in the square itself)—and click to place the image of two pears. If you need to reposition the graphics frame to match the following image, do so now.

This is what a vector path looks like in Photoshop, showing the points and curves of the clipping path.

4 Choose Object > Clipping Path > Options. Move the Clipping Path dialog, if necessary, so that you can see the pear image.

5 Choose Photoshop Path from the Type menu. If Preview is not selected, select it now. Choose Two Pears from the Path menu. The background is now hidden, or clipped out, by the path. Click OK.

6 Choose Object > Fitting > Fit Frame To Content.

7 Switch to the Selection tool (▶) and double-click the pears image. Press Shift+Ctrl (Windows) or Shift+Command (macOS), and then click the lower-right corner handle. Drag up and to the left to scale both the frame and its contents. Make the pears image about the size shown, and then drag it toward the bottom of the blue square, also as shown.

▶ **Tip:** You can switch to the Selection tool by pressing the V key.

8 Press Alt (Windows) or Option (macOS) and drag up and to the right. This creates a copy of the image. Choose Object > Clipping Path > Options, and then choose Right Pear from the Path menu and click OK. Then, choose Object > Fitting > Fit Frame To Content. Switch back to the Selection tool (▶), then click to select the frame (at first, the content will be selected), and use the same technique to scale this pear to about 80% of the original size (the Control and Properties panels show the scale amount as you scale the object). You can also type **80** in the X scale field in the Control or Properties panel and press

● **Note:** Notice the double arrows (▶) that appear when you press Alt (Windows) or Option (macOS) and click an object, indicating that a copy of the object will be made when you drag, leaving the original object in place.

Enter or Return to apply the same scale number to the Y dimension when Same Settings (⬚) is on. If Different Settings (⬚) is on, add Ctrl (Windows) or Command (macOS). Move the image slightly inside and below the top of the blue frame as shown. Finally, move the pointer outside the bounding box until it changes to the rotate pointer (↱). Rotate the photo to the right about −28 degrees.

9 Press Alt (Windows) or Option (macOS) and drag down and to the left to create another copy of the single pear. Choose Object > Clipping Path > Options, choose Photoshop Path, and this time choose the Left Pear path and click OK. Then choose Object > Fitting > Fit Frame To Content. Switch back to the Selection tool, click to select the frame, and move the pointer outside the bounding box until it changes to the rotate pointer (↱). Rotate the photo to the left to about 22 degrees, and then move it down and position it between the two pears at the bottom as shown.

● **Note:** You can also type **22** in the Rotation Angle box in the Control or Properties panel.

10 Notice how a clipping path allows an image to overlap multiple other objects. You can also move images in front of or behind other objects. Take a few moments to experiment.

11 Choose File > Save to save the file.

Working with transparent backgrounds from Photoshop in InDesign

1 Navigate to the leftmost page of this spread (page 2) by sliding page 4 to the right. Do this by holding down the spacebar. The hand icon (✋) appears. Keep the spacebar pressed and drag until page 2 is centered in your window.

2 Select the Rectangle Frame tool (⊠) in the Tools panel and draw a frame in the lower area crossing over the border between page 2 and page 3 and extending into the pasteboard below the document pages.

3 You can choose fitting options for a frame before you place a graphic. Choose Object > Fitting > Frame Fitting Options. In the Frame Fitting Options dialog, choose Fit Content Proportionally from the Fitting menu and then click the top-center reference point in the Align From area. Click OK.

This is what a transparent background looks like in Photoshop.

4 With the frame still selected, choose File > Place and double-click the Tulips.psd file in the Lesson11 folder. InDesign fits the image proportionally to the frame as specified. Choose Edit > Deselect All.

5 Now we want to scale the picture without scaling the frame. Switch to the Selection tool and click the photo over the circle of the content grabber (⊚) to select the contents of the frame, in this case the photo of the tulips. The handles of the bounding box of the photo (not the frame) will be active. You'll see that this bounding box is a contrasting color to the frame bounding box. In the Control or Properties panel, set the reference point to the top center (⊞) position, make sure Same Settings (🔒) is on, type **70** in the Scale field, and press Enter or Return.

▶ **Tip:** You can press the Esc key when you have content selected to switch to the Selection tool and select the frame instead. You can also toggle between selecting the content and selecting the frame by double-clicking with the Selection tool.

6 The photo scales downward from the top center, resulting in the image being larger but also further down. Drag or use the arrow keys to nudge the position of the photo so that most of the image is cropped out, with just the tops of the flowers and leaves showing on the page. Refer to the figure below for reference. Press Esc to select the graphic's frame again, and use the Selection tool to make the frame wider or taller if necessary.

Notice how different the edges of the tulip image are compared to the edges of the pears image. The edges of the tulips and leaves blend softly into the background. This is the purpose of using transparency in Photoshop to remove a background rather than a vector path: to create a soft edge between the image and any background onto which it is placed.

● **Note:** It may be helpful to press the W key to change to Preview mode to see where the photo crosses the trim edge of the page. Then press the W key again to toggle back to Normal mode.

Importing native Adobe graphic files

When you import files saved from Adobe applications such as Photoshop (.psd), Illustrator (.ai), and Acrobat (.pdf), InDesign allows you to work with these files in unique ways that you can't do with other file formats. For example, you can turn the visibility of layers off and on in InDesign.

Working with a Photoshop file with layers

Next, we'll work with a layered Photoshop file and adjust the visibility of the individual layers.

● **Note:** You can open the Links panel to confirm that this is the image you select.

1 Navigate to page 1, the cover panel. If you locked the Background photos layer in the previous exercise, go to the Layers panel and unlock it now. Using the Selection tool, click the background image, Cover-RedFlower.psd, and choose View > Fit Page In Window. This file, which you relinked in a previous exercise, has four layers.

2 Choose Object > Object Layer Options to open the Object Layer Options dialog. This dialog allows you to show and hide layers.

3 Move the Object Layer Options dialog so that you can see as much as possible of the selected image. Select the Preview option to view changes while keeping the dialog open.

4 In the Object Layer Options dialog, click the eye icon (●) to the left of the Cobblestones layer. The layer is turned off, leaving only the Red Poppy layer visible.

5 Click the eye icon (●) to the left of the Sky with Clouds layer. Click OK.

6 Choose File > Save to save your work.

Creating an anchored graphics frame

An anchored graphics frame moves with the text to which it's anchored if editing causes the text to reflow. In this exercise, you'll anchor the CD title to a text frame on the center page.

● **Note:** If the Anchored Object Control square is not visible when selecting the logo, choose View > Extras > Show Anchored Object Control.

1 In the Pages panel, double-click the second spread, and choose View > Fit Spread In Window. At the bottom of the pasteboard is the Songs of the Garden logo. You'll insert this graphic into a paragraph on the page.

2 Press and hold Z to temporarily access the Zoom tool, or select the Zoom tool (🔍) and click to zoom in on the logo and the text frame above it.

3 Choose Type > Show Hidden Characters to view the spaces and paragraph returns in the text. This helps you locate where you want to anchor the frame.

4 Select the Type tool (T) and click in front of the word "Addie" at the beginning of the second paragraph. Press Enter or Return, creating an empty paragraph. Press the up arrow, which moves the cursor to the beginning of the empty paragraph, and then type three or four spacebar spaces.

5 Return to the Selection tool (▶), and click the logo. (Be careful to click outside the content grabber so that you select the frame and not the graphic within.) Notice the small solid-red square near the upper-right corner of the frame. You can drag this square into a text frame to anchor an object to text.

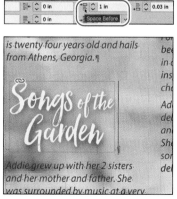

6 Hold down the Shift key, and drag the red square near the upper right of the logo frame to the beginning of the empty second paragraph, within the space characters. Holding the Shift key creates an inline graphic that flows within the text (as opposed to floating outside the text frame). You'll see a thick cursor indicating the point where the graphic will be inserted. Release the mouse button. After the graphic is anchored, the red square on the graphic's frame changes to an anchor symbol. The graphic will stay between the first and third paragraphs and move up or down if text is added or deleted without you having to also move the graphic each time.

Once a graphic is anchored, you can select it with the Type tool and apply text attributes that affect its position. Now you'll create space between the graphic and the surrounding text with the Space Before option.

7 Select the Type tool (T), and then click to the right of the inline graphic at any of the space characters to establish the insertion point in that paragraph.

8 Click the Paragraph Formatting Controls button (¶) in the Control panel. Hold down the Shift key and click the up arrow button to the right of the Space Before icon (↑≡) four times to change the value to 1 in. As you increase the value, the anchored graphics frame and the text below it shift downward. Note that the cursor also gets longer, reflecting the large Space-Before value.

9 To see how the anchored graphic flows when text is edited, click to the right of the period that ends the first paragraph, and then press Enter or Return twice. Notice how the graphic moves down each time you press the key. Press Backspace (Windows) or Delete (macOS) twice to remove the extra paragraph returns, and the graphic moves back up.

10 Choose File > Save to save your work.

Adding text wrap to an anchored graphics frame

You can customize how the paragraph text wraps around an anchored graphics frame. The text wrap settings offer many different options to flow text around a frame or the shape of the graphic within the frame.

1 Using the Selection tool (▶), select the graphics frame with the Songs of the Garden logo you placed in the previous exercise.

2 Press Shift+Ctrl (Windows) or Shift+Command (macOS), and drag the upper-right handle of the frame up and to the right until you've scaled the graphic and its frame to cover roughly 15–20% of the second column. With the graphic still selected, drag it downward so that the top is below the first paragraph.

● **Note:** An animation may play that demonstrates Subject-Aware Wrapping, which is the default setting under Contour Options, in the Type menu, where it's called Select Subject. You'll learn about this feature later in the lesson. Click OK to close the animation.

3 Choose Window > Text Wrap to access the Text Wrap panel. Position the panel so that you can see the changes as you apply settings. In the Text Wrap panel, select Wrap Around Object Shape (▦) to flow the text around the graphic.

4 Under Wrap Options, choose Right Side from the Wrap To menu. Under Contour Options, choose Same As Clipping from the Type menu. To increase space between the text and the graphic, click the up arrow button in the Top Offset option () three times to change the value to 0.1875 in.

Text can also wrap around a graphic's shape rather than around the rectangular bounding box.

5 With the Text Wrap panel still open, under Contour Options, choose Detect Edges from the Type menu. The other settings will stay the same. Detect Edges creates a vector path around the objects. The text wrap is determined by the shape of the objects in this graphic, in this case by the letters.

6 To view the results clearly, choose Edit > Deselect All, and choose Type > Hide Hidden Characters to hide the paragraph returns and spaces. You could toggle back and forth between normal and preview modes as well, all while leaving the Text Wrap panel open.

7 In the Text Wrap panel, experiment with the available options from the Wrap To menu. Return to Right Side as your final choice.

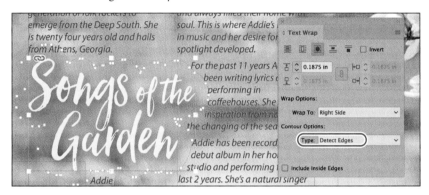

The path created when using the Detect Edges contour option is an editable vector path with points and handles as shown above. For example, you can manually adjust the anchor points by dragging them to a new position. You can also add or delete points and convert them from corner points to smooth points (and vice versa) with the Pen tool (). You can change the shape of curves by adjusting the anchor point handles with the Direct Selection tool (▷).

8 Select the Direct Selection tool (▷), and then click the graphic to view the anchor points used for the text wrap. Experiment with moving individual points and notice how that reflows the text.

9 Examine this path in the 11_End.indd file, where many points along the bottom of the graphic were deleted to better control the text flow of the first line of the paragraph below the anchored graphic. You don't have to follow this path exactly, but use it as an example.

▶ **Tip:** When you hover over an anchor point with the Pen tool, the icon adds a minus sign to indicate that if you click that point, it will be deleted.

10 Close the Text Wrap panel, and choose File > Save.

Importing an Illustrator file

InDesign takes full advantage of the smooth edges of vector graphics, such as those from Illustrator. When you use the High Quality Display setting, vector graphics and type appear with smooth edges at any size or magnification.

1 In the Layers panel, select the Graphics layer. Choose Edit > Deselect All to make sure nothing is selected in your document.

2 Choose View > Fit Spread In Window to see the entire spread.

3 Choose File > Place, and select the Illustrator file Garland.ai from the Lesson11 folder. Make sure that Show Import Options is not selected. Click Open.

● **Note:** If an Illustrator file imports with a white background, delete it and import it again, but turn on Show Import Options and then turn on Transparent Background.

4 InDesign shows the loaded vector graphics icon (). Click in the upper-left corner of the spread to add the Illustrator file to the page. Use the Selection tool (▶) to position it as shown here. Graphics created in Illustrator have transparent backgrounds by default.

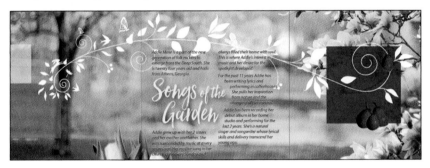

5 Choose File > Save to save your work.

Importing an Illustrator file with layers

You can import native Illustrator files with layers into an InDesign layout and control the visibility of the layers. One way this feature is used is to publish different versions of a document. The part that changes is set up on different layers that can be turned on only in the matching version, while the main design stays the same.

1 Deselect all objects by clicking in the pasteboard of the document window. Click the empty graphics frame to the left of the red frame on the far left of the spread.

2 Choose File > Place. In the lower left of the Place dialog, select Show Import Options. Select the file Flower-Title.ai, and click Open. The Place PDF dialog appears when Show Import Options is selected (because Illustrator files are written in PDF file format).

3 In the Place PDF dialog, make sure that Show Preview is selected. Click the General tab and choose Bounding Box (All Layers) from the Crop To menu and make sure that Transparent Background is selected.

4 Click the Layers tab to view the layers. This file has three layers: a background image of a flower (Flower Drawing), a layer of text in English (English Title), and a layer of text in Spanish (Spanish Title).

Although you can now designate which layers you would like to display in the imported graphic, the small Preview area makes it difficult to see the results.

5 Click OK. You'll select the layers to display while working in the layout.

6 Press Ctrl+= (Windows) or Command+= (macOS) a couple of times to zoom in and center the graphic on your screen.

7 In the Control or Properties panel, click the center reference point (⊞) and then click the content grabber (◎) to scale the graphic (content) within the frame (container). Click the downward open triangle (˅) to the right of either the X or the Y scale percentage field and choose 75%. InDesign scales the graphic and centers it in the frame. (If you use the Properties panel, you may need to click the three dots at the lower right of the Transform area to reveal the More Options area, which contains the scaling entry fields.)

Scaling presets in the Properties panel, left, and in the ., center.

8 Press the Esc key to select the frame, press the Shift key, and click the translucent red frame. Click the red frame again to make it the Key Object. Use the horizontal and vertical center buttons in the Control, Properties, or Align panel to center the graphics frame with the flower over the translucent red frame.

9 Choose Edit > Deselect All, click the flower graphic, and choose Object > Object Layer Options. Move the dialog, if necessary, so that you can see the graphic in the document.

10 Select Preview, and then click the eye icon (👁) next to the English Title layer to turn it off. Click the empty box next to Spanish Title to turn on that layer. Click OK, and then choose Edit > Deselect All.

Using layered Illustrator files allows you to store variations of an illustration in one file without having to create separate files for each variation.

Using Subject-Aware Text Wrap

Subject-Aware Text Wrap, similarly to Content-Aware Fit, uses artificial intelligence to find the subject of a photo and then creates a text wrap path around that subject. It works on images that do not have a dropped background.

1 Navigate to page 6, and choose View > Fit Page In Window to center page 6 on your screen.

2 Using the Selection tool (▶), click the sunflower image under the text frame that contains a numbered list with white text (the songs on this disc).

3 Choose Window > Text Wrap to open the Text Wrap panel if you closed it after the previous exercise. Position the panel so that you can see the changes as you apply settings. In the Text Wrap panel, select Wrap Around Object Shape (▦) to flow the text around the graphic.

4 This time, from the Type menu under Contour Options, choose Select Subject, which may be turned on as the default setting.

An animation demonstrating Subject-Aware Wrapping may play when you use the Text Wrap panel. Click OK to close the animation.

5 A path has been created around the petals of the sunflower, and the text of the song list is now wrapping around the flower, following this path. To make the text flow more smoothly, we'll change the offset. Click the up arrow four times, or type **.25** in the Top Offset field. Close the Text Wrap panel.

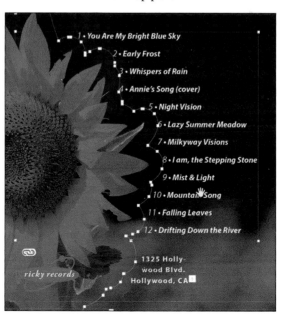

Similarly to Content-Aware Fit, which you used in an earlier exercise, Subject-Aware Text Wrap uses artificial intelligence to determine the subject of an image.

6 The song list is now wrapping around the flower in an appealing way. But the address in the text frame below is also being affected by the text wrap setting on the sunflower image, and that's not what we want. To prevent that text frame from following the wrap path, use the Selection tool (▶) to select the text frame that contains the address to the right of the Ricky Records logo.

7 Choose Object > Text Frame Options, and click Ignore Text Wrap at the bottom of the dialog. Click OK. The text of the address returns to its previous position, while the song list remains wrapped around the flower.

Filling type with a graphic

A striking design element is to fill a headline or accent letters with a graphic, such as a photograph or vector art. Next, you'll learn this technique.

1 Navigate to page 2. Select the Type tool (T) in the Tools panel or press the T key. In the Layers panel, select the Graphics layer.

2 Draw a large text frame just to the left of the Flower-Title graphic (mostly or entirely in the pasteboard) and type a capital letter **A** and **M**. Then press the Esc key to select the text frame.

● **Note:** It's not important for part of the graphic to be touching the page when you convert to outlines. If you are in the general area to the left of page 2, it will be easy to drag the new graphic into position.

3 Using the Character, Control, or Properties panel, choose Myriad Pro for the font and Bold for the style. Enter **130** for Font Size. If you see a plus sign in the lower right of the frame after you change the font size, drag the frame handles to make the text frame large enough to contain the large letter. Set the tracking (🔠) to **-50** so that the letters almost touch.

4 With the text frame still selected, choose Type > Create Outlines. InDesign changes the font to a vector graphic. Letters like this capital A become compound paths where you can see any background art through the triangle that forms the inner part of the letter. Switch to the Direct Selection tool to see the vector path points, and then switch back to the Selection tool.

5 Set Fill Color () to [None] in the Swatches, Control, or Properties panel.

6 Choose File > Place. In the lower left of the Place dialog, deselect Show Import Options. Select the file Blue-Hydrangea.psd, and double-click to place the image. Both letters are filled with the image, excluding the cutout of the triangle in the center of the capital A. InDesign treats both letters as one compound path object. To understand this structure, choose Object > Paths > Release Compound Path. The M is no longer filled with the image, and the center of the A is no longer cut out. Choose Edit > Undo Release Compound Path.

7 Hover your pointer over the letter frame and click the content grabber ().

8 In the Control or Properties panel, set the reference point to the top center () position, set the scale to 150% by using the menu or by typing in the value, and then click the Flip Horizontal button ().

9 Click the content grabber again and drag the image to position it within the letters as you wish.

10 Press the Esc key to select the frame again, and drag the frame to the right and above the red Flower-Title graphic. Scroll to the right if needed to see more of the page. Then choose Object > Arrange > Send To Back.

Notice that the letter graphic moves behind the garland graphic but that it's still in front of the background image. This is because the Arrange commands move objects within a layer and not between layers. The photo behind the letter graphic is on a different layer (Background photos) that is under (behind) the Graphics layer.

11 Choose Edit > Deselect All, and then choose File > Save.

Using an InDesign library to manage objects

▶ Tip: You might use a library to store boilerplate text, a photo of each writer who contributes to a publication, or frequently used page elements such as a logo or an image with a caption.

InDesign libraries let you store and organize graphics, text, and design elements that you use frequently. InDesign libraries are stored as files on your hard drive or a shared device. You can also add ruler guides, grids, drawn shapes, and grouped images to a library. Each library appears as a separate panel that you can group with other panels any way you like. You can create as many libraries as you need—for example, different libraries for each of your projects or clients. In this section, you'll import a graphic currently stored in a library, and then you'll create your own library.

1 Move to the left of the letter graphic you created in the previous exercise until you see a light blue square that's partially transparent.

2 Choose View > Fit Page In Window to see the entire page.

3 Choose File > Open, select the file Lesson_11_Elements.indl in the Lesson11 folder, and then click Open to open the library file.

● Note: When you open it, the Lesson_11_ Elements Library may be grouped with the default Sample Buttons And Forms library. You can drag the default library off the docked panel and close it.

4 In the Lesson_11_Elements Library panel menu, select Show Subset. In the Show Subset dialog, in the last entry field for Parameters, type **flower**, and click OK. InDesign searches the library for all objects that have the word "flower" in their name and finds three objects.

● Note: After you drag the flower image onto the page, the Links panel may display a missing link icon (●) or a modified link icon (▲) because you moved the Blue-Flower.ai file from its original location to your hard drive. To remove the warning, click the Update Link button in the Links panel, or click the Relink button in the Links panel and navigate to the Lesson11 folder to find Blue-Flower.ai.

5 In the Layers panel, make sure the Graphics layer is selected.

6 Of the three objects visible in the Lesson_11_Elements Library panel, drag Blue-Flower.ai anywhere on the page. The file is added to the page. Open the Links panel and notice that the filename appears in the Links panel.

7 Using the Selection tool (▶), position the Blue-Flower.ai image so that it's on top of the light blue background frame on the far left of the page.

8 Close the Lesson_11_Elements Library panel, and choose File > Save to save your work.

Creating an InDesign library

Now you'll create your own library and add text and a graphic to it. When you add a graphic to an InDesign library, the original graphic file is not copied into the library; instead, InDesign maintains a link to the original source file. Graphics stored in a library still require the original, high-resolution file for high-resolution display and printing.

1 Choose File > New > Library. (If the CC Libraries alert appears asking whether you want to try out CC libraries now, click No.) Type **CD Projects** as the library filename, navigate to the Lesson11 folder, and click Save.

● **Note:** See the sidebar on the next page for more information about CC Libraries.

2 Navigate to page 6 (the back cover of the CD insert). Using the Selection tool (▶), drag the Ricky Records logo to the library you just created. The logo is now saved in the library for use in other InDesign documents.

3 In the CD Projects library, double-click the Ricky Records logo. In the Item Information dialog, type **Ricky Records Logo** in the Item Name field, and click OK.

▶ **Tip:** If you Alt-drag (Windows) or Option-drag (macOS) an object into a library, the Item Information dialog box appears as soon as you drag the item into the library. You can assign a name to the object as you add each item.

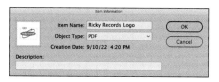

4 Using the Selection tool, drag the address text frame to the CD Projects library.

5 In the CD Projects library, double-click the address text block in the Library panel. For Item Name, type **Ricky Records Address**, and click OK. Click the panel menu and choose Large Thumbnail View so that it's easier to see the items.

Now your library contains both text and graphics. As soon as you make changes to the library, InDesign saves the changes.

6 Close the CD Projects library by clicking the close button at the top of the library panel group.

Congratulations! You have completed this lesson.

Creating and using CC Libraries

Creative Cloud Libraries make your favorite assets available to you anywhere. You can use CC Libraries to create and share colors, character and paragraph styles, graphics, Adobe Stock assets, and more using your favorite Creative Cloud desktop and mobile apps. You can then access them across other Creative Cloud apps whenever you need them. You can also share libraries with anyone who has a Creative Cloud account, so it's easy to collaborate, keep designs consistent, and create shared style guides to use across projects.

CC Libraries work much like the InDesign libraries you used in this lesson. To create a new CC Library, follow these steps:

1 Choose Window > CC Libraries to display the CC Libraries panel, or click the CC Libraries panel button (🔲). Click OK to close the introductory window.

2 Click + Create New Library.

3 Enter **CD Elements** in the Library Name field, and then click Create.

▶ **Tip:** The CC Libraries menu includes several commands that let you create and manage CC Libraries and control how library elements are displayed in the panel, including the ability to group items.

4 Use the Selection tool (▶) to select the text frame with the address at the bottom of page 6, and drag it into the Library panel. The formatted text will be added to the library. If you click the plus sign at the bottom of the CC Library panel, you can choose to add individual elements such as a paragraph style.

5 Scroll to the right and select the "Songs of the Garden" graphic on the cover, and then drag it into the library window. Double-click the name "Artwork 1" and change the name to **Songs of the Garden logo**. Be sure to click the name and not the icon of the graphic itself. Rename Text 1 to **Company Address**. Drag another graphic to the library and name it, such as the red maple leaf at the top of the cover. Examine the organization of the library.

After you've saved assets to a CC Library, you can use them in other InDesign documents, as well as in other Adobe CC applications, such as Photoshop and Illustrator.

6 Choose File > New > Document to open a new InDesign document.

7 Drag the "Company Address" asset in the CC Library to the page and click. The Centered White paragraph style uses Paper as the fill color, so you'll need to add a fill color to the text frame to see the white text. This paragraph style is also added to the list of styles in the Paragraph Styles panel in the new document.

8 Drag the "Songs of the Garden logo" asset from the CC Library to the page, and then click with the loaded graphics icon to place the graphic. Notice that the graphics retain the settings applied when they were added to the library.

9 Close the document without saving changes and return to the document you were working on.

You can also share CC Libraries with team members and other colleagues. For more information, see the "Exploring on your own" section at the end of this lesson.

Using snippets

A snippet is a file that holds objects and describes their location relative to one another on a page or page spread. Snippets are a way to conveniently reuse and place objects in position, and they can be shared with others. You create a snippet by exporting objects to a snippet file, which has the .idms extension. When you place a snippet file in InDesign, you can determine whether the objects are placed in their original positions or where you click. You can store snippets in an InDesign library as well as on your hard drive. Artwork added to CC Libraries from InDesign is also stored as a snippet.

To create a snippet, do one of the following:

- Using a selection tool, select one or more objects, and then choose File > Export. From the Save As Type (Windows) or Format (macOS) menu, choose InDesign Snippet. Type a name for the file, and click Save.

- Using a selection tool, select one or more objects, and then drag the selection to your desktop. A snippet file is created. Rename the file.

To add a snippet to a document, follow these steps:

1 Choose File > Place.

2 Select one or more snippet files, and then click Open.

3 Click the loaded snippet cursor where you want the upper-left corner of the snippet file to be.

 If you placed the insertion point in a text frame, the snippet is placed in the text as an anchored object.

 All objects remain selected after you place the snippet. By dragging, you can adjust the position of all objects.

4 If you loaded more than one snippet, press the arrow keys to change the snippet loaded in the cursor, and click the loaded snippet cursor to place the currently selected snippet.

Rather than place snippet objects according to where you click on a page, you can place them in their original locations. For example, a text frame that appeared in the middle of a page when it was saved as a snippet can appear in the same location when you place it as a snippet. To place snippets in their original location:

- Open the File Handling area of the Preferences dialog. In the Snippet Import area, choose Original Location from the menu.

 The default is Position At: Cursor Location, which places the object based on where you click on a page.

- Or press Alt (Windows) or Option (macOS) when you click with the loaded snippet cursor to override the current Snippet Import settings. If your preferences are set to Current Location, the snippet will be placed in its original location instead.

Exploring on your own

Now that you've had some practice working with imported graphics, here are some exercises to try on your own:

- Place different file formats with Show Import Options selected in the Place dialog, and see what options appear for each format. You can use any of the sample graphic files for this lesson or any other lessons or other available graphics. For a full description of all the options available for each format, see InDesign Help.

- Place a multiple-page PDF file or an Adobe Illustrator (.ai) file with multiple artboards. Turn on Show Import Options in the Place dialog, and import different pages from the PDF or different artboards from the Illustrator file.

- Open the InDesign document Vector-Raster.indd inside the folder RR_logos within the Lesson11 folder. This document contains the Ricky Records logo in both vector and raster formats, scaled up to 300%. Notice the difference in clarity. Experiment with further scaling these two versions of the logo. The clarity of the vector logo is maintained no matter how large you make it.

- During this lesson, you created a CC Library named "CD Elements." In addition to being able to access assets in CC Libraries using several Adobe graphics applications, you can share these libraries with team members and other colleagues to ensure that everyone is using the latest iterations.

 Choose Window > CC Libraries to open the CC Libraries panel, and then select CD Elements from the Libraries menu at the top of the panel. Choose Invite People from the panel menu. In the Invite To window that opens in the Creative Cloud app, enter the email addresses of the colleagues with whom you want to share your library. Choose Can Edit or Can View from the menu to specify whether recipients can view and edit elements (Can Edit) or view only (Can View). Click Invite. The recipients will receive an email invitation to collaborate on the library.

- Another way to import Illustrator graphics into InDesign is to copy the vector shapes from Illustrator and switch over to InDesign and paste. The Illustrator vector objects are converted into InDesign vector objects. You can use these objects as if you had drawn them in InDesign. If you have Illustrator, try this yourself. After you paste the objects into InDesign, change the color with the colors from your InDesign Swatches panel. Then use the Pen tool to select points and change the vector shape.

 If you do not have Illustrator, you can use the vector art of a butterfly that is in the pasteboard of the Start.indd file, to the left of the first spread.

Review questions

1 How can you determine the filename of an imported graphic in your document?

2 What is the difference between dropping a background with a clipping path versus with transparency?

3 What is the difference between updating a graphic file's link and relinking the file?

4 When an updated version of a graphic becomes available, how do you make sure that it's up to date in your InDesign document?

5 How do you scale an imported graphic and its frame at the same time?

6 What is a quick technique to make a duplicate of an object and place it in position at the same time?

Review answers

1 Select the graphic, and then choose Window > Links to see the graphic's filename highlighted in the Links panel. The graphic appears in the Links panel if it was imported by choosing File > Place or dragged into the layout from Explorer (Windows), Finder (macOS), or Bridge.

2 Clipping paths are vector drawn paths that create a crisp, sharp edge. Photoshop images that use transparency to remove the background create a soft, blended edge between the graphic and the background.

3 Updating a file's link simply uses the Links panel to update the onscreen representation of a graphic so that it represents the most recent version of the original. Relinking a selected graphic uses the Place command to allow you to insert a different graphic in place of the selected graphic.

4 In the Links panel, make sure that no modified link icon is displayed for the file. If a modified link icon is displayed, you can simply select the link and click the Update Link button. If the file has been moved, a missing link icon appears in the Status column in the Links panel, and you must locate it again using the Relink button.

5 Press Ctrl (Windows) or Command (macOS) and drag to scale either larger or smaller. Adding the Shift key keeps the graphic from being distorted.

6 With the Selection tool, press Alt (Windows) or Option (macOS) and drag to the desired location. A copy of the object is created at the new location, and the original object remains in place.

12 WORKING WITH TRANSPARENCY

Lesson overview

In this lesson, you'll learn how to do the following:

- Change the opacity of objects drawn in InDesign.

- Apply transparency settings to imported graphics.

- Apply transparency settings to text.

- Apply blending modes to overlapping objects.

- Apply feathering effects to objects.

- Add a drop shadow to text.

- Apply multiple effects to an object.

- Copy effects between objects.

- Apply an effect to one layer of a Photoshop file.

- Edit and remove effects.

 This lesson will take about 75 minutes to complete. To get the lesson files used in this chapter, download them from the web page for this book at adobepress.com/InDesignCIB2023. For more information, see "Accessing the lesson files and Web Edition" in the Getting Started section at the beginning of this book.

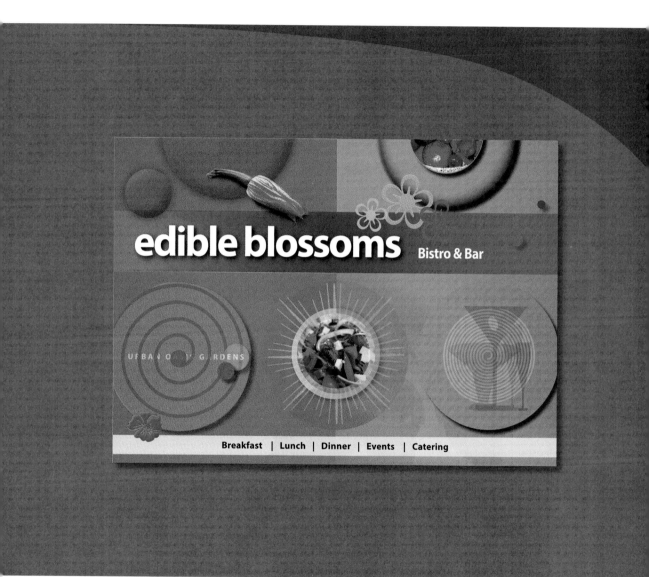

Adobe InDesign offers an array of transparency features to feed your imagination and creativity. These include controls over opacity, special effects, and color blends. You can also import graphic files that use transparency and apply additional transparency effects.

Getting started

The project for this lesson is the cover of a menu for a fictional restaurant, Edible Blossoms Bistro & Bar. By applying transparency effects and using multiple layers, you'll create a visually rich design.

● **Note:** If you have not already downloaded the project files for this lesson to your computer from your Account page, make sure to do so now. See "Getting Started" at the beginning of the book.

1 To ensure that the preferences and default settings of your InDesign program match those used in this lesson, move the InDesign Defaults file to a different folder following the procedure in "Saving and restoring the InDesign Defaults file" on pages 3–4.

2 Start InDesign. Click Open from the Home screen, or choose File > Open, and open the 12_Start.indd file in the Lesson12 folder, which is located within the Lessons folder in the InDesignCIB folder on your hard drive.

3 Choose File > Save As, name the file **12_Menu.indd**, and save it in the Lesson12 folder.

The menu appears as a blank page because all the layers that contain objects are currently hidden. You'll reveal these layers one by one as you need them, so it will be easy to focus on the specific objects and tasks in each exercise.

● **Note:** To better view the interface onscreen or in print, the screen captures in this book reflect the Medium Light interface rather than the default setting of Medium Dark. In addition, some screen captures illustrate User Interface Scaling for a closer look at interface elements. You can modify interface settings in Preferences.

4 To ensure that the panels and menu commands match those used in this lesson, choose Window > Workspace > [Advanced], and then choose Window > Workspace > Reset Advanced.

5 To see what the finished project looks like, open the 12_End.indd file in the Lesson12 folder.

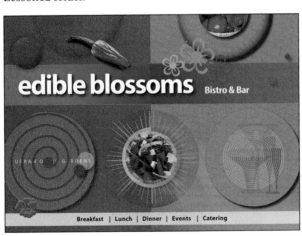

6 When you are ready to start working, either close the 12_End.indd file or leave it open for your reference. Then return to your lesson document by choosing 12_Menu.indd from the Window menu or by clicking the 12_Menu.indd tab in the upper-left corner of the document window.

Creating a background graphic

By applying transparency effects, you can create see-through objects that reveal any objects underneath. You'll begin by working with the bottommost layer, which will interact in different ways with the objects on layers above. This layer serves as a textured background visible through the objects above it that have transparency effects applied.

Because nothing is below the bottommost layer in the layer stack, there are no objects that would be revealed by applying transparency, so you won't apply any transparency effects to objects on this layer. Since this is the bottommost layer, any objects above this layer will interact with objects on this layer when transparency effects are applied to those objects stacked above.

1 Choose Window > Layers to display the Layers panel, or click the Layers panel icon (❤) in the panel dock.

2 In the Layers panel, select the layer labeled Background, scrolling as necessary to find it at the bottom of the layer stack. You'll import an image onto this layer.

3 Make sure that the two boxes to the left of the layer name show that the layer is visible (the eye icon [👁] appears) and unlocked (the layer lock icon [🔒] does not appear).

 The pen icon (✐) to the right of the layer name indicates that this is the layer on which any imported objects will be placed and new frames will be created.

● **Note:** Many of the steps in this lesson refer to the Control panel. You can use the Properties panel if you prefer, but it is not part of the default [Advanced] workspace. To open it, choose Window > Properties. To save screen space, dock it with the rest of the panel dock.

4 Choose View > Grids & Guides > Show Guides. You'll use the guides on the page to align the background image that you import.

5 Choose File > Place, and then open the 12_Background.tif file in your Lesson12 folder. This file is a grayscale TIFF.

▶ **Tip:** TIFF stands for Tagged Image File Format, a common bitmap graphic format often used for print publishing.

6 Move the loaded raster graphics icon (🖼) slightly outside the upper-left corner of the page; then click the corner where the red bleed guides meet so that the placed image fills the entire page, including the margins and bleed area. Keep the graphics frame selected.

7 Choose Window > Color > Swatches or click the Swatches icon () in the panel dock. You'll use the colors saved in the Swatches panel to apply color to the graphics frame and the image.

▶ **Tip:** InDesign offers many convenient ways to apply colors. You can also double-click the Fill box at the bottom of the Tools panel, and you can choose a fill color from the Fill menu in the Control and Properties panels.

8 In the Swatches panel, select Fill Color (). Scroll down the list of swatches to find the Green-Bright-Medium swatch and select it. Click the arrow to the right of the Tint field, and drag the slider to 80%.

The white background of the graphics frame is now an 80% tint of the green color, but the gray areas of the graphic remain unchanged.

After applying a fill color and tint to the frame.

▶ **Tip:** You can also use the Direct Selection tool to select the graphic; move the pointer within the frame and click when the hand pointer appears.

9 Using the Selection tool (), double-click the image or move the pointer within the frame and click the content grabber () to select the graphic instead of the frame. Select Green-Medium in the Swatches panel. Green-Medium replaces gray in the image, leaving the fill color for the frame unchanged. Set the tint of the image color to **73%**.

After applying a fill color and tint to the content (the image).

InDesign can apply color to grayscale or bitmap images saved in PSD, TIFF, BMP, or JPEG format. When you select the graphic within a graphics frame and then apply a fill color, the color is applied to the gray portions of the image rather than to the background of the frame.

10 In the Layers panel, click the empty box to the left of the Background layer name to lock the layer. Leave the Background layer visible so that you can see the results of the transparent objects you will be placing above this layer.

11 Choose File > Save to save your work.

You've just learned a quick method for colorizing a grayscale image. Although this method works well for some purposes, you may find the color controls available in Adobe Photoshop more effective for creating your final artwork.

Applying transparency settings

InDesign has extensive transparency controls that, when applied to an object, enable you to reveal underlying objects and control how those objects interact with objects below them. Additional transparency features, such as drop shadows, glows, and other effects, provide a wide range of possibilities for creating visual effects. You'll learn about these additional features later in the lesson.

In this part of the project, you'll practice using a variety of transparency features on several objects placed on the various layers in the menu file.

About the Effects panel

You use the Effects panel (Window > Effects) to specify the opacity and blending mode of objects and groups, apply a transparency effect, isolate blending to a particular group, and knock out objects in a group. The Effects panel (*fx.*) is also available in the panel dock as part of the default [Advanced] workspace.

Changing the opacity of solid-color objects

With the background graphic complete, you can start applying transparency effects to objects on layers stacked above it. You'll start with a series of simple shapes that were drawn using InDesign.

1 In the Layers panel, select the Art1 layer so that it becomes the active layer, and click the lock icon (🔒) to the left of the layer name to unlock the layer. Click

● Note: The shapes mentioned are named by the color swatch applied to the fill of the object. If the Swatches panel is not open, choose Window > Color > Swatches to open it, or open it from the panel dock.

the empty box on the far left of the Art1 layer name so that the eye icon (👁) appears, indicating that the layer is now visible.

2 Using the Selection tool (▶), click the circle filled with the Red-Dark swatch in the center of the page. This ellipse frame was drawn in InDesign and filled with 100% of the Red-Dark color.

3 Choose Window > Effects to display the panel or click the Effects icon (*fx.*) in the panel dock to the right of the document.

Effects panel overview

Blending mode—Specifies how colors in transparent objects interact with the objects behind them.

Opacity—Determines the opacity of an object, stroke, fill, or text, from 100% (completely opaque) to 0% (completely transparent). As you lower the opacity value of an object, the object becomes increasingly translucent and underlying objects become increasingly visible.

Levels—Indicates the opacity settings and any transparency effects applied to the selected page element (object, stroke, fill, text)—for example, an object's stroke may have 20% opacity and an effect applied, while the fill has no transparency settings. Click the triangle to the left of the word "Object" (or "Group" or "Graphic") to hide or display these level settings. The FX icon (*fx.*) appears on a level after you apply transparency settings there, and you can double-click the FX icon (*fx.*) to edit the settings.

Clear effects—Clears effects (object, stroke, fill, or text) from an object, sets the blend mode to Normal, and changes the Opacity setting to 100% throughout the object—that is, removes all transparency.

FX button—Displays a list of transparency effects.

Delete—Removes effects, but not a blending mode or opacity, from an object.

Isolate Blending—Applies a blending mode to a selected group of objects.

Knockout Group—Makes the opacity and blending attributes of individual objects in a group knock out, or block out, underlying objects within the group, while effects set on the group will still interact with objects outside the group.

— Adapted from InDesign Help

4 In the Effects panel, click the arrow on the right side of the Opacity percentage. An Opacity adjustment slider appears. Drag the slider to 70%. Alternatively, enter **70%** in the Opacity field, and press Enter (Windows) or Return (macOS).

Note: The FX icon (*fx*) is displayed in the Effects panel when you select the Red-Dark circle because it already has a drop shadow effect applied.

After you change the opacity of the Red-Dark circle, it becomes translucent. In the right half of the circle, the resulting color is a combination of the Red-Dark fill of the circle and the purple rectangle below. The left half of the circle combines the Red-Dark fill of the circle with the background image that shows through because the circle is no longer 100% opaque.

5 Select the semicircle in the upper-left area of the page filled with the Blue-Bright swatch, and in the Effects panel set the Opacity value to 50%. The semicircle now appears as a subtler variation in color against the background because it's now partially transparent, and you can see the leaves from the background image. Note that the opacity is applied at the Object level, which is the default behavior.

Before applying 50% Opacity. After applying 50% Opacity.

6 Select the full circle at the lower left filled with the Green-Medium swatch, and in the Effects panel set the Opacity value to 60%.

7 Choose File > Save to save your work.

Applying a blending mode

Changing an object's opacity creates a color that combines the color applied to an object with the colors applied to objects below it. Different blending modes change how the colors in stacked objects interact.

In this exercise, you'll apply a blending mode to objects on the page.

1 Using the Selection tool (▶), again select the circle in the center of the page filled with the Red-Dark swatch.

2 In the Effects panel, choose Overlay from the Blending Mode menu. Notice how the appearance of the colors changes.

70% opacity, Normal blending mode.

Same opacity with Overlay blending mode.

3 Select the Blue-Bright-filled semicircle in the upper-left corner of the page (the same object you set to 50% opacity in the previous exercise). In the Effects panel, choose Multiply from the Blending Mode menu.

50% Opacity, Normal blending Mode.

50% Opacity, Multiply blending Mode.

4 Choose File > Save.

For more information on the different blending modes, see "Specify how colors blend" in InDesign Help.

Adding transparency effects to imported vector and bitmap graphics

So far in this lesson, you have applied various transparency settings to objects drawn using InDesign. You can also apply opacity values and blending modes to imported graphics created with other applications, such as Adobe Illustrator and Adobe Photoshop.

Applying transparency to a vector graphic

1 In the Layers panel, select the Art2 layer. Unlock this layer and make it visible.

2 In the Tools panel, choose the Selection tool (). On the left side of the page, select the graphics frame that contains the black spiral image by clicking within the frame. This frame is in front of a Green-Medium-colored circle.

3 With the black spiral frame still selected, hold down the Shift key and click to select the graphics frame that contains a black spiral on the right side of the page. This frame is in front of a Purple-Cool-colored circle. Both of the graphics frames with spirals should now be selected.

4 In the Effects panel, choose Color Dodge from the Blending Mode menu, and set the Opacity value to 30%.

● **Note:** The effects display more clearly when you use High Quality Display. However, this may slow down your computer. To set the whole document to High Quality Display, choose View > Display Performance > High Quality Display. To set High Quality Display on individual objects, choose Object > Display Performance > High Quality Display while an object is selected.

Selected frames before applying blending mode and opacity.

After applying blending mode and opacity.

Next you will apply a blending mode to a stroke, separately from the rest of the object.

1 With the Selection tool (▶), select the circular graphics frame with the salad image in the center of the page.

2 A level indicates which part of an item has opacity settings or a blending mode, as well as whether transparency effects have been applied. It can be the item as a whole (Object), or it can be only parts of the item (Stroke, Fill, or Text). Levels enable you to apply different transparency settings or effects to different parts of the same object.

▶ **Tip:** You can hide or display level settings in the Effects panel by clicking the triangle to the left of the word Object (or Group or Graphic, depending on the selection).

In the Effects panel, click the triangle to the left of Object to reveal the levels (it may already be open). Click Stroke (beneath Object) to select it. Selecting the Stroke level applies any blending mode or opacity changes you make only to the stroke of the selected object.

3 From the Blending Mode menu, choose Hard Light. Notice how the result is different where the stroke is over different backgrounds. Because the stroke is over different objects, the left and right sides of the circle now look different. Compare the inside of the stroke that is over the image (the content of this frame) to the outside of the stroke that is not over the image.

● **Note:** Each area of an object interacts with what's behind it. Different blending modes produce different interactions.

4 Choose Edit > Deselect All, and then choose File > Save to save your work.

Applying transparency to a bitmap graphic

Next you'll apply transparency effects to an imported bitmap graphic. Although this example uses a monochromatic image, you can apply transparency settings to multicolor photographs as well. The process is the same as applying transparency effects to any other InDesign object.

1 In the Layers panel, select the Art3 layer. Unlock this layer and make it visible. You can lock either the Art1 layer or the Art2 layer to make it easier to prevent them from being modified accidentally.

2 Using the Selection tool (), select the graphics frame with the black starburst image in the center of the page. Because it's on the Art3 layer, the frame edge is displayed in blue, the color of the layer.

3 In the Effects panel, enter **70%** as the Opacity value, and press Enter or Return.

4 Double-click within the black starburst image to select the content rather than the frame, or click the content grabber (). You'll know when the content is selected rather than the frame, because the content boundaries change color and show the size of the content rather than the frame.

5 In the Swatches panel, select Fill Color (), and then select the Red-Bright color swatch. That color replaces the black areas of the image.

6 In the Effects panel, choose Screen from the Blending Mode menu, and leave the Opacity value at 100%. The starburst changes colors based on how the Screen blending mode interacts with objects beneath it.

Content selected and color swatch applied.

Effect applied to content.

7 Choose Edit > Deselect All, and then choose File > Save to save your work.

Importing and adjusting Illustrator files that use transparency

When you import Adobe Illustrator (.ai) files into an InDesign layout, InDesign recognizes and preserves any transparency settings that were applied in Illustrator. You can also adjust opacity, add a blending mode, and apply additional transparency effects in InDesign.

Now you will place a vector image of some drinking glasses that have transparency applied in Illustrator and then add additional transparency in InDesign.

1 Choose View > Fit Page In Window, if necessary.

2 In the Layers panel, make sure that the Art3 layer is the active layer and that the Art3, Art2, Art1, and Background layers are visible (👁).

3 Lock the Art2, Art1, and Background layers if not yet locked to prevent them from being modified.

4 Choose the Selection tool (▶) in the Tools panel, and then choose File > Place. Locate the 12_Glasses.ai file in your Lesson12 folder, press the Shift key and then double-click, or click Open. Adding the Shift key opens the Place PDF dialog showing the import options without the need to click Show Import Options in the Place dialog first.

5 In the Place PDF dialog, choose Bounding Box (All Layers) from the Crop To menu, and make sure that Transparent Background is selected.

6 Click OK. The dialog closes, and the pointer becomes a loaded vector graphics icon (⌐) with a preview of the file.

▶ Tip: When you're repositioning the image, Smart Guides can help you center the image perfectly within the purple circle.

7 Position the loaded vector graphics icon (⌐Ҭ) within the Purple-Cool-colored circle on the right side of the page and then click to place the graphic at full size. Drag the graphics frame to center it within the purple circle. Smart Guides are displayed when the frame is centered.

▶ Tip: To show only the Art3 layer and hide all other layers, Alt-click (Windows) or Option-click (macOS) the Toggle Visibility icon for the Art3 layer in the Layers panel.

8 In the Layers panel, click to hide the Art2, Art1, and Background layers so that only the Art3 layer is visible. This shows the placed image on its own, and you can see that the transparent color interactions within the Illustrator image itself are visible (no effects have been applied in InDesign).

9 Click to redisplay the Art2, Art1, and Background layers. Notice that the white "olive" shape is completely opaque, whereas the other shapes of the drinking glasses are partly transparent.

10 With the glasses image still selected, change the Opacity setting in the Effects panel to **60%**. Choose Color Burn from the Blending Mode menu. Now the colors and interactions of the image take on a completely different appearance, and the olive shape has become transparent as well.

11 Choose Edit > Deselect All, and then choose File > Save.

Applying transparency settings to text

Changing the opacity of text is as easy as applying transparency settings to graphic objects in your layout. You'll try the technique now as you change the color of text.

1 In the Layers panel, lock the Art3 layer, and then unlock the Type layer and make it visible. Click the Type layer to make it the active layer (🖋).

2 Using the Selection tool (▶), click the text frame "URBAN OASIS GARDENS" in the lower left. If necessary, zoom in so that you can read the text easily.

To apply transparency settings to text or to a text frame and its contents, you must select the frame with the Selection tool. You cannot specify transparency settings when text is selected with the Type tool.

3 In the Effects panel, select the Text level so that any opacity and blending mode changes you make will apply to the text only.

4 Choose Overlay from the Blending Mode menu, and change Opacity to **70%**.

▶**Tip:** Effects are applied to all text within a text frame. You cannot apply an effect to some words and not others. To achieve that look, the words with an effect applied must be in separate text frames from the words without an effect applied.

5 Double-click the Hand tool (✋) to fit the page in the window, and then choose Edit > Deselect All.

Now you'll change the opacity of a text frame's fill, separately from the text.

1 Using the Selection tool (▶), click the text frame at the bottom of the page that contains "Breakfast | Lunch | Dinner | Events | Catering." If necessary, zoom in so that you can read the text easily.

2 Select the Fill level in the Effects panel, and change Opacity to **70%**. Notice that this changes the white background while the text remains black.

3 Try the same effect with the Object level selected, and notice how this time the text turns gray, which is not what we want.

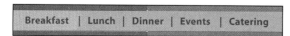

You've now seen the advantage of being able to apply effects to different parts of the same object. Choose Edit > Undo Set Transparency Parameters.

4 Choose Edit > Deselect All, and then choose File > Save.

Working with effects

So far in this lesson, you've learned how to apply transparency by changing the blending mode and the opacity of objects drawn in InDesign, imported graphics, and text. Another way to apply transparency is by using the nine transparency effects in InDesign.

You'll try some of these effects now as you fine-tune the menu's artwork.

Applying a basic feather to the edges of an image

Feathering is another way to apply transparency to an object. Feathering creates a subtle transition from opaque to transparent so that any underlying object or the page background is visible through the feathered area. InDesign features three types of feathering:

- **Basic Feather** softens or fades the edges of an object over a distance that you specify.

- **Directional Feather** softens the edges of an object by fading the edges to transparent from directions that you specify.

- **Gradient Feather** softens the areas of an object by fading them to transparent.

First, you'll apply Basic Feather, and then you'll move on to Gradient Feather.

1 In the Layers panel, unlock the Art1 layer if it's locked, and ensure it's the active layer.

2 If necessary, choose View > Fit Page In Window to see the entire page.

3 With the Selection tool (▶), select the Purple-Warm-filled circle on the upper-right side of the page.

▶ **Tip:** You can also open each of the effects dialogs from the Effects panel menu.

4 Choose Object > Effects > Basic Feather. The Effects dialog appears, displaying a list of the transparency effects on the left and an accompanying set of controls on the right.

5 Make sure that Preview is selected and, if necessary, move the dialog to view the effects of your changes. In the Options area of the Effects dialog, set these options:

- In the Feather Width field, type **0.3125 in**.

- Change both the Choke value and Noise value to **10%**.

- Leave the Corners option set to Diffused.

Transparency effects

Drop Shadow—Adds a shadow that falls behind the object, stroke, fill, or text.

Inner Shadow—Adds a shadow that falls just inside the edges of the object, stroke, fill, or text, giving it a recessed appearance.

Outer Glow and **Inner Glow**—Add glows that emanate from the outside or inside edges of the object, stroke, fill, or text.

Bevel and Emboss—Adds various combinations of highlights and shadows to give text and images a three-dimensional appearance.

Satin—Adds interior shading that makes a satiny finish.

Basic Feather, **Directional Feather**, and **Gradient Feather**—Soften the edges of an object by fading them to transparent.

—From InDesign Help

Transparency...	
Drop Shadow...	⌥⌘M
Inner Shadow...	
Outer Glow...	
Inner Glow...	
Bevel and Emboss...	
Satin...	
Basic Feather...	
Directional Feather...	
Gradient Feather...	

► **Tip:** In addition to applying transparency effects by choosing Object > Effects and then choosing an option from the submenu, you can add effects from the Effects panel menu, or you can click the Effects button (*fx.*) at the bottom of the Effects panel and then choose an option from the submenu.

6 Notice how the edges of the purple circle are now shaded and look more dimensional.

7 Click OK to apply the settings, and close the Effects dialog.

8 Choose Edit > Deselect All, and then choose File > Save.

Applying a gradient feather

You can use the Gradient Feather effect to fade an object from opaque to transparent.

1 Using the Selection tool (►), click the Purple-Warm-filled vertical rectangle that covers the right half of the page.

2 At the bottom of the Effects panel, click the FX button (*fx.*) and choose Gradient Feather from the menu.

3 The Effects dialog appears, displaying the Gradient Feather options.
In the Gradient Stops area, click the Reverse Gradient button () to reverse the location of solid and transparent colors.

4 Click OK. The purple rectangle will now be solid on the right and fade to transparent on the left.

Now you will use the Gradient Feather tool to adjust the direction of the fade.

● **Note:** You can also set an exact angle in the Effects dialog as seen in step 3. Using the Gradient Feather tool allows you to work more visually and experiment with the result of dragging at different angles.

5 In the Tools panel, select the Gradient Feather tool (). (Be careful not to choose the Gradient Swatch tool.) Drag the pointer up from the bottom left of the purple rectangle toward the right about halfway up to the top of the rectangle to change the gradient direction.

Left, the gradient feather moves horizontally from right to left—that is, the fill is solid on the right and fades to transparent as it moves left.

Right, the direction has been changed. The purple fill is solid at the top right and fades to transparent at the bottom left.

6 Choose Edit > Deselect All, and then choose File > Save.

Adding a drop shadow to text

When you add a drop shadow to an object, the result is a 3D effect that makes the object appear to float above the page and cast a shadow on the page and objects below. You can add a drop shadow to any object, and you have the option to assign a shadow independently to an object's stroke or fill or to the text within a text frame.

Now you'll try this technique by adding a drop shadow to the "edible blossoms" text. A key concept to understand when applying effects to text is that effects can be applied only to a whole text frame, not to some of the words within a frame. You work with the Selection tool and select the text frame, not the Text tool.

1 Using the Selection tool (), select the text frame that contains the words "edible blossoms." Hold down the Z key to temporarily access the Zoom tool, or select the Zoom tool () and magnify the frame so that you can see the text clearly.

2 At the bottom of the Effects panel, click the FX button (*fx.*), and choose Drop Shadow from the menu.

3 In the Blending area of the Effects dialog, enter **85%** for Opacity. In the Position area, enter **.06 in** for both X Offset and Y Offset. In the Options area, enter **0.125 in** for Size and **5%** for Spread. Make sure that Preview is selected so that you can see the effects on your page.

▶ **Tip:** By making sure the shadow is tucked under the object, the shadow is creating the desired 3D effect on the object. When there is space between the shadow and the object, too much visual attention is drawn to the shadow itself.

You can also adjust the distance and angle of a drop shadow with the settings in the Position area, either by typing numbers in the settings or by dragging the line in the angle circle to a new position.

4 Click OK to apply the drop shadow to the text.

5 Choose Edit > Deselect All, and then choose File > Save to save your work.

Next, you will apply multiple effects to a single object and then edit them.

Applying multiple effects to an object

● **Note:** The Effects dialog allows you to apply multiple effects to a single object and shows you which effects are applied to a selected object (indicated by a checkmark on the left side of the dialog).

You can apply more than one transparency effect to an object. For example, you can create the impression that an object is embossed and that it has a glow around it by applying two transparency effects.

In this exercise, you'll apply an embossed effect and an outer glow effect to two vector objects on the page.

1 Choose View > Fit Page In Window. In the Layers panel, turn off the visibility of the Art3 layer.

2 Using the Selection tool (▶), select the Blue-Bright-filled semicircle in the upper-left corner of the page.

3 At the bottom of the Effects panel, click the FX button (*fx.*), and choose Bevel And Emboss from the menu. If necessary, move the dialog so that you can preview the effects.

4 In the Effects dialog, make sure that Preview is selected so that you can view the effects on the page. Then specify the following settings in the Structure area:

Size: **0.3125 in**; Soften: **0.25 in**; Depth: **60%**

You can also click the up arrow to click through increments and stop at these values for the Size and Soften settings and use the slider for the Depth setting.

5 Leave the rest of the settings as they are, and keep the Effects dialog open.

6 From the list on the left side of the dialog, click the words "Outer Glow" to add another effect to the semicircle. The box next to Outer Glow will be checked, and the settings dialog will change to display the options for Outer Glow rather than for Bevel And Emboss. Specify these settings:

Mode: **Multiply**; Opacity: **80%**; Size: **0.25 in**; Spread: **10%**

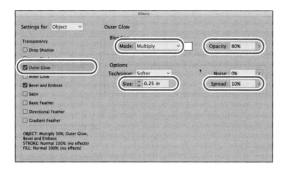

7 Click the Set Glow Color box to the right of the Mode menu. In the Effect Color dialog, make sure that Swatches is selected in the Color menu, choose Black from the list of colors, and then click OK.

8 Click OK again in the Effects dialog. This object now has multiple effects applied.

Next, you will apply the same effects to another object on the page in the simplest way: select the object with the effect you want to copy, drag the FX icon (*fx*) next to this effect in the Effects panel, and drop it on another object.

Copying effects between objects

1 Double-click the Hand tool (✋) to fit the page in the window, if needed.

2 Using the Selection tool (▶), select the blue semicircle in the upper-left corner of the page again, if necessary (it should still be selected).

3 With the Effects panel open, drag the FX icon (*fx*) on the right side of the Object level in the panel directly on top of the small green circle on the page to the left of the semicircle with the multiple effects. A gripping hand icon with a plus sign will appear. Release the mouse button. The same effect settings are now applied to the small green circle. Note that only the effects are applied; the color of the green circle is not changed.

▶ **Tip:** When nothing is selected (Edit > Deselect All), you can press the W key to toggle between Preview and previous screen modes.

4 Choose Edit > Deselect All, and then choose the Preview screen mode from the menu at the bottom of the Tools panel to see the results without guides and frame edges. Return to Normal mode.

5 Choose File > Save.

You can use the same technique to apply effects to objects in other documents:

1 Choose File > Open and open the file 12_Start.indd again. If you left the 12_End.indd file open for reference, close it now.

2 Choose Window > Arrange > 2-Up Vertical so that you can see the 12_Menu.indd and 12_Start.indd files side by side.

3 In the file 12_Start.indd, make sure that the Background layer is active (since it is already unlocked).

4 Draw a shape, such as a rectangle or ellipse frame, with one of the drawing tools, and choose any color for the fill from the Swatches panel.

5 Select the tab of the 12_Menu.indd file to make it the active file, and using the Selection tool (▶), select the same Blue-Bright-filled semicircle in the upper-left corner of the page, which now has multiple effects applied.

6 Use the same technique as in step 3 of the previous exercise: with the Effects panel open, drag the FX icon (*fx.*) on the right side of the Object level, and drop it directly on top of the shape you just drew in the other InDesign file. Release the mouse button when you see the gripping hand with a plus sign. The effect settings are applied to the object in the other document. Notice again that it's the effects that are copied, not the fill color or other attributes.

7 Close the 12_Start.indd file without saving.

Another way to apply effects to other objects is to create an object style, as you learned in Lesson 9. You can then import that object style into other documents by using Load Object Styles in the Object Styles menu.

Transparency settings and options

Many transparency effect settings and options are the same across different effects. Common transparency settings and options include the following:

Angle and Altitude—Determines the lighting angle at which a lighting effect is applied. A setting of 0 is equivalent to ground level; 90 is directly above the object. Click and drag the angle radius or enter a degree measurement. Select Use Global Light if you want a uniform lighting angle for all objects. Used by the Drop Shadow, Inner Shadow, Bevel And Emboss, Satin, Directional Feather and Gradient Feather effects.

Blending Mode—Specifies how colors in transparent objects interact with the objects behind them. Used by the Drop Shadow, Inner Shadow, Outer Glow, Inner Glow, and Satin effects.

Choke—Along with the Size setting, determines how much of the shadow or glow is opaque and how much is transparent; large settings increase opacity, and small settings increase transparency. Used by the Inner Shadow, Inner Glow, Basic Feather and Directional Feather effects.

Distance—Specifies the offset distance for the Drop Shadow, Inner Shadow, or Satin effect.

Noise—Specifies the amount of random elements in the opacity of a glow or shadow as you enter a value or drag the slider. Used by the Drop Shadow, Inner Shadow, Outer Glow, Inner Glow, Basic Feather and Directional Feather effects.

Opacity—Determines the opacity of an effect; drag the slider or enter a percentage measurement. Used by the Drop Shadow, Inner Shadow, Outer Glow, Inner Glow, Gradient Feather, Bevel And Emboss, and Satin effects.

Size—Specifies the amount of shadow or glow. Used by the Drop Shadow, Inner Shadow, Outer Glow, Inner Glow, Bevel And Emboss and Satin effects.

Spread—Determines the transparency of the blur within the shadow or glow effect as established by the Size setting. A higher percentage makes the blur more opaque. Used by the Drop Shadow and Outer Glow effects.

Technique—These settings determine how the edge of a transparency effect interacts with background colors. Softer and Precise are available for the Outer Glow and Inner Glow effects:

> **Softer**—Applies a blur to the edge of the effect. At larger sizes, doesn't preserve detailed features.

> **Precise**—Preserves the edge of the effect, including its corners and other sharp details. Preserves features better than the Softer technique.

Use Global Light—Applies the global light setting to the shadow. Used by the Drop Shadow, Bevel And Emboss, and Inner Shadow effects.

X Offset and Y Offset—Offsets the shadow on the x- or y-axis by the amount you specify. Used by the Drop Shadow and Inner Shadow effects.

—From InDesign Help

Applying an effect to a layer of an imported image

In Lesson 11 you learned how to turn layers in an imported Photoshop file off and on. We'll use that technique and also apply an InDesign effect to one of the layers.

1 In the Layers panel, make sure the Art3 layer is visible and unlocked.

2 Using the Selection tool (▶), click the squash blossom image above the words "edible blossoms." Press Ctrl+= (Windows) or Command+= (macOS) a few times to zoom in on the image.

Notice that the shadow on this image doesn't look right. The grays are on top of the background colors without interacting with them. The technique to correct this requires two copies of the image placed exactly on top of each other. You'll do that first.

3 Ensure that the frame with the squash blossom image (Squash-Blossom.psd) is selected. Choose Edit > Copy, and then choose Edit > Paste In Place. There are now two copies of this image exactly on top of each other.

4 Choose Object > Hide. The topmost copy of the image is now hidden.

5 Click to select the remaining copy of the image. Choose Object > Object Layer Options. If necessary, move the dialog so that you can preview the effects. Click the Preview button so that you can watch the change, and then turn off the Foreground layer so that only the Shadow layer is visible and click OK.

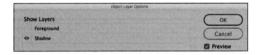

● **Note:** To see the results most clearly, switch to the Preview screen mode by pressing the W key. Then press the W key again to switch back to Normal screen mode so that you can see the frame edges.

6 Open the Effects panel and change Blending Mode to Multiply. Notice the dramatic difference in how the grays of the Shadow layer now interact with the colors below.

Bottom copy of the squash blossom image with the foreground layer turned off.

Shadow layer of the bottom copy set to Multiply blending mode.

7 Choose Object > Show All On Spread. The second copy of the squash blossom image is visible again. Now you need to make sure you are selecting the topmost copy of the image. One easy way to be sure which one you are selecting is to click a different object and then click back on the squash blossom. The second copy will be selected because it's on top.

8 Choose Object > Object Layer Options again. This time turn the Shadow layer off and click OK. Now the shadow to which you applied the Multiply effect is the only one that's visible. The result is much more visually pleasing because the gray values in the shadow are now interacting with the colors below them.

● **Note:** The Object Layer Options visibility settings work like they do in the Layers panel. You make a layer visible by clicking in the left square next to the layer name to make the eye icon visible. You make a layer invisible by clicking the eye icon so that it disappears, turning that layer off.

9 Lock all of the layers below Art3. Then drag across an edge of the squash blossom image. Because the two images are exactly on top of each other, you'll select both instances of the image. Choose Object > Group. Grouping both instances makes it easy for you to reposition this image while keeping them aligned exactly on top of each other.

10 Experiment with moving this object above different backgrounds. For example, while the group is selected, open the Layers panel and move the solid blue square from the Art3 layer to the Type layer. Then drag the squash blossom down so that part of the shadow crosses the white letters of "edible blossoms." Notice that the shadow blends with the green colors while remaining black only where it crosses the white areas. Using only the black channel for shadows in Photoshop ensures that they will stay a neutral gray when printed.

▶ **Tip:** By using this technique, you can blend the shadow with background colors, while at the same time ensuring that the shadow will print with black ink only when it's over white (the paper).

11 Move the image back to the Art3 layer and position it above the "edible blossoms" type, near its original location. The position does not have to be exact.

12 Choose Edit > Deselect All, and then choose File > Save.

Editing and removing effects

Applied effects can easily be edited or removed. You can also quickly check whether any effects have been applied to an object.

First you'll edit the gradient fill behind the restaurant title, and then you'll remove the effects applied to one of the circles.

▶ **Tip:** To quickly see which pages in your document contain transparency, choose Panel Options from the Pages panel menu, and then select Transparency. A small icon (⬚) is displayed next to any pages containing transparency.

1 In the Layers panel, make sure that the Art1 layer is unlocked and that it is visible and active. If you switched to Preview screen mode in the previous exercise, switch back to Normal mode. Choose View > Fit Page In Window.

2 Using the Selection tool (▶), click the frame with the gray gradient fill that's behind the text "edible blossoms."

3 Choose Window > Properties to display the Properties panel. One of the properties available is Effects. In this case, the effect is Gradient Feather, which is displayed with an underline to the right of the Effects button (*fx.*). Click it, and the Effects panel opens. In the menu that appears, the Gradient Feather effect has a checkmark next to it, which indicates that it is already applied to the selected object.

4 In the Effects dialog, turn on Preview and move the dialog so that you can see this object (if necessary). Under Options, change Type to Radial. Under Gradient Stops, click the midpoint (the small diamond shape above the gradient ramp). Slide it left and right, and watch how it changes the look. The black color radiating from the center spreads farther across the page or becomes much smaller. The setting is shown as a percentage in the Location field. Set the midpoint to about 35%. Click OK to update the Gradient Feather effect.

5 Click the Fill button in the Appearance area of the Properties panel. Change the fill color to Blue-Dark and press the Enter key. Choose Edit > Deselect All. Close the Properties panel.

When not to use transparency

Transparency vs. tints: Transparency effects are great creative tools, but they do result in a more complex file. They should be used purposefully and not when the visual style can be accomplished more simply.

The most common scenario is when you want to make the color of a frame lighter and that frame has nothing behind it that needs to show through, such as when it's on a white background. In those cases you should use a tint of the color, not an Opacity setting. Use the slider in the Color or the Swatches panel, or use a tint swatch. See Lesson 5 for more details on tints.

100% of a color. Tint of that color on a Opacity setting applied
 white background. to that color on a white
 background.

> **Tip:** If you like to use the sliding function of the Opacity slider to see a color change before making a choice, note that you can also use the same slider functionality in the Swatches panel to make tints. Click the arrow to the right of the Tint value and use the slider that pops up. You can see the tint change as you move the slider.

Now you will remove the effects applied to an object.

1 In the Layers panel, turn on visibility for all layers and unlock all layers.

2 Select the Selection tool (▶). While holding down the Ctrl key (Windows) or Command key (macOS), click the small Purple-Warm circle to the right of and below the salad image in the center of the page. Your first click may select the rectangular frame above the circle. Click again within the small circle to select it. Or lock the Art3 layer (the larger rectangle is on this layer) to more easily work with objects on the Art2 layer below (the Purple-Warm circle is on this layer).

3 In the Effects panel menu, choose Clear Effects. This will remove the Drop Shadow effect applied to the circle while leaving the Opacity setting applied. That's why the purple color of the circle is still interacting with the objects below.

> **Tip:** When you hold down the Ctrl key (Windows) or Command key (macOS) and click overlapping objects, the first click selects the topmost object, and each successive click selects the next object below in the stacking order.

> **Tip:** The Clear Effects button (▨) at the bottom of the Effects panel also removes blending mode and opacity settings from the object (clears all transparency) in addition to clearing effects.

4 Choose Edit > Deselect All, and then choose File > Save.

5 Double-click the Hand tool (🖑) to fit the page in the window, and change to the Preview screen mode to admire your work.

Congratulations! You have completed the lesson.

Exploring on your own

Try some of the following ways of working with InDesign transparency options:

1 Navigate to page 2. Experiment with the buttons at the bottom of the Effects panel, Isolate Blending and Knockout Group, which work only with grouped objects. The objects at the top of the page show the difference between these options; the resulting effects are the opposite of each other. In the example, each leaf has a blending mode applied, and the three leaves are grouped.

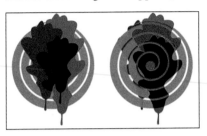

Left, Isolate Blending is turned on; objects in the group interact with one another, but not with objects below.

Right, Knockout Group is turned on; objects in the group interact with objects below, but not with one another.

2 Experiment with changing the blending modes and effects applied to the text frame and objects at the bottom. The text frame is filled with a gradient, and an effect is applied, but the text is editable, so you can select the text and type whatever you'd like.

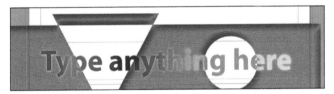

3 Now create some shapes yourself on a new layer (by using the drawing tools, by copying objects from page 1, or by importing new copies of some of the image files used in this lesson). Apply fill colors to any shapes that don't have content, and position your shapes so that they overlap each other, at least partially. Then:

 • Select the uppermost object in your arrangement of shapes. Using the controls in the Effects panel, experiment with other blending modes, such as Luminosity, Hard Light, and Difference. Then select a different object and choose the same blending modes in the Effects panel to compare the results.

 • In the Effects panel, change the Opacity value of some of the objects but not others. Then select different objects in your arrangement and use the Object > Arrange > Send Backward and Object > Arrange > Bring Forward commands to observe different results.

 • Experiment with combinations of different opacities and different blending modes applied to an object. Do the same with other objects that partially overlap the first object to explore the variety of effects you can create.

Review questions

1 How do you apply a transparency setting or effect to different parts of an object?

2 If you've applied transparency effects to an object, what is the easiest way to apply the same effects to a different object?

3 What is the importance of the stacking order of layers and of objects within layers when you work with transparency?

4 What's the quickest and easiest way to remove transparency effects from an object to which multiple effects are applied?

5 What is a limitation of applying effects to text?

6 When is it better to use a tint instead of an opacity setting?

Review answers

1 Choose one of the levels in the Effects panel: Object level applies to the object as a whole, but you can also choose Stroke, Fill, or Text levels and apply separate settings to each.

2 Select the object to which you've applied transparency effects, and then drag the FX icon displayed on the right side of the Effects panel to another object.

3 The transparency of an object affects the view of objects below (behind) it in the stacking order and the appearance of the front object. For example, objects below a semitransparent object can be seen behind it—like objects behind a colored plastic film. By changing which objects are above (in front) or below (behind), the resulting color and/or effect can be quite different.

4 Select the object, and then click the Clear Effects button at the bottom of the Effects panel. This clears effects, blending modes, and opacity settings. The trash can button clears only effects. You can also choose Clear All Transparency from the Effects panel menu.

5 Effects can be applied to the entire text frame only. They cannot be applied to separate words within a text frame.

6 It's better to use a tint when the object has nothing below it with which a transparency effect will interact, such as when it's on top of a white background. In other words, if you simply want to make the object lighter and not have anything behind show through, use a tint.

13 PRINTING AND EXPORTING

Lesson overview

In this lesson, you'll learn how to do the following:

- Check a document for potential printing issues and fix them.

- Manage the colors used in a document.

- Confirm that an InDesign file and all of its elements are ready for printing.

- Preview a document onscreen before printing.

- Create different Adobe PDFs for proofing and for press.

- Create an Adobe PDF preset for press-ready PDFs.

- Print a proof of a document.

- Create a print preset to streamline the printing process.

- Assemble all necessary files for printing or delivery to a service provider or commercial printer.

- Export graphics for the web and other digital destinations.

 This lesson will take about 50 minutes to complete. To get the lesson files used in this chapter, download them from the web page for this book at adobepress.com/InDesignCIB2023. For more information, see "Accessing the lesson files and Web Edition" in the Getting Started section at the beginning of this book.

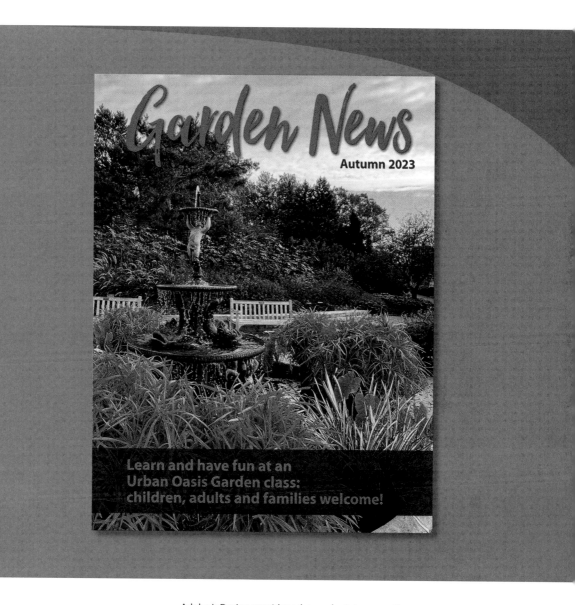

Adobe InDesign provides advanced print-preparation and printing controls to help you manage the printing process, regardless of the output device. You can easily output your work to a laser or inkjet printer, an onscreen proof PDF, or a press-ready PDF.

Getting started

In this lesson, you'll do some print-preparation work on a magazine cover and spread. The document will be printed on a color inkjet or laser printer for proofing and also on a high-resolution imaging device, such as a platesetter used in commercial offset printing. Prior to printing, you will export the document to a PDF file that can be used in a review process.

● **Note:** If you have not already downloaded the project files for this lesson to your computer from your Account page, make sure to do so now. See "Getting Started" at the beginning of the book.

1 To ensure that the preferences and default settings of your InDesign program match those used in this lesson, move the InDesign Defaults file to a different folder following the procedure in "Saving and restoring the InDesign Defaults file" on pages 3–4.

2 Start InDesign. Choose File > Open and open the 13_Start.indd file in the Lesson13 folder, located inside the Lessons folder within the InDesignCIB folder on your hard drive.

3 An alert message informs you that the document contains one modified link. Click Don't Update Links. You will correct this problem later in this lesson.

When you print an InDesign document or export a PDF file for printing, InDesign must access the original artwork that was placed in the layout. If imported artwork has been moved, graphic filenames have changed, or the original files are no longer available, InDesign alerts you that the original artwork cannot be located or has been modified. This alert appears when a document is opened, printed, exported, or checked for printing using the Preflight panel. InDesign shows the status of all files necessary for printing in the Links panel.

4 To ensure that the panels and menu commands match those used in this lesson, choose Window > Workspace > [Printing And Proofing], and then choose Window > Workspace > Reset Printing And Proofing.

● **Note:** To better view the interface onscreen or in print, the screen captures in this book reflect the Medium Light interface rather than the default setting of Medium Dark. In addition, some screen captures illustrate User Interface Scaling for a closer look at interface elements. You can modify interface settings in Preferences.

5 Choose File > Save As, rename the file **13_Press.indd**, and save it in the Lesson13 folder.

6 To see what the finished project looks like, open the 13_End.indd file in the Lesson13 folder. For this lesson, the difference between the Start and End files is not visible in a preview; instead, you'll need to examine the Links and Color Swatches panels to see the differences.

7 When you are ready to start working, either close the 13_End.indd file or leave it open for your reference. Then return to your lesson document by choosing 13_Press.indd from the Window menu or by clicking the 13_Press.indd tab in the upper-left corner of the document window.

Preflighting files

InDesign provides controls for performing a quality check on a document prior to printing, handing off the document to a print service provider, or publishing to a digital format. "Preflight" is the standard industry term for this process. In "Preflighting as you work," in Lesson 2, "Getting to Know InDesign," you learned how you can take advantage of the live preflight capabilities in InDesign. This lets you monitor a document as you create it to prevent potential problems.

You can use the Preflight panel to confirm that all graphics and fonts used in the file are available for printing and exporting and that there are no instances of overset text. Now you'll use the Preflight panel to identify a modified graphic and overset text in the sample layout.

1 Choose Window > Output > Preflight, or click the Preflight icon (🐾) in the panel dock.

▶ **Tip:** You can also access the Preflight panel by double-clicking "2 errors" at the bottom of the document window or by choosing Preflight Panel from the menu to the right of "2 errors."

2 In the Preflight panel, make sure that On is selected and confirm that [Basic] (Working) is selected in the Profile menu. Notice that two types of errors are listed: LINKS and TEXT. The number following in parentheses indicates one link-related error and one text-related error.

3 Click the triangle to the left of LINKS and then to the left of TEXT to reveal more information about the errors. Click the triangle to the left of Modified Link to display the name of the modified graphic file. Double-click the Lily.jpg link name; this centers the graphic in the document window and selects the graphics frame. (In this case it goes to page 8 because that's where this graphic is placed.) The Info area at the bottom of the panel displays details about the selected problem and how to fix it. If you look carefully at the frame that contains the magazine title, you'll notice a yellow triangle in the upper-left corner (the modified link alert (▲) badge), which indicates that the graphic file has been modified after it was placed into the layout.

4 You can click the Link badge or double-click the modified link icon in the Links panel to update this graphic. Click one of those now.

● **Note:** Modified or missing graphics are displayed in low resolution regardless of the current Display Performance setting.

Notice that after you update the link to the Lily.jpg graphic, the color has changed. A typical scenario in production is that color correction was done to this photo after the design was approved to go to press. Also notice that the modified link alert in the upper-left corner has changed to a link symbol, meaning that the graphic is linked to the InDesign file and is not missing or modified.

Modified graphic before updating.

After updating.

Tip: The Display Performance area of the Preferences dialog lets you change default settings for the display of raster images, vector graphics, and objects to which transparency is applied, independently of each other. Choose Edit > Preferences > Display Performance (Windows) or InDesign > Preferences > Display Performance (macOS) to open the Preferences dialog.

5 To display the document at high resolution, choose View > Display Performance > High Quality Display. It's a best practice to view a document at High Quality Display when checking it for production quality.

6 Open the Preflight panel again by clicking the icon in the panel dock (). Notice that there is now a single TEXT error. In the same way you clicked the missing or modified graphic to locate it, click the triangle to the left of Overset Text (1). Then click the page number to the right of the listed text frame. This navigates to the text frame and selects it, centering it in the document window.

7 The red square with a plus sign inside indicates that there is more text that does not fit into the frame. There should be no overset text in a file that is ready to be reviewed, published, or printed.

8 Using the Selection tool (), pull down the center handle on the text frame enough to display the last line of the paragraph. Now the Preflight panel status shows No Errors (No errors) at the bottom. Every document should have No Errors in the preflight status when you are finished preflighting.

Note: If any links remain modified at this point, open the Links panel menu and choose Update All Links.

9 Choose File > Save to save the changes you've made to the document, and close the Preflight and Links panels.

Two other important aspects of preflighting for printing on press are the color space and resolution of the images. Some workflows use the CMYK color space for press, and others use RGB and convert to CMYK at different points in production. Images for press need to be high resolution, where the effective resolution is at least 300 ppi. Since such files can be very large, the image files in this lesson are small so that the lesson can be easily downloaded. See "Viewing information about linked files" in Lesson 11, "Importing and Modifying Graphics," for how to customize the Links panel to show the information important to your workflow, which will help you add color space and resolution to your preflighting process. You can also create custom preflight profiles suited to your workflow and to different output destinations (see the sidebar on the next page).

Creating a preflight profile

When the live preflight feature is enabled (that is, when On is selected in the Preflight panel), the default working profile, called [Basic], is used to preflight your InDesign documents. This profile checks for basic output conditions, such as missing or modified graphic files, unresolved caption variables, inaccessible URL links, overset text, and missing fonts.

You can also create your own custom preflight profiles or load profiles from your print service provider or another source. When you create a custom preflight profile, you specify the conditions you want to detect. Here's how to create a profile that alerts you when non-CMYK colors are used in a layout:

1 If the Preflight panel is not open, choose Window > Output > Preflight, and then choose Define Profiles from the Preflight panel menu.

2 Click the New Preflight Profile button (+) on the lower-left side of the Preflight Profiles dialog to create a new preflight profile. In the Profile Name box, enter **CMYK colors only**.

3 Click the triangle to the left of Color to display color-related options, and select Color Spaces And Modes Not Allowed.

4 Click the triangle to the left of Color Spaces And Modes Not Allowed, and then select all of the available options except CMYK and Gray (RGB, Lab, Spot Color, and HSB). Gray works with CMYK because it prints on the black plate only. Deselect Cyan, Magenta Or Yellow Plates Not Allowed. (This would be used for a preflight profile for documents printing with spot colors only.)

5 Leave existing preflight criteria for Links, Images And Objects, Text, and Document as is. Click Save, and then click OK.

6 Choose CMYK Colors Only from the Profile menu in the Preflight panel. Notice the additional errors listed in the Error area of the panel.

7 Click the triangle next to Color to expand the display, and then click the triangle next to Color Spaces And Modes Not Allowed to see a list of objects that do not use the CMYK color model. Click various objects to view information about the problem and how to fix it. (Make sure the Info area of the Preflight panel is visible. If not, click the triangle to the left of Info to display it.)

8 When you're done viewing information, choose [Basic] (Working) from the Profile menu to return to the default profile used for this lesson.

Previewing separations

If your documents need to be prepared for commercial printing, you can use the Separations Preview panel to check whether the colors are set up properly for the particular printing process that will be used for this document. For example, will the document be printed with process CMYK inks, with spot-color inks, or with a combination of those? The answer determines what you need to check for and fix.

1 Navigate to page 1, and choose Window > Output > Separations Preview. Or click the Separations Preview icon () in the panel dock to open the panel.

2 Choose Separations from the View menu in the Separations Preview panel. Adjust your view so that you can see the page, and adjust the panel's height so that all the listed colors are visible. If necessary, choose View > Fit Page In Window.

▶ **Tip:** If you choose Ink Limit from the View menu in the Separations Preview panel, InDesign displays in red any areas that exceed the specified maximum ink percentage. (The default Ink Limit value is 300%.)

3 Click the eye icon () next to CMYK to hide all page elements that use CMYK colors. The elements that are still visible are elements that use something other than CMYK color. In this case, spot colors are applied.

▶ **Tip:** Because the printing process works by laying each ink down exactly on top of each other, you want to avoid using multiple inks on very small objects such as body text. This is because if there is the slightest variance in the inks being positioned exactly on top of each other (mis-registration), the text will look blurry. When small objects like text use only one ink, this problem is avoided.

4 Click the eye icon next to Bright Green. The text at the bottom disappears, which means it's using this spot color. This should be the process color version of the design's theme color. You'll correct this later in the lesson.

5 Click the eye icon next to CMYK to show all colors again, and navigate to page 2. Click the eye icon next to Black to turn it off. The headline disappears, but some of the body text is still visible. The intention is for the body text to be black only, but because it's still visible when the black plate is off, it will print on several plates.

6 To investigate why this is and fix it, slide the page to the left so that you can see part of the body text from page 3. The text on both pages is supposed to be the same, but something is wrong. Neither story should be visible when the Black plate is turned off. Turn Black back on, open the Paragraph Styles panel (Window > Styles > Paragraph Styles), and click in the body text on page 3 using the Type tool (T,). The style Body Copy No Indent is highlighted. Now click in the body copy on page 2. The [Basic Paragraph] paragraph style is highlighted. Somewhere in the creative process, this text was formatted without using the paragraph style.

Select some text at the end of the first paragraph and drag through the beginning of the third paragraph. Click the Body Copy No Indent paragraph style to apply it to all paragraphs.

7 Press the Esc key to exit the Type tool. Turn off Black again in the Separations Preview panel. Now all of the text that you expect to be black disappears. This is because the character color is part of the paragraph style, and that color is 100% Black. You can see how using paragraph styles can prevent many errors, including accidentally styling text in the wrong color.

8 Choose Off from the View menu in the Separations Preview panel to enable viewing of all colors, and then close the panel. Then close the Paragraph Styles panel, choose Edit > Deselect All, and choose File > Save.

Coated vs. uncoated ink names

The widely used PANTONE ink libraries include both Coated (C) and Uncoated (U) versions. The ink names include (C) or (U) to indicate the difference.

This difference in appearance onscreen is to approximate the way the ink will look printed on these different types of paper. In the vast majority of projects printed with spot color inks, there is only one plate for each ink. Therefore, if you have a file using these colors, you'll need to make sure only one instance of the same color is in the document so that only one printing plate for that color will be produced.

▶ **Tip:** Sometimes special effects are achieved in printing with spot color inks by printing the same ink twice. This is called a "second hit" and must be set up in the file like an additional color.

Coated vs. uncoated paper

The photo to the right shows how different the same CMYK ink mix looks when printed on coated paper (left) and on uncoated paper (right). The same difference happens with any kind of ink, including PANTONE inks.

This difference in appearance is caused by the physical characteristics of the paper. Uncoated paper absorbs more ink than coated paper, so it looks more matte and less glossy when the ink dries. The same color can look darker on uncoated paper and brighter on coated paper.

Managing colors

One of the best practices when making sure a file is ready for commercial printing is to ensure that the colors used—and only those colors—appear in the Swatches panel. This is one of the first checks a service provider will do when they receive your files.

▶ **Tip:** Notice the color called TRUMATCH 8-b. TRUMATCH is a library of color swatches built into InDesign that is specific to the CMYK printing process. Printed swatch books for both coated and uncoated paper are available.

1 Choose Window > Color > Swatches to open the Swatches panel. Pull the panel down so that it's long enough to see all of the colors. Notice that there is another blue color just below Blue-Bright that looks nearly identical. This commonly happens in the creative process, but the intention is to use the same color for this blue throughout, so this must be fixed in production. Drag the Swatches panel to the dock for easy access later. You can close the Color and Gradients panels. Then click the icon () in the panel dock to open the Swatches panel again.

2 First, we'll find all unused swatches. Before starting, make sure that both Fill Color () and Stroke Color () are set to [None]. Then choose Select All Unused from the Swatches panel menu. Choose Delete Swatch from the panel menu to remove the unused swatches. If this second blue color was not used, the problem would be solved. But since it remains, we'll have to take another step.

Select All Unused Colors.

3 Select the blue just below Blue-Bright, C=67 M=43 Y=0 K=0. Again choose Delete Swatch from the panel menu. This time, because this color is used somewhere in the document, a dialog opens that enables you to replace the swatch being deleted with a different swatch. From the menu, choose Blue-Bright. Because we know that the intention of the design is that this color be

consistent throughout the document, it's not necessary to find each instance where it might be used. Click OK.

Select Bright Green and notice the symbol to the right of the name (). This indicates that this is a spot ink. But we've been instructed that this project is printing with CMYK inks only. Click the trash can at the bottom of the Swatches panel to delete this color. In the Delete Swatch dialog, replace it with the design's theme color Green-Brightest, which is a process (CMYK) color. Click OK. This fixes the separation issue we saw on the cover in the Preflight exercise.

4 Next we want to find out whether any additional colors are in the file that were not saved as swatches. Choose Add Unnamed Colors from the Swatches panel menu. Three colors appear that were not there before. (This happens when you create colors in the Color panel and use them in the file but don't take the step of adding them to the Swatches panel.) The important thing is whether these colors are using inks that will or will not work with this file's printing process. These are CMYK colors, so they are not a problem.

Add Unnamed Colors.

Locating colors

You can find colors in your InDesign document using the Find/Change dialog. The two major uses of this ability are 1) to find objects of a particular color and change them to another color as a design decision, and 2) to find objects that are using colors that will cause problems in the printing process or other media so that you can change these objects to the correct colors.

In this exercise, you'll use this feature to find colors that will cause problems in the printing process.

1 Return to the Swatches panel and scroll to the top. Select the color below the default Black swatch, c70m67y64k74. From the panel menu, choose Find This Color. In the Find/Change dialog, click Find Next. InDesign selects the first object it finds that uses this color, the grasshopper graphic to the left of the story at the top of page 2. (You may remember that the grasshopper was still visible when you turned off the black plate in a previous exercise. If an object is made with black ink only, it will disappear when you turn off the black plate.)

The grasshopper looks like it's black, but it's colored with this swatch that actually consists of all four inks. Colors like this one are a typical result of working in the RGB color space in Adobe Illustrator, converting the file to CMYK color space, and then pasting the object into InDesign. Any objects using this color need to be the default [Black] so that they print on the black plate only.

2 Under Change Color, choose [Black] and click Change. You won't see a visible change because onscreen the colors look the same. But in the Swatches panel, [Black] will now be selected. You can change the color of this graphic because it's an InDesign vector object, not a linked graphic.

● **Note:** With the Find Color feature, you can find objects and text during the same search.

3 Click Find Next again. InDesign selects the next object that uses the c70m67y64k74 swatch. The type in the return address on the back page will be selected. Click Change and then click Find Next again. InDesign returns a message that says the search is complete and lists how many instances were found. Click OK in this message and then click Done to close the Find/Change dialog. Choose Edit > Deselect All.

4 Choose Select All Unused from the Swatches panel menu again to confirm that the c70m67y64k74 swatch is no longer in the document. Click the Delete button (🗑) at the bottom of the Swatches panel, and choose File > Save.

Finding graphics with spot colors

The Locate Colors feature can also find imported graphics with spot colors. You'll have to open them in their original application to fix this if InDesign's Ink Manager features won't work for the situation (such as spot colors with transparency effects) or if your preference is to correct the color in the graphic file.

1 Open the Swatches panel again if necessary, and then choose Sort > All Swatches By Name from the Swatches panel menu.

2 Notice that there is one Pantone spot color, PANTONE 130 C. Select this color, and choose Find This Color from the panel menu.

3 The Find/Change dialog will open, and PANTONE 130 C will be selected for Find Color. Click Find Next. InDesign selects the next object that is PANTONE 130 C. In this case, it moves to page 3 and selects the yellow flower graphic.

4 To quickly check whether this is InDesign vector art that you can change within InDesign or if it's an imported graphic, choose Window > Links or click the Links button (✏) in the panel dock. YellowFlower.ai is selected in the Links panel. Your choice is to open this graphic in Illustrator and change the colors to process colors or use the Ink Manager in InDesign to convert this color to process when the document is printed or exported.

5 Close the Links panel and the Find/Change dialog.

Next you will learn to use the Ink Manager to set this graphic to output with process inks without opening it in Illustrator.

Using the Ink Manager

The Ink Manager provides control over the inks used at output time. Changes you make using the Ink Manager affect only the output. They do not change how the colors are defined in the document.

The Ink Manager options are especially useful for controlling how inks will print without having to go back and change imported graphics. For example, if a publication will be printed with CMYK process inks but a graphic uses a spot color, the Ink Manager provides the option of changing the spot color to the equivalent CMYK process color.

1 Open the Separations Preview panel, choose Separations from the View menu, and then turn off PANTONE 130 C. Parts of the flower graphic disappear, which are the objects colored with PANTONE 130 C. Then turn PANTONE 130 C back on. Choose Ink Manager from the panel menu.

2 In the Ink Manager dialog, click the spot icon (◼) to the left of the PANTONE 130 C color swatch. It changes to a CMYK icon (◼). The color will now print as a combination of CMYK colors instead of printing on a separate color plate. Click OK to close the Ink Manager.

▶ **Tip:** If a document contains two similar spot colors when only one is required or if the same spot color has two different names, the Ink Manager lets you map the variations to a single spot color. This is called an "ink alias."

3 Now open the Separations Preview again and select Separations from the View menu. You see that PANTONE 130 C is no longer there. Set View to Off and close the Separations Preview panel.

▶ **Tip:** If the file will in fact print with spot color inks, you can use transparency effects without a problem, as long as you are careful that the effect uses the same inks as the rest of the file.

The All Spots To Process option at the bottom of the Ink Manager dialog lets you convert all spot colors to process colors. This is a good solution if you want to limit the printing to the CMYK process without having to change the spot colors in the source files of the imported graphics. However, if the spot color graphics use transparency, the results from the Ink Manager are not reliable. In those cases, you must open the graphic and change the spot colors to process in the original application.

In many workflows, you'll have both CMYK and spot versions of the same art so that you can link to the one that is correct for the printing process of each particular document. If the project is printing in CMYK and spot colors and transparency effects are used in imported graphics, you can't convert to CMYK in InDesign because there will be errors such as white boxes where the effect is supposed to be. In this case, you must use a CMYK version of the imported graphic.

Previewing transparency effects

In the past, documents that contain objects to which transparency effects had been applied needed to undergo a process called *flattening* when they were printed or exported. Flattening divides the objects into vector-based areas and rasterized areas, which are further divided into squares called "tiles." Even if you use the High Resolution setting when flattening, rasterized areas will be a much lower resolution than the image processor at a commercial printer, and the effect won't look as good when printed compared to not flattening. The flattening strategy was needed before image processors at commercial printers could process transparency.

Modern image processors *can* process transparency without flattening. The best final appearance is achieved by *not* flattening at any point in the production process. The Flattener Preview panel can help you see which objects in the file are using transparency effects so that you can make sure you've used them intentionally and not by accident. It enables you to quickly find objects with transparency and check the settings.

Next, you'll use the Flattener Preview panel to determine the objects to which transparency effects have been applied.

1 Navigate to page 1, and choose View > Fit Spread In Window.

2 Choose Window > Output > Flattener Preview, or click the Flattener Preview icon () in the panel dock, and then position the Flattener Preview panel so that you can see the entire page.

3 In the Flattener Preview panel, choose Transparent Objects from the Highlight menu and click the Refresh button. The entire page is displayed with a dimmed grayscale preview, except for the areas with transparency effects.

4 If it's not already selected, choose [High Resolution] from the Preset menu. Notice how the masthead at the top of the page is displayed with a red highlight. This object has a drop shadow, which is a transparency effect.

▶ **Tip:** Transparency can be applied in Adobe Photoshop, in Illustrator, or directly in an InDesign layout. The Flattener Preview panel identifies transparent objects, regardless of whether the transparency was created using InDesign or in an imported graphic.

5 Scroll or click through to the next spread. Now nothing is highlighted in red, and the spread looks the same as when Flattener Preview is off. That's because there are no objects with transparency on this spread.

6 Choose None from the Highlight menu to disable Flattener Preview, and then close the panel.

Previewing the pages

Now that you've previewed the color separations and areas of transparency in the layout, you'll preview the page to get an idea of how the magazine will look when printed.

1 At the bottom of the Tools panel, press and hold the Screen Mode icon (🖵) and then choose Preview from the menu. The guides, frame edges, invisible characters, pasteboard, and other nonprinting items are hidden. This is the best onscreen view of how the document will look when it is printed and trimmed. It also enables you to quickly preview a page, rather than turning the nonprinting items off one at a time.

2 Press and hold down the Screen Mode icon again, and then choose Bleed. Additional space outside the perimeter of the final document trim size is displayed. This view is used to confirm that objects that need to bleed do in fact extend beyond the edge of the document. After the job is printed, this excess area is trimmed to the final printed size.

● **Note:** For more information about bleed, review the section about printing to the edge of the paper in Lesson 3, "Setting Up a Document and Working with Pages."

3 Scroll through the entire document and look over everything before printing or exporting. In Bleed mode, you can see whether items at the edge are extended far enough into the pasteboard, in addition to looking at everything else you

can see in Preview mode. Confirm once again that the Preflight status shows No Errors (■ No errors).

Normal Screen Mode. Preview Screen Mode. Bleed Screen Mode.

4 Choose Normal from the Screen Mode menu, and then choose File > Save.

After confirming that the file looks acceptable, you are ready to print it.

Creating an Adobe PDF proof

● **Note:** PDF is the acronym for Portable Document Format, which is the industry-standard way to share layouts throughout the creative and production process.

If your documents need to be reviewed by others, you can easily create Adobe PDF files to transfer and share. Those with whom you share the PDF can review the project without having InDesign or the fonts and links. PDFs can be compressed to a smaller size; all fonts and graphics are self-contained in a single composite file, and files are displayed onscreen and print the same whether opened in Windows or in macOS. InDesign exports directly to Adobe PDF.

Exporting your publication as an Adobe PDF document also has many advantages for commercial printing. You can create a compact, reliable file that contains all the elements in the InDesign file, including high-resolution graphics and all the fonts, so that your service provider can work with the file and get the same high-quality results they would from working directly with the InDesign file, and you don't have to send all the fonts and links. A properly exported PDF from InDesign is ready for your service provider to use with the tools for commercial printing such as preflight checks, trapping, imposition, and color separation.

These two purposes for using a PDF have different requirements. You can use presets to save settings that are appropriate for various purposes so that you don't have to select multiple choices in the Export dialog each time you export. In other words, presets allow you to set up requirements for different purposes and then use them reliably every time. You can also share presets with colleagues to ensure that all PDFs are exported with the same settings by everyone.

You will now create an Adobe PDF file suitable for review and proofing purposes using one of the built-in presets.

1 Choose File > Export.

2 Choose Adobe PDF (Print) from the Save As Type (Windows) or Format (macOS) menu. For the filename, type **13_Proof.pdf**. If necessary, navigate to the Lesson13 folder, and then click Save. The Export Adobe PDF dialog opens.

3 In the Adobe PDF Preset menu at the top of the dialog, choose [High Quality Print]. This setting creates PDF files suitable for output on desktop printers and for onscreen proofing without creating a file that is too large to easily share, while also being a high enough resolution for a reviewer to evaluate the quality of pixel-based (raster) graphics.

► **Tip:** The presets available in the Adobe PDF Preset menu are used for creating a range of Adobe PDF files, from small files suitable for onscreen viewing to press-ready files suitable for high-resolution output.

Select View PDF After Exporting. This will open the PDF file in Adobe Acrobat as soon as it's finished exporting, which saves you the step of switching to Acrobat and opening the file. Leave the default choices for the remaining settings.

● **Note:** Adobe PDF (Print) export in InDesign is performed in the background, which enables you to continue working while an Adobe PDF is being created. If you try to close your document before the background process is completed, InDesign will display a warning message.

4 Click Export. A progress circle rotates in the upper right of the menu bar (⟳). An Adobe PDF file is generated and displays on your monitor in Adobe Acrobat Pro DC or Adobe Acrobat Reader DC.

5 Review the Adobe PDF. This type of PDF is appropriate to share with colleagues or customers for review purposes or to print to an office printer for review on paper.

► **Tip:** You can also view the PDF export progress by opening the Background Tasks panel (Window > Utilities > Background Tasks).

► **Tip:** To learn more about the review process, explore the Share For Review feature and the PDF Comments feature. Start by choosing Help > InDesign Help to access Adobe's InDesign support website.

Creating a press-ready PDF and saving a PDF preset

InDesign files are submitted to commercial printers either as native files (which you'll learn about later in this lesson) or as press-ready PDFs. Press-ready PDFs are high resolution and include the bleed area. In this exercise, you will learn about creating an Adobe PDF file suitable for commercial printing.

InDesign includes a PDF export preset called [Press Quality] that has most of the necessary settings already defined. However, it's not correct for documents that include any objects that bleed. You will start with that preset and modify it so that you have a press-ready preset that includes the bleed.

1 Choose File > Adobe PDF Presets > Define. The Adobe PDF Presets dialog opens. Scroll down to [Press Quality], select it, and click New. This enables you to create a new preset based on the options already set up in the default Press Quality preset.

2 In Preset Name, type **Press Quality With Bleed**.

● **Note:** You can also choose Use Document Bleed Settings, but by setting a bleed amount in the preset, even documents without a bleed amount set in Document Setup will export with the specified bleed area.

3 Click Marks And Bleeds on the left and make the following changes: Under Marks, select Crop Marks. In Offset, type **.125**. In the Bleed And Slug area, for Bleed enter **.125** in the Top field, and make sure the Same Settings icon (⟦⟧) is turned on to set the same bleed settings on all sides.

4 Click OK and then Done. This preset will now be available whenever you export to PDF.

5 Choose File > Adobe PDF Presets > Press Quality With Bleed. This is a faster way to use PDF presets than choosing File > Export. Name the file **13_Press_HighRes.pdf**, and then click Save. The Export Adobe PDF dialog opens. Make sure that View PDF After Exporting is selected, and then click Export.

When the PDF opens in Acrobat, notice how the cover photo extends past the crop marks. The crop marks indicate where the blade will cut through the paper to trim the magazine to the final size. In this case, it will cut through the printed image and produce a clean edge with no unprinted paper showing.

The most important required characteristics of a PDF for commercial printing are:

- High-resolution pixel-based (raster) graphics

- Bleed included

- PDF compatibility of at least Acrobat 5 so that transparency effects are not flattened

The preset you have made does all of these things. However, you may want to edit it. For example, you may want to increase the version of Acrobat compatibility because you know that everyone in your production workflow is up to date and there is no reason to be compatible back to Acrobat 5.

To check whether a PDF will have live transparency or will be flattened, examine the different options available when compatibility with Acrobat 4 is selected rather than later versions of Acrobat. Since Acrobat 5 was the first version to support transparency, the Acrobat 4 file format uses the strategy of flattening to approximate the visual appearance of transparency effects.

1 Switch back to InDesign, and choose File > Adobe PDF Presets > Define. The Adobe PDF Presets dialog opens. Scroll down to Press Quality With Bleed, and choose Edit.

2 Click the Advanced category on the left. Notice that the Transparency Flattener settings are dimmed and not available. This means the transparency will not be flattened. Now change the Compatibility setting to Acrobat 4. The Transparency Flattener settings are now available because exporting to Acrobat 4 means exporting to a file format that can't process transparency effects, and therefore you must compensate for that by flattening these effects. Click Cancel and then Done to exit the dialog.

▶ **Tip:** If you need to create a flattened press-ready PDF, use the [High Resolution] Transparency Flattener preset in the Advanced panel of the Export Adobe PDF dialog.

 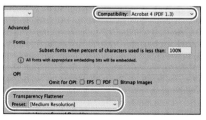

Sharing a preset

1 Choose File > Adobe PDF Presets > Define. The Adobe PDF Presets dialog opens. Scroll down to Press Quality With Bleed. Click this name and then choose Save As.

2 Choose a name for your preset and navigate to a location on your hard drive where you wish to save it. Click Save. You can now share this file with others.

3 To import a preset, you use the Load button in the Adobe PDF Presets dialog. Click Load and navigate to the Lesson13 folder on your hard drive. Select Proof-Facing-Pages.joboptions, and then click Open. Click Done to exit the Adobe PDF Presets dialog. The preset is now available.

This preset creates a high-quality proof that will display in Acrobat with the left and right pages of a spread next to each other on the screen.

4 Choose File > Adobe PDF Presets > Proof Facing Pages and export the file again, naming it as you wish. In Acrobat, scroll or click through the file to the first spread after the cover to see it displayed as a spread rather than single pages. Controlling the view this way ensures that the reviewer will see the document in the closest parallel to paging through the printed magazine.

Printing a proof and saving a print preset

● **Note:** If you do not have access to a printer, you can choose PostScript File from the Printer menu. You can then choose an Adobe PDF PPD (if available) and complete all the steps in the remainder of the lesson. If no other PPDs are available, you can choose the Device Independent PPD; however, some controls covered in the remainder of the lesson are not available if you choose Device Independent.

In this section, you'll create a print preset to save settings—and save time in the future—without having to individually set each option for the same device each time. The process is similar to saving a PDF preset. You will use this preset for proofing on your office printer, assuming the printer has only Letter or A4 paper.

1 Choose File > Print.

2 From the Printer menu in the Print dialog box, choose your inkjet or laser printer.

The options you see throughout this exercise will be different depending on the device selected. Follow the steps with your printer's options as best you can.

3 From the left side of the Print dialog, select Setup, and then choose the following options:

- Paper Size: US Letter (or A4)

- Orientation: Portrait

- Scale To Fit

4 From the same list on the left side of the Print dialog, select Marks And Bleed, and then choose these options:

- Crop Marks

- In the Offset field, enter **.125**.

- Page Information

- In the Bleed And Slug area, the Use Document Bleed Settings option will be selected because this document was set up with a bleed amount in Document Setup.

● **Note:** If you want to enter a bleed amount yourself, deselect Use Document Bleed Settings.

Notice the preview in the lower left of the dialog. This illustrates the options you've turned on and how the document will fit on the paper.

The crop marks print outside of the page area and provide guides showing where the final document is trimmed after printing, just as we saw in the press-ready PDF. The page information automatically adds the document name and the page number, along with the date and time it was printed, to the bottom of the printout. Since the document itself is already letter size, and the crop marks and page information are printed outside the page edges, you must select Scale To Fit in order to fit the page, bleed, and marks onto a Letter or A4 piece of paper.

5 On the left side of the Print dialog, select Output. Choose Composite RGB or Composite CMYK from the Color menu. (If you are printing to a black-and-white printer, choose Composite Gray.)

Choosing Composite CMYK causes any RGB colors, including those in RGB graphics, to be converted to CMYK at the time of printing. This setting changes neither the original, placed graphic files nor any colors applied to objects. Which setting you should choose depends on your device.

▶ **Tip:** If your document contains transparency that is flattened during the printing process, select Simulate Overprint in the Output area of the Print dialog when printing to achieve the best printed result.

6 On the left side of the Print dialog, select Graphics. Choose Optimized Subsampling from the Send Data menu.

When Optimized Subsampling is selected, InDesign sends only the image data necessary for the printer selected in the Print dialog. This can reduce the time it takes to send the file to print. To send the complete high-resolution graphic information to the printer, which may take longer to print, select All from the Send Data menu.

● **Note:** The Optimized Subsampling option cannot be selected if you are using the Device Independent PPD, because this generic driver can't determine what information a selected printer may need later.

7 Choose Subset from the Fonts Download menu. This causes only the fonts and characters that are actually used in the document to be sent to the output device and can reduce the time it takes to print single-page documents and short documents without much text. This option may be dimmed with your device.

8 Leave the settings in the Color Management and Advanced categories at their defaults for this lesson.

▶ **Tip:** To quickly print using a preset, choose File > Print Presets and select the desired preset. Holding down the Shift key while doing this will print using the settings in the selected preset without opening the Print dialog.

9 Click Save Preset at the bottom of the Print dialog, name the preset **Proof Fit To Page** in the Save Preset dialog, and click OK. InDesign returns to the Print dialog with your settings in place. Next time you want to print with these settings, you can do so in one step by choosing the preset you just made.

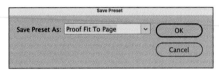

10 Click Print to print the file or click Cancel.

Creating a print preset saves Print dialog settings so that you don't need to individually set every option each time you print with the same requirements to the same device. You can create multiple presets to meet various quality capabilities of individual devices and to meet your various project needs. When you want to use these settings in the future, you can choose them from the Print Preset menu at the top of the Print dialog. You can also share print presets with colleagues.

Print Booklet

A very useful way to proof documents that will be stitched into a booklet is to use the Print Booklet feature. This feature enables you to make a proof on paper that will be constructed similarly to the commercially printed booklet. When you print a document this way, you can fold the stack of pages in half, staple them on the fold (spine), and page through the proof to review it.

1 Choose File > Print Booklet to open the Print Booklet dialog.

2 Click the Print Settings button at the bottom of the dialog. In the Print dialog, select the Setup category, and change Orientation to Landscape (Horizontal). Click OK. InDesign returns to the Print Booklet dialog.

3 Leave Booklet Type set to 2-Up Saddle Stitch, and then click Preview on the left side of the dialog. Notice how the last page is next to the cover. This is called a "printer's spread"—in this case, the outside covers. Click Cancel (or print the document if you choose).

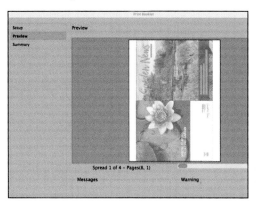

Printer's spread of the outside covers from the lesson file.

4 Open the file named 13_SixteenPager.indd. Choose File > Print Booklet, and follow steps 2 and 3. Click through the spreads using the slider at the bottom of the preview window. This file is set up with large page numbers so that you can easily see how the pages fit together in printer spreads. Click Cancel (or print the document if you choose), and then close the 13_SixteenPager.indd file.

Printer's spread of the outside covers of a sample 16-page file.

Printer's spread of the inside covers of a sample 16-page file.

Printer's spread of an interior spread in the sample 16-page file.

Printer's spread of the center spread in the sample 16-page file.

Packaging files

The Package feature assembles a copy of your InDesign document, all linked graphics, and the fonts needed for printing into a single folder. Packaging a document ensures that a project can be provided to a vendor with no worry that something might be missing and cause a delay in the production process. InDesign packaged projects and press-ready PDFs are the two industry-standard ways of providing an InDesign project to a commercial printer.

Packaging is also used to share the project with others and to archive finished projects in a way that gathers all components together.

Now you'll package the files for the magazine in preparation for sending them to your print provider.

● **Note:** Adobe Fonts available as part of your Creative Cloud membership are not included when you use the Package command.

1 Choose File > Package. The Summary area of the Package dialog notifies you of one more printing-related issue.

Because the document contains RGB images, InDesign alerts you to their presence. This alert is standard because some printers want you to convert all images to CMYK before submitting the file. But others want to do the conversion from RGB to CMYK using standards for their presses, so read this alert but don't change anything. A best practice is to talk to your print provider and ask what they prefer.

Leave Create Printing Instructions unselected.

▶ **Tip:** InDesign can create a text file of instructions and your contact information that will accompany the InDesign file, links, and fonts in the package folder. The recipient of the package can use the instructions file to better understand what you want done and how to contact you if questions arise.

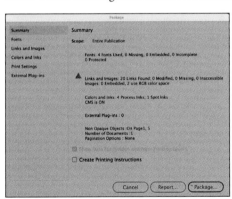

2 Click Package. If asked to save the document, click Save.

3 In the Create Package Folder dialog, browse to locate the Lesson13 folder. Notice that the folder that will be created for the package is named 13_Press Folder. InDesign automatically names the folder based on the document name, which you assigned at the beginning of this lesson. You can change this name if you wish.

4 Confirm that the following options are selected:

- Copy Fonts (Except Activated From Adobe Fonts And Non-Adobe CJK Fonts)
- Copy Linked Graphics
- Update Graphic Links In Package (relinks the packaged InDesign file to the links in the packaged Links folder, not their original location)
- Include IDML (so that others can open the file in a previous version of InDesign if necessary)
- Include PDF(Print) (so that you can't forget to send a PDF proof along with the native files)

```
☑ Copy Fonts (Except activated from Adobe Fonts and non-Adobe CJK fonts)
☑ Copy Linked Graphics
☑ Update Graphic Links In Package
   Use Document Hyphenation Exceptions Only
   Include Fonts and Links From Hidden and Non-Printing Content

☑ Include IDML
☑ Include PDF(Print)        Select PDF Preset:   [High Quality Print]        ⊟

   Instructions...
   View Report

New Folder                                              Cancel    Package
```

5 Choose [High Quality Print] from the Select PDF Preset menu.

6 Click Package.

7 Read the warning message that informs you about the licensing restrictions that may affect your ability to include the fonts when you send the file, and then click OK.

8 Switch to File Explorer (Windows) or the Finder (macOS), and then navigate to the 13_Press Folder in the Lesson13 folder (located inside the Lessons folder within the InDesignCIB folder on your hard drive). Open the folder.

Notice that InDesign created a duplicate of the InDesign document, the IDML file, and the PDF of your document. It also copied all fonts into a Document Fonts folder and all graphics and other linked files necessary for high-resolution printing into a Links folder. Because you selected Update Graphic Links In Package, the duplicate InDesign file now links to the copied graphic files located in the package folder instead of to the original linked files on your hard drive or server. This makes the document easier for a printer or service provider to manage and also makes the packaged folder ideal for archiving and sharing.

9 Review the PDF created by the packaging process to check that all text and graphics are correct. When you have finished viewing its contents, close the 13_Press Folder and return to InDesign. Typically, this folder is zipped and uploaded to the service provider, with the included PDF serving as the proof for them to check their work.

Exporting graphics for the web and other digital destinations

You can export graphics from InDesign into files that can be used by a web developer or for other digital purposes. The advantage of doing this is that the developer does not have to spend time re-creating your work, and you'll know that objects you've spent a lot of time and care creating in InDesign will be correctly represented on a web page, mobile device, social media, or email graphic.

You'll want to talk to the developer who'll be working with your files and ask what specifications they prefer, such as for resolution. For example, the old 72 dpi standard for the web may not apply to projects that are intended for display on modern tablets that have a much higher screen resolution.

You'll try a couple of examples using general settings for this exercise.

1 Navigate to page 5. There are two graphics that were created with InDesign objects and type. The red one also includes InDesign effects.

2 Select the yellow graphic. Choose File > Export, and from the Save As Type (Windows) or Format (macOS) menu, choose PNG. This format is better for graphics with clean edges such as these circles and type. Use JPEG for photographic objects. Name the file **Tomatoes-Peas-Carrots-Yellow.png** and save it to the Lesson13 folder.

3 In the Export area of the Export PNG dialog, click Selection so that only this object is exported, and in the Image area, choose:

- Quality: Maximum

- Resolution (ppi): 150

- Color Space: RGB

In the Options area, choose:

- Transparent Background (because this object is a circle and has an inner circle cutout)

- Anti-alias (creates smoother edges)

- Simulate Overprint (to preserve the look of effects)

Then click Export.

4 Switch to the desktop and locate the file you just exported. Drag it over the icon of a web browser to view it. If you have Photoshop, you can open it there as well.

5 Switch back to InDesign and select the red circle graphic. Repeat steps 2–4, naming this file **Tomatoes-Peas-Carrots-Red.png**. When you view this file in a web

browser or Photoshop, notice that the appearance of the applied InDesign effect is preserved, as is the transparency in the middle and outside of the circle.

Original objects in InDesign. Exported PNG file in Photoshop.

Another method is to export multiple objects at once. To do this, you'll use a couple of features that you may not have used before. One is the Export To HTML feature, but for the purpose of exporting graphics, you don't have to know anything about HTML coding. We'll use the feature just to get the images it generates. The second is the Articles panel, which is a way to organize elements in InDesign files that are intended for digital output such as EPUB or web pages.

1 Navigate to page 4 by holding down the spacebar and clicking. The hand icon (🖑) appears. Keep the spacebar pressed and drag until you can see the images on page 4. These are some of the final images from Lesson 11.

2 With the Selection tool (▶), drag across all four images to select them.

3 Choose Window > Articles. The Articles panel opens. It's empty except for some instructional text.

4 Drag the selected images over the Articles panel window. A gripping hand with a + sign appears. Release the mouse button. A dialog appears allowing you to name this article; type **Flowers** and click OK. The Articles panel shows the name of the article and the four images you just added.

5 Choose File > Export, and from the Save As Type (Windows) or Format (macOS) menu, choose HTML. Name the file **Flowers-for-web**. Navigate to the Lesson13 folder, and click Save.

6 The HTML Export Options dialog box opens. In the first panel, General, choose Same As Articles Panel in the Content Order area.

7 Choose Image from the list at the left. Make sure that Copy Images is set to Optimized (the default). Click Preserve Appearance From Layout (For Graphic/Media Objects). This is what will keep the cropping, sizing, and positioning within the frame of the images, as well as any InDesign effects that may have been applied. For Resolution, select 150, and for Image Conversion, select PNG. The PNG file format will preserve transparency, and objects that are not rectangles will export with a transparent background. You'll see this with the circular picture frame in this example.

8 Click OK. The images will open in your default web browser. This is part of the default setting for exporting to HTML. Close this browser window, switch to your desktop, and open the Lesson13 folder. There will be a new folder called Flowers-for-web-web-resources and a file called Flowers-for-web.html.

9 Open the Flowers-for-web-web-resources folder and the image folder inside. The four images you added to the Articles panel are there, converted to PNG, and they have other web-required characteristics such as RGB color. These files are ready to use in a digital format. You can delete the other files generated by the HTML export.

10 If you have Photoshop, open the images to examine the results. Notice that the images look exactly the same as in InDesign (cropping, size, and position within the frame) and that the round picture frame is transparent outside the circle.

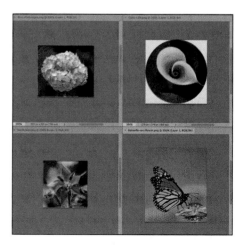

You can also export whole pages for use in emails and social media posts. A variation of the menu cover from Lesson 12 is an example.

1 Choose File > Open, navigate to the Lesson13 folder, and open Edible-Blossoms-Cover.indd inside the Edible-Blossoms-Cover Folder. Choose File > Export, and from the Save As Type (Windows) or Format (macOS) menu, choose JPEG and click Save. JPEG is the usual format when exporting whole pages.

2 In the Export area, click Range, and choose 1 (since there is only one page in this document it will be selected automatically). In the Image area, choose:

- Quality: Maximum

- Format Method: Baseline

- Resolution (ppi): 72

- Color Space: RGB

In the Options area, choose:

- Embed Color Profile

- Anti-alias (creates smoother edges)

- Simulate Overprint (to preserve the look of effects)

Then click Export.

3 Switch to the desktop and open the folder where you saved this file. You can view it in a browser or Photoshop.

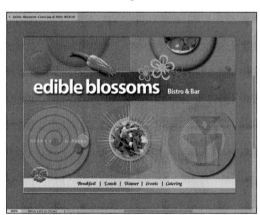

Congratulations! You've completed this lesson.

Exploring on your own

- Create new print presets by choosing File > Print Presets > Define. Define presets to use for oversized formats or for printing to various color or black-and-white output devices you may use. For example, if you have a printer that uses tabloid paper, create a preset that allows you to print letter-size pages at full size with a specified bleed amount. Or create a preset for a small format, such as a postcard, that will fit on letter size paper at 100%.

- Practice using the Press Quality With Bleed preset you saved with other documents, such as those from other lessons in this book or your own files.

- Practice using the Package feature with other documents, such as those from other lessons in this book or your own files. Examine the contents of the resulting folder to become familiar with what is needed when sending your file to a service provider such as a commercial printer.

- Learn how to open imported graphics that need to be fixed for printing. Click a graphic from the Links panel. Choose Edit With from the Links panel menu. Choose Photoshop to open raster images and Illustrator to open vector graphics. Make changes to the imported art, and then save and close the file. Go back to InDesign, and notice how the links have updated.

- Practice exporting for social media platforms. Open the folder Social Media Posts inside the Lesson13 folder. Inside is the front of the postcard from Lesson 1 reformatted to fit the differing dimensions of each platform, Facebook, Instagram, Pinterest, and Twitter. Open each file and export using the JPEG settings used in the previous exercise. Try uploading to any platform of your choice.

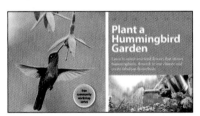
Facebook, 1200 x 630 pixels.

Twitter, 1200 x 675 pixels.

Pinterest, 1000 x 1500 pixels.

Instagram, 1080 x 1080 pixels.

Review questions

1 What problems does InDesign look for when using the [Basic] (Working) profile in the Preflight panel?

2 What elements does InDesign gather when it packages a file?

3 How can you find where a color is used in an InDesign file?

4 What functions does the Ink Manager provide?

5 What are the two industry-standard ways of preparing final files to send to a service provider such as a commercial printer?

Review answers

1 By default, the [Basic] (Working) profile in the Preflight panel confirms that all fonts used in the document or inside placed graphics are available. It also looks for linked graphic files and linked text files to confirm that they have not been modified since they were initially imported, and it warns you of missing graphic files and overset text frames (as well as unresolved caption variables, inaccessible URL links, and missing fonts).

2 InDesign gathers a copy of the InDesign document along with copies of all the fonts and graphics used in the original document. The original files remain untouched. If you choose Update Graphic Links In Package, the links in the packaged InDesign file will be linked to the packaged links folder and not to their original location. If you select Include IDML, InDesign creates an IDML version of the document that can be opened in previous versions of InDesign. If you select Include PDF(Print), InDesign creates an Adobe PDF (Print) version of the document. If you choose to include a PDF, you can also choose a PDF preset. Note that Adobe Fonts are not packaged.

3 Click the swatch in the Swatches panel and then choose Find This Color from the panel menu. It's helpful to first choose Add Unnamed Colors so that all colors in the document are displayed in the Swatches panel. Or open the Find/Change dialog and click the Color tab. Then choose a color from the Find Color menu.

4 The Ink Manager provides control over inks at output time, including the ability to convert spot colors to process colors and to map individual ink colors to different colors, without changing the colors in InDesign or in imported graphics.

5 The two standard methods are using a press-ready PDF with bleed and using the InDesign Package feature to create a folder with all components the service provider needs to work with the file (InDesign file, fonts, and linked graphics).

14 CREATING ADOBE PDF FILES WITH FORM FIELDS

Lesson overview

In this lesson, you'll learn to do the following:

- Set up a workspace for forms.

- Add and configure various form field types.

- Learn the differences between the types of form fields.

- Use prebuilt form elements.

- Set the tab order of form fields.

- Add a Submit button to a form.

- Export an Adobe PDF (Interactive) file with form fields.

- Test your form in Adobe Acrobat Reader.

 This lesson will take about 45 minutes to complete. To get the lesson files used in this chapter, download them from the web page for this book at adobepress.com/InDesignCIB2023. For more information, see "Accessing the lesson files and Web Edition" in the Getting Started section at the beginning of this book.

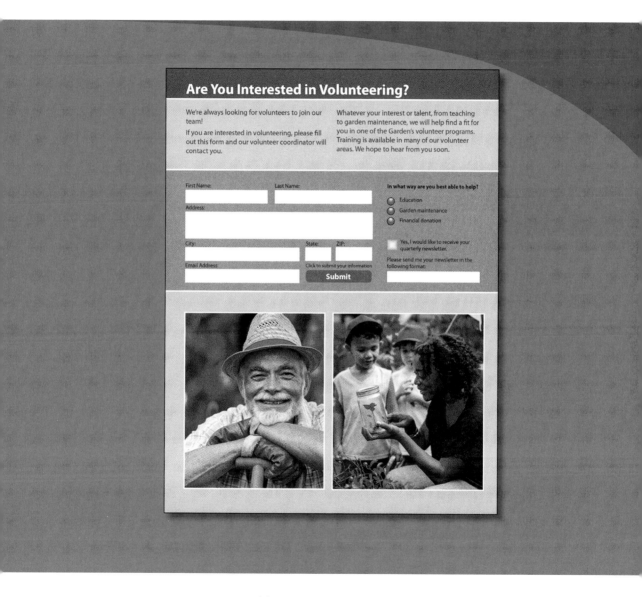

Adobe InDesign provides all the tools you need to create simple PDF forms, and you have the option of using Adobe Acrobat Pro DC to add features and functionality that aren't available in InDesign.

Getting started

In this lesson, you'll add several different types of form fields to a volunteer registration form, export an Adobe PDF (Interactive) file, and then open the exported file in Adobe Acrobat Reader and test the fields you created.

● **Note:** If you have not already downloaded the project files for this lesson to your computer from your Account page, make sure to do so now. See "Getting Started" at the beginning of the book.

1 To ensure that the preferences and default settings of your InDesign program match those used in this lesson, move the InDesign Defaults file to a different folder following the procedure in "Saving and restoring the InDesign Defaults file" on pages 3–4.

2 Start InDesign. Choose File > Open, and open the 14_Start.indd file in the Lesson14 folder, located inside the Lessons folder within the InDesignCIB folder on your hard drive. This one-page document is a registration form.

● **Note:** If an alert informs you that the document contains links to sources that have been modified, click Update Modified Links.

3 To ensure that the panels and menu commands match those used in this lesson, choose Window > Workspace > [Interactive For PDF], and then choose Window > Workspace > Reset Interactive For PDF.

4 To see what the finished document looks like, open the 14_End.indd file in the Lesson14 folder.

5 Close the 14_End.indd file after you have finished examining it, or you can leave this document open for reference.

● **Note:** To better view the interface onscreen or in print, the screen captures in this book reflect the Medium Light interface rather than the default setting of Medium Dark. In addition, some screen captures illustrate User Interface Scaling for a closer look at interface elements. You can modify interface settings in Preferences.

Start file.

Completed document.

PDF form in Acrobat.

6 Return to the 14_Start.indd file and choose File > Save As, rename the document **14_PDF_Form.indd**, and save it in the Lesson14 folder.

Setting up a workspace for forms

When creating a fillable form with InDesign, you'll start with a page that has already been designed. The process of taking a designed form and turning it into a form that can be filled out in a PDF uses specific tools. The Interactive For PDF workspace has many of the tools you'll need readily available. You will be even more efficient if you customize the workspace a little.

1 First, drag panels off the panel dock that are not needed for forms: Page Transitions and Bookmarks. Drag each panel to the left over the pasteboard. These panels are useful for other types of interactive PDFs but are not needed for forms. Also drag the Links, Color, and Gradient panels to the pasteboard, as they won't be used for this exercise. You'll be adding form functionality to a document that is already designed and built. It doesn't matter if some of the panels dock together as you drag them.

2 Close each of the panels you just dragged off the panel dock.

3 Choose Window > Styles > Object Styles to open the Object Styles panel. Choose Window > Properties to open the Properties panel. Then drag each of these panels to the bottom of the panel dock so that you can open and close them as needed while conserving screen space.

4 Save this workspace so you can use it again. Choose Window > Workspace > New Workspace. Use a name like **PDF Forms-Basic** or whatever makes sense to you. (For more complicated and long forms, you might want to save a separate workspace with additional tools.) Click OK.

Throughout this lesson, you'll use the Buttons And Forms panel very often. Arrange your screen so that there is room to leave it open as you work, if possible. Or, open and close it (🗐) from the panel dock as often as needed.

Adding form fields

Some of the setup work on the form fields has already been done. You'll complete the form by adding more fields and then modifying some of them.

Adding text fields

In a PDF form, a text field is a container into which the person who fills out the form can enter text. All but two of the frames have already been converted into text fields. You'll add two new frames and convert them into text fields.

● **Note:** You can simplify the display of the page by hiding Layer 1 in the Layers panel. Only the objects in the form area are displayed when you hide Layer 1.

● **Note:** If you do not see the icons (⟦I⟧) in the text fields, zoom in more. Try working at 150% zoom or higher.

1 Open the Layers panel by clicking the Layers icon (❧) in the panel dock. Notice that the file is set up with a separate layer, Form Elements. The objects that are part of the form are on this layer. Lock the other layer, Layer 1, so that you can work with the form objects without accidentally moving anything else.

2 Use the Zoom tool (🔍) to zoom in on the area in the top half of the page that contains the form objects. This is where all of your work in this lesson will be done.

3 Using the Selection tool (▶), move the pointer over the white rectangle below "First Name." Notice that a red dotted line is displayed around the object, and a small icon is displayed at the lower right. The dotted line indicates that the object is a PDF form element; the icon of the text frame indicates that the type of PDF form element is a text field. Click in the text field to select the object.

4 Click the Buttons And Forms icon (🗏) in the panel dock to display the Buttons And Forms panel. Notice the settings for the text field. Text Field is selected as the type, and the name of the element is First Name. The Description field is displayed to the form user when the pointer hovers over a field, which means you can provide additional guidance to users who fill out a form. The Description field is also set to First Name. Printable is selected by default to enable printing of this form. Leave Font and Font Size at the defaults.

Different types of form fields have different icons in the lower-right corner. This is a text field icon.

5 Select the frame of the First Name form field (if necessary), press Alt (Windows) or Option (macOS), and drag a copy of it below Last Name. Resize the field to make it longer, aligning it with the fields below, by dragging the center-right handle to the right. The Smart Guides will appear when the pointer is aligned.

6 In the Buttons And Forms panel, notice that the name of this field is First Name 1. This is an InDesign behavior you must be aware of when creating forms: no fields can have the same name. InDesign enforces this rule by adding sequential numbers to the name of duplicated fields. To make this a unique field with the correct information, change both the Name and Description fields to **Last Name**.

7 To create a field from scratch, select the Rectangle tool (▢,) in the Tools panel and draw a frame under the Email Address text frame. Align the right edge with the City frame above and the top edge with the bottom of the Email Address text frame. Use the Smart Guides to make the frame the same height as the City frame. You can convert any kind of frame—text, graphics, or unassigned—into a PDF form field. A text field does not have to be made from a text frame.

Notice how the Smart Guides help you align and size objects.

8 Now we will assign the same fill and stroke as the other text fields. An object style for the text field boxes has already been created for this lesson. Open the Object Styles panel by clicking the Object Styles icon (⬚) in the panel dock. Using the Selection tool (▶), click the box you just drew if it's not still selected. Select the object style Text Field Box, and then close the Object Styles panel. The same fill and stroke have now been applied to the new frame. Next, make the text field the same height and width as the City field by dragging the rectangle handles slightly. The size has changed slightly because the object style added a stroke to the frame. Watch for the Smart Guides to display again. Confirm that the size of the field is the same as the City field by checking the measurements in the Control or Properties panel.

● **Note:** Whenever you add a stroke to a frame, you can set the stroke to align to the center, outside, or inside of the frame edge. The center and outside options change the height and width measurements of the frame.

9 With this new frame still selected, in the Buttons And Forms panel choose Text Field from the Type menu, and assign it the name and description **Email Address**. Set Font Size to Auto. Auto is a good choice for fields such as email addresses that can be very long; the setting decreases the font size as needed to fill the frame. This functionality prevents any text from being clipped off when the page is printed. This time, choose a different font from the default.

10 Choose File > Save.

Adding either/or choices: radio buttons

● **Note:** Use radio buttons for either/or (mutually exclusive) choices when the user must specify a status that can have only one answer—for example, whether they are a member, nonmember, or student member of an organization.

Radio buttons present the person filling out the form with two or more choices, but only one choice can be selected as the response. A group of radio buttons functions as one field, with a unique value for each button. Checkboxes can appear similar to radio buttons, but every checkbox in the list can be either on or off.

Radio buttons are often simple circles; however, you can design your own buttons or choose from several sample buttons included with InDesign. In this exercise, you'll use one of the sample radio buttons. The prebuilt buttons in this library are vector shapes with various attributes for fill, stroke, and effects.

1 Choose View > Fit Page In Window, and then use the Zoom tool (🔍) to magnify the "In what way are you best able to help?" portion of the form.

▶ **Tip:** Choose File > Open, and navigate to the InDesign 2023 application folder. Inside, open Presets > Button Library. This library contains many preconfigured objects you can use in interactive projects.

2 Slide your view to the right so that you can also see part of the pasteboard. The three circles there are a set of radio buttons that is included with InDesign in a library.

3 Using the Selection tool (▶), drag across the three radio buttons to select them and move them from the pasteboard to a position below the text frame with the text "In what way are you best able to help?" Left-align them with the question and top-align the top one with the first answer. Refer to the following figure for the correct position.

4 In the Control or the Properties panel, and with the three buttons still selected, make sure that the upper-left reference point is selected in the reference point locator (▦), enter **40%** in either of the Scale Percentage fields, make sure that the Make All Settings The Same icon (🔗) is selected, and then press Enter (Windows) or Return (macOS). If necessary, move the buttons to match the figure shown.

Radio buttons before being scaled.

5 With all three buttons still selected, open the Buttons And Forms panel, enter **Form of Assistance** in the Name field and **In what way are you best able to help?** in the Description field, and then press Enter or Return. Notice that Type is already set to Radio Button because each circle was already set up as a radio button. By giving them the same name, you ensure that only one can be selected at a time.

After being scaled to 40%.

6 Choose Edit > Deselect All, or click an empty area of the page or pasteboard.

Each button must have a unique value, which you'll do now.

7 Use the Selection tool (▶) to select the first radio button (to the left of Education).

8 At the bottom of the Buttons And Forms panel, enter **Education** in the Button Value field at the bottom of the panel, and then press Enter or Return. Under Appearance, scroll up to [Normal Off] and click to select it. Make sure that Selected By Default is not selected.

9 Repeat steps 7 and 8 to change the Button Value setting of the middle button to **Garden maintenance** and of the bottom button to **Financial donation**. Notice that the name of the field is the same for all three buttons; only the Button Value changes. The second and third buttons should already be set to the state [Normal Off] in the Appearance area.

Note: The states listed under Appearance in the Buttons And Forms panel control the look of the radio buttons when you move the pointer over the button in the PDF form.

Adding yes or no choices: checkboxes

A checkbox presents a yes-or-no choice for an individual item. A user of the form can click the empty checkbox to add a checkmark or leave it unselected (the default setting in the exported PDF). Now you'll add a checkbox.

1 In the pasteboard to the right is a square with a checkmark. This is also a pre-configured button from the Button Library included with InDesign. Use the Selection tool to drag it to the left of the text frame that contains "Yes, I would like to receive your quarterly newsletter," which is just below the radio buttons you created in the previous exercise. Align the checkbox so that the top of the checkmark frame aligns with the top of the text frame.

2 Press Shift+Ctrl (Windows) or Shift+Command (macOS) and drag the lower-right handle to scale the checkbox graphic so that it is the same height as the text frame to the right. Use the following image as a guide to position the graphic.

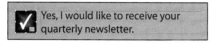

Checkbox graphic after being scaled.

3 With the checkbox graphic still selected, open the Buttons And Forms panel by clicking the icon (🖰) in the panel dock. Enter **Receive Newsletter** in the Name field, and then press Enter or Return. Notice that Type is already set to Check Box and that Button Value is Yes. Under Appearance, click [Normal Off]. In the Description field, enter **Check here if you'd like to receive our newsletter**. Make sure Selected By Default is not selected.

4 The checkbox and radio buttons will have red highlights because they are on the Form Elements layer. As you work on any form, it's a good practice to check that elements are on the layer where they belong. Doing so helps keep your work organized and becomes especially important when you work on complicated forms. This file is set up with all of the form objects on a separate layer from the other elements. Choose Edit > Deselect All, and then open the Layers panel (◈). Click the square next to the Form Elements layer and all objects on that layer are highlighted, allowing you to ensure that the objects are on the correct layer.

5 Choose Edit > Deselect All again, and then choose File > Save.

Adding a list of choices: combo box

A combo box creates a menu that lists multiple predefined choices. The user can select only one of the choices. Next, you'll create a combo box that offers three choices.

1 Use the Selection tool (▶) to select the text frame below the "Please send me your newsletter in the following format:" heading.

2 In the Buttons And Forms panel (⬛), choose Combo Box from the Type menu, and then enter **Newsletter Format** in the Name field. In the Description field, enter **Choose which way you'd like to receive our newsletter**. Change Font Size to **10**. To provide the viewer of the PDF form with different choices, you'll add three list items.

3 In the lower half of the Buttons And Forms panel, in the List Items field enter **Print Publication: Standard Mail**, and then click the plus sign (+) to the right of the field. Notice that the text you entered is now displayed in the list below the field.

4 Repeat the previous step to add **Adobe PDF: Email Attachment** and **Link to online newsletter: Email** to the list. Select the Sort Items option to sort list items alphabetically.

5 Click Print Publication: Standard Mail in the list of items to make it the default selection. When the user opens the exported PDF file, Print Publication: Standard Mail will already be selected.

6 Choose Edit > Deselect All, and then choose File > Save.

Setting the tab order of the fields

The tab order you establish for a PDF form determines the order in which fields are selected as a user presses the Tab key. To make the form user-friendly, the order must be logical to the user. You would not want the tab to move from First Name to ZIP and skip the fields in between. Next, you'll set the tab order for the fields in this form.

1 From the Object menu, choose Interactive > Set Tab Order.

2 In the Tab Order dialog, click Last Name (the name of the text field you created that holds the surname of the person filling out the form), and then click Move Up until Last Name appears below First Name near the top of the list. Use the Move Up and Move Down buttons or drag field names up or down to rearrange them to match the order on the page. Click OK to close the dialog.

Tab order before being rearranged.

You can drag more than one field at a time.

After being rearranged.

3 Choose File > Save.

Adding a button to submit the form

If you distribute a PDF form, you'll want to include a way for anybody who fills out the form to return it to you electronically. To accomplish this, you'll create a button that sends the filled-out PDF form to your email address.

1 Use the Selection tool (▶) to select the rounded-corner text frame with a red fill and the text "Submit," scrolling to the left to see this frame if needed.

2 In the Buttons And Forms panel (📑), choose Button from the Type menu, enter **Submit Form** in the Name field, and then press Enter or Return. In the Description field, enter **Send the completed form via email**.

3 Click the plus sign (+) to the right of "Actions:" and then choose Submit Form from the menu.

4 In the URL field, enter **mailto:**. Make sure you enter a colon after "mailto." Do not enter a space or a period before or after the colon.

5 Enter your email address (for example, pat_smith@domain.com) after mailto:. This will return the completed form to you.

▶ **Tip:** Any object or group can be converted into a button. The example in this lesson is a text frame with a fill color and the text "Submit." To convert a selected object or group into a button, choose Button from the Type menu in the Buttons And Forms panel.

▶ **Tip:** The ability to add an action to a button is one of the most versatile tools for interactive PDFs.

Tip: A button's appearance can have three different states. The state that's displayed depends on the user's interaction. The Normal state is the default display when no interaction occurs, the Rollover state displays when the pointer is over the button, and the Click state displays when the mouse button is clicked.

Tip: If you don't want the Submit button itself to appear on a printout of the form, deselect the Printable option in the Buttons And Forms panel for the button.

6 To cause the button's appearance to change when a user moves the pointer over the Submit button, you'll add a Rollover appearance.

Click [Rollover] in the Appearance area of the Buttons And Forms panel. Click the arrow to the right of Fill Color in the Control panel, and enter **50** in the Tint field. Press Enter or Return to accept the change and close the fill area of the panel. (Using the Control panel will leave the Buttons And Forms panel open at the same time.)

7 Return to the Buttons And Forms panel. Notice that the [Rollover] appearance is now lighter than the [Normal] appearance, reflecting the tint change you just made. Click [Normal] to display the default appearance.

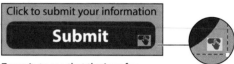

Zoom in to see that the icon for a button is a finger pointing to a rounded-corner rectangle.

Users will see this visual cue when hovering over the button.

8 Open the Layers panel by clicking the icon (✿) in the panel dock, or choose Window > Layers and make sure all layers are visible (in case you hid Layer 1 earlier in the lesson).

9 Choose Edit > Deselect All, and then choose File > Save.

Form field types

Button: The most versatile interactive element. A button can trigger many actions.

Checkbox: For yes-or-no choices, a checkbox is either selected or unselected. Use checkboxes for "Check all that apply" questions.

Combo box: The user can choose only one answer from a list.

List box: Similar to a combo box except that the user can choose more than one answer.

Radio button: For either/or choices, the user can choose only one answer.

Signature field: Enables the user to sign a form with a digital signature.

Text field: Allows the user to type text information.

Exporting an interactive PDF file

Now that you've finished work on the form fields, you're ready to export an interactive Adobe PDF file and then test the exported file.

1 Choose File > Export. In the Export dialog, choose Adobe PDF (Interactive) from the Save As Type menu (Windows) or Format menu (macOS). Name the file **14_PDF_Form.pdf** and navigate to the Lesson14 folder, located inside the Lessons folder within the InDesignCIB folder on your hard drive.

2 Click Save. The Export To Interactive PDF dialog opens.

3 In the Export To Interactive PDF dialog, click the General tab. In the Options area, make sure that Include All is selected for Forms And Media. This is the most important setting to make the form fields work in the PDF.

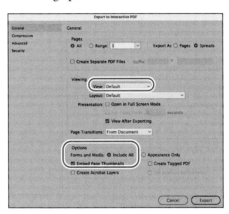

4 Choose Fit Page from the View menu to display the entire page when the exported PDF is opened. Click Export.

● **Note:** You may not need to enter a filename because the default behavior is to name the exported file with the name of the InDesign file. That means the PDF name may automatically be 14_PDF_Form.

▶ **Tip:** In many scenarios where you'll create a form, you'll need to complete the Title, Author, Subject, and Keywords fields. You do so in Acrobat after the file is exported from InDesign. In Acrobat, choose File > Properties and then click the Description tab to fill out these fields.

Testing your form in Adobe Acrobat Reader

You should always test your forms in Acrobat Reader because the end user is most likely to use that version of Acrobat when filling out the form. If you do not have Acrobat Reader, install it now. The current version is Adobe Acrobat Reader DC. It's a free download at https://get.adobe.com/reader.

1 Open Acrobat Reader and open the PDF you just exported. Zoom in to the form area of the page. First, click in the First Name field and press the Tab key. Continue to tab through all the fields to make sure that the tab order is correct. Fill out each field with sample information before tabbing to the next field. Be sure to type in a very long email address in that field and notice how the text size gets smaller once you type beyond the length of the field at the original font size. Also check whether this field has a different font than the rest as you specified.

2 Next, click the radio buttons under "In what way are you best able to help?" and notice that you can make only one choice at a time.

3 Click the box beside "Yes, I would like to receive your quarterly newsletter" to see that the checkmark appears. Then choose one of the newsletter formats from the drop-down menu.

● **Note:** If you have Acrobat Pro DC as part of your Creative Cloud subscription, that is the professional version of Acrobat, which most users of the form probably will not have.

4 Move the pointer across each field, pausing for a moment, and notice the tips that appear (called "tool tips"). These are the descriptions that you entered in the Buttons And Forms panel for each field.

If you find any errors, go back to the InDesign file and fix them. Then export and test again.

● **Note:** A security warning dialog may display when Acrobat creates an email message with the completed form as an attachment. Click Allow.

5 When you're done, click the Submit button that emails the filled-out form to you. A dialog will open asking which email program you want to use. Make your choice and then click Continue. Your email software will open with the filled-out form attached to a new message. Send the form and then return to InDesign.

6 Look at the email you received and notice the subject line: Form Returned: 14_PDF_Form.pdf. This is a default function of the Submit Form action of the Submit button. Therefore, it's important to consider the name of the PDF when you create forms to be emailed.

Congratulations! You've created a PDF form and tested it.

Exploring on your own

• Use the Ellipse tool (⬤) to create a small circular frame. Choose a fill color from the Swatches panel and use the Buttons And Forms panel to convert the frame into a button. Assign the Go To URL action to the button and enter a complete URL in the URL field (for example, https://www.adobepress.com). Assign a different fill color to the Rollover state. To test this button, export an Adobe PDF (Interactive) file and click the button.

• There is a sample List Box in the pasteboard to the right of the Newsletter field. Drag this frame and the text frame above it onto the page. Export an Adobe PDF (Interactive) file and test selecting more than one choice.

• Experiment with the other actions that can be applied to a button for interactive PDFs. Note the section of actions in the middle of the list that work only with EPUB or Publish Online files, not PDFs. Export and test the result.

Review questions

1 What panel lets you convert an object into a PDF form field and specify settings for form fields?

2 What is the difference between a radio button and a checkbox?

3 What action can you assign to a button that enables a viewer of the exported PDF form to send a copy of the filled-out form to an email address?

4 What programs can be used to open and fill out an Adobe PDF form?

5 What are the three most important things to do when exporting your InDesign file to create a fillable PDF form?

6 How do you control the order in which a user can tab through the fields when filling out a form?

Review answers

1 The Buttons And Forms panel (Window > Interactive > Buttons And Forms) lets you convert objects into PDF form fields and specify settings for them.

2 Radio buttons are for questions that have an either/or answer; the user of the form can choose only one. Checkboxes are for questions whose answer is a simple yes when the box is selected.

3 To enable the viewer of a PDF form to return a filled-out form, use the Buttons And Forms panel to assign the Submit Form action to the button. After you assign the Submit Form action, enter **mailto:** followed by an email address (for example, mailto:pat_smith@domain.com) in the URL field.

4 You can open and fill out PDF forms using Acrobat Pro DC or Acrobat Reader DC, as well as third-party apps.

5 First, in the Export dialog, choose Adobe PDF (Interactive) from the Save As Type menu (Windows) or Format menu (macOS). Then in the Options area of the General tab, make sure that Include All is selected for Forms And Media. Then test the form in an app the intended audience is likely to use, such as Acrobat Reader.

6 From the Object menu, choose Interactive > Set Tab Order. Then move the field names up or down so that they follow the visual order that the user will see.

15 CREATING A FIXED-LAYOUT EPUB AND PUBLISHING ONLINE

Lesson overview

In this lesson, you'll learn how to do the following:

- Create a new document for mobile delivery.

- Create animations using a motion preset and a motion path.

- Configure the timing of multiple animations.

- Create buttons that trigger various actions.

- Preview animations and interactivity within InDesign.

- Add a movie, a sound, a slideshow, buttons, and a hyperlink.

- Export a fixed-layout EPUB and preview it in a viewing app.

- Use the Publish Online feature.

 This lesson will take about 60 minutes to complete. To get the lesson files used in this chapter, download them from the web page for this book at adobepress.com/InDesignCIB2023. For more information, see "Accessing the lesson files and Web Edition" in the Getting Started section at the beginning of this book.

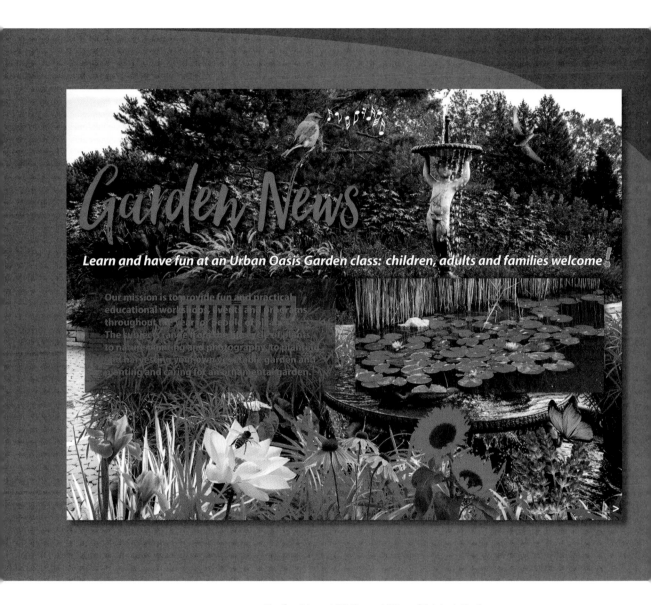

Garden News

Learn and have fun at an Urban Oasis Garden class: children, adults and families welcome

Our mission is to provide fun and practical educational workshops, events and programs throughout the year for gardeners. The subjects vary from identification to nature painting and photography, to planting and harvesting your own vegetable garden and planting and caring for an ornamental garden.

The fixed-layout EPUB capabilities of Adobe InDesign let you create media-rich publications with animations, movies, slideshows, sounds, and hyperlinks, and you can include buttons that enable viewers to perform a variety of actions, from clicking through a slideshow to playing a sound file.

Getting started

● **Note:** If you have not already downloaded the project files for this lesson to your computer from your Account page, make sure to do so now. See "Getting Started" at the beginning of the book.

In this lesson, you'll begin by creating a new InDesign document using settings appropriate for a fixed-layout EPUB. After you've set up the new document, you'll open a partially completed version of the publication, add several multimedia and interactive elements, and then save and preview a fixed-layout EPUB that can be viewed on a variety of EPUB readers.

1 To ensure that the preferences and default settings of your InDesign program match those used in this lesson, move the InDesign Defaults file to a different folder following the procedure in "Saving and restoring the InDesign Defaults file" on pages 3–4.

2 Start InDesign. To see what the finished document looks like, open the 15_End.indd file in the Lesson15 folder. If an alert informs you that the document contains media content that may not have playback controls in the Interactive PDF, click Continue. (We are not creating an Interactive PDF in this lesson.)

3 To ensure that the panels and menu commands match those used in this lesson, choose Window > Workspace > [Digital Publishing], and then choose Window > Workspace > Reset Digital Publishing. This optimizes the panel arrangement for the work you'll do in this lesson and provides quick access to several of the controls you'll use.

● **Note:** To better view the interface onscreen or in print, the screen captures in this book reflect the Medium Light interface rather than the default setting of Medium Dark. In addition, some screen captures illustrate User Interface Scaling for a closer look at interface elements. You can modify interface settings in Preferences.

4 Navigate through the finished document to view the cover page and the page that follows.

In all previous lessons that use sample print documents, the completed InDesign layouts look the same onscreen and in print; however, because the exported publication in this lesson is intended for display in an EPUB reader or online, what you see onscreen when you open the sample files in InDesign doesn't exactly match the appearance of the exported EPUB. The following images show what the completed lesson file looks like in InDesign.

Page 1.

Page 2.

5 Close the 15_End.indd file after you have finished examining it, or you can leave this document open for reference.

Creating a new document for fixed-layout export

Because exported EPUBs are viewed onscreen (on mobile devices such as tablets or on desktop computers, for example) and can include elements such as buttons, animations, and video that can't be included in print documents, creating a document that's intended for export in the EPUB format differs in some ways from creating a print document. That said, all the typographic and page-layout features covered in this book are available and work the same when creating digital publications. To begin, you'll create a new mobile document.

1 Choose File > New > Document.

2 In the New Document dialog, click the Mobile tab; then click View All Presets+, and select iPad Pro (10.5 in) from the available choices. In the Pages field, type **2**, choose Landscape Orientation, and deselect Primary Text Frame. Leave all other settings unchanged, and click Create.

Note: Setting a new document's Intent to Mobile (or Web) deselects the Facing Pages option and changes the unit of measurement to pixels. It also sets the Transparency Blend Space (Edit > Transparency Blend Space) to RGB and the default color swatches in the Swatches panel to Process RGB for the new document.

3 Choose File > Save As, name the file **15_Setup.indd**, navigate to the Lesson15 folder, and click Save.

 Rather than creating the remainder of the document from scratch, you'll continue this lesson by opening a partially completed document that already contains most of the required objects. Close the 15_Setup.indd document.

EPUB: Fixed-layout versus reflowable

An EPUB is a document created for viewing on a device such as a tablet rather than for printing on paper. This allows for capabilities such as adding many kinds of multimedia elements and interactive features or reflowing text for the particular device.

The biggest difference between a fixed-layout EPUB and a reflowable EPUB is that a fixed-layout EPUB retains the design of the InDesign document (like a PDF) regardless of the device on which it's displayed. In contrast, a reflowable EPUB displays content in a continuous thread and reflows the content based on the size of the reader screen and the zoom level. Readers of reflowable EPUBs can change the font and font size to suit their preference.

Viewers of fixed-layout EPUBs can view the pages as they were designed and can interact with the multimedia elements. The fixed-layout format lets you include buttons, animations, video, and audio in your publications. For example, you can present another version of a printed publication with these rich media features added. Fixed-layout EPUBs can also be published online and viewed on devices. This format is better suited for more design-intensive publications in which the visual layout is critical to the experience for the reader. The reflowable format is the preferred choice for text-intensive publications such as fiction and nonfiction books where the visual layout is not as important, though they can include video and audio that flow inline with the text.

Adding animation

Animation effects let you add movement and other visual effects to InDesign objects and groups. For example, you can animate a frame by making it fly into place from outside the page, or you can fade in a text frame so that it turns from invisible to opaque. InDesign includes several "motion presets," which are preset animations that you can quickly apply to objects. You can also use objects as a motion path to animate another object or group.

Next, you'll examine a group that has already been assigned animation settings that cause it to "fly" onto the page when a viewer opens the exported EPUB file. You'll preview this animation within InDesign and create some animations of your own that automatically play when the page is displayed. Then you'll adjust the timing of the animations so that they play in the desired sequence.

Using a motion preset to create animation

The quickest and easiest way to animate an object or group is to apply any of more than 40 built-in motion presets. After you apply a preset, you have several options for controlling how the animation is played, including the event that triggers the animation and the duration.

1 Choose File > Open, and then open the 15_FixedLayout_Partial.indd file in the Lesson15 folder.

2 Choose File > Save As, name the file **15_FixedLayout.indd**, and save it in the Lesson15 folder. Dismiss the alert about Interactive PDFs again (if necessary).

Before you create your own animation, you'll take a look at a group that's already had animation effects applied to it.

3 Press the Z key to temporarily activate the Zoom tool and zoom in on the text that begins with "children, adults and families" in the right half of page 1. Then use the Selection tool (▶) to click the text frame.

Notice the small icon () in the lower-right corner of the group. This indicates that an animation has been applied to the group. Also notice that a horizontal green line extends from the pasteboard to the center of the group. This line is the motion path used for the animation. The circle is the starting point, and the arrowhead is the endpoint of any motion path.

Note: Below are enlarged views of the start and end points of a motion path.

The icon in the lower-right corner indicates that the group has been animated.

The green line indicates the path along which the group will move.

4 Choose Window > Interactive > Animation or click the Animation icon () in the panel dock to open the Animation panel. Notice that the group has a name (Welcome Animated Group) and that Custom (Fly In From Right) is selected in the Preset menu. (The word "Custom" at the beginning of the preset name indicates that the default settings for this preset have been modified. You'll modify other presets later in this lesson.) On Page Load is selected in the Event(s) menu, indicating that the animation will start playing automatically as the page is displayed.

Note: The panel dock is located on the right when you use the [Digital Publishing] workspace.

Clicking the triangle next to Properties in the Animation panel expands the panel and provides access to several additional animation controls.

5 To preview the animation, click the Preview Spread: EPUB button () at the bottom left of the Animation panel. The EPUB Interactivity Preview panel opens. Drag the lower-right or left corner of the panel to make it large enough to view the publication. Click the Play Preview button, which is the leftmost button along the bottom of the panel. The animated headline flies in from the right side of the page.

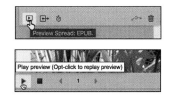

Tip: To see the animation again, press Alt (Windows) or Option (macOS) and click the Play Preview button again.

6 Drag the EPUB Interactivity Preview panel to the bottom of the dock, since you'll use it throughout this lesson. The panel icon (⬛) displays in the dock. For a full explanation of the EPUB Interactivity Preview panel, see the following sidebar.

The EPUB Interactivity Preview panel

The EPUB Interactivity Preview panel lets you preview an InDesign document that includes multimedia, animation, and interactivity without having to switch to a separate program. You can display the panel by choosing Window > Interactive > EPUB Interactivity Preview or by clicking the Preview Spread button in the lower-left corner of the Animation, Timing, Media, Object States, or Buttons And Forms panel.

You can perform the following functions in the EPUB Interactivity Preview panel:

- Play Preview (▶): Click to play a preview of the selection, spread, or document. Alt-click (Windows) or Option-click (macOS) to replay the preview.

- Clear Preview (■): Click to clear the preview.

- Navigate between previous page (◀) and next page (▶): Click the left or right arrows to navigate between previous and next pages. Preview Document Mode must be chosen to navigate to the previous or next page. Click Play Preview to enable the previous page and next page buttons.

- Set Preview Spread Mode (▯): Click to set the mode to Preview Spread Mode. This is the default mode and is used to test interactive elements on the current page.

- Set Preview Document Mode (▱): Click to set the mode to Preview Document Mode. This mode allows you to click through each page of the document and test the interactive elements.

- Collapse/Expand panel (◊): Click to expand/collapse the EPUB Interactivity Preview panel. This icon is in the upper left next to the panel title.

Next, you'll add a preset to another group and then to a text frame, and you'll customize the settings of both animations.

1 Choose View > Fit Page In Window. With the Selection tool (▶), click any of the flower graphics at the bottom of the page except the one on the far left, which you will work with separately later in the lesson. Clicking any of the graphics selects the group of four graphics.

2 Open the Animation panel (•ː) and choose Fly In From Bottom from the Preset menu. The pink butterfly image in the preview area shows you what the preset does. Try several presets and then return to Fly In From Bottom. Ensure that On Page Load is selected in the Event(s) menu.

3 Select the blue text frame with green text. Choose the Fade In preset and set Duration to **2** seconds. The word "Custom" will appear before Fade In when you change the duration from the default preset values.

4 Open the EPUB Interactivity Preview panel (🖾) and click the Play Preview button (▶) in the lower-left corner of the panel to view the animations. Notice that the headline appears first, followed shortly by the group of graphics at the bottom of the page, and finally the blue text frame. The sequence is a result of the order in which the animations were created. Next, you'll modify the order in which these animations play. Close the EPUB Interactivity Preview panel (»).

Adjusting the timing of animations

The Timing panel lists the animations on a page or spread and lets you change the order in which animations are played, play animations simultaneously, or delay animations. You'll use the Timing panel to change the order in which the three animations on page 1 are played and to play two of the animations simultaneously.

1 Choose Window > Interactive > Timing or click the Timing icon (⏱) to open the Timing panel from the panel dock. Ensure that On Page Load is selected in the Event menu. The three animations you've worked with so far are listed.

2 Click Welcome Animated Group in the list of animations. Because it was created first, it's at the top of the list and will play first.

3 Drag Welcome Animated Group to the bottom of the list so that it plays last. A thick line appears when you drag. Release the mouse button when the thick black line is below "Our mission..." (the name of the text frame set to Fade In).

4 Select Flower Group, and then Shift-click the animation named "Our mission ..." to select both objects.

5 Click the Play Together button (⇥) at the bottom of the Timing panel.

6 Click Flower Group, specify a delay of **1.5** seconds, and press Enter (Windows) or Return (macOS). This will delay the display of this animation when the page opens. After the delay, the Flower Group will fly in, and the blue text frame will simultaneously fade in.

7 Click the Preview Spread button (⊡) at the bottom of the Timing panel to open the EPUB Interactivity Preview panel, and then click the Play Preview button (▶) to preview the page and check the timing changes.

8 Close the EPUB Interactivity Preview panel (»), and choose File > Save.

Buttons

Buttons are one of the most versatile tools for adding interactive features to a publication because a button can trigger many actions. Next, you'll configure buttons to play animations and add two buttons using two different methods. The graphics that you will use to make buttons are on a layer named Buttons above the layer with the rest of the content. This practice ensures that the buttons will not disturb the other content and will always be above that content in the stacking order, which is a good way to keep your files organized and the button objects easily accessible.

Using buttons to play animations

The animations you worked with in the previous section are configured to play automatically when the page is displayed (Event: On Page Load). You can also create animations that play when you perform other actions, such as moving the pointer over an animated object or clicking an object or group that's been configured to work as a button.

In this section, you'll first examine an object that's already been animated and converted into a button that plays an animation. Then you'll create a new button that plays an already-animated object.

1 Scroll down so that you can see the pasteboard at the bottom of the page. You'll see two images. Zoom in to see the lower-left area of the page. Use the Selection tool (▶) to position the monarch butterfly image on top of the purple iris, matching the following screenshot.

● **Note:** If you don't see two icons on the butterfly image, zoom in more and ensure View > Screen Mode is set to Normal.

Notice the two icons in the lower-right corner of the butterfly image's bounding box. The icon on the right indicates that the group is animated; the icon on the left indicates that the group is also a button.

2 With the monarch butterfly selected, open the Animation panel (•̇•). The animation is named Monarch Butterfly.

The Dance preset has been applied and On Release is selected in the Event(s) menu. The symbol to the right of the Event(s) menu (⊕) indicates that a button will trigger the animation. The Duration and Play values show that the animation will take one second to play and will play two times.

3 Click the Buttons And Forms icon (⧉) in the panel dock. Or choose Window > Interactive > Buttons And Forms. Notice that the group has been configured to work as a button and that the action is to play the Monarch Butterfly animation.

4 Click the Preview Spread button (⊡) at the bottom of the Buttons And Forms panel to open the EPUB Interactivity Preview panel, or open it from the panel dock. Then click the Play Preview (▶) button. After the opening animations are displayed, click the butterfly image to play the animation and then close the panel.

● **Note:** Throughout this lesson, if you have trouble with the interactivity not working correctly in the EPUB Interactivity Preview panel, click the Clear Preview button (■) and then click the Play Preview button (▶) again.

Next, you'll configure a button that animates a different object.

1 Choose View > Fit Page In Window, and select the blue butterfly image in the lower-right corner of the page. Note that it already has a motion path, the green curved vector path, because it's already configured as an animation.

The icon in the lower-right corner of the graphic () indicates that this image is animated; however, you may have noticed that when you preview the page, the image is not visible. That's because although the image is configured to fly in from above the page, there's no way to play the animation. To address this, you'll convert the accompanying flower graphic into a button.

▶ **Tip:** Creating a separate frame with the stroke and fill color set to None in the Buttons layer results in a button that looks like it's the artwork but that is actually a different object on a separate layer. This ensures that you don't disturb the artwork and keeps your buttons organized and easy to access.

2 Select the Rectangle Frame tool (⊠) in the Tools panel and draw a frame over the purple flower in the lower-right corner of the page. You should still be on the Buttons layer, but if not, open the Layers panel (◆) and move the new frame to the Buttons layer. Set the frame's color to [None] for Fill and Stroke.

The size of the frame becomes the tappable or clickable area in the EPUB, so you can use a frame with no fill and no stroke to make a button with a larger tappable or clickable area than the graphic might have. This technique makes using the EPUB easier for your audience.

3 With the rectangle still selected, open the Buttons And Forms panel, click the + sign (+.) next to Actions, and choose Animation from the menu. Then from the Animation menu, which shows the animations in the current file, choose Blue Butterfly. (It may already be selected at the top in the list of animations.)

4 Name the button **Lavender and Butterfly**. Make sure On Release Or Tap is selected in the Event menu.

A best practice is to always name your buttons; otherwise, InDesign will automatically name them Button 1, Button 2, and so on. Give your buttons meaningful names to make sure they are easily recognizable as you build your EPUB—for example, when setting the control of interactions in animations. Looking for a specific button based on InDesign's automatic naming would be very confusing.

In the Buttons And Forms panel, you don't need to choose a type first, because when you add an action, the selected object is automatically turned into a button. Review the list of possible actions, and note that the bottom group is only for PDFs. Click the triangle next to PDF Options at the bottom of the panel to close that area. You won't need those actions while working on an EPUB.

5 Click the Preview Spread button () at the bottom of the Buttons And Forms panel to open the EPUB Interactivity Preview panel, and click the Play Preview button. After the opening animations are displayed, move the pointer over the photo of the lavender flower at the lower right. Notice that the arrow pointer changes to a pointing finger when you hover over something that the reader can click to activate, such as this new button. Click the lavender flower image to play the new animation. Then close the panel.

6 Choose File > Save to save your work.

Using a button to trigger custom motion paths for animations

Many of the motion presets in InDesign cause an object to move along a path. In addition to using this type of preset to animate an object, you can use any InDesign object as the path for animating another object by converting it to a motion path. Next you'll convert a path to a motion path and configure a button to play the animation with the custom path; then you'll create a custom path of your own and use it as a motion path.

1 Navigate to the pasteboard area at the top of the right side of the page. You'll see an image of a flying bird and a curved path with a black stroke. Using the Selection tool (), drag to select both the bird image and the path.

2 Drag the bird image and the path onto the page so that the bird is within the empty red graphics frame. This frame is on the Buttons layer, and the bird image and the path are on the Graphics layer.

3 With the bird and path still selected, open the Animation panel () and click the Convert To Motion Path () button at the bottom of the panel. The black path changes to a green motion path. The shape of the path will determine where the animation moves. On Page Load is selected in the Event(s) menu. Deselect it by choosing On Page Load again so that Choose is displayed instead.

4 Click the Create Button Trigger () button to the right of the Event(s) line. A diamond-shaped icon with crosshairs inside appears.

Click the red graphics frame. The frame is converted to a button, the Buttons And Forms panel opens, and the Swift.psd animation is automatically selected.

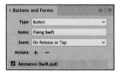

5 Name the button **Flying Swift**. Make sure On Release Or Tap is selected in the Event menu.

6 Open the EPUB Interactivity Preview panel (▣), and click the Play Preview button. After the opening animations are displayed, move the mouse over the photo of the bird in flight. Notice that the pointer changes to a pointing finger because it is sensing the button you just created. Click to play the new animation; the bird flies across and off the page, along the path. Close the panel.

Now that you know how a custom motion path works, you'll create your own custom animation path and then configure a button to play it.

1 Navigate to the pasteboard area at the bottom of the page. You'll see a bee image below the white flower. Move the bee image up onto the page and then on top of the white flower.

2 Zoom in to the middle bottom area of the page. Use the Pencil tool (✏.) to draw a path starting from the center of the bee image and then up and over to the next flower and up and over again to the sunflower.

Use this screenshot for guidance.

3 Use the Selection tool to select the bee image and the path you just created, open the Animation panel (•ː), and click the Convert To Motion Path (⌒) button at the bottom of the panel. On Page Load is selected in the Event(s) menu. Deselect it by choosing On Page Load again, and set Duration to **2** seconds. The motion path has been connected to the bee image to create an animation. Notice that the path has a dot at the start on top of the bee image and an arrow at the end on top of the sunflower image, indicating the direction of the animation.

4 Select the Rectangle Frame tool (⊠.) and draw a frame over the photo of the bee, making sure that its fill and stroke color are set to [None] and that it is on the Buttons layer. Make the frame a little larger than bee image.

5 Open the Buttons And Forms panel (⊟), click the + sign (+.) next to Actions, and choose Animation from the menu. Then choose Bee-Spread-Wings.psd from the Animation menu. (The Animation panel automatically used the name of the image file.) Name the button **Flying Bee**.

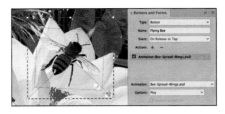

6 Click the Preview Spread button (⊡) at the bottom of the Buttons And Forms panel to open the EPUB Interactivity Preview panel, and click the Play Preview button. After the opening animations are displayed, click the bee image (which is the button you just configured to play the new animation) to verify that the animation is playing correctly, and then close the panel.

7 Experiment with changing the motion path. Select the button frame and choose Object > Lock so that you can select the path by clicking the bee image. Switch to the Direct Selection tool (▷) to modify points or segments of the path that will change the flight path of the bee. You can add or delete points, move points, or change the shape with the point handles. In the 15_End.indd document, the path has been modified to be more irregular. Preview the changes you've made in the EPUB Interactivity Preview panel, noticing how the change to the shape of the path changes the motion of the animation.

● **Note:** If you have trouble selecting the motion path points or segments, zoom in so that you can more easily click the green line.

8 Close the panel and then choose File > Save to save your work.

Creating a navigation button

The next button you'll create will be a navigation button for the reader to move through the pages. This is one of the most common uses for buttons.

1 Select the Rectangle Frame tool (⊠.) and draw a frame over the blue tab with the right-pointing open triangle in the lower-right corner of the page, making sure that it has no stroke and no fill and that it is on the Buttons layer. Make it larger than the tab so that the reader does not have to click exactly on the tab.

▶ **Tip:** Many apps for viewing EPUBs include navigation buttons, but each app will perform navigation differently. They might be small and hard to see, on the side or on the bottom of the screen. Adding your own buttons ensures that the reader will easily see the navigation buttons.

2 Open the Buttons And Forms panel () and click the + sign () next to Actions. Choose Go To Next Page. Name this button **Next Page**.

▶ **Tip:** In a long document, create the navigation buttons on the parent page. If there are several parent pages, use the first parent so that you can create the buttons once and ensure that they are consistent on all pages.

3 Open the EPUB Interactivity Preview panel (), and this time click the Set Preview Document Mode button () at the far right so that you can preview all pages in the document. Click the Clear Preview button () and then click Play Preview ().

4 After the opening animations are displayed, click the navigation button you just created, and the next page will display. You will see other animations on page 2 that you'll work with later in this lesson.

5 Click the green tab in the lower left to navigate back to the first page, and then close the EPUB Interactivity Preview panel (>>).

Creating a pop-up caption

Pop-up captions are frequently used in EPUBs. There are many ways to create them. Using InDesign's ability to hide and show objects is one of the simplest methods. You'll learn this technique next.

1 Use the Selection tool () to select the frog image on top of the photo of the lily pads. First you'll add some animation so that the reader is prompted to click it.

Note: Scale Width and Height are set to keep settings the same by default (). If yours has been changed, click the Same Settings icon to scale the frog image proportionally.

2 Open the Animation panel (). Choose the Zoom In (2D) preset, and set Duration to **1.5** seconds and Play to **3** times. In the Properties area, set Scale to **150**% and press Enter (Windows) or Return (macOS).

3 Open the Buttons And Forms panel (), click the + sign () next to Actions, and choose Show/Hide Buttons And Forms. Name the button **Caption Trigger**.

4 Select the flower shape with the words "Meet me at the Lily Pad Garden!" This is a group of InDesign text and path objects that will become the pop-up caption. Click the + sign () next to Actions, and again choose Show/Hide Buttons And Forms in the Buttons And Forms panel (). Name this button **Caption**.

▶ **Tip:** The Visibility menu in the Show/Hide action lists all the buttons on the current page or spread. You can't use the Show/Hide Buttons And Forms action to work with buttons elsewhere in a document.

5 In the Visibility area, leave everything on Ignore (✖) except Caption and Caption Trigger. Click the Ignore symbol (✖) next to Caption and click again to cycle through the options until it is set to Hide (). Do the same with Caption Trigger until it is set to Show (). Also select Hidden Until Triggered in the Appearance area. This setting ensures that the caption object is invisible when the reader opens the page.

6 Select the frog image that you converted to a button in step 3. In the Buttons And Forms panel (⏏) (which will still be open), change the Visibility setting of Caption to Show (👁) and change Caption Trigger to Hide (🚫).

Trigger button object.

Caption button object.

Settings for the trigger object (the frog).

Settings for the caption object (the flower with text).

When the reader opens the page, the trigger object will be visible, and the caption object will be hidden. When the trigger object is clicked or tapped, it will disappear, and the caption object will appear. When the caption object is clicked or tapped, it will disappear, and the trigger object will reappear.

7 Open the EPUB Interactivity Preview panel, and if needed, click the Clear Preview button (■). Change the preview mode to Preview Spread Mode (🗋), and press Play Preview (▶). Test this pop-up caption by clicking the frog image trigger object and then the caption.

8 Close the EPUB Interactivity Preview panel (≫), and choose File > Save.

Adding multimedia and interactive elements

The ability to add movies and sounds to an InDesign document that will be exported as a fixed-layout EPUB is another way that you can create media-rich, interactive publications that aren't possible with print publishing.

In many ways, imported movies and sounds are like other InDesign objects. For example, you can copy, paste, move, and delete movies and sounds just like other objects—but they also have unique properties that you can adjust within InDesign.

Adding a movie

Tip: You can import video files in H.264-encoded MP4 format and audio files as MP3 format. You can use the Adobe Media Encoder application that is part of a Creative Cloud membership to convert other video or audio formats to MP4 or MP3.

Adding a movie to a fixed-layout EPUB InDesign document is similar to adding a photo or illustration to a print document. Next, you'll import a movie into the document and use the Media panel to choose a poster image that's displayed when the movie isn't playing.

1 Navigate to page 2. Choose View > Fit Page In Window, and then choose File > Place. Select the Bee-Pollination-Video.mp4 video file in the Links folder in the Lesson15 folder and click Open.

Note: A warning may display stating that video and audio playback controls may not work in Interactive PDFs. Since the destination of this project is not PDF, you can disregard this warning and close the alert window.

2 Click the loaded video icon () where the blue ruler guides meet in the upper-left area of the page. The video is placed at full size, just as a still image would be. It's important to prepare video images before placing them, including planning the size dimensions. Keep the movie selected.

3 A static image, called a poster, is displayed in an EPUB reader before the video plays. The default is to display the first frame of the movie when the movie is not playing, but you can choose other images. The poster image can be a frame from the movie or a separate file. To set a poster image, choose Window > Interactive > Media to open the Media panel. You can use the controls below the movie image to preview the movie and choose a frame to be the poster. We'll try choosing a different image instead of the first frame.

4 From the Poster Frame menu in the Media panel, select Choose Image. Navigate to the Links folder in the Lesson15 folder, and double-click the file named Bee-Pollination-Poster.jpg. Click the content grabber and then choose Object > Fitting > Fill Frame Proportionally.

Note: Each EPUB reader app will have different video player controls. After you export your EPUB, test the video player in different readers. Another option is to create your own play/pause buttons in InDesign and hide the default buttons with a filled frame.

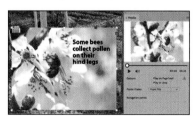

5 Click the Preview Spread button () at the bottom of the Media panel and then click the Play Preview button. In the preview, click the Play/Pause button at the left of the video player controls at the bottom of the video poster image to play

and pause the movie. There is a separate control to adjust the sound volume at the right (there is no sound in this video).

▶ **Tip:** When you use a video in an EPUB, it is embedded in the final file. Be aware that video files can be large and make the resulting EPUB file large as well; therefore, you need to balance the quality level of the video with the file size.

6 Drag the Media panel to the dock to add it for easy access later (if necessary). Close the EPUB Interactivity Preview panel (»), and choose File > Save.

Creating a slideshow

A slideshow is a sequence of stacked images displayed one at a time as a viewer taps Previous and Next buttons. The sample document for this lesson already includes the graphics you need to create an interactive slideshow. You'll arrange these graphics in a stack, convert them into a format that can configure the slide-show (a multi-state object), and then set up buttons that enable a viewer to navigate through the slides. Using multi-state objects is a way to create an object that has multiple versions.

1 On the right side of page 2 is an image of a seed underground with several other picture frames to the left of it. Using the Selection tool (▶), drag to select all of the frames by dragging your pointer across the middle area of the images so that you do not also select the arrow graphic or the grasshopper image.

2 Choose Window > Object & Layout > Align to open the Align panel, or use the Align area in the Properties or the Control panel. Click the leftmost frame again to make it the key object. Choose Align To Key Object (▦.) from the Align To menu if it's not already selected. Click the Align Left Edges button (▌), and then click the Align Bottom Edges button (▙). Close the Align panel (or Properties panel).

Tip: Always name multi-state objects; otherwise, InDesign will automatically name them Multi-state 1, Multi-state 2, and so on.

3 With the graphics frames still selected, choose Window > Interactive > Object States to display the Object States panel, or click the Object States icon (⬚) to open it from the dock. Then click the Convert Selection To Multi-State Object button (⊞) at the bottom of the panel. If necessary, lengthen the panel to display the names of all objects. (The panel looks empty until you do the conversion.)

Graphics frames combined into a multi-state object. Each object appears as a separate state in the Object States panel.

Tip: Each state in a multi-state object can be named. The stack is like a layer stack, and the order of the objects can be changed by dragging them up or down in the panel.

4 In the Object States panel, enter **Germination** in the Object Name field, and then press Enter (Windows) or Return (macOS).

Now that you've created a multi-state object, you'll create a way for viewers to click or tap through the images in sequence.

1 Use the Selection tool to select the white arrow graphic to the left of the multi-state object and open the Buttons And Forms panel (⬚). This will be the button used to scroll backward through the slides.

2 In the Buttons And Forms panel, click Convert To Button (⊙) at the bottom of the panel and enter **Previous** in the Name field.

Note: When there are several multi-state objects on a page, you may need to choose the correct multi-state object from the Object menu in the Buttons And Forms panel. In this file, InDesign automatically selects the Germination multi-state object because it's the only one on the page.

3 Click the + sign (+) next to Actions and choose Go To Previous State from the menu. (The Germination multi-state object was automatically added to the list of objects.)

4 Don't select Stop At First State. When it's not selected and the user clicks to the last slide and clicks the arrow again, the first slide will display. In other words, you can keep clicking through the

slides in a loop. When this option is selected, nothing happens when the user clicks the arrow again after the last slide is displayed.

5 Select the right-pointing black arrow graphic, and repeat steps 2–4 to configure a button named **Next**. To make a button that scrolls forward through the slides, when you click Add New Action For Selected Event, choose Go To Next State from the Actions menu, and then select Stop At Last State (or not, as you choose).

6 Open the EPUB Interactivity Preview panel (⌨), click the Play Preview button, and then click the Previous and Next buttons you created to view the slideshow.

7 Close the EPUB Interactivity Preview panel (»), and choose File > Save.

Creating a hyperlink

Hyperlinks let viewers jump to other locations in a document, to other documents, or to websites. A hyperlink includes a source element (text, a text frame, or a graphics frame) and a destination, which is the URL, email address, page, or text anchor to which the hyperlink jumps. Next, you'll create a hyperlink to a website.

Urban Oasis Garden is a fictional place, so we will create a hyperlink to a URL of a real organization, the Arbor Day Foundation. This nonprofit is dedicated to planting trees in communities and forests.

1 Use the Selection tool (▶) to select the picture of the apples on the branch, the rightmost picture along the bottom.

2 Choose Window > Interactive > Hyperlinks to display the Hyperlinks panel, or click the Hyperlinks icon (🔗) to open it from the dock.

3 In the URL field, replace the default text with **https://www.arborday.org**. Press the Enter key. InDesign recognizes this as a web address, and you'll see the circle under the status column turn to green, indicating that the web address is available. The name InDesign assigns to the hyperlink is the name of the object—in this case, the name of the image.

● **Note:** The Status column in the Hyperlinks panel uses a traffic light indicator for hyperlinks to web addresses to indicate whether the entered web address is available (green) or not (red). Some addresses might be flagged as unavailable (red light) if the network you are connected to prohibits access to certain sites.

4 Choose Rename Hyperlink from the panel menu. Change the name to **Arbor-Day-Foundation** and click OK. If you create a document with many hyperlinks, you'll want to name them in a way that's clear rather than leaving the default name.

5 Test the link by choosing Go To Destination from the Hyperlinks panel menu. Your default web browser will open and load this page.

6 Switch back to InDesign, open the EPUB Interactivity Preview panel (⌨), and click the Play Preview button (you may need to click Clear Preview (■) first). Move the pointer over the picture of the apples on the branch. The pointer changes to a pointing finger, indicating a clickable object. Click to test the hyperlink. The Arbor Day Foundation home page is once again displayed in your browser.

▶ **Tip:** You can also click the green icon in the status column to go to the hyperlink's destination URL.

7 Return to InDesign, close the EPUB Interactivity Preview panel (»), choose Edit > Deselect All, and then choose File > Save.

Adding a sound

Adding a sound to a page is the same as adding a movie, but the options for controlling how sounds are displayed and played are a little different from those for movies because movies and sounds are different types of media.

Next, you'll add a sound to the cover page, and then you'll convert one of the objects on the page into a button that plays the sound when clicked. You'll also hide the sound object so that it's not visible on the page.

● **Note:** A warning may display stating that video and audio playback controls may not work in Interactive PDFs. Since the destination of this project is not PDF, you can disregard this warning and close the alert window.

1 Navigate to page 1 and zoom in on the upper-center area near the title. Choose File > Place, select the BirdSounds.mp3 sound file in the Links folder in the Lesson15 folder, and then click Open.

2 Click the pasteboard above the top of the page, near the bluebird image. Don't worry about placing the sound precisely because you'll hide this object later.

3 Open the Layers panel (✿) and move this object up to the Buttons layer; then position the sound frame on top of the bluebird image. Close the Layers panel.

● **Note:** By default, a controller is displayed for a sound file. The Media panel doesn't include an option that enables you to turn off the display of the controller for a sound file.

4 Click the Media panel icon (▤) in the panel dock to open the panel and examine the options available for a sound file. If you want, use the Play and Pause buttons to preview the sound. Leave the default settings unchanged. Close the Media panel.

This is all you need to do to add a sound, but for this lesson, instead of displaying sound controls in an EPUB reader, as would happen if you left the object where it is, you'll hide it and then configure a button to play it.

5 Choose Object > Arrange > Send To Back (the sound object should still be selected).

6 Select the Rectangle Frame tool (⊠) in the Tools panel and draw a frame over the bluebird image that's now in front of the sound frame. This frame will become the button that activates the sound to play. The objects are layered so that the empty frame is in front, the bird image is behind that, and the sound file is behind the bird image.

7 With the empty graphics frame still selected, open the Buttons And Forms panel (). Click the + sign (+) next to Actions and choose Sound. Because the page has only one sound, the sound object you just placed is automatically selected in the Sound menu (BirdSounds.mp3).

8 Enter **Play Bird Sounds** in the Name field. Make sure On Release Or Tap is selected in the Event menu and that Play is selected in the Options menu.

9 Click the Preview Spread button (▣). In the EPUB Interactivity Preview panel, click the Clear Preview button (■) and then click Play Preview (▶). Click the bluebird image to play the sound. The audio clip (24 seconds in length) will play once and stop. Close the EPUB Interactivity Preview panel.

Next, we'll set up the music notes to move while the sound is playing. They each have had an animation setting already assigned.

1 With the Play Bird Sounds button still selected, open the Buttons And Forms panel (). Click the + sign (+) next to Actions, and select Animation. Then from the Animation menu, choose Music Note 1. Repeat these steps until you have added each Music Note animation in order, 1–8. Each time you click the + sign (+) next to Actions and select Animation, InDesign will automatically assign the first animation in the list. After it does so, select the next Music Note in the sequence from the Animation menu. The result is a list of nine actions assigned to this button, one sound at the top of the list, followed by eight animations.

Note: The empty graphics frame should still be selected, even after previewing the sound in the last exercise.

2 Open the Timing panel (⏱) and pull the panel down so that you can see all the animations. Click BirdSounds.mp3 at the top, press the Shift key, and click the last Music Note at the bottom so that all are selected. Click the Play Together button (▶⚏) at the bottom right. Open the EPUB Interactivity Preview panel again, click the Clear Preview button (■), and then click Play Preview (▶). Click the bluebird image to play the sound. Now the animation will play along with the sound.

3 Close the EPUB Interactivity Preview panel (»), and choose File > Save.

Exporting a fixed-layout EPUB file

Much as the settings in the Print dialog control the appearance of printed pages, the settings you use when you export an InDesign document as an EPUB control the appearance of the EPUB.

In this exercise, we'll use some simple settings, but be aware that when you create an EPUB to be published via an online service, you must meet specific requirements or the EPUB will fail the publisher's standards, and you'll have to fix it and resubmit until it passes the publisher's validation process. You should get all the requirements from your publisher at the beginning of a project.

1 Choose File > Export.

2 In the Export dialog, choose EPUB (Fixed Layout) from the Save As Type menu (Windows) or the Format menu (macOS).

3 In the File Name field (Windows) or the Save As field (macOS), name the file **15_FixedLayout.epub** and save the file in the Lesson15 folder, located inside the Lessons folder within the InDesignCIB folder on your hard drive. Click Save.

4 In the General area of the EPUB – Fixed Layout Export Options dialog, notice that EPUB 3.0 is automatically displayed for Version. This is the only EPUB version available for fixed-layout EPUBs. Leave all settings at their defaults.

Rasterize First Page (in the General area of the dialog) creates an image that will be used as an icon for the publication in the ebook reader app and on an ebook storefront.

5 Click Metadata in the list on the left of the EPUB – Fixed Layout Export Options dialog. In the Title field, enter **Garden News**, and type your name in the Creator field.

If your EPUB will be formally published, the information in the Metadata dialog is very important. Ebook sites require that this information be provided. Download the metadata specifications from the publisher.

6 Click Conversion Settings from the list. Choose PNG from the Format menu to ensure that the graphics in grouped objects and objects with transparency are displayed correctly in the exported EPUB.

7 Click Viewing Apps from the list. The System Default setting in the Viewing Apps area will vary depending on your operating system. When the EPUB is exported, it is automatically opened in the selected program. Click the Add Application button if you would like to use a different EPUB reader app.

8 Click OK to export. If InDesign displays an alert warning that certain objects might not appear as expected after export, click OK to continue and view the EPUB.

The EPUB file will open automatically in the specified viewing app, and you can navigate through it to view the content and work with the multimedia and interactive elements you created. You can also open the EPUB file on any device that supports the EPUB format.

There will be differences in the interface between different ebook readers (frame, style and location of controls, fit in window, etc.).

Opened in Books app.

Part of the process of creating a digital publication such as a fixed-layout EPUB is to test the functionality on the various devices the target audience might use.

9 Try exporting again, and choose a slightly different filename, such as **15_FixedLayout_Auto.epub**. This time change the Format option in Conversion Settings to Automatic. Under JPEG Options, verify that Progressive is selected in the Format Method menu and High in the Image Quality menu, and leave the other options as they are.

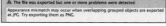

10 Click OK. A warning displays about appearance mismatch when overlapping grouped objects are exported as JPEG. Click OK and the export will finish. The file will open in the specified viewing app. Compare the results to the EPUB exported with PNG settings. Then compare file size in File Explorer (Windows) or the Finder (macOS).

11 Return to InDesign. Choose File > Save.

InDesign Publish Online

The Publish Online feature in InDesign allows you to distribute digital versions of your InDesign documents on the internet. Documents you publish online can be viewed on any desktop or mobile device and easily shared on Facebook and Twitter. You can easily provide hyperlinks to these documents in emails or embed the hyperlinks in web pages.

The InDesign documents you publish online are visually identical to the original layouts, and all interactive features are supported.

1 To publish the currently displayed document online, click the Share button on the right side of the menu bar, and then choose Publish Online or File > Publish Online.

2 In the General area of the Publish Your Document Online dialog, enter **Garden News** in the Title field, and in the Description field enter **Interactive multimedia version of Garden News magazine**. The Advanced tab of the Publish Your Document Online dialog lets you choose a cover page and specify image export settings. Leave all the settings at their defaults for this exercise; then click Publish.

▶ **Tip:** The Title field text appears as information in search engine results and appears as the text in the browser window title bar or tab. It is also used when you share the online publication on social media, such as Facebook, and as the subject line for email sharing.

A window displays as the document uploads and provides a preview of the first page, the name of the document, the description (if any), a status bar showing the progress of the upload, and the opportunity to cancel the upload.

3 When the upload is complete, click View Document to display the document in a web browser. Your default web browser opens and displays the publication.

Notice the different controls available. In this browser (Safari), controls appear along the bottom right of the window. Every browser will have a different configuration of controls. Test the functionality of all the interactive elements.

Also note that the URL is indd.adobe.com. Publish Online documents are hosted on Adobe servers. Each published document is assigned its own unique URL.

4 Return to InDesign. Notice the other options available in the Publish Online dialog that will still be displayed. These include the ability to copy the URL to the Clipboard, as well as buttons for Facebook, Twitter, and email to share the link on social networks or to open a new email in your default email program.

5 Close the Publish Online window, and choose File > Save.

After you publish documents online, you can easily access the five most recently published documents from within InDesign by choosing File > Recently Published. (The Recently Published menu does not appear until after you have published your first document.)

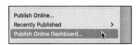

The Publish Online Dashboard lets you view, share, and delete all published documents. If you want to remove a document that you've published online, choose File > Publish Online Dashboard. A web page opens in your default browser and displays in chronological order a list of the documents you've uploaded, with the most recent at the top. To delete a published document, click the more options button (⋯) at the far right and then click Delete.

Congratulations! You've finished the lesson and created a fixed-layout EPUB with multimedia and interactivity.

Exploring on your own

For additional practice, try some of the following exercises. You can continue working on the sample document and save your changes, or you can choose File > Save As and save a new document with a new name to the Lesson15 folder.

Adding animation properties

You may have noticed that when the animations on page 2 play, the grasshopper image gets progressively smaller as it moves across the page. This characteristic is controlled in the Properties area of the Animation panel.

1 Navigate to page 2. Using the Selection tool, select the grasshopper image.

2 Open the Animation panel () from the panel dock and examine the Properties area in the lower area of the panel. If necessary, click the triangle next to Properties to reveal the settings.

3 Notice that Scale W and H are set to 50% in the Animate To area. This means the object will scale while it's performing the animation from the current size to 50% of that size.

4 On this object or any objects in the document, experiment with other settings such as Rotate or Hide After Animating in the Animation Properties panel.

Creating a slide-in caption

Another type of effect is the slide-in caption. You can examine the finished effect to see how it works and then try creating it yourself. This effect is created using three duplicate object states with different button actions, animation, and timing settings.

A step-by-step guide to creating this caption effect is available with the lesson download, 15a_slide_in_caption_step_by_step.pdf.

1 Open the file 15_FixedLayout-Alternate. The frame with the mission statement has been changed to a slide-in caption.

● **Note:** The clickable or tappable area is larger than the triangles, but they are the signal to the user that there is something to click or tap.

2 Open the EPUB Interactivity Preview panel and click the red triangles above the words "Our Mission" on the far left of the page. A text frame containing the mission statement slides in from the left.

3 Click the red triangles again and the mission statement slides back off the photo and the button returns to the start position. Close the EPUB Interactivity Preview panel.

Review questions

1 What's the primary difference between a reflowable EPUB and a fixed-layout EPUB?

2 InDesign provides two methods for animating objects. What are they, and how do they differ?

3 By default, animations play in the order in which they were created. How can you change the order in which animations are played, and how can you play multiple animations simultaneously?

4 How can you preview multimedia and interactive elements within InDesign?

5 How do you create a slideshow?

Review answers

1 The reflowable EPUB format allows the EPUB reader to optimize the content depending on the display device. For example, the viewer of a reflowable EPUB can adjust the display size of the text, which affects the amount of text on a given page and the flow of text from page to page. In fixed-layout EPUBs, the dimensions of the original InDesign pages are maintained, as is the fidelity to the original layout design.

2 You can animate objects by choosing a motion preset in the Animation panel, or you can create a motion path. A motion path consists of two elements: the animated object or group and the path along which the animated object moves.

3 The controls in the Timing panel let you control when animations are played. All animations associated with the selected Event (such as On Page Load) are displayed. You can drag the names within the list to change the order in which they're played. To play them simultaneously, you can select multiple animations and click the Play Together button ().

4 The EPUB Interactivity Preview panel lets you preview and test multimedia and interactive elements. The Animation, Timing, Media, Object States, and Buttons And Forms panels all include a Preview Spread button (), and you can also display the panel by choosing Window > Interactive > EPUB Interactivity Preview.

5 To create a slideshow, first create a stack of objects, and then use the Object States panel to create a multi-state object. Next, create and configure two buttons: one that displays the previous state of the multi-state object and one that displays the next state.

INDEX

J

jump lines, 184–186, 187
justified text, 225

K

Keep Options dialog, 209
kerning, 223–224, 235
key objects, 119–120, 129
keyboard shortcuts
 magnification controls, 24, 97
 number pad used for creating, 246
 single-letter for tools, 11
 styles applied with, 244
 text formatting with, 240
 troubleshooting, 26
Keyboard Shortcuts dialog, 32

L

Layer Options dialog, 95
layers, 91–96
 creating new, 95
 effects applied to, 350–351
 explanation of, 91–92
 hiding or displaying, 92
 Illustrator files with, 316–318
 moving items between, 93, 94, 96
 naming/renaming, 95
 Photoshop files with, 312
 reordering, 95
 selecting objects on, 93
Layers panel, 91–93, 95
leaders, tab, 229, 235
lesson files, 3
Levels setting, 334
libraries
 Creative Cloud, 158–160, 324
 InDesign, 322–323
ligatures, 214
line breaks, 225–226
line styles (nested), 250
Line tool, 11, 125
lines
 arrowheads on, 125
 drawing, 11, 125
linked files
 listed in Links panel, 297–298
 relinking multiple, 307
 revealing the location of on disk, 298
 viewing information about, 297–298, 300

Links panel, 296–300
 caption options, 109–110
 detaching from panel group, 297
 link status icons in, 300
 list of linked files in, 297–298
 managing links in, 296–298
 relinking files in, 300, 307
 replacing images in, 299–300
 updating revised files in, 299, 300
list boxes in forms, 394, 396, 398
lists, numbered/bulleted, 231
Live Preflight feature, 51–53
Load Styles dialog, 263–264
loaded graphics icon, 46, 103–105, 302, 331
loaded text icon, 40, 165, 170–171, 173
local overrides, 43, 244, 253
Locate Color feature, 149–150, 365–367
locked layers, 95–96, 103

M

magnification controls, 24–26, 33, 97
margins
 hanging punctuation outside, 221–222
 specifying settings for, 60, 68
mask shapes, 308
math calculations, 66, 108, 127–128
Measure tool, 74–75
measurement units, 59, 313
Media panel, 416–417, 420
Medium Light interface, 8, 30–31
Menu Customization feature, 23, 32
menus
 context, 29
 customizing, 23
 panel, 29–30
Merge Cells option, 277
metadata
 caption, 109–110
 EPUB file, 422
Missing Fonts dialog, 192, 204–205
missing links, 300, 307, 322, 360
Mixed Ink colors, 144
modified link icon, 299, 322, 327
monitor calibration, 136
motion paths, 405, 409, 411–413, 427
motion presets, 404–407
movies in EPUBs, 416–417
multicolumn text frames, 101, 218
multimedia in EPUBs, 415–419, 420–421
multi-state objects, 417–418, 427

text frames, 96–102
 aligning text in, 102
 Auto-Size feature, 166–167
 columns in, 41, 101, 218–219
 creating, 96–98, 170–173
 formatting options, 39
 importing text into, 165
 inset spacing options, 102
 parent page, 65–67
 reshaping, 98–99
 resizing, 98, 99, 166–167
 threaded, 54, 168–175
Text Wrap panel, 111, 314–315, 318–319
threaded text frames, 54, 168–175
TIFF file format, 331
Timing panel, 407–408, 427
tint swatches, 150–151, 353
Tool Hints, 32
tool tips, 10, 194, 239, 253, 398
tools
 displaying info about, 32
 overview of using, 10–13
 selecting, 10–13, 33
 viewing hidden, 12–13
Tools panel, 9, 10–13, 21–22
tracked changes, 202–203
tracking, typographical, 223–224
training resources, 4–5
Transform panel, 63–64
transforming objects, 121
transparency, 330–355
 effects utilizing, 342–353
 graphics settings for, 336–338
 Illustrator files with, 339–340
 overview of features for, 333–336
 Photoshop backgrounds with, 310–311
 previewing, 368
 settings and options for, 349
 text settings for, 340–341
 using tints vs., 353
 viewing pages with, 350
Transparency Flattener settings, 373
trifold layout, 85–86
Type 1 fonts, discontinued, 212
Type On A Path tool, 123–124
Type tool, 11
 editing text with, 38–39, 191–193
 formatting text with, 166
 loading with multiple files, 169
 tables and use of, 271, 290

typography, 209–235
 column options, 218–219
 composition methods, 227
 drop cap creation, 222–223
 fonts and type styles, 211–214
 fraction characters, 216–217
 line break adjustments, 225–226
 paragraph alignment, 220–222
 paragraph rules, 233
 shading paragraphs, 232
 stroke and fill effects, 216
 tab settings, 228–231
 tracking and kerning adjustments, 223–224
 vertical spacing adjustments, 209–210
 See also text

U

Undo command, 8
Update Link button, 299, 300, 322, 327
updating
 InDesign program, 2
 revised graphics, 299–300
 styles, 183–184, 262–264
User Interface Scaling, 31

V

Variable Font format, 212
vector graphics, 295–296, 336–337
Vertical Justification options, 39, 66, 102, 181, 209
vertical spacing adjustments, 181, 209
videos in EPUBs, 416–417
view commands, 24
View Threshold menu, 182
viewing environment for color, 134

W

Web Edition of book, 3
workspace, 9
 creating your own, 23, 32, 389
 customizing, 23
 Interactive For PDF, 9, 23, 388, 389
Workspace Switcher menu, 23
wrapping text, 110–112, 314–315, 318–320

Z

zoom, animated, 26
Zoom tool, 16, 25–26, 33
zooming in/out, 24, 97